The Political Economy
of Sino-American Relations

A Greater China Perspective

The Political Economy of Sino-American Relations

A Greater China Perspective

Edited by Y.Y. Kueh
with the assistance of Brian Bridges

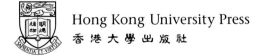

Hong Kong University Press
香港大學出版社

Hong Kong University Press
The University of Hong Kong
Pokfulam Road, Hong Kong

© Hong Kong University Press 1997

ISBN 962 209 440 6

All rights reserved. No portion of this publication may
be reproduced or transmitted in any form or by any recording,
or any information storage or retrieval system, without permission
in writing from the publisher.

Printed in Hong Kong by Condor Production Co., Ltd.

Contents

Preface

This volume has its origin in the appreciation that one of the most significant relationships in the Asia-Pacific region in the 1990s is that between the United States and the dynamic economies of China, Taiwan and Hong Kong. It was with the intention of trying to analyse the recent trends and future prospects for Sino-American economic relations that Lingnan College's Centre for Asian Pacific Studies decided to hold an international conference in Hong Kong in June 1995. The College was particularly happy to have the opportunity to cooperate with the Institute of American Studies of the Chinese Academy of Social Sciences in organizing this conference, which followed on from an earlier conference held in Shenzhen in November 1993. Paper presenters, discussants and participants not only from the United States, China, Taiwan and Hong Kong but also from Europe, Australia, Japan and other Asian countries joined in the wide-ranging and stimulating discussions.

This volume draws together a number of the papers presented at that conference, and falls into four parts. The first provides two overview papers by American scholars; they examine aspects of the Chinese reform process and its impact on the political economy of the state of Sino-American relations. The second part provides a range of perspectives from Taiwanese and Hong Kong scholars on their regions' relations with the United States and the interaction with Sino-American relations. The third part examines in detail particular trade, investment and technological cooperation issues, as well as setting out some of the key features of the triangular economic relationship in what has popularly come to be called 'Greater China'. The fourth part sets the Sino-American relationship in the broader regional context, looking at the impact on, and the perspectives of, other Asian Pacific nations, as well as discussing China's role in the global economy.

All chapters have been revised and updated during 1996 in the light of comments made at the conference; in the case of Harry Harding, his chapter has been updated to March 1997. We believe that this volume provides a timely and insightful examination of the key issues in Sino-American economic relations.

I would like to thank the various sponsors who have given valuable financial and administrative support to the original conference: The Bank of China Group; The Lingnan Foundation (New York); The Ford Foundation (Beijing); The Bank of East Asia (Hong Kong); The Chinese Association for

American Economic Studies, Beijing; International Golf and Yacht Club, Hong Kong; Hong Kong Society of Asia and Pacific 21; Hong Kong Kwun Tong Industries and Commerce Association; and The World-wide Chinese Friendly Association. In particular, I would like to give special mention to the Institute of American Studies at the Chinese Academy of Social Sciences, Beijing, which played an invaluable role in arranging the Chinese participation in the original conference.

Last but not least, I am most grateful to my colleague, Dr Brian Bridges, who has graciously helped to edit many of the chapters and rendered them much more readable and to Dr Raymond C.W. Ng (Assistant Research Officer at the Centre for Asian Pacific Studies) as well, for his painstaking work on the entire manuscript.

Y.Y. Kueh
Lingnan College
March 1997

Contributors

Bridges, Brian	Associate Professor, Department of Politics and Sociology, Lingnan College; formerly Head of East Asian Studies Department, Royal Institute of International Affairs, London
Chai, Joseph C.H.	Senior Lecturer, Department of Economics, The University of Queensland
Cheng, Leonard K.	Professor of Economics, Hong Kong University of Science and Technology
Cheung, Kui-yin	University Lecturer, Department of Economics, Lingnan College, Hong Kong
Chung, Chin	Associate Research Fellow, Chung Hua Institution for Economic Research, Taipei
Dernberger, Robert F.	Professor of Economics Emeritus and Director, Center for Chinese Studies, University of Michigan
Harding, Harry	Dean, Elliott School of International Affairs, The George Washington University; formerly Senior Fellow, Brookings Institution, USA
Kueh, Yak-yeow	Chair Professor of Economics, and Dean, Faculty of Social Sciences, Lingnan College, Hong Kong; formerly Foundation Director, Centre for Chinese Political Economy, Macquarie University, Sydney
Lei, Kai-cheong	University Lecturer, Department of Economics, Lingnan College, Hong Kong
Noland, Marcus	Senior Fellow, Institute of International Economics, Washington DC
Sinha, Radha	Professor of International Economics, Sophia University, Tokyo; formerly Professor of Political Economy, University of Glasgow, UK
Sung, Yun-wing	Professor and Chairman of Department of Economics, The Chinese University of Hong Kong
Voon, Thomas	Associate Professor, Department of Economics, Lingnan College, Hong Kong
Yamamoto, Hiromi	Professor of East Asian Economics, Faculty of Economics, Kyoto University
Yu, Tzong-shian	Professor and former President, Chung Hua Institution for Economic Research, Taipei

Introduction

In the 1980s the Asia-Pacific region was the world's fastest growing region economically and its record to date in the 1990s, despite occasional hiccups in some countries, suggests that that status will be maintained in this decade as well. The impressive growth rates of recent years are founded both on heightened flows of trade and investment within the region and on an ever-broadening range of commercial contacts with external trading partners. Both have taken place within an increasingly congenial regional political context, especially after the collapse of the Soviet Union which has brought about a basically favourable power realignment on a global scale.

Within this overall pattern of Asia-Pacific economic dynamism, one aspect which has attracted particular attention in recent years has been the intensification of trade and investment linkages between mainland China, Hong Kong and Taiwan; so much so that observers have come to talk of 'Greater China' as a way of characterizing this new phenomenon.* Although it was the decision of the Chinese government in the late 1970s to adopt 'open-door' policies for economic modernization which acted as the trigger, the private sector in Hong Kong and Taiwan have been quick to see the commercial potential of ventures in and with China. While it is true that political sensitivities (most notably between China and Taiwan) have not been completely eliminated, economic logic has remained a powerful driving force behind this integration between the three economies.

Individually, the three Chinese economies are in any case important players in global trade and investment relations. China, Hong Kong and Taiwan have been occupying in recent years the eleventh to thirteenth positions amongst the world's trading nations; and China has now become one of the world's largest recipient countries of foreign direct investment (FDI), second only to the United States, while Hong Kong has assumed the status of the fourth largest FDI supplier in the world. With the emergence of 'Greater China', however, external trading partners are increasingly being faced with the need

---

* Throughout this study, the term, mainland China, the Chinese Mainland, China and the People's Republic of China are used interchangeably; and 'Greater China' is used as an economic concept to capture the precipitous increase in economic interaction and integration between the three Chinese economies since 1979.

to carry out business activities and construct trade policies which take account of the complex set of economic linkages between the three economies. This means that they are no longer able to deal with one economy in isolation from the others. Clearly for all three economies, the United States figures as one of their most important external partners. This volume therefore endeavours to examine in detail, both from the perspective of the 'Greater China' economies as well as from the side of the Americans, many of the complexities of the Sino-American relationship.

The end of the Cold War profoundly affected the pattern of international relations and led to assessments that the preoccupation of the previous half century with geopolitics and security would be replaced by enhanced concern about economic, social and environmental issues. However, in reality as the 1990s have progressed, it has also become clear that economic issues are still closely linked with political questions. This means that any discussion of the economic dimensions of the Sino-American relationship needs to be set against the broader background of Sino-American political relations.

As one of America's leading China watchers, Harry Harding, demonstrates in the opening chapter, there has been a range of troublesome political issues which have plagued Sino-American relations in the 1990s — some of these date back a long way, others are new on the agenda. The conference from which this edited volume derives was itself held at a time when relations between the United States and China were particularly tense in the aftermath of the visit to the United States by President Lee Teng-hui of Taiwan. Tensions actually heightened even further in the spring of 1996 at the time of Taiwan's presidential elections with Chinese military activity near Taiwan being counterbalanced by US naval deployments. However, as Harding argues, despite these problems, there are a number of internal and international factors which still provide durability and resilience to the relationship. Indeed, there are signs, in the second half of 1996, that some measure of stability is being restored to the Sino-American relationship. Thus, although there inevitably will exist a blend of divergent and convergent interests in the relationship, the prospects for cooperation are once again becoming more favourable.

While Harding's analysis primarily covers post-Cold War policies and perceptions on both sides, the chapter by Radha Sinha, an Indian scholar now based in Japan, sets the current Sino-American relationship against a much longer historical and intellectual background. He notes various stages in the development of Sino-American relations over the past century and a half, from US imperialism (albeit a moralistic one), through benign neglect to the *rapprochement* of the 1970s. He characterizes the present period as one of constructive dialogue and argues for patience, caution and reduced reliance on rhetoric in developing the Sino-American relationship.

While not losing sight of the important political context, the other chapters of the volume concentrate on key aspects of the economic interactions between the various economies. The starting point has to be the profound changes which have taken place in the Chinese economy since the late 1970s. Based on his long-time observation of the Chinese economy, Robert Dernberger offers a thoughtful assessment of the pattern of economic reforms in China over nearly two decades. He sees a considerable — and relatively successful — transformation of the Chinese economy, but notes that some key issues, particularly in the banking and legal systems, will be difficult challenges for the new post-Deng Xiaoping leadership. Turning to how these changes have had and are having an impact on relations with the United States, Dernberger anticipates a slowdown in Chinese trade and investment growth, but argues that China will inevitably play an ever larger role in the Asian economy; as such, US businessmen will not want to miss out on the commercial opportunities on offer.

Two other overview chapters approach the Sino-American relationship from the perspective of the other components of 'Greater China': Taiwan and Hong Kong. The senior Taiwanese economist Tzong-shian Yu compares the state of economic relations between Taiwan and the United States with that of mainland China with the United States. He argues that for both Taiwan and China the United States will remain an important export market, but that by contrast with the 1980s it is now China rather than Taiwan which will be running large — and controversial — trade surpluses. But he also notes that with the burgeoning of economic ties between Taiwan and mainland China, any US trade policy measures taken against China will have an impact not just on Taiwanese investment in China but also on industrial growth in Taiwan itself.

Hong Kong, even more closely linked with China, is bound to be most profoundly affected by any major US-China trade disputes. The chapter by Y.Y. Kueh and Thomas Voon clearly brings to light, in quantitative terms, the pivotal role Hong Kong plays in facilitating two-way US-China trade, and hence the enormous economic importance to Hong Kong of a favourable Sino-American political relationship. Of particular interest is the rigorous analysis made to reconcile the long-standing conflicting US versus China claims over trade deficits against each other. Kueh and Voon show that by an absolutely overwhelming proportion, the discrepancy can be explained away by Hong Kong's imputed earnings from export processing commissioned to the Chinese hinterland which by American reckoning are, however, treated grossly as Chinese exports to the United States. Kueh and Voon also conclude that the exaggerated US trade deficit claims against China appear to assume a political overtone, given that, by contrast, similar, persistent and massive US trade deficits *vis-à-vis* Japan, and South Korea and Taiwan as well, have never really inspired the American government to any serious trade disputes with these established political allies.

The chapter by Kui-yin Cheung takes a closer look at the Hong Kong-China trade links by focusing specifically on the role that fluctuating exchange rates have played in affecting two-way trade flows including, in particular, the all-important 'outward processing' trade initiated from Hong Kong. Against the background of his findings, Cheung argues that, as part of China's bid to join the new World Trade Organization (successor to the General Agreement on Tariffs and Trade), reform of its foreign exchange system, in particular the movement towards full convertibility of the renminbi, are essential. He also remains optimistic that Hong Kong's rediscovered role as an entrepôt and gateway to China for foreign, including American, companies will continue for the foreseeable future.

Of course, investment activities are closely intertwined with trading relationships and two chapters address these linkages. Leonard Cheng, a Hong Kong specialist on China's investment issues, takes a detailed look at the record of US companies investing in China and highlights some of the areas where there have been disagreements between China and the United States. Some of the disputes, he argues, are really about the speed of Chinese economic reform, but he does note some aspects, such as industrial policy, where standpoints differ more widely. Nonetheless, like Dernberger, he feels that US companies will want to continue to invest and be active in the China market.

Taiwanese scholar Chin Chung examines in detail the nature and function of FDI from both Taiwan and Hong Kong in the Chinese mainland in light of available international experience. She compares how the associated relocating of export-oriented manufacturing activities has been brought to bear on both the relative shares of the Chinese Trio in the US and Japanese markets (in favour of the Chinese Mainland), and the industrial structure of Taiwan, as well as that of Hong Kong. She argues that, for reasons of a lack of 'firm-specific assets' on the part of the investing firms, increased FDI outflows to the Mainland tend to result in a 'hollowing-out' of the manufacturing sector. While, however, the vacuum left in Hong Kong can be rapidly filled by the bourgeoning service economy taking advantage of the booming China re-export trade, Taiwan, because of both political and geographical constraints, however, should look for ways of replenishing lost capital and entrepreneurship, if it wants to make up foregone chances for industrial upgrading and restructuring.

A crucial issue which still hangs over China's economic and trading relationship with the United States and the world at large obviously concerns China's resumption of membership of the GATT/WTO. Given that the potential impact is expected to be enormous, Hong Kong trade specialist Yun-wing

Sung discusses, in his chapter, specifically how it may bring about drastic changes in China's own economic system and economic stability, and hence in its commodity and services trade relationship with the outside world on the one hand, and, on the other, how it may further help to enhance economic integration between the 'Socialist' (China) and 'Capitalist' (Hong Kong and Taiwan) parts of China. Sung argues that an economically integrated 'Greater China' will inevitably continue to be outward-oriented, relying on the United States as the largest export market and Japan as the largest supplier of capital goods and technology — a conviction shared indeed by Kueh and Voon as well. Of particular analytical interest in Sung's chapter is the attempt made to disentangle the intriguing trade relationship between the Chinese Mainland and Taiwan. He contends that despite the official ban by the Taiwanese government, 'direct trade' has already been flourishing, by way of 'nominal' transhipment via Hong Kong, by Taiwan exporters in a frenzy to cash in on both emerging Chinese consumerism and the heightened export-oriented FDI demand for input equipment and materials. Thus, as Sung argues, the advent of a WTO status may not make too much difference in this respect.

Needless to say, the Sino-American economic relationship is also affected by, and in turn has an impact on, economic relationships between other economic powers in the Asia-Pacific region. Clearly, Japan, by the very size of its economy and its own intense trading and investment relationships with both China and the United States, cannot be ignored. One of Japan's leading scholars on the Chinese economy, Hiromi Yamamoto, carefully charts the growing trade, aid and investment links between Japan and China and sets them in the context of Japan's gradual shift away from reliance on the United States as its major trading partner to the booming Asia-Pacific economies. He also detects a tendency in the 1990s for Japan to slowly move away from following the US lead in relations with China, suggesting that in future the dynamics of the Sino-Japanese economic — and political — relationship will be less influenced by the state of US-Japan and US-China relations.

Of course, Japan and the United States are competitors not just in the China market but also in the smaller markets of Hong Kong and Taiwan. Kai-cheong Lei uses an econometric analysis to examine the exact state of this competition in these two latter markets. He demonstrates that, although the Japanese and US combined shares of these two markets has been slowly declining over the past two decades in the face of new competitors, Japan's share of both markets remains larger than the US share and indeed in the more sophisticated Hong Kong market, its lead over the United States is growing.

An Australia-based specialist in Chinese economic studies, Joseph Chai, adopts a different perspective, taking as his starting point the debate within Australia about the likely trade-diverting and trade-creating effects for Australia of Sino-American contention. He concludes that even if the United States feels it necessary to balance its trade with China by increasing exports to China this would not necessarily mean greater competition with Australian commodities, such as agricultural products, in the China market.

While scholars and government officials do still argue about the differing methods of computation and consequently differing projections of the size of the Chinese economy and its future role in world trade, even under conservative calculations it is clear that China has become one of the world's major economies. How can the international economic system adjust to the emergence of this new economic power and the associated 'Greater China'? The final chapter in the volume, by the American international trade specialist Marcus Noland, tries to speculate on the changing role of China in the international economy. He argues that the sheer size of China, its sustained rapid growth and the still incomplete nature of reform there means that integrating it into the international economic order will be at times both problematic and painful for other states, including the United States. As such he feels that China should be encouraged to join actively in bodies such as the WTO and APEC (Asia Pacific Economic Cooperation), to make it prepared to assume obligations while receiving benefits from these groupings.

There is no doubt that with China being increasingly assimilated into the world system of market economies and free trade, by way of economic reform, trade decentralization and enhanced trade and investment relations, any major economic and trading decision-making by the Chinese government is bound to be increasingly subject to the dictates of universally established rules and procedures, and customs governing multilateral or bilateral relations. The continuous concessions made by the Chinese government in recent years in response to US requirements for compliance with intellectual property rights and for opening up the market (in terms of the market access agreement) are a good case in point.

At the same time, the Chinese domestic system of production, investment and trading can be expected to be closely woven into the global system of labour division, industrial specialization and trade exchange. Any readjustments made in trading and investment policies on the part of the Chinese government, will then likely become increasingly constrained and hence marginal in extent, within the global context of private enterprises, decentralized trading autonomy, banking, financial and investment liberalization, and competition. Thus, if global economic interdependence continues to increase, it will be more difficult for China, or any other major country, to disturb the world economic order.

Of course, in the case of Sino-American economic relations, as in the case of other important relationships, international trade and investment cannot be entirely free of political influence. Issues such as Taiwan, Tibet, arms sales, nuclear non-proliferation and human rights, coupled with a growing perception by the US government of China as a 'threat' to South-east Asia and the world at large, do cast a shadow over normal economic exchanges. Geopolitics and regional security considerations apart, clearly differences of value imperatives, over human rights for example, which set the Chinese belief in the rights of existence and development against the American belief in individual freedom and democracy, do threaten to spill over into the economic arena, despite the delinking by the Clinton administration of annual most-favoured-nation (MFN) renewal from the human rights issue.

Taking a longer-term perspective, political change can perhaps be seen as a function of economic development, and just as Taiwan has changed politically in recent years with its economic growth, so too change may even come to China in the twenty-first century. However, the situation with mainland China is clearly dissimilar by virtue of its sheer size and its highly diversified and complex economic and social structure. The stark contrasts between the coastal and interior provinces, in terms of economic disparity, as well as the long-standing industry-agriculture dichotomy, have ever since the communist takeover in 1949, compelled the Chinese leadership to regard a certain degree of political centralism as necessary to hold together the fabric of the state. In fiscal terms this clearly implies forced transfer from the relatively richer eastern to the poorer western regions — a basic policy which has gained greater currency in recent deliberations over the current five-year plan. Equally, if not even more forcefully, there has been a consistent draining of resources, ironically conversely from the poor agricultural sector to the relatively rich urban industrial sector, as part of the forced-draft industrialization for catching up with the Western industrial powers. Both types of forced transfers clearly presuppose centralized political control one way or the other, necessarily implying forced savings and pervasive suppression of consumption and consumer choice, and, by extension, deprivation of individual freedom and consumer voting American-style.

Our short introduction does not intend to digress into domestic Chinese politics and economics, but these few points about the fundamentals should be sufficient to highlight the very sources and rationale underlying the enormous gap between the Chinese and the Americans in their respective value perceptions and moral standards.

Is the gap between the Chinese and the Americans really unbridgeable? In terms of value imperatives, it is quite unlikely to be bridged in the foreseeable future. Nonetheless, with China emerging as a major geopolitical factor and, even more rapidly, becoming a global economic power, *realpolitik* would certainly lend substance to Harding's argument that in the coming years China and the United States would be neither friend nor foe.

On a positive note, trade and investment relations between the United States and China, or more importantly indeed between the United States and

'Greater China' at large, have accumulated to a scale these days that was unthinkable fifteen years ago. Although in a way China may be economically more dependent on the United States than vice versa, it is safe to assume that neither country would really be prepared to risk the potentially wide-ranging negative consequences of rocking the 'economic' boat. There is therefore a real element of truth in Harding's contention that the enhanced economic interdependence between the two countries, especially since the early 1990s, must be seen as an important factor in providing some durability and resilience to Sino-American relations. Therefore, as President Clinton begins his second term of office, there are signs that the tensions of the 1995–96 period can be put behind us and that a new more productive phase in Sino-American relations can begin.

Y.Y. Kueh and Brian Bridges
March 1997

1

US-China Relations, 1995–97:
From Crisis to Hope to Uncertainty

Harry Harding

In 1995–96, Sino-American relations reached what many observers regarded as their lowest ebb since the two countries' rapprochement in the early 1970s. The most immediate issue was Taiwan. In May 1995, the United States permitted Taiwan's president, Lee Teng-hui, to visit Cornell University, there to make a major public address. Beijing feared that this decision presaged a major change in American relations with Taiwan — perhaps a willingness to support Taiwan's quest for enhanced international status or even formal independence. To deter both Taipei and Washington from moving in these directions, Beijing launched a major series of military exercises in the Taiwan Strait in late 1995 and early 1996, and the US moved two aircraft carrier battle groups to the seas off Taiwan to illustrate its continuing commitment to the island's security. For the first time since the 1960s, there was a chance, however remote, of direct military confrontation between the US and China over Taiwan.

By the end of 1996, however, the situation appeared to have stabilized. Military tensions in the Taiwan Strait had been reduced, and Taiwan and the mainland had agreed to establish some direct shipping links between them. The United States had reaffirmed its commitment to a one-China policy, and reassured Beijing that future visits by top-ranking Taiwan officials would be low-keyed and infrequent. Washington had also announced a new strategic framework to guide its relations with Beijing: a policy of integrating China into the international community with all the rights and responsibilities of a major power. And, perhaps most important, the two countries had agreed to resume bilateral summit meetings, which had been suspended ever since the Tiananmen Crisis of 1989.

Despite these welcome developments, it was uncertain how far, or how fast, Sino-American relations could improve. The bilateral agenda remained burdened with a plethora of controversial issues: human rights, Taiwan, trade, proliferation, and Hong Kong. Powerful sceptics in both capitals warned against 'appeasement' and called for a tougher policy towards the allegedly hegemonic policies of the other. Neither government could spend unlimited amounts of political capital to challenge the sceptics, reassure its publics, and rebuild the relationship. By the spring of 1997, Washington was enmeshed in an inquiry as to whether the Chinese government had made improper political campaign contributions so as to influence the American Congress and even the White House itself. This deepened the doubts that the United States could take any decisive positive steps towards Beijing.

Together, these developments raised some fundamental questions: What are the causes of strain in US-China relations? How fragile is the relationship likely to be, now that China has entered the post-Deng era?[1] Can we be confident that the two countries can avoid confrontation in the years to come? And what can be done to stabilize the Sino-American relationship?

A TROUBLED RELATIONSHIP, 1995–96

China and the United States entered 1995 with a highly troubled relationship. The most immediate cause of strain was the sheer number of controversial issues on their bilateral agenda. The United States was concerned with three sets of issues: trade, security, and human rights. China was vexed by American obstruction of its bid to join the World Trade Organization, by constant American pressure on such issues as human rights, market access, and non-proliferation, and above all by unwelcome signs of change in American policy towards Taiwan.

In the commercial realm, in 1995 the US bilateral trade deficit with China reached $40 billion according to American measures, nearly equal to that with Japan, thereby becoming a significant irritant in Sino-American relations. This was true even though the two countries could not agree on the size, or even the direction, of the trade imbalance, primarily because so much of their trade was being conducted through Hong Kong. It was also true even though most economists regard bilateral trade balances as an irrelevant measure of the health of an international economic relationship. The trade deficit stimulated American concern with a variety of secondary problems that allegedly promoted Chinese exports to the US and restricted American exports to China, such as inadequate Chinese protection of intellectual property rights, barriers to access to the Chinese market, Chinese evasion of American textile import quotas, and the export of Chinese goods produced by prison labour.

In the strategic area, proliferation of weapons of mass destruction remained a major problem. The United States government was concerned by reports that China had delivered the components of the M-11 medium-range missile to Pakistan and had transferred nuclear power plants and missile technology to Iran. Periodically, there were reports of Chinese exports of the precursors of chemical weapons as well. The Congress and the press — and to a somewhat lesser degree the US government — also criticized China's programme of underground nuclear testing, in defiance of the moratorium announced by Russia, Great Britain, and the United States, until Beijing finally halted testing at the end of 1996.

Increasing attention was also paid to China's behaviour in the South China Seas. Although the United States did not challenge China's claims to the Spratly or Paracel Islands, it was concerned that China might claim the entire South China Seas as its territorial waters, and on that basis might interfere with freedom of navigation through the area. Like other Southeast Asian nations, the United States also disapproved of China's use of force to pursue its claims, first by seizing disputed islands from the Vietnamese, and then by establishing and defending an outpost on Mischief Reef, claimed by the Philippines.

More generally, many American analysts expressed concern about the rise of Chinese military power. They pointed to the steady increases in China's official military budgets after 1989 — increases that outstripped both the growth in the total national budget and the official rate of inflation. They cited China's professed desire to acquire greater force projection capability, particularly a blue water navy. And they also noted China's purchase of Su-27 fighter-bombers, and the technology to manufacture them, from Russia.

Third, human rights retained a prominent place on the American agenda with China. This was not just a matter of Beijing's suppression of dissent through the harassment and arrest of political activists, although this issue remained extremely important to many Americans. There was also concern about a much longer list of human rights abuses, including the restrictions on religious practices, the revival of coercive birth control campaigns in the Chinese countryside, and the limitations on cultural autonomy in Tibet. With the return of Hong Kong to Chinese sovereignty in mid-1997, there was growing American attention to the fate of that territory, and criticism of the Chinese decision to dissolve the local legislature elected in 1995 and to create a new one using different, unspecified electoral mechanisms.

China, for its part, had its own list of grievances about the United States. The most significant economic issue was the slow progress being made on China's application for membership in the World Trade Organization by the working party headed by the United States. Beijing accused Washington of violating its pledge, part of the 1992 bilateral agreement on market access, to support Chinese membership in the WTO. It also resented the American reluctance to treat China as a developing country, and to grant it all the benefits and exemptions in the WTO that normally accompany such a status. And, although the Clinton administration ultimately decided not to retain a linkage between China's human rights record and the renewal of its most-favoured-nation status, Beijing still criticized Washington for refusing to grant China permanent, unconditional most-favoured-nation treatment, which it regarded as the cornerstone of the world trading order.

Beijing also resented American criticism on human rights. The Chinese government, of course, regarded American concern with this issue as an unwarranted intervention in its internal affairs. But even ordinary Chinese regarded the American position as ill-informed and ill-intentioned. Americans seemed to ignore China's progress on many economic and social dimensions, including the degree of freedom that most Chinese enjoyed in their daily lives, and focused instead on the arrests of a small number of political dissidents, conditions in Chinese prisons, the suppression of unauthorized churches, and the absence of free elections. Many Chinese concluded that, by focusing so sharply on the suppression of dissent, the hidden American intention was to foster political instability in their country, so as to prevent China's emergence as a major power that could challenge American interests.

The growing interest of some Americans, including prominent Hollywood celebrities, in the violations of human rights in Tibet particularly worried the Chinese. Many felt that this issue was a pretext for promoting Tibet's independence from China. The greater willingness of top American officials to meet with the Dalai Lama in recent years, the regular Congressional resolutions criticizing the Chinese 'occupation' of Tibet, and growing public support for the Tibetan government in exile provided, in the Chinese view, ample evidence of this intention, even though the US government had never challenged Chinese sovereignty over Tibet.

Still, the issue of greatest concern to China in 1995 was Taiwan. As noted above, the crisis in Sino-American relations in that year was due primarily to the decision by the Clinton administration to grant a visa to Taiwan's president, Lee Teng-hui, to make an unofficial visit to Cornell University. From Beijing's perspective, this was the third time in as many years that the United States had upgraded its relations with Taiwan. In the summer of 1992, the Bush administration had agreed to sell 150 F-16 fighters to Taiwan. A few months later, the Bush administration had sent Carla Hills, the US Trade Representative, to Taipei for the first cabinet-level visit since 1978. Then, in the late spring of 1995, the United States permitted a visit by Taiwan's head of state — the highest-level visitor from Taiwan since diplomatic relations were terminated at the end of 1978.

In each case, Beijing charged that Washington had violated an explicit promise to China. In the eyes of Chinese leaders, the F-16s violated the 1982 communique on American arms sales to Taiwan, which prohibited sales of higher quality military equipment than Taipei had been receiving at the time of the normalization of US-China relations; the visit by Carla Hills violated the 1978 agreement on normalization, which limited Taiwan and the United States to 'unofficial' relations; and the visa for Lee Teng-hui violated the Clinton administration's own Taiwan policy review of 1994, which had concluded that high-level Taiwanese officials could only pass through the United States in transit to third countries. (Indeed, up until one week before the decision was made, the State Department had been reassuring the Chinese embassy in Washington that Lee Teng-hui would not be allowed to make even an unofficial visit to the US.)

In short, the Sino-American relationship in 1995 was burdened by a large number of controversial questions, from trade to Tibet, from human rights to Taiwan, and from non-proliferation to the South China Seas. But cataloguing these issues separately cannot adequately account for their cumulative impact. Four additional points are critically important in understanding the fragility of US-China relations during this period.

First, many of these issues carried great emotional weight in the two countries. Beijing's record on human rights, especially after the Tiananmen Crisis of 1989, challenged the long-standing American interest in promoting human rights abroad, especially in China. Conversely, US policy on Taiwan and Tibet seemed to defy the even more enduring Chinese commitment to maintaining its own sovereignty and territorial integrity. In other words, these problems did not simply raise practical difficulties that could easily be resolved through compromise, but invoked core values that were of fundamental importance to both sides and could not easily be reconciled.

Second, old controversies continued to plague Sino-American relations, long after promising agreements on them had been reached. Thus, Beijing thought that the various bilateral communiques on the Taiwan question had set enduring limits on American relations with Taipei, and that the agreement on US access to the Chinese market had provided a framework for promoting China's speedy membership in the World Trade Organization. Conversely, the United States thought that previous negotiations with China had resolved the issues of the transfer of missile technology and the protection of intellectual property rights. But none of these apparent agreements was fully or steadfastly implemented, at least to the satisfaction of the aggrieved party. This created a vicious cycle, in which each side increasingly doubted the other's credibility and good faith, and in which each government therefore felt justified in violating its own commitments to the other.

Third, these troublesome issues spanned the full range of Sino-American relations, such that there was no longer any area that is devoid of controversy. With the common threat posed by the Soviet Union gone, the strategic realm was plagued by disagreements over proliferation, over the South China Seas, and (to a lesser degree) over the future of the Korean peninsula. Trade and investment, which had appeared seemed to replace the united front against the Soviet Union as the principal basis for Sino-American relations in the 1980s, had fallen victim to quarrels over market access, intellectual property rights, and China's membership in the World Trade Organization. And the American hope that China was embarked on a path of political reform that would soon lead to democracy was dashed by the Tiananmen Crisis of 1989 and by the cessation of further political liberalization thereafter. There was no single issue, in short, that could provide a solid foundation or persuasive rationale for a cooperative Sino-American relationship.

Finally, in 1995 there was no commonly accepted framework to undergird Sino-American relations. The United States spoke of 'comprehensive engagement' with China. But this seemed simply to involve a parade of high-level officials to China, each carrying the demands or requests of their Cabinet departments. No overarching framework linked the various strands together. And the emphasis of the dialogue seemed to be on the areas of disagreement, rather than common ground — so much so that some Chinese wondered whether 'comprehensive engagement' meant a wide-ranging process of diplomatic interaction, as the Americans intended, or an ongoing series of political confrontations, which the term could also conceivably denote.

Together, the large number of emotional issues plaguing Sino-American relations, the failure to resolve them effectively, and the absence of a compelling set of common interests at the heart of the relationship had produced serious mistrust on both sides of the Pacific. Each country increasingly viewed the other as a threat to important national interests.

In China there was a growing perception, expressed quite explicitly by political leaders and foreign policy analysts alike, that America was deliberately trying to keep China weak. In this interpretation, the United States, victorious in the Cold War against the Soviet Union, desired to perpetuate its status as the world's sole superpower. The rise of China — the world's most populous state, and potentially the world's largest economy — would be the principal obstacle to this ambition.

Accordingly, many Chinese believed that the United States was engaged in a deliberate attempt to block China's rise to major power status. It was trying to accomplish this through a coordinated three-pronged strategy of destabilization, division, and containment. The American promotion of democratization and the support for Chinese dissidents was intended not to enhance the human rights of the Chinese people, but rather to foster disunity and disorder. The upgrading of America's relations with Taiwan, and the growing US interest in Hong Kong and Tibet, allegedly embodied the intention to secure the geographical fragmentation of China. Blocking China's participation in the WTO, preventing it from hosting the Olympic Games in 2000, and expanding America's diplomatic and military contacts with Vietnam were all regarded as US attempts to contain China's political and strategic influence.

Although only a minority of Chinese specialists on American affairs believed that the United States had a deliberate and coordinated strategy to keep China in its place, this view was much more widely held among Chinese leaders, intellectuals, and ordinary people. Beginning in 1993, some of the Chinese students and scholars in the United States — presumably those who best understood the United States and were the most sympathetic to it — began to express their concern that American human rights policy was intended not to improve the lot of ordinary Chinese, but to keep China weak and divided. Many of these same younger Chinese intellectuals also saw American criticism of their country, on issues ranging from violations of human rights to the use of illegal drugs by Chinese athletes, as reflecting a persistent American refusal to acknowledge Chinese as equals. Chinese analysts of international affairs reported that there was a widespread view among ordinary urban Chinese that the US felt threatened by the rise of Chinese power, and was adopting various strategies to prevent it. Several popular books, many written by young Chinese intellectuals, embodied these concerns, the most notable being one entitled *China Can Say No*.

Moreover, there were persistent reports that the Chinese military shared this view of US intentions. Although many Chinese officers admire American military technology and would like to see the restoration of dialogue and exchanges with their American counterparts, they were also pressing their government not to compromise with Washington on matters of principle in the bilateral relationship.[2]

Similarly hostile perceptions of China began to emerge in the United States as well. China began to be seen not only as a repressive regime, as had been the case since the Tiananmen Crisis of 1989, but as a threatening one as well. Some Americans regarded the rise of Chinese power as a strategic menace to the United States, with different observers presenting different reasons for alarm. Some believed that authoritarian political systems, like China, are more likely than democracies to adopt aggressive foreign policies. Others pointed to China's political culture, arguing that China historically has been reluctant to engage in enduring international cooperative relationships, especially those that would significantly constrain Chinese sovereignty. Still others simply looked at the sheer size of China, arguing that the emergence of an economic and military power of such magnitude will inevitably be a destabilizing factor in the Asia-Pacific region, and thus a threat to American interests, whatever its political system or political culture. Regardless of their reasoning, proponents of this hypothesis warned that China would become a 'second Soviet Union' — a rising expansionist power that would ultimately challenge the dominant American position in Asia.

Another group of Americans saw China as a threat for economic, rather than military, reasons. From this perspective, China would become a major economic rival of the United States within a relatively short period of time. It would combine its own low-cost labour with advanced imported technology to produce, for export to the United States, a wide range of manufactured goods with which American industry will be unable to compete. At the same time, it would also prevent US exporters or investors from gaining extensive access to the Chinese domestic market, even as it encouraged both foreign and domestic entrepreneurs to produce for exports abroad. In short, China would follow the same neo-mercantilist strategies of promoting exports and restricting imports as the other successful economies of East Asia. But, because of the size of its labour force, it would be a vastly greater threat to the American economy than either Taiwan or South Korea. China would become, in this interpretation, a 'second Japan', albeit one with much lower labour costs.

These suspicions were reflected in American public opinion, as well as in elite analysis. A poll conducted towards the end of 1994 for the Chicago Council of Foreign Relations found that 57% of the American public regarded the 'development of China as a world power' to be a 'critical threat' to the United States, up from 40% in the previous poll in 1990.[3] A second poll, conducted for Potomac Associates in 1994, showed that 37% of Americans regarded China as 'unfriendly' or as an 'enemy', although this figure was down from 49% in 1991.[4]

The Potomac Associates poll also confirmed that a large number of Americans viewed China as an economic threat. Of those surveyed, a bit more than half — 53% — saw China as an 'unfair' trading partner, up from 27% in 1989. These results were similar to American perceptions of Japan in 1986, although still not as critical as American views of Japan in 1994, when fully three-quarters of Americans saw Japan as an unfair trading nation.

These views were increasingly reflected in Congress, among both Democratic liberals and Republican conservatives. The Democrats took up the China issue after the Tiananmen Crisis of 1989, accusing the Bush administration of 'coddling dictators' in Beijing. Now, even with a Democratic president in the White House, they continued their criticism of China, seeking to hold Clinton to his campaign promises to take a tougher line against unacceptable Chinese conduct at home or abroad.

For their part, the Republicans became even more vocal after Clinton's election in 1992. In the early 1990s, they focused more on Taiwan, arguing that the United States should agreed to upgrade its relations with Taipei, sell more sophisticated arms to the island, and reaffirm its commitment to Taiwan's security. Shortly after his election as Speaker of the House in 1995, Newt Gingrich even advocated the restoration of diplomatic relations with Taiwan, until he was persuaded by Henry Kissinger to revoke his proposal.

To be sure, neither the Republicans nor the Democrats regarded the revocation of China's most-favoured-nation status as the most appropriate instrument for exercising influence over Beijing. They understood that the economic cost to the United States would be high, and the risk of strategic confrontation with China would be great. They also saw that more and more

Chinese dissidents, both in China and overseas, favoured the maintenance of normal trade and investment relations with China. They also understood that, because of these considerations, it was unlikely that the termination of China's most-favoured-nation status would ever achieve enough Congressional support to override a Presidential veto.

Accordingly, the Congressional sceptics took a different approach. They introduced a variety of bills in Congress that would either prod or require the executive branch to toughen its policy towards China in other ways. These included a declaration that Tibet is a sovereign-occupied country, a request that the President appoint a special US envoy to Tibet, the establishment of a 'Radio Free Asia', the insistence that it draw on the 'expertise' of Chinese dissidents overseas in designing its broadcasts to China, and a provision that the Taiwan Relations Act should 'supersede' the August 1982 communique on US arms sales to Taiwan.[5] More generally, the Congress was highly sceptical of any efforts by the Clinton administration to improve relations with China, especially if they involved any sort of American 'concessions' to Beijing.

FROM CRISIS TO HOPE, 1995–96

By the end of 1995, these tensions and suspicions had erupted into crisis. Angered at Taiwan's attempts to upgrade its international standing, fearful that some other countries might be willing to follow the American example and permit visits by high-level Taiwanese officials, and apprehensive about the outcome of the March 1996 presidential elections on Taiwan, Beijing launched a series of military exercises in the Taiwan Strait that lasted from late 1995 through 1996. The exercises involved large multi-service manoeuvres, aimed at convincing Taipei that the PRC could exert direct military pressures against either Taiwan or the offshore islands it controls. They culminated with the launching of surface-to-surface missiles, targeted in the ocean just off some of Taiwan's major ports, suggesting the possibility that the mainland could impose some kind of blockade against the island.

China's military exercises did not seem to be aimed at preventing Taiwan from carrying out its presidential elections. Instead, they were designed to influence the outcome of those elections, by showing the Taiwanese electorate the risks of voting for a candidate, like Peng Ming-min of the Democratic Progressive Party, who supported Taiwanese independence, or even for a candidate, like Lee Teng-hui, who sought to increase Taiwan's role in the world — a policy that Beijing regarded as just one step short of independence. In addition, the military exercises were also intended to send a signal to the United States: that there was the possibility of a military confrontation in the Taiwan Strait into which the US might be drawn. Beijing assumed that

Washington wanted to avoid such a conflict, and would try to forestall it by stabilizing its relations with the mainland and by imposing restraint on Taiwan.

The military exercises did not achieve all of the mainland's objectives. To the extent that they affected the outcome of presidential elections, or the positions of Taiwan's major political parties on policy towards the mainland, then Beijing's gambit was only a partial success. It probably did cause a drop in electoral support for the DPP, at least relative to that party's showing in the previous legislative elections. That, in turn, may have persuaded the party to downplay its advocacy of independence and to focus on domestic issues, a step that it took shortly after the March presidential elections. But the military exercises also increased popular support for Lee Teng-hui, despite his sponsorship of flexible diplomacy. It also caused a second opposition party, the New Party, formerly an advocate of early reunification with the mainland, to back away from that position. In short, the military exercises pushed Taiwan public opinion towards the middle of the political spectrum, away from independence, but also away from reunification, and certainly closer to Lee Teng-hui.

Internationally, the military exercises also had mixed consequences. The scale and duration of the manoeuvres sent shockwaves through the region, as did Beijing's ability to coordinate naval, air, ground, and missile forces in large-scale exercises. Few governments were willing to express their concerns publicly, but many Asian analysts said privately that they thought Beijing's actions were excessively belligerent. Japan was one of the few countries that criticized China's actions directly, and the crisis in the Taiwan Strait greatly exacerbated the growing suspicion in Japan that China might be emerging as the principal threat to national security. It also dampened local criticism of the US-Japan Mutual Security Treaty, which had come under fire because of the rape of a Japanese schoolgirl by US servicemen on Okinawa, and enabled Tokyo and Washington to reaffirm the vitality of their alliance later that spring.

In the United States, however, the crisis had a paradoxically salutary effect on thinking about China, at least in the short run. One might have thought that, in the US as in Japan, it would have reinforced the arguments of those who had been warning of the rise of Chinese military power and calling for the containment of Beijing. And, indeed, the Clinton administration did respond to the missile tests in the latter phase of the military exercises by sending two aircraft carrier battle groups to the seas east of Taiwan, so as to signal the continued American commitment to a peaceful resolution of the Taiwan issue. On balance, though, the crisis persuaded the administration, and much of the Congress and the public as well, that the US needed to take new initiatives to halt the deterioration of the American relationship with China. For what had begun as an ideological dispute over human rights in 1989, and had become a broader political dispute over a wider range of issues by the mid-1990s, was now threatening to become a military confrontation.

Thus, in the middle of 1996, the US unveiled a new approach to China. To begin with, it restated its commitment to a 'one-China' policy, and assured Beijing that future visits by top-level Taiwanese leaders to the United States would be low-keyed and rare. In addition, for the first time since 1989, Washington presented an overall strategic framework for its policy towards China: to promote China's full integration into the international community, with both the privileges and the responsibilities of major power status. By announcing this objective, the Clinton administration meant to reassure Beijing that its aim was not to contain the rise of Chinese power nor to undermine China's internal stability, while also satisfying critics at home that the US would continue to oppose Chinese behaviour that violated international norms. In the words of Secretary of Defence William Perry, the policy was thus neither 'containment' nor 'appeasement', but rather an attempt to 'work together where we agree and reduce tensions where we disagree'.[6]

Moreover, the Clinton administration also suggested more clearly than ever before that it saw cooperation, rather than conflict or competition, as the principal element in the Sino-American relationship. Previously, Washington had only identified secondary issues, such as the prevention of international drug-trafficking, as areas in which the two countries might cooperate. In doing so, it had implied that it regarded the differences between the two countries over issues such as trade and human rights as the primary aspect of the relationship. Now, in mid-1996, Washington started to affirm the common interests of the two countries in promoting economic cooperation and regional stability, suggesting that the differences between them were less fundamental.

Finally, also for the first time since 1989, Washington proposed the resumption of regular bilateral summit meetings between Chinese and American leaders. This marked the culmination of the gradual restoration of the official bilateral dialogue that had been suspended after the Tiananmen Crisis of 1989. Although the US had resumed regular Cabinet-level contact in 1993, as part of its policy of 'comprehensive engagement', and although Presidents Bush and Clinton had met their Chinese counterpart, Jiang Zemin, in multilateral settings such as the United Nations or the annual APEC conference of economic leaders, Washington had previously been reluctant to restore the exchange of official visits at the summit. Now, in 1996, the US proposed a series of such visits, beginning with a trip by Vice President Al Gore to Beijing in early 1997, to be followed by reciprocal visits by Jiang Zemin and Bill Clinton over the subsequent eighteen months. The proposed frequency of summit diplomacy was reminiscent of the earlier attempt to rebuild Sino-American relations in 1983–84, following the resolution of the dispute over American arms sales towards Taiwan.

These new American initiatives were reasonably well-received in Beijing. Given the priority that Chinese leaders assign to personal relationships with their foreign counterparts, the American proposal to restore regular Sino-American summit meetings was especially appreciated. The conceptual framework proposed by the US — the integration of China into a community of nations — also proved acceptable, particularly after Washington made clear that China would have a major role in writing the rules of the international community, and would not simply be expected to follow norms developed by others. And the American formula that the common interests of the two countries were more fundamental than their differences echoed the line that Beijing had been taking on Sino-American relations for several years. Thus, shortly after the Clinton administration conveyed its new policy to Beijing — principally by an exchange of visits between National Security Adviser Anthony Lake and his Chinese counterpart, Liu Huaqiu — Chinese spokesmen began saying that the atmosphere for Sino-Americans had significantly improved.

On the American side, too, the response to the Clinton administration's initiatives was surprisingly positive, considering the intensity of the criticism of China's domestic and international behaviour in the previous years. Although there was some criticism in the press of the proposed restoration of bilateral summit meetings between American and Chinese leaders, overall the idea gained widespread acceptance. Through the series of Cabinet-level visits undertaken since the end of 1993, the Clinton administration had proved that it could conduct meetings with its Chinese counterparts in a businesslike manner, avoiding excessive effusiveness, so that official dialogue would not be seen as 'kowtowing' to Beijing.

Accordingly, the annual renewal of Beijing's most-favoured-nation status passed through Congress with surprisingly little debate in the summer of 1996, and without significant Congressional attempts to force the Administration to adopt a tougher approach to China in other areas. There seemed to be a growing realization, in fact, that the annual reconsideration of the economic relationship with China was generating little leverage over Beijing, once it had become evident that the US would not revoke China's most-favoured-nation status except in the most extreme of circumstances. There was even an emerging willingness in Congress to consider granting permanent most-favoured-nation status to China, as part of the agreement on Beijing's accession to the World Trade Organization.

Nor did Senator Robert Dole, the Republican candidate for President in 1996, make China policy a major issue in his campaign. Although accusing the Clinton administration of vacillation towards China, he did not express any significant reservations about the new policies of engagement with Beijing or the integration of China into the international community. Moreover, Dole did not propose any major changes in America's policy towards Taiwan, such as upgrading official relations or supporting Taiwanese independence, although he did suggest a willingness to provide the island with a theatre missile defence system. Dole's failure to challenge the Clinton administration's new China policy led some observers to speak of a 'new consensus' in the United States on how best to deal with Beijing.

RENEWED UNCERTAINTY, 1997

But it soon became clear that consensus on China policy would be illusive. By early 1997, it seemed more likely that vexing problems would continue to bedevil the relationship, that powerful sceptics in each country would continue to question the intentions of the other, and that Beijing and Washington would disagree on the definition and application of the strategic framework for their relationship.

The problems that have plagued Sino-American relations over the past decade are likely to continue to do so in the years ahead. America's trade deficit with China, at least as measured by official US statistics, is almost certain to exceed its bilateral trade deficit with Japan — although this development may be somewhat delayed by the recent depreciation of the yen against the dollar. This will exacerbate the accusations in the United States that China is engaging in the same unfair, mercantilist trade practices that Japan practised in earlier decades: seeking to expand its exports to the United States while restricting American access to its own markets.

At the same time, the US will be deeply concerned with conditions in Hong Kong, as that territory returns to Chinese sovereignty in the middle of 1997. Beijing's decision in January 1997 to repeal part of the bill of rights that the Hong Kong government enacted in the early 1990s, to adopt new laws against sedition, and to dismantle the legislative council elected in 1995 have heightened apprehensions that China will restrict civil and political liberties in Hong Kong once it regains control. Any suppression of dissent, interference in the judicial system, or restrictions on the press in Hong Kong could have severe repercussions on US attitudes towards China.

The Taiwan issue is also likely to complicate Sino-American relations, as it has done for the last five decades. Although there is some hope for improvement in cross-Strait ties, as reflected in Taipei's decision to permit some forms of maritime links between Taiwan and the mainland, it is also virtually certain that Lee Teng-hui will continue his attempts to expand Taiwan's international relationships, both bilaterally and multilaterally. It is also highly probable that Lee will adopt certain political reforms, such as the effective dismemberment of the provincial government on Taiwan, that will be interpreted in Beijing as a step towards independence. These developments could again provoke mainland China to use military pressure to prevent any significant movement towards independence.

Other issues could also disrupt US relations with China. The suppression of political dissent in China, further restraints on nationalism in Tibet, Chinese arms sales to what the US regards as 'rogue regimes', Chinese attempts to seize disputed territory in the South China Seas, a further confrontation between China and Japan over the Senkaku or Diaoyutai islands, or evidence that the Chinese government was indeed involved in making illegal campaign contributions to American politicians — all these could intensify the concern that China is becoming more repressive at home or more aggressive abroad.

In the future, environmental problems could also emerge as still another controversial issue between China and the United States. Already, the Three Gorges Dam project has been condemned by a coalition of environmentalists and human rights activists: the former for the dam's impact on the environment, the latter for the Chinese government's suppression of criticism of the project and for the forced relocation of millions of people living in the areas that will be flooded.[7] Other environmental problems in China — especially those, like acid rain, that have international consequences — could also be the subject of censure in the US. The fact that Vice President Gore's visit to China in March 1997 focused on environmental issues raised the hope that the two countries could establish, from the outset, a cooperative framework for dealing with this issue. But it also gave this potentially controversial issue much greater centrality and visibility than ever before.

Partly as a result of these concrete issues, there will remain powerful sceptics in both countries who will continue to challenge any efforts to rebuild Sino-American relations. Not all Chinese observers, for example, have been reassured that American intentions towards their country are benign. Many conservative analysts in China continue to regard international organizations and regimes as devices designed by rich and powerful nations in their own interests, so as to keep poor and weaker countries like China in their place. The American concept of integrating China into the international community is therefore seen as a form of 'soft containment' — of enmeshing China in institutions that were designed to advance Western interests, not Chinese.[8] Although Jiang Zemin appeared reasonably secure in his positions just after the death of Deng Xiaoping in February 1997, he may not always be able to ignore the political pressures from those who favour a tougher policy towards the United States.

In the US, in turn, there are still analysts who believe that the rise of Chinese power will inexorably pose a fundamental challenge to American interests, particularly in the security sphere, and that the resulting competition between the two countries will never be effectively constrained or regulated by international rules or institutions.[9] Another school of American thought is more enthusiastic about the policy of integrating China into the international community, but expects full and immediate results, despite the fact that this strategic framework cannot resolve all of the issues in the relationship quickly or completely.

Both groups of sceptics will continue to have a strong voice in Congress, especially since it will have a Republican majority at least through 1998, that will remain highly critical of China's violations of human rights, its acquisition of force projection capabilities, and its mounting trade surplus with the United States. In early 1997, the sceptics seized on charges that the Chinese government was attempting to acquire political influence in Washington by funnelling money to both the Democratic National Committee and to individual members of Congress, using Asian-Americans with business connections in China as its conduit. Thus, despite President Clinton's remarkable victory in the Presidential elections of 1996, he may not be able to rebuild America's relations with China quickly or decisively, particularly if such progress requires steps that his critics will portray as 'appeasing China' or 'kowtowing to Beijing'.

Moreover, even under the best of circumstances, the new strategic framework proposed by the United States will not overcome the reservations of these sceptics, because it will not provide a guarantee of harmony between the two countries. Beijing and Washington will not necessarily agree on the content of the international norms that are supposed to guide their relationship. The United States, for example, may suggest that China should refrain from the use of force against Taiwan, on the grounds that such disputes should be resolved peacefully; but China will respond that Taiwan is a part of its territory, and that any American intervention violates the principle of national sovereignty. Similarly, Washington will continue to insist that certain aspects of Beijing's internal behaviour represent a violation of internationally-accepted human rights; China will again respond that its pattern of governance is its internal affair, in which the US has no right to intervene.

Relatedly, the two countries will likely address the enforcement of international norms from quite different perspectives. China, for example, may expect side-payments from the US in return for agreeing to abide by international principles. Already, for example, Beijing has asked for a *quid pro quo* in exchange for honouring the Missile Technology Control Regime: first the cessation of the sale of American F-16s to Taiwan, and more recently a ban on American theatre missile defence systems to the island. It also has suggested that it would sign the two major United Nations covenants on human rights if the US agrees not to sponsor resolutions critical of China before the UN Commission on Human Rights. In contrast, the American approach tends to be that compliance with international norms is a matter of automatic obligation, and should not be subject to negotiation. There will be little sympathy in the US for Chinese demands for compensation.

Conversely, the US will certainly expect that it has the right to impose sanctions against China when it believes that Beijing is violating international norms. Indeed, sanctions for violations of the Missile Technology Control Regime are already written into American law, as are certain sanctions (such as termination of arms sales and official development assistance) for countries that engage in gross violations of human rights. If China enters the World Trade Organization, it is likely that many in the US Congress will insist upon some kind of unilateral enforcement mechanism that can be activated if Beijing reneges on its obligations.

Even if China and the US agree on the definition of international norms, and even if Beijing faithfully complies with all of them, this will not resolve all issues in Sino-American relations. After all, some Chinese actions of which the US disapproves, such as the sale of safeguarded nuclear power equipment or conventional weapons systems to Iran, are not illegal under international law, but simply conflict with American interests and policies. And international law does not prohibit the United States and Japan from strengthening their security alliance, even though China increasingly finds this to run counter to its national interests.

On the other side of the ledger, there are grounds for optimism, at least of the cautious variety. First, both countries remain pre-occupied with domestic problems, each having its own form of budgetary crisis that discourages costly foreign commitments. The United States is still grappling with the issues of fiscal retrenchment and economic readjustment, with few Americans eager to take on costly international obligations. China faces the challenge of overcoming various obstacles to continued economic growth — shortages of arable land, depletion of energy reserves, inadequate water supplies, growing environmental pollution, economic, congested transportation systems, and the like — when its banking system is insolvent and its government revenues represent a declining share of GNP.

Second, the economic and societal interdependence between the two countries has increased substantially over the last several years, and stands in sharp contrast to the mutual isolation of the Soviet Union and the United States during the Cold War. US firms have now invested more than US$4 billion in China, and have committed more than $10 billion more. By US count, bilateral trade has risen to more than $50 billion, making China one of America's most significant trading partners. According to Chinese statistics, the US is China's third largest trading partner, with around 15% of China's global trade, and China's third largest source of foreign investment, albeit with less than 10% of new contracts. Tens of thousands of Chinese, including close relative of China's top leaders, now work and study in the United States, with a smaller but still significant number of Americans resident in China. This means that each side would suffer a huge cost if their relations were disrupted, and gives both governments an important stake in maintaining a stable bilateral relationship.

Third, the international environment also encourages restraint. At this point, most other countries in the Asia-Pacific region want to prevent a confrontation between the United States and China, in which they might be forced to choose sides. It would be virtually impossible for the US to persuade any other Asian country to join it in a strategic alignment against China. Conversely, belligerent Chinese behaviour towards Taiwan, Korea, or the South China Seas would alienate far more countries than just the United States. This environment encourages both Beijing and Washington to pursue cooperation and to avoid confrontation.

These factors provide some durability and resilience to Sino-American relations. They make it unlikely that the relationship between the two countries will degenerate to the point of mutual isolation or strategic confrontation, as they did in the 1950s and 1960s. The fact that both sides sought to improve their relations following the Taiwan Strait crisis of 1995–96, despite the fact that both governments were facing domestic demands to adopt a tougher posture in the Sino-American relationship, illustrates all these considerations at work.

PROSPECTS

Even under the best of circumstances, however, China and the United States will not experience a second honeymoon, as they did first in the early 1970s, or again in the mid-1980s. The differences of interest and perspective are simply too great. Rather, the two sides must expect that their relationship will entail both convergent and divergent interests, and thus will remain a blend of cooperation, competition, and even occasional conflict.

Some years ago, I predicted that China and the United States would, in the 1990s, be 'neither friend nor foe'.[10] A Chinese colleague has recently used a similar, although more eloquent, formulation: *he erh bu re, fen erh bu lie* (the two countries will cooperate, but not be close; they will have differences, but not split apart). The question is what aspect will dominate this contradictory relationship: the cooperative or the conflictual.

The answer will depend on two main factors. The first is whether the governments of the two countries can use the more positive atmosphere of early 1997 to resolve some of the major problems in the relationship. In this, China's application for membership in the WTO presents an important opportunity, since a successful negotiation on this issue would bring benefits to many parties. For China, it would mean membership in a major international organization. For Washington, it would entail meaningful commitments by the Chinese government to reduce the barriers to trade and investment in their country, and would provide safeguards and enforcement mechanisms if they failed to honor their promises. And, for Taipei, China's membership in the WTO would pave the way for Taiwan to join the same organization as a separate customs territory. The problem, as of the spring of 1997, was whether the US Congress would endorse any agreement on MFN that involved giving China permanent, unconditional most-favoured-nation status — a *quid pro quo* upon which Beijing seemed almost certain to insist.

The second key factor is whether new issues emerge, or old issues intensify, in ways that further weaken the relationship. Here, the suppression of popular protests in mainland China, signs that Beijing is limiting human rights in Hong Kong, or evidence of Chinese violations of non-proliferation regimes could all exacerbate American suspicions of China. And pressure from Taiwan to enhance its international standing in the world, especially if encouraged or supported by the United States, would heighten Chinese mistrust of the United States. Any of these developments would lead the sceptics in both countries to renew their demands for a tougher policy towards the other.

NOTES

1. The notion that Sino-American relations have been fragile since the *rapprochement* of the early 1970s is one of the principal theses of Harry Harding, *A Fragile Relationship: The United States and China Since 1972* (Washington, DC: The Brookings Institution, 1992).
2. For two major articles on the military's reviews, both from the Hong Kong Press, see *Hsin Pao*, 8 July 1994, p. 23; in *Foreign Broadcast Information Service Daily Report: China* (hereafter *FBIS*), 13 July 1994, pp. 1–2; and *Cheng Ming*, 1 July 1995; in *FBIS*, 17 July 1995, pp. 8–11.
3. The intensity of concern about China among opinion leaders was lower, but the trend was the same: 46% of these opinion leaders, as opposed to 57% of the public, saw the development of China as a world power as a 'critical threat' to the United States, up from only 16% in 1990. These 'opinion leaders' include a sampling of members of Congress, officials in the executive branch, and those in key positions in business, the media, academia, policy research institutions, labour unions, churches, and interest groups active on foreign policy issues. See John E. Rielly, *American Public Opinion and U.S. Foreign Policy* (Chicago: Chicago Council on Foreign Relations, 1995).
4. William Watts, 'National security: A key to extending MFN to China', *Update* (Honolulu, HI: The East-West Centre, 16 May 1994). These figures are somewhat mitigated, however, by the fact that Americans tend to express concern about China only if asked. When requested to volunteer the international issues they thought were of greatest importance to the United States, well under 6% of opinion leaders identified China or the rise of Chinese power. See Rielly, *American Public Opinion and U.S. Foreign Policy*, op.cit.
5. Although the sponsors of the amendment believed that the term 'supersede' meant to take precedence, in fact the term means to nullify.
6. Speech to the Washington State China Relations Council, 30 October 1995.

7. See, for example, Human Rights Watch/Asia, 'The Three Gorges Dam in China: Forced resettlement, suppression of dissent, and labour rights concerns', *Human Rights Watch/Asia Reports,* Vol. 7, no. 2 (New York: Human Rights Watch, February 1995).
8. The title chosen for a Council on Foreign Relations report advocating this policy, *Weaving the Net,* simply reinforced suspicions that the American strategy is aimed at ensnaring Beijing in institutions that will prevent it from pursuing China's national interests. See James Shinn (ed.), *Weaving the Net: Conditional Engagement with China* (New York: Council on Foreign Relations Press, 1996).
9. The most comprehensive statement of this view is Richard Bernstein and Ross H. Munro, *The Coming Conflict with China* (New York: Alfred A. Knopf, 1997).
10. Harry Harding, 'Neither friend nor foe: A China policy for the nineties', *Brookings Review,* Vol. 10, no. 2 (Spring 1992), pp. 6–11.

2

China's Economic Reforms and Their Impact on US-China Trade Relations

Robert F. Dernberger

I welcome the invitation to present my 'assessment of the current state of the Chinese economic reform programme' and speculate on 'how the reforms are impacting on trade and economic relations with the United States'. It is, however, becoming increasingly difficult to say anything original about China's economic reforms. Almost any issue of our traditional economic journals now contain several theoretical and empirical studies of the Chinese economic reform programme. This literature has been enriched by the contributions of our colleagues in political science and sociology — both China specialists and non-China specialists alike. In short, we are accumulating a vast amount of both theoretical and empirical studies on China's economic reforms. The purpose of these introductory remarks is to recognize the existence of this vast amount of literature, to admit that I have not been able to read all of it, and to argue that I have read enough of it to know it will be very hard for me to say much about the Chinese economic reform programme that you have not already heard or read; but I will try.

As for an assessment of the impact of the Chinese economic reform programme on future Sino-American economic relations, I do not believe my record as a forecaster is any worse than of my colleagues. Most forecasts of China's future have been wrong because they were based on trends existing up to the time the forecast was made. Developments in China's economy over the past four decades, however, reveal the lack of any persistent trend for more than three or four years. Rather than past trends, the most crucial influences on developments in China's future have been endogenous and exogenous shocks. These endogenous and exogenous shocks, by definition, are very difficult to anticipate and predict.

Yet, these problems have never prevented me from making speculative predictions in the past and I will not shirk my assignment here.[1] Of course, the world of the past four decades is changing dramatically and developments in the economies of Asia are a major reason for these changes. Obviously, these economies and these changes will help define the new world economic order. Any forecast we make about the future of this region, therefore, must recognize the possibility that the new world order they are a part of will be defined by them and not be a replication of our own egocentric and culturally biased view of what that new world order will be or even should be.

CHINA's ECONOMIC REFORMS

In the search for a general theory, much of the economic literature on the transition in the formerly communist economies involves rather sterile debates over the speed and the sequence of the reforms to be implemented. The transition was simply viewed as a matter of abandoning the well-known Soviet-type economy and the creation of a free market economy. We now realize that not all these societies have the objective, or are willing to bear the pain, of simply abandoning their old economic system for a free market economy. Furthermore, rather than exhibiting a single, uniform model, each of these economies already held to be free market economies vary in the extent and variety of the government regulations they place on their market economy. Thus, the market economies of the West have long been designated by specialists in the field of comparative economics as regulated, market economies, rather than free market economies.

Even if we were to assume that the formerly communist countries desired to adopt a model of a free market economy, they obviously could not do so instantly or in a single leap or 'big bang'. With regard to 'marketization', even if prices are suddenly set free, how can markets — complete with contract law and property rights and the courts to enforce them, competition on both sides of the market with the free flow of goods and factors, and developed capital markets to allow freedom of entry and enforcement of the exit of losers — be created overnight? With regard to 'privatization', the attempt to sell off all state enterprises overnight would resemble a fire sale, even assuming buyers could be found with the funds to buy them. And how could we be sure that ownership would be placed in the hands of those who desired to operate the enterprises efficiently in competitive, free markets, not cannibalize the assets or operate them as price-fixing monopolies?

Those who acknowledge the need for gradualism moved on to a debate over the proper sequence of reforms. These discussions do introduce a greater emphasis upon empirical analysis than the normative-driven arguments about 'big bangs'. However, these discussions also rely on theoretical arguments to draw up the necessary sequence of reforms for the transition to be successful.[2]

These debates in the literature are of little help in understanding the Chinese economic reform programme. Rather, the Chinese economic reform programme is best understood as a series of policy responses to the particular problems the policymakers faced. And their responses to those problems were taken within the constraints and pressures of their environment at the time. Much has been made of the lack of a master plan for their economic reform programme in Western writings, but there was no need for a master plan. Unlike the situation in Eastern Europe and Russia, there was no economic crisis facing the Chinese in 1978. The leadership crisis was resolved with the success of Deng Xiaoping at the Third Plenum of the Eleventh Central Committee at the end of 1978. That same meeting is said to have launched the economic reform programme. But what was produced at that meeting was far from a programme. Rather, that meeting produced what was a somewhat simple policy response to the most serious economic problem faced by China's leaders at the end of 1978: the problem of agriculture.

AGRICULTURAL REFORMS

Collectivized agriculture proved to be a failure in the communist countries, but the Maoist version of collectivized agriculture made the situation in China even worse. By the end of the 1970s, per capita consumption of many agricultural foodstuffs was below the level of the mid-1950s, while attempts to increase output by increasing modern, purchased inputs often reduced the income of the peasant. The post-Mao leadership in 1978 was obviously concerned over the need to feed the Chinese people and with the growing discontent of the peasantry. Thus, although hardly a programme of economic reform, the Third Plenum at the end of 1978 simply called for a dramatic increase in the prices paid to peasants for their output. It is true, however, that the simultaneous circulation of a revised version of the '60 Articles', a document that expressed the agricultural policy views of the more moderate wing of the party, did generate the evolution of economic reform in the countryside.[3] In reaction to the release of this document, local cadres and the peasants began to adopt the 'contract responsibility system', and this return to family, leasehold farming soon spread throughout China.

While the Chinese economic reforms are said to represent a strategy of gradualism, I fail to see how the successful transition of China's agricultural sector, the largest in the world, from an extreme form of collectivization into essentially a system of household leasehold farming in five years can be judged to be gradual. Marketization of farm activities and output took a little longer and even today local cadres retain significant control over agriculture if and when they desire to exercise that control. Yet, by the mid-1980s, China's agriculture was well on the way to being 'privatized and marketized', the objective of many well-planned reform programmes.

China's leaders reluctantly gave in to this initial wave of reform from below and, in fact, to complement and facilitate the changes taking place in the countryside, the commune and brigade was transformed into the township and village level of government. The quotas of assigned deliveries were transformed into negotiated contracts on a voluntary basis; the peasants were given tenant rights for periods of more than one generations and were allowed to leave the land to find work outside crop production in local towns and villages.

A major reason for the leadership's acceptance of these reforms from below in agriculture was that they were a smashing success and agriculture quickly became the most dynamic sector of the economy in the early 1980s.[4] Unfortunately, however, this record of initial success was not sustained after the mid-1980s.[5] Thus, the agriculture sector, that is, farming, remains a problem faced by China's current leaders and is becoming more critical as time passes. Nonetheless, the success of the initial reforms in this sector did provide China's leaders with more than a decade before they had to come to grips with this problem once more.

OPENING

Reform of the agricultural sector was not the only pressing need facing the Chinese leaders at the time of the Third Plenum in 1978. During the Cultural Revolution, self-dependency was adopted as a major element of the Maoist development strategy. China's trade in 1970 represented one of the lowest ratios of foreign trade to national income in the world: 5.9 percent. When rehabilitated by Zhou Enlai to administer the economy in 1972, Deng Xiaoping increased China's foreign trade, quickly generating a sizable deficit in the balance of trade.[6] When Deng argued that the deficit could be paid for by exports of oil and coal, he was attacked by the radicals as wanting to turn China into a colony of the industrial powers. Deng also argued for the restoration of China's science and technology establishment, which included the need to rely on help from the foreigner for this purpose. Attacked for these 'poisonous weeds' (that is, greater foreign dependence), Deng fell from power again in 1975. Inasmuch as the Third Plenum played a significant role in returning Deng Xiaoping once more to power, it also led to the reforms opening China to greater foreign economic interdependency.[7]

Despite several pauses and even a few steps backwards from time to time, the open-door reforms have been the most continuous and remarkable of all the reforms. Within a decade the Chinese dismantled their centralized and monopoly control of both trade and loans, although transactions in certain sectors or of certain types, along with those above certain amounts, require the approval of the central authorities. Trade negotiations can now be carried out at the local level so that direct contacts between buyers and suppliers are possible. Special economic zones, open ports, technology and development zones have been created all over China where local officials intensely compete for foreign investment.

Those who would claim that the Chinese have been gradual in their economic reforms would have to explain how a communist country with a Soviet-type economy at a low level of development, one of the lowest ratios of foreign trade to national income, and no foreign direct investment, could make the transition, in a little more than a decade, to an open economy that is now the largest participant in the world economy among the developing countries, as well as one of the largest among the industrialized countries. China now also receives the largest amount of foreign direct investment and soft loans in the developing world and also ranks high among the industrial countries as a recipient of large capital flows. Obviously, the open-door reforms have been a dramatic and relatively rapid success.[8] Although starting from a very low base, when the agricultural sector began to fade as the leading growth node in China's economy, the growth of exports assumed a major role as the stimulus to economy-wide growth in the last half of the 1980s. By the 1990s, the rapid expansion of the 'three-investment' sector (the use of foreign funds in creating wholly-foreign owned enterprises, joint-ventures, and co-operatives) also became a dynamic centre of growth.

As already noted, the agricultural and open-door reforms still leave government and party officials with considerable controls and the ability to interfere in economic decisions in the agricultural and foreign trade sectors if and when they want to. Yet, it should be noted that the impressive record of success of the reforms in these two sectors owes much to the central government's willingness to restrict its role to adopting and specifying the general principles and guidelines for the reforms, leaving it up to local governments and cadres to adapt these principles to fit their needs and objectives in implementing the reforms. Many observers interpret this increased role of the localities in administering the reform programme as merely representing the central government's loss of its control over the localities, but I believe it is more a successful strategy of 'reform from below'.[9] In addition, it should be recognized that the reforms in agriculture and in the foreign sector were enhanced by the tremendous support given to them by two very powerful interest groups that were essential to China's successful economic development: the peasants in the case of the agricultural reforms and the foreigner, especially the overseas Chinese, in the case of the open-door reforms.

PRIVATIZATION AND MARKETIZATION

The Chinese leaders did indeed adopt a gradual strategy in regard to both 'privatization' and 'marketization'. One the one hand, I do not believe that the Chinese leadership, or any significant element of the leadership, has ever advocated the 'privatization' of the state enterprise sector. On the other hand, the Chinese gradual approach to marketization may be one of the most successful examples of marketization reforms to be found. As argued above, China's economic reforms were a progressive and sequential series of policies adopted to cope with real problems.

By the mid-1980s, the state enterprise sector and the traditional system of economic planning were under ever growing strains. Originally, China's leaders believed that the state enterprise sector could be 'fixed-up' by reforming the system of management. This approach ended in failure. Nonetheless, while the state sector as a whole was not a disaster, at the same time it was not a dynamic centre of growth. Most importantly, already bloated with surplus workers, it was not able to provide employment for the increasing numbers of unemployed in the urban areas.[10] This growing problem of urban unemployment was a serious threat to a third major source of support for the regime — the urban labour force. In addition, the attempt to decentralize decision-making and liberalize trade flows in the economy after 1978 was not only making the existing system of planning an anachronism, but the attempt to retain the scheme of artificially set and irrational prices threatened to make the economic system being created by China's economic reforms even worse than the economic system that was being reformed.

There were obviously many unresolved disagreements among the leadership in the mid-1980s, and the urban and industrial reform document adopted by the party in October 1984 only put forth the general direction to be followed.[11] The problem of unemployment was to be alleviated by the expansion of the non-state sector. Local governments, especially the township and village governments that had inherited the commune and brigade industries, were urged to expand the 'community' enterprises under their control.[12] The urban and industrial reform document of 1984 also recognized the existence of a private sector.[13]

Many Western observers believe the lack of well-defined and defended property rights in the local sector is a major weakness of China's economic reforms. But this ignores the fact that property rights being well-defined depends on the prior existence of well-defined markets. In the absence of well-defined markets, the township and village enterprises (TVE) sector, or 'community', or cooperative sector, has been China's unique and effective response to a second-best solution. As a result, even in the absence of well-defined property rights, this sector has become a dominant growth node in China's economy since the mid-1980s.

As for the process of marketization, or achieving well-defined markets, the 1984 document on urban and industrial reform created a path of transition that has also proved to be effective. Centralized, mandatory planning was to be progressively reduced as lower level, negotiated plans ('guidance planning') were to be expanded, with market allocations to be significantly increased for most products. After a decade of transition, mandatory planning has been greatly reduced to a rather minimal level and market transactions have become the dominant force in China's economy.[14] How did this transition from a planned economy to what are essentially market-forces take place without the disruptions and even collapse of the state enterprise sector? Many Western observers cite the two-tier price system introduced by the urban and industrial reform document of 1984 as a source of serious inefficiencies and corruption. While this is true, they also see the two track price system as preventing the 'marketization' of the industrial sector. What they fail to see is that the two-tier price system was the only way to marketize the economy, while at the same time preserving the state enterprise sector, one of the leaderships primary objectives.

What the two-tier price system did was to assure the state enterprises that a significant part of their capacity could still be used to produce output 'according to the plan', and that the state would supply the necessary inputs and buy the output at the old, planned prices. At the same time, the process of pushing these state enterprises onto the market was begun, that is, the rest of their capacity was to be used to produce for the market with inputs purchased on the market.[15] Once introduced, the portion of capacity covered by the mandatory plans and administered prices was steadily reduced and the planned prices were adjusted upward towards their market equivalent. In this manner, China's state enterprises were successfully shifted a considerable way from the planned economy to a market economy in about a decade.

Although there is no evidence the Chinese leaders want to privatize the state sector, state enterprises now do feel pressure from market forces.[16] As a whole, the state enterprise sector is incurring ever-growing financial losses and these losses can cause the manager of the loss making enterprise considerable problems.[17] The losses suffered by state enterprises, that is, those suffering losses, increased by 40 percent a year in 1985 and 1993. The total profits of the state industrial sector as a whole in 1993 were only 50 percent what they had been in 1985 (in current prices!).[18] Obviously, although being pushed onto the market, the state enterprises were not doing very well in adjusting to market forces.

Can we say it really is their fault if no one forces them to be profitable and efficient? In other words, contrary to dominant thinking in the West, I agree with those who, like Barry Naughton,[19] believe the state industrial sector is still a very significant and viable economic sector in China's economy and produces many products vital to the economy. The problem is that having pushed them onto the market, the state has proceeded very slowly in making the state enterprises live up to the discipline of market forces.

MACROSTABILITY

It is the losses of the state enterprises that have generated the urgent need for the final category of economic reforms — macrostability. China's budget has not been balanced throughout the economic reform period and the deficit has even increased over time, but this was not a critical problem for China's leaders until the 1990s. China's budget is a unified budget, that means it includes revenues and expenditures at all levels of government, and the problem that has become serious is to be found in the revenues and expenditures of the central government alone. Traditionally, the central government's main source of revenue was the profits of state enterprises. The economic reforms introduced market prices, that is, higher prices for inputs and lower prices for some outputs; increased competition for both the state and non-state-sector enterprises alike; and led to significant increases in the wages and bonuses paid to their bloated labour force. Thus, the profits of state enterprises fell dramatically.[20]

Local budgets in 1993 were about twice the level of the central budget and, in the aggregate, were in surplus, while the central budget was in deficit, **even when foreign loans and domestic bond sales are included as revenue in the central budget**. Obviously, the economic reforms had made the fiscal system of China an anachronism of the pre-reform economic system and by 1993 the central budget accounted for less than 20 percent of national income and was suffering an ever-growing deficit. Once more, when the problem became serious enough, the Chinese leaders reacted with additional reforms, introducing a completely new system for raising government revenues as of 1 January 1994.

While retaining commodity and business taxes, a new value added tax of 17 percent was introduced and the profits tax was made uniform for all enterprises at 33 percent. The income tax was restructured to give it more bite, especially at the higher incomes. Equally important, rather than having to rely on their share of taxes collected by local tax collectors; taxes due to the central government were to be collected directly by the central government.[21] Implementation of this new tax system obviously will not be totally effective in the immediate future, but I do not believe this problem is the most vulnerable area in China's economic reform programme at the present time.

A major reason why the Chinese leaders were able to wait so long before introducing their fiscal reforms was their success in reducing the share of investment and operating funds which the state enterprises received from the budget, shifting the source of these funds to bank loans. However, this merely shifted the problem of inefficient and loss-making enterprises to the banking system. Thus, the banks were now carrying on their books a large amount of unpaid loans, some extended to state enterprises that had uncollectable unpaid bills due from other enterprises. Attempts to clear up the problem of these 'triangular debts' and unpaid loans held by banks, even when somewhat successful, would find the problem recurring as the basic cause of the problem has never been cured. The basic problem of the state enterprises not being profitable or economically sound is not to be found in the enterprises or their operations, but in the failure of the banking system to refuse loans to those enterprises that are clearly loss leaders and white elephants.

When the economic reform programme was initiated in the early 1980s, microstability was not a major problem because demand was sustained and increased in keeping pace with increases in output, while there was no serious problem of an 'overhang'. After a decade of reforms and rapid growth of per capita incomes, the public had built up a tremendous amount of liquid savings. With few assets to invest in due to the poor development of China's capital markets, the public has willingly held those funds in bank deposits.

How lucky can the Chinese economic reformers be? The old economic system relied on the 'forced savings' of the public to finance the inefficient state enterprise sector, but because of the marketizing reforms, those 'forced savings' are no longer available. Nonetheless, the economic reform period has seen a significant increase in per capita incomes and growth in non-state enterprises and an equally spectacular increase in 'voluntary savings' by these non-state enterprises and the public. These savings have been 'voluntarily' placed in banks, which have then been able to use these 'voluntary savings' to finance the inefficient state enterprise sector. However, this windfall for China's reformers has only postponed the inevitable, the need for the banking system to discipline the state enterprise sector so as to make it much more efficient and profitable. Thus, after fifteen years of relative success and a considerable transformation of their economic system to a market system, which retains considerable elements of central administrative control, political interference and state enterprises, the Chinese now have come face-to-face with the critical problem that will determine their continued success.

CURRENT SITUATION

The Chinese leaders are aware of the need for a significant reform of their banking system and have even specified a model for those reforms, some elements of which have been introduced.[22] The central bank (the People's Bank of China) has been set free from the Ministry of Finance and no longer has to finance the budget deficit of the central government.[23] To effectively control the commercial banking sector and the money supply that sector creates, the central bank has introduced a reserve requirement, has established a rediscount rate, regulates an intra-bank fund market, and can operate in the bond market, powers similiar to those used by the Federal Reserve System in the United States.[24] Except for three special banks, all other banks in China are to become commercial banks, making loans on the basis of the ability of the borrower to repay the loan, that is, earn a sufficient rate of return on the use of the loan. The three specialized banks that have been set up are for the purpose of 'policy loans' in the agricultural sector, for development projects and for foreign trade. The loans made by these specialized banks admittedly will have lower rates of return, but are to be based on calculations of social costs and benefits and not based on political pressure and interference as was true of the many 'policy loans', that is, the bad loans, made in the past.[25]

While reform of the banking system presently is the most critical obstacle to the continued success of the economic reform programme, these reforms will take time, even in the best of circumstances. Obviously the banks will need to be freed from the routine interference of representatives of the government and the Party. Unfortunately, those government and Party officials recognize that they have lost their direct control over the allocation of resources and goods at the micro level of the economy and that their ability to exercise indirect control at that level is mainly through their control of the banking system. On the other hand, giving the banking system its freedom is a move that is necessary to cope with the two major economic problems that face the Chinese leadership: the need to apply the hard budget constraint on the most inefficient of the state enterprises and the need to control the money supply to prevent inflation.

There are, of course, many different reforms that must be introduced or continued to bring the economic reform programme to its successful conclusion. Factor markets are yet to be marketized, but except for capital markets, promising initial steps have already been taken and I remain optimistic. Then there is the need to develop the legal system necessary for a true market economy and the need to create a new Chinese capitalist ethic of entrepreneurial behaviour, that is, the utilization of new technology and innovations in the production of goods and services for the sake of consumer satisfaction and profit, rather than depending on political protection and favours for earning rents. These transformations to the legal and behavioural norms of a true market system, of course, will take a generation or more to achieve, but I am optimistic here too.

However, even if we are optimistic about their successful transformation to a market economy, there are two fundamental economic problems that remain for Chinese leaders to cope with in the immediate future. These same two problems beset any market economy in the West, but due to China's size, level of development and flawed economic policies of the Maoist era, the nature of these two problems in China is quite severe. These are the problems of agriculture and of unemployment. The growth of jobs in the non-agricultural sectors and the demand for agricultural products has never increased fast enough in any market economy to absorb surplus labour or to maintain stable levels of income in the agricultural sector. Thus, all Western market economies have found it necessary to adopt price supports and/or an income policy for the labour force in their agricultural sectors. The problem in China, of course, is much worse, because the Chinese are beginning to develop a market economy with as much as 200 million disguised unemployed already located in agriculture and a need to lay off workers in the industrial sector to restructure that sector in their move to a market economy. This will be a long-term problem over the foreseeable future, but one cannot be too optimistic about their willingness to come to grips with it. It will not go away and the sooner they begin to deal with it the better.

By allowing the non-state sector to grow rapidly in the 1980s, China's leaders believed they had found a way out of the problem of urban unemployment.[26] With the retrenchment in credit in 1989, the number of enterprises and employment in the rural collective sector declined, but with the return of an expansionary phase of the cycle in China's economy, the rural collective sector is once more generating jobs at a rapid pace. Yet growth in this and the state enterprise sector cannot be relied upon to create full employment of China's huge labour force in the near future. Thus, as all other market economies in the West have had to provide, a funded system of unemployment insurance and retirement payments must be developed for China's labour force. The Chinese leaders are beginning to take the necessary steps to put such a system in place, but even they admit it will take a generation or more before they have such a system in place.[27]

These three critical problems — the need to transform the banking system into an independent commercial banking system, the need to provide either price supports or an income policy for the peasants, and the need to develop a funded system of unemployment insurance and retirement programmes for the Chinese urban labour force — certainly will be a challenge for China's future leaders. But there is more — the problem of the political succession: determining who China's leaders will be in the future. Predicting leadership transitions in China has never been easy and tackling and solving any of these three problems has been the undoing of many skilled political leaders in the Western market economies. Whoever emerges as China's future leader in the post-Deng era, in my judgement, none of the potential political leaders who are likely to survive the succession crisis has the popular support and influence necessary to carry out the reforms that are needed to solve these three problems successfully. Thus, the Chinese could easily end up in a rather long period of muddling through in their attempts to cope with these problems. If so, this would mean the Chinese would fail to realize the promise of the past fifteen years; a most impressive record of completing many of the necessary initial stages in the transition from a Soviet-type economy to a 'socialist market economy'.

IMPACT OF THE REFORMS ON SINO-AMERICAN ECONOMIC RELATIONS

Having presented my views on the current problems in China's economic reform programme with a somewhat uncertain forecast as to the future of the reforms, let me now turn to a forecast of the impact of that uncertain future on Sino-American economic relations in the future. Obviously, the latter forecast will be even more uncertain than the former.[28] Thus, our discussion in this part of the chapter will be more speculative in nature, consisting of a review of those factors I believe will affect Sino-American economic relations in the future, rather than an attempt to provide any quantitative 'guestimate' of what that future will be.

My forecast of the future of China's foreign economic relations made in 1988 was made in response to the many calls then being made for the creation of a formal economic bloc of Asian economies to foster greater intra-Asian trade. Relying on past trends, my argument was simple. Firstly, the rapid growth of world trade in the last half of the 20th century was one of the most beneficial economic developments in history. Secondly, that growth was dominated by growth in trade between the industrial countries. Thirdly, those developing countries that promoted their export trade to, and economic relations with, the industrialized countries were the success stories in the developing world. And fourthly, the growth in trade between the developing countries was an insignificant share of this dramatic and vital story of trade and development. Therefore, my prediction then was that any attempt to realign that existing pattern of trade in favour of a customs or economic union among the developing countries of Asia would be a third or fourth best solution to their trade and development problems and would be based more on parochial, short-sighted political objectives rather than sound economic reasoning.

Seven years later it is obvious my arguments in 1988 were flawed by too great an emphasis on past trends. While I still believe attempts to form regional economic unions are not first or even second best solutions, I had completely failed to recognize three very important and dramatic developments then at work in an interdependent manner which would change the very nature of my forecast.

Firstly, the Japanese have been rethinking their role as just another 'Western' economic power and are asserting a greater say in how the new world economic order should work. Their position can be expected to reflect an Asian position, allowing for greater government participation in export promotion and the regulation of trade, with a lack of transparency in protecting the domestic market. Equally important with their policy position is the fact that Japan has begun to redirect foreign investment, along with trade, towards greater economic relations with their neighbours in Asia.

Secondly, several countries in Asia (the NIEs) have become industrialized and others are following in their wake. Thus, even though trade among the industrialized countries will remain the mainstay of world trade, some of this trade can now take place completely within Asia. The same is true of foreign investment, that is, capital flows from the industrialized countries of Asia to the developing countries of Asia.

Thirdly, as a result of their economic reform programme, China has joined the world economy in a major way, but has joined the world economy by means of trade with, and the receipt of foreign investment from, China's neighbours in Asia. In fact, much of the dynamic growth in intra-Asian trade is due to the rapid growth in China's trade with its neighbours. The economic flows between the three elements that make up Greater China (the PRC, Taiwan and Hong Kong) alone accounts for a significant share of the intra-Asian trade and investment flows. [29]

Quite simply, with no formal organization to manage these changes, they have begun to create a natural intra-Asian economic bloc of growing interdependence. It would be a gross exaggeration to say this economic bloc is now self-sufficient and has marginalized the United States and Europe, but we are speculating about the future. Certainly the emergence of this new intra-Asian economic bloc has weakened the position of dominance the United States formerly held in the world economy. As the value of our dollar falls and our trade deficits with the economies of Asia grow, the United States has pursued two reactions to cope with this problem. Unfortunately, both are based on domestic politics, rather than on sound economic reasoning or reality.

Despite the fact that most US businessmen are telling the US government that the economic future of the US lies in Asia, others are arguing that the US should build its economic future on renewed emphasis on our traditional economic ties with Europe and/or, via NAFTA, building up our intra-hemisphere economic relations with Central and South America. These arguments are unlikely to amount to much as the world's dynamic centre of future growth will be in Asia, not in Europe or the American hemisphere. The other US reaction, dictated largely by our domestic political debates and search for votes in the next election, has seen the United States make unilateral demands and threats for transparency, the removal of various obstacles to our exports, acceptance of quotas on our imports, requests for bilateral agreements negotiated in confrontational meetings with deadlines or we will impose this or that penalty, and so on. Our grievances are real and much of the rest of the world agrees with our objectives, but the methods and unilateral nature of our dealing with these problems is a very poor strategy for a major participant in the WTO and we are in danger of losing support for our cause. Furthermore, the United States has chosen to fight a two-front economic war with the two most powerful economies in Asia, while the harm they could do to our economy is steadily increasing **in comparison** to the harm we could do to their economy. Finally, this strategy may play well to American voters and special interest groups, but it does not play well with most US businessmen who just want to make money.[30]

Over the past fifteen years, the economic reform programme has made China one of the major economic powers, along with Japan, in the Asian economic bloc of countries. Over that same period in the United States, the failure to balance the budget, or even come close to balancing it, and the US life-style of high consumption and low savings means that the US budget deficit has had to be financed by the foreigner, that is, capital inflows in the balance of payments. This is reflected in large import surpluses, especially in US trade with the Asian economies. Seeing our failure to put our own house in order, the foreigner is losing interest in financing our budget deficit and this puts pressure on the US dollar. The Group of Seven still feels the need to come to the rescue of the dollar to save the existing world economic system, but each such attempt is carried out less and less enthusiastically. Yet the United States keeps making unilateral demands and threats in the attempt to solve the problem by getting the Japanese and the Chinese to open their markets for our exports and to restrict their sales to the United States.

The United States, of course, can be proud of how we, and many others, have worked hard and successfully to bring the world economy closer to the state of free trade, with tremendous benefits to us all. It would be tragic if we were the country to disrupt this process now. Yet, learning from my attempt at forecasting in 1988, I will not base my forecast of future Sino-American economic relations on these pessimistic past trends, especially those not based on sound economic forces and reasoning. Thus, I am willing to make the optimistic assumption that the confrontational level of intergovernmental negotiations between China and the United states will be rather temporary and that the United States will learn that the strategy of 'brinkmanship' with threats and unilateral demands are losing us support among our friends who are important members of the WTO. China, of course, has already identified the United States as the major obstacle to their being among the major members of the WTO. And it may well be the WTO itself that ultimately has to assume the role of convincing the United States to accept economic reality and negotiate our grievances with China and Japan to achieve a 'playing field' that **both sides** believe is level and beneficial to the economies of both countries.

More important and to the point, however, I do not believe these squabbles at the governmental level should cause us to lose sight of an even more significant development in the economic relations between the United States and China (and Japan, India and Vietnam, as well). Despite the actions and statements of the political leaders in both the United States and China, US businessmen and local authorities in China have been more influenced by the basic economic forces for making deals which are of benefit to both sides, and I strongly believe these forces will win out in the long run. Of course, the long run can be terribly long and the action of politicians on both sides can place constraints on the growth of Sino-American economic relations. Furthermore, the impressive record of growth in China's domestic economy and foreign trade and in foreign investment in China over the past few years is most likely to be somewhat reduced to a lower level in the future. Nonetheless, despite these caveats, as a result of the economic reforms, China's economic growth will continue to be impressive and it will play an ever larger role in the Asian economy. As far as US businessmen are concerned, they definitely want to be a part of that future as well. Unless they are prohibited from doing so by their own government, they will play a significant role in both China's trade and in investment in China in the future.[31] Whether that participation works so that the aggregate volume of trade and capital flows work to alleviate the current problems experienced in Sino-American economic relations has more to do with actions taken by American economic policymakers in putting their own house in order than with developments in Asia. With regard to American economic policy decisions in the future, my forecast in 1988 informs me I should heed the lesson learned and not be too pessimistic because of trends in the past. I wish I could heed that lesson, but it is not easy for me to do so.

NOTES

1. One of my earlier forecasts, published in 1988, probably is not known of or remembered by anyone at this conference and may best be left forgotten. Robert F. Dernberger, 'Economic cooperation in the Asia-Pacific region and the role of the PRC', *Journal of Northeast Asian Studies,* 7, 1 (Spring 1988): pp. 3–21. Inasmuch as that earlier attempt at forecasting provides us with a most useful lesson in forecasting, I will refer to that earlier forecast and the lessons it provides us in a later section of this chapter.
2. The above two paragraphs obviously present a simplification of what has come to be called 'the view of the transition from Cambridge, Massachusetts'. The views of this school are well-summarized in a two-volume collection of papers by the members of that school, Olivier Jean Blanchard, Kenneth A. Froot, and Jeffrey D. Sachs (eds.), *The Transition in Eastern Europe,* 2 vols. (Chicago: University of Chicago Press, 1994). It was the members of this school that began to question the ability of any economy to achieve the transition in one 'big bang' and to present much longer timetables and the sequence of reforms to be implemented at various stages of the much longer timetable. There is, of course, a significant voice in opposition, with which I agree. Those in opposition argue that the unique history,

institutions and cultural environment of each of these countries plays a very significant role in determining the path of economic reform they follow and the success they achieve. Arguments based on universal theories and timetables derived from theoretical principles, on the other hand, may not be very helpful to either the outside analysts or the internal policymaker. For a clear statement of the opposition point of view, see Peter Murrell, 'The transition according to Cambridge, Mass', *Journal of Economic Literature*, 33, 1 (March 1995): pp. 164–78 (this is a review article of the two-volume work cited above).

3. The original version of this document had been released in the early 1960s arguing for a much more decentralized system of collectivized farming, with the production team (25–45 households) being made the basic decision-making and income allocating unit. The team was to be protected against expropriation without reimbursement of its factors of production, output and income and be given a relatively low and fixed tax assessment. This document was the moderate answer to the more centralized, extractive and income levelling policies of the Maoists.

4. The gross value of farming output in real terms increased by 6.4 percent a year from 1978 to 1986; grain output by 3.2 percent a year over the same period. Per capita consumption of foodstuffs increased for almost all of the population, as did the quality of the diet. Equally important, the incomes of the peasants increased dramatically (rural household income increased in real terms by 9.9 percent a year from 1978 to 1985),reducing the urban-rural income gap. Statistics in this chapter are from MEAS, Macro Economic Application System, a software package of data, graphics, and econometrics developed and distributed by the State Information Centre of China. This data set contains over 2000 variables on 3.5" disks, issued quarterly. Monthly data are included and disks for provincial data sets are available.

5. The gross value of farming output and grain output increased by only 4.7 percent and 2.2 percent a year, respectively, from 1986 to 1993. Furthermore, grain output actually fell in two years during that period; grain output in 1993 being only 2.3 percent higher than it was three years earlier. Moreover, peasant household income increased by only 2.8 percent a year from 1985 to 1993, less than one-third the rate of increase in the period 1978–85.

6. One can feel some sympathy for Deng here. Coming back to power in the midst of a serious drought period and faced with the need to feed the Chinese people, Deng quickly increased the imports of grain (it is said that over one-third of urban grain consumption in some of China's large coastal cities was being supplied by foreigners), of fertilizer to grow more grain (it is said that China's purchases of fertilizer from Japan left Japan with no excess supply), and complete fertilizer plants (these purchases were the first purchases of complete plants from a US company by China). Unfortunately, the OPEC oil cartel got its act together in the early 1970s and significantly raised the price of energy throughout the world. Grain and fertilizer being energy intensive products, the cost of China's import bill increased rapidly and an import surplus of over one billion US dollars was incurred by China in 1974.

7. It should be noted that both the agricultural and opening reforms focused on a key issue in high-level political struggles over the entire three decades after 1949. Therefore, it is not surprising that the Third Plenum, a significant watershed in the history of those struggles, quickly led to the agricultural reforms and the opening of China.

8. During the period 1978–93, total foreign trade grew by 26 percent a year, as did exports and imports separately. Thus, by 1993, China was the seventh largest foreign trader in the world. Between 1983 and 1993, the utilization of foreign capital increased by 35 percent a year, foreign loans utilized by 27 percent a year and direct foreign investment by 46 percent a year. By 1990, China's external debt was sixth in the world, but the foreign debt service ratio (required debt service

payments to total exports) was only 8.5 percent by far the lowest among those countries with large foreign debts. As for international reserves, China's non-gold international reserves ranked ninth in the world and gold reserves ranked sixth in 1992.

9. On a research trip to China in January 1995, one of the question asked of officials visited at all levels of the administrative hierarchy concerned this loss of control over the localities. I was considerably surprised to learn that most officials could readily identify the various areas of China that had been 'given' greater freedom to act on their own by the central government, the uniformly recognized ability of the central government to step in if any locality overstepped the guidelines specified, the recognition of which guidelines were soft and which were hard, and the entrepreneurial and innovative energy spent on working within the guidelines for the best interests of the locality. All this has led to a lot of experiments in the reforms, but I gained the distinct impression that all believed the central government was watching and had the authority and power to choose which experiments to call off and which to support.

10. New classes of graduate were coming out of China's schools and many students who had been sent down to the countryside in an earlier period were now being allowed to return to their families in the city.

11. 'Decision of the Central Committee of the Communist Party of China on reform of the economic structure' *Xinhua* (20 October 1984), translation in *Foreign Broadcast Information Service* (22 October 1984), pp. K1–19.

12. This was done with a vengeance. Output of the TVE and joint-rural industries grew by 32.7 percent a year in the period 1985–93, compared to the 23.5 percent rate of growth in the state industrial sector. By 1993, the state sector accounted for less than 50 percent of total industrial output. While the cooperative sector, three-fourths of which is TVE and joint-rural enterprises, accounted for almost 40 percent.

13. Even though that sector has been continually subject to high-level policy swings and low-level harassment by local cadres (to the extent that many private entrepreneurs willingly allow the local governmnent and officials a share of the enterprise for protection, becoming part of the TVE or collective sector), the officially designated private industrial sector has grown by 49.2 percent a year during the period 1985–93 and accounted for almost 10 percent of industrial output at the end of this period.

14. The role of 'guidance planning' continues to be important today and the industrial ministries retain considerable power to control and interfere in state industries they control. There can be little doubt, however, that this control has been considerably weakened as a result of the reforms and that the production and distribution of industrial products in China today is no longer under the control of the planner. Also, the ability of the government and cadres at all levels to interfere either by means of officially approved regulatory powers (and these are often transparent) or ad hoc self-appointed powers is a major weakness of the Chinese economic reform programme and prevents us from saying that industrial output and its distribution is determined only by market forces. Hopefully, this interference is not what the Chinese mean when they say they are seeking to develop a 'socialist market economy' or 'markets with Chinese characteristics'.

15. If the state enterprise was afraid of the market, they could always volunteer for a share of the 'guidance plan', which also bought their output and supplied their inputs at non-market prices.

16. While it is true that the Chinese are not privatizing their large and medium sized-enterprises, there are many experiments in selling shares of stock in these enterprises. Yet, these experiments are more a means of raising funds for the enterprise than for transferring control of the enterprise or its management to the

stockholders. The government or state sector of the economy that controlled the enterprise in the past ends up holding a majority of the shares. Also, there are strict limits on the amount of shares that can be held by any one individual. The few stockholders meetings that have been held have been described as a 'joke' by those stockholders 'invited' to attend. This does not deny, however, that once the shares are circulated, the stock market may develop so that various groups interested in greater efficiency and profits gain effective control over the managers of the state enterprise. The managers of the state enterprises that I have met do not seem to feel any pressure from the stockholders at the present time and few seem to fear that they will in the near future.

17. Despite these losses, we must note that the number of state enterprises increased by 12 percent between 1985 and 1993 and that the output of these enterprises increased by 17.4 percent a year (9.2 percent in real terms) over that same period.

18. We can sympathize with the managers of the loss-making enterprises as they inherited a bloated work force and obsolete equipment, producing obsolete or unwanted products, with no sales experience, and accounting practices that did more to reflect engineering information, rather than financial flows in the enterprise.

19. For an excellent analysis of the data to support this claim, see Barry Naughton, 'What is distinctive about China's economic transition? State enterprise reform and overall system transformation', *Journal of Comparative Economics*, Vol. 18, No. 3 (June, 1994): especially Part III, pp. 475–486.

20. By 1993, revenue from enterprises was less than 10 percent of total revenue in the state budget, while subsidies to loss-making enterprises were about ten times the level of revenues from enterprises in the budget.

21. For a good summary of the various elements of the 1994 tax reforms, see Ma Junlei and Luo Liqin, 'Important reform in China's tax system', *China Newsletter* (JETRO), No. 110 (May–June, 1994), pp. 12–17, 21. The success of this reform, of course, depends upon a considerably reformed method of accounting and record keeping by the economic units and the tax collector, while — like taxes anywhere — will rely upon the compliance of those taxed and capabilities of those collecting the taxes. Nonetheless, the reform is based on sound economic arguments for a modem tax system in a market economy.

22. For a good, but brief, review of the banking reforms currently being introduced, see John Wong, 'Assessing China's economic reform progress in 1994', *China Newsletter* (JETRO), No. 114 (January–February, 1995), pp. 8–14, especially the section on Banking Reform.

23. The Ministry of Finance is to finance the budget deficit of the central government with bond sales, but these will be allocated and assigned to various units throughout the economy, as in the past. Bond sales by any other unit will not be allowed until the bond sales of the Ministry of Finance have been subscribed.

24. To make these reforms more effective the central bank must close its many branches at the local level throughout the economy, eliminating a major source of the loans made to the state enterprise sector, loans that are not always based on the prospect of economic returns, but due to political pressure and interference on behalf of the borrower.

25. These policy loans, or bad loans, on the books of the banking system are said to have been as much as 40 percent of the loans of the banking system in the past. Unfortunately, early reports claim that the loan activities of the specialized banks represent more a continuation of past practices in making policy loans, than in basing loan decisions on calculations of social costs and benefits.

26. Employment in rural collectives, which includes the TVE sector, increased by about 13 percent a year, or by an average of 7 million workers a year, during the period 1978–88.

27. For a very good discussion of the recent steps that have been taken to provide a

funded unemployment compensation and retirement programme, see Zhang Jixun, 'Labour reforms and new labour-management relations', *China Newsletter* (JETRO), No. 115 (March–April, 1995), pp. 8–17, 24.

28. For the purpose of our forecast of the future of Sino-American economic relations, we assume a slightly more optimistic outcome of the economic reforms in the future than is indicated by our discussion of the major problems now facing the Chinese leadership. Although not as outstanding a record as accomplished in the past, we expect the level of economic activity in China's economy, the level of total foreign trade and foreign investment, and the standard of living of the average Chinese to continue growing in over the near future. Thus, we assume the transition in the political leadership at the top of the political system will be accomplished without serious crises as well.

29. Compare this with Russia, where the flow has been largely of entrepreneurial talent leaving, not returning. Cuba also suffers from the same problem as Russia, while Vietnam is beginning to enjoy the same advantage as China.

30. Unfortunately, US economic policy in the area of international economic relations throughout the post-war period has been influenced by the State Department (with embargoes applied here and there for this or that foreign policy objective), the Pentagon (much foreign aid consisting of military aid and with little promise of economic payoff) and by special interest groups (the relatives of MIAs and human rights advocates).

31. In talking with US businessmen involved in investment and trade with China, one gets several impressions despite the horror stories reported in the popular press and journals. I can sum that up with a few phrases that you hear in talking with them: 'even if they drive you crazy and you are losing your shirt, if you want to be a player of significance in the world economy, you have to be in China as that is where the action is', 'we have more to fear from the actions of our own government' than we do from actions by the Chinese government. Most of the joint-venture and wholly-owned US businesses could and would tell you about problems they were having in doing business in China, but none were pulling out and most were expanding their business. Some were even very pleased with the results of their business in China, so much so that they were moving their operations in third counties to China. All those who were optimistic had a longer-term perspective, the short-term bottom line was not very impressive and even downright depressing for a businessman interested in a 'quick' buck.

3

Taiwan's Perspective on Sino-American Economic Relations

Tzong-shian Yu

INTRODUCTION

The purpose of this chapter is to attempt to provide a perspective from Taiwan on recent developments in Sino-American economic relations. Since 1950, Sino-American economic relations have meant both the economic relations between Taiwan and the United States and the economic relations between China and the United States. So, it is logical for us to start our exploration with an assessment of the background and current status of Taiwan's economic relations with the United States, and to proceed to an examination of the recent development of economic relations between China and the United States, and then to consider the prospects for the further development of the triangular relationship between Taiwan, China and the United States.

When dealing with the issue of Sino-American economic relations, one cannot ignore the fact that the economic relationship between Taiwan, China, and the United States has continued even though the two countries broke off diplomatic relations in 1979. The economic relationship between China and the United States, on the other hand, has become more important since 1979, when the US government recognized the People's Republic of China and the latter started to adopt its open-door policy. It should also be noted that the recent developments in Sino-American economic relations are mainly part of the overall US strategy towards Asia. According to the US strategy, Taiwan is a key card for the United States to play against China. China is a counterweight for the United States to employ to balance Japan, since Japanese power has gradually reemerged since World War II and is once again considered a potential threat to US security. And, according to the US view, only China has the capacity to check Japan in the Asia-Pacific region.

Based on the above considerations, it can be understood that the same US trade policy used towards Taiwan in the 1980s, when Taiwan enjoyed a big trade surplus with the United States, will now be applied to China in the 1990s, as China starts to accumulate an increasing trade surplus with the United States. As for US direct investment in the two parts of China, the mainland and Taiwan, this depends completely on private enterprises' profit-making motives and is independent of US government policy.[1]

To explore Sino-American economic relations, our analysis will proceed from the point in time before 1979, when no diplomatic relations existed between China and the United States, and then move on to the period after 1979, when the United States established diplomatic relations with China, and China initiated its open-door policy and economic reform strategy. In addition, the prospects for this continuing triangular relationship will be discussed.

SINO-AMERICAN ECONOMIC RELATIONS BEFORE 1979

As stated above, Sino-American relations before 1979 include the economic relationship between Taiwan and the United States, and the economic relationship between China and the United States.

The Economic Relationship Between Taiwan and the United States

Since 1951, Taiwan has had a close economic relationship with the United States, not only because Taiwan received US aid amounting to US$1.5 billion (1951–65), and has been host to many US-sponsored foreign direct investment (FDI) projects, but also because the United States has been the largest market for Taiwan's products.[2] For instance, exports to the United States accounted for 41.9 percent of Taiwan's total exports in 1972, and 39.5 percent of Taiwan's total exports in 1978. Conversely, imports from the United States to Taiwan made up 21.6 percent of Taiwan's total imports in 1972, and 21.5 percent in 1978.[3] As a result, Taiwan enjoyed a trade surplus every year. In 1978, the trade surplus with the United States accounted for 52.6 percent of exports to the United States, but this was only a small proportion of the US trade deficit, so the US government did not pay special attention to Taiwan's increasing trade surplus, and Taiwan still enjoyed a favourable trade status with the United States.

With regard to foreign direct investment in Taiwan, the United States and Japan together were the biggest foreign investors prior to 1979. While the latter's FDI accounted for less than one-third, the former accounted for about one-third of total FDI, which indicates that US investment in Taiwan was significant and helpful for the continued expansion of Taiwan's exports.

During this period, Taiwan had no economic relations with China, the Taiwan Strait was completely blocked by military forces, and no triangular relations among Taiwan, China and the United States had been formed.[4]

Economic Relations Between China and the United States

Before 1972, no substantial trade existed between China and the United States. However, since that year, when the late US president Richard M. Nixon visited Beijing and opened China's door, bilateral trade between the two countries increased irregularly until 1978 when the Beijing government announced its intention to adopt the open-door policy. Accordingly, their bilateral trade suddenly increased. For instance, total bilateral trade nearly tripled between 1973 and 1978. Imports from the United States increased 340 percent, while exports to the United States increased 580 percent, reflecting improved diplomatic relations between the two countries.

During the period of time under discussion, except for 1977 when China had a small trade surplus, China suffered a trade deficit with the United States every year. Even though the growth rate of Chinese exports to the United States was very high, the United States was not concerned (for details, see Table 3.1).

Sino-American Economic Relations After 1979

Before 1979, the Sino-American economic relationship was rather simple. Both Taiwan and China enjoyed favourable trade treatment from the United States. However, in the period from 1979 to the early 1990s, the Sino-American relationship became more complicated than ever before. Sino-American economic relations are no longer entirely peaceful; trade disputes have arisen instead. More importantly, triangular economic relations have been formed.

Economic Relations Between Taiwan and the United States

Since 1979, when the diplomatic relationship between Taiwan and the United States was terminated, many people in Taiwan have become extremely worried about the economic relationship between the two countries. Actually, the interruption of diplomatic relations has had little to do with their economic relations. For instance, total trade between the two still increased substantially by 31.9 percent in 1978 and 26.6 percent in 1980. Exports to and imports from the United States both had a rapid growth rate. From 1983 to 1987, in every year except for 1985, Taiwan posted a sharp increase in its exports to the United States. This, in turn, resulted in such a large trade surplus with the United States, accounting for more than 15 percent of Taiwan's gross domestic product (GDP), that the US government took some retaliatory trade measures against imports from Taiwan. Although the growth rate of exports to the United States has fallen since 1988 with the occurrence of a 'bubble' economy

Table 3.1 Commodity Trade of China With the United States

Unit: US$ Millions

Year	Total Trade		Imports from the US		Exports to the US		Balance of Trade
	Value	Growth Rate (%)	Value	Growth Rate (%)	Value	Growth Rate (%)	
1972	13	–	3	–	10	–	7
1973	260	–	220	–	40	–	-180
1974	476	83.08	373	69.55	103	157.50	-270
1975	471	-1.05	342	-8.31	129	25.24	-213
1976	317	-32.70	161	-52.92	156	20.93	-5
1977	294	-7.26	114	-29.19	180	15.38	66
1978	992	237.41	721	532.46	271	50.56	-450
1979	2452	147.18	1857	157.56	595	119.56	-1262
1980	4813	96.29	3830	106.25	983	65.21	-2847
1981	5888	22.34	4382	14.41	1506	53.20	-2876
1982	5336	-9.38	3717	-15.18	1619	7.50	-2098
1983	4027	-24.53	2321	-37.56	1706	5.37	-615
1984	5963	48.08	3663	57.82	2300	34.82	-1363
1985	7025	17.81	4373	19.38	2652	15.30	-1721
1986	5994	-14.68	3527	-19.35	2467	-6.98	-1060
1987	7860	31.13	4830	36.94	3020	22.42	-1800
1988	10010	27.35	6630	37.27	3380	11.92	-3250
1989	12250	22.38	7860	18.55	4390	29.88	-3480
1990	11770	-3.92	6590	-16.16	5180	18.00	-1410
1991	14200	20.65	8010	21.55	6190	19.50	-1810
1992	17490	23.17	8900	11.11	8590	38.77	-310
1993	27650	58.09	10690	20.11	16960	97.44	6270
1994	35431	28.14	13970	30.68	21461	26.54	7491

Note: All figures are in nominal terms.
Source: 1972–80 : (1) *China Statistical Yearbook,* State Statistical Bureau, Beijing.
1981–6   : (2) *Yearbook of China's Foreign Trade.*
1987–93 : (3) Chow, Shi-Chien, 'The Sino-American Economic Relations: Retrospects and Prospects', *International Trade,* No. 9, 1994.
1994   : (4) *China's Customs Statistics* (monthly), No. 12, 1994.

cycle,[5] the trade surplus is still very large compared to Taiwan's total exports or Taiwan's GDP. In response to these US trade measures, the government of Taiwan has opened its market as wide as possible to its trade partners (see Table 3.2).

The big trade surplus with the United States is the main reason that the United States has had trade disputes with Taiwan. For many years, the United States has suffered from two deficits: one is its fiscal deficit, and the other the trade deficit. Both have steadily increased, and have been considered the main factors weakening the US economy. Alan Tonelson, in his article 'US policy is

Table 3.2 Commodity Trade of Taiwan With the United States

Unit: US$ Millions

Year	Total Trade		Imports from the US		Exports to the US		Balance of Trade
	Value	Growth Rate (%)	Value	Growth Rate (%)	Value	Growth Rate (%)	
1972	1794.7	–	543.4	–	1251.3	–	707.9
1973	2629.6	46.52	952.5	75.29	1677.1	34.03	724.6
1974	3716.5	41.33	1679.9	76.37	2036.6	21.44	356.7
1975	3474.8	-6.50	1652.1	-1.65	1822.7	-10.50	170.6
1976	4836.2	39.18	1797.5	8.80	3038.7	66.71	1240.2
1977	5600.2	15.80	1963.9	9.26	3636.3	19.67	1672.4
1978	7386.5	31.90	2376.1	20.99	5010.4	37.79	2634.3
1979	9033.0	22.29	3380.8	42.28	5652.2	12.81	2271.4
1980	11433.8	26.58	4673.5	38.24	6760.3	19.60	2086.8
1981	12928.9	13.08	4765.8	1.97	8163.1	20.75	3397.3
1982	13322.2	3.04	4563.3	-4.25	8758.9	7.30	4195.6
1983	15980.1	19.95	4646.4	1.82	11333.7	29.40	6687.3
1984	19909.3	24.59	5041.6	8.51	14867.7	31.18	9826.1
1985	19479.7	-2.16	4746.3	-5.86	14733.4	-0.90	10 027.1
1986	24446.5	25.50	5432.6	14.46	19013.9	29.05	13 581.3
1987	31332.8	28.17	7648.0	40.78	23684.8	24.57	16 036.8
1988	36473.9	16.41	13006.7	70.07	23467.2	-0.92	10460.4
1989	36039.0	-1.19	12002.8	-7.72	24036.2	2.42	12033.4
1990	34357.7	-4.67	12611.8	5.07	21745.9	-9.53	9134.1
1991	36434.6	6.04	14113.8	11.91	22320.8	2.64	8207.0
1992	39342.6	7.98	15771.0	11.74	23571.6	5.60	7800.6
1993	40359.9	2.59	16772.6	6.35	23587.3	0.07	6761.9
1994	42380.6	5.01	18042.7	7.57	24337.9	3.18	6295.2

Note: All figures are in nominal terms.
Source: Monthly Statistics of Exports and Imports, Taiwan.

paralyzed on Asia', provides a very clear explanation. He points out that 'the longer our [American] Asian deficits last, the longer US economic growth and job creation will lag, the weaker the dollar will become'. So he suggests that 'Asians may doubt America's military credibility but they still urgently need American capital, technology and, above all, markets. Thus, tightly regulating Asian access to these assets is America's best bet for expanding its access to Asian markets and helping to shape Asia's future.'[6] From this statement, it can be understood why the US government has become so concerned about its trade deficit and is trying to force its trade partners to reduce their trade surplus with the United States as soon as possible.

In 1968, Taiwan first started to run a trade surplus with the United States. However, it accounted for just 4.9 percent of Taiwan's total exports and 33.9 percent of Taiwan's total trade surplus, while in 1986, it accounted for 34 percent of Taiwan's total exports and 86.6 percent of Taiwan's total trade surplus, indicating that the trade surplus with the United States had become extremely significant to Taiwan's balance of trade.

In order to reduce its trade deficit with Taiwan, the US government, in October 1986, made use of Section 301 of its trade law to ask Taiwan to reduce its tariffs on the import of cigarettes and wine, and to eliminate the constraints on the marketing of these products. In December 1988, the US government again employed Section 301 to ask Taiwan to abolish its import quota on turkey meat. In the same year, the US Congress passed the 'Special 301' provisions of the Omnibus Trade and Competitiveness Act so as to develop an overall strategy to ensure adequate and effective protection of intellectual property rights both at home and abroad, and equitable market access for US goods which rely on intellectual property rights protections, such as copyrights, patents and trademarks. Since then, Taiwan, due to its big trade surplus with the United States, has become a target for the United States to utilize these 'Special 301' provisions. In May 1986, Taiwan was placed on the 'priority watch list' because US videos were appearing in Taiwan's MTV houses without the permission of their producers. In May 1992, because of widespread counterfeiting of computer software, Taiwan was again placed on the priority watch list and this time was also subject to the new 'Special 301 provisions'. In response to these requests, the government in Taiwan set up an examination system for its exports. In May 1993, Taiwan was once again placed on the priority watch list under the Special 301 provisions because of continuing violation of intellectual property rights. Correspondingly, the government in Taiwan had to agree to the prohibition of the unauthorized parallel import of copyrighted or patented products. In April 1995, Taiwan was downgraded onto the general watch list because of improved protection of intellectual property rights.

Economic Relations Between China and the United States

The year 1979 was very significant in the development of economic relations between China and the United States. In that year the US government formally recognized the People's Republic of China, which led to the rapid growth of bilateral trade. Also in that year, the Beijing government embarked on the open-door policy, which was an important first step on its way to a new era of outward development. Consequently, total trade between the two countries in 1979 increased by more than 147 percent. Imports from the United States increased by 158 percent, while exports to the United States increased by 120 percent. China was granted Most-Favoured-Nation status by the United States in February 1980, which raised China's competitiveness in the US market. From 1979 to 1994, total trade with the United States increased steadily and substantially. There was only one year, 1990, in which it dropped by 4 percent because of the Tiananmen Square Incident on 4 June 1989. In 1990, imports from the United States declined by 16 percent, yet exports to the United States increased by a further 18 percent, which helped to narrow China's trade deficit with the United States. The trade deficit with the United States started to fall in 1990, and then turned into a trade surplus as from 1993. In that year, the trade surplus with the United States accounted for 22.7 percent of total trade between the two countries (see Table 3.1).

As with Taiwan, China started to have trade disputes with the United States in the 1980s. The United States partially reduced its quota on the import of textiles from China in January 1983. In response to this action, China immediately stopped signing contracts for the import of cotton and chemical fibre from the United States. Over the last decade, the trade disputes between the two countries have included: quotas set by the US government on the import of textiles from China, disputes regarding the protection of intellectual property rights, anti-dumping measures on imports from China, and complaints about the lack of transparency of trade law and regulations in China. To settle these trade disputes, the US government has made use of the Special 301 provisions to force China to make concessions.

In April 1991, the US government announced that China, India and Thailand were to be placed on the priority watch list and investigated for their poor implementation of regulations on intellectual property rights over chemical products and copyrights. After much negotiation the Beijing government had to end the trade dispute with a compromise. In February 1992, the Beijing government signed a memorandum of understanding regarding the protection of intellectual property rights under the Special 301 provisions. Although the two sides held many talks, the United States remained unsatisfied with China's implementation in this regard. So, in June 1994, China was placed on the priority watch list under the Special 301 provisions. After a six-month investigation, the two countries failed to reach an agreement on the implementation of intellectual property rights safeguards in China, and again, this resulted in trade sanctions being imposed against Chinese products by the United States. In February 1995, in view of the continued lax implementation of intellectual property rights regulations in China, the US government announced its intention to increase tariffs on the import of 35 products from China by 100 percent. This announcement attracted great attention, not only from China, but also from Hong Kong and Taiwan. Finally, the two countries reached an agreement and settled the dispute.[7]

Direct investment by the United States in the Mainland was negligible before 1979, even though the two countries started to have various exchange programmes in 1972. The main reason for this delay was that during that period of time, China was still a closed country and foreign direct investment was considered an invasion by capitalists. However, from 1979 on, China opened its doors and many developed countries became interested in making investments in China. They were very cautious at the beginning in the early 1980s but became more confident in the late 1980s. According to the *Almanac of China's Economy*,[8] the United States was third in accumulated investment in China up to 1993, with Hong Kong being first and Taiwan second. Since 1992, when Deng Xiaoping visited the Pearl River Delta and demonstrated his unambiguous approval of the rapid growth of southern China, people in China have been eager to accelerate their industrial development, and Korea, Japan, Germany and others have started to increase investment in the coastal areas of China.

The Economic Relationship Between Taiwan and China

Prior to 1979, when the United States recognized the People's Republic of China, no economic relations were allowed between the two sides of the Taiwan Straits. However, since that time the economic relationship between the two sides has changed completely. Although exchanges between the two sides were still illegal, smuggling activities in the Taiwan Strait were increasingly undertaken. Then, in 1987, the government in Taiwan began to allow its people to visit their relatives in the mainland. During this period of time, exports to China from Taiwan were larger than imports from China, so Taiwan enjoyed a trade surplus with the Mainland. In 1987, the bilateral trade between the two sides increased substantially. Exports to China increased by 51.3 percent, while imports from China increased by 100.5 percent. It should be noted that this bilateral trade was conducted through Hong Kong.[9] A proportion of the trade probably also passed through other harbours, but no customs data was registered. During the last two years (1993–5), Taiwan has made use of its trade surplus with China to offset the trade deficit with Japan. Otherwise, Taiwan would have suffered an overall trade deficit.

Taiwan's trade with China is closely related to Taiwan's investment there. Since 1987, many small Taiwanese firms have invested in factories in China. Because this behaviour is not legal, they have to establish 'paper companies' in Hong Kong, with new names in order to avoid interference from the government in Taiwan.

Initially, these companies usually brought old machinery and equipment with them from Taiwan, but, more recently, they have been purchasing new machinery and equipment. Due to the fact that many parts domestically produced in China do not meet the quality requirements for production, many parts and upstream products for these operations are imported from Taiwan. Recently, local markets in China also are demanding components from Taiwan, so that imports from Taiwan have increased greatly in China. As for Taiwan's imports from China, they are still subject to many regulations.[10] This is why, every year since 1980, Taiwan has enjoyed a trade surplus with China (refer to Table 3.3).

Table 3.3 Commodity Trade of Taiwan With China

Unit: US$ Millions

Year	Total Trade		Imports from China		Exports to China		Balance of Trade
	Value	Growth Rate (%)	Value	Growth Rate (%)	Value	Growth Rate (%)	
1979	76	–	55	–	21	–	-34
1980	320	–	78	–	242	–	164
1981	466	45.63	76	-2.82	390	61.07	314
1982	297	-36.27	89	17.90	208	-46.65	119
1983	264	-11.11	96	6.77	168	-18.98	72
1984	552	109.09	127	33.04	425	152.38	298
1985	1103	99.82	116	-9.16	987	132.13	871
1986	955	-13.42	144	24.25	811	-17.91	667
1987	1515	58.64	289	100.47	1226	51.27	937
1988	2720	79.54	478	65.68	2242	82.81	1764
1989	3482	28.01	586	22.60	2896	29.18	2310
1990	4043	16.11	765	30.41	3278	13.18	2513
1991	5793	43.28	1126	47.10	4667	42.40	3541
1992	7407	27.86	1119	-0.60	6288	34.70	5169
1993	8689	17.31	1104	-1.40	7585	20.60	6481
1994	9809	12.89	1292	17.10	8517	12.30	7225

Note: Value only includes the trade which pass through Hong Kong customs to and from China. The proportion which passed through other harbours to and from China is not included.
All figures are in nominal terms.

Source: 1. *Re-exports by origin country and by destination country*, Census and Statistics Department, Hong Kong government.
2. *Monthly Statistics of Exports and Imports*, Taiwan.
3. *Statistical Yearbook of China*, various years.

PROSPECTS FOR TRIANGULAR RELATIONS BETWEEN TAIWAN, CHINA AND THE US

So far, economic relations between Taiwan and the United States, China and the United States, and Taiwan and the Mainland have been are closely interconnected with one another. These relations can be described as follows:

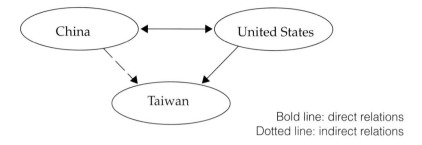

Bold line: direct relations
Dotted line: indirect relations

The economic relationship between Taiwan and China is based on the economic complementarity of the two regions, that is, Taiwan provides capital, technology, management skill and marketing channels, while China provides labour, land and raw materials. This combination can create comparative advantage for a company and enhance products' competitiveness in the world market. In fact, almost all the products made by Taiwanese firms in China are for export and a large proportion of them are going to the US market. The United States has long been the biggest market for Taiwan's exports. Even in 1994, exports to the United States still accounted for 26 percent of Taiwan's total exports. By contrast, since 1990, Taiwan's trade surplus with the United States has started to decline, while at the same time, China's trade deficit with the United States has started to narrow, and, since 1993, has turned into a trade surplus. This may imply that some proportion of China's trade surplus (or reduction in trade deficit) with the United States may be attributable to the reduction in Taiwan's trade surplus with the United States.

Both Taiwan and the United States have undertaken direct investment in China, and have been helpful to China's economic growth. However, the final goal of their production efforts is not only to serve foreign markets but also to gain access to China's domestic market. Through its rapid growth, China has become a big market, and it is natural that this attracts foreign investors to make more direct investment there.

Due to the close relationship between China's foreign trade and Taiwan's investments in China, Taiwan has become very sensitive to US sanctions against exports from China to the United States. For instance, in the spring of 1995, when the Beijing and Washington governments could not reach an agreement in their dispute on intellectual property rights, the US government attempted to make use of the Special 301 provisions to punish China. This action attracted great attention and concern in Taiwan. This reaction by Taiwanese businesses was due to the fact that if China was punished by the Special 301 provisions, not only would Taiwan's investments in China be unfavourably influenced, but Taiwan's own domestic industry would also be adversely affected.

At present, both Taiwan and China have trade surpluses with the United

States. Although the former's trade surplus with the United States has gradually declined, the US government still makes use of the Special 301 provisions to make Taiwan further reduce its trade surplus. In the mid-1990s China started to run a trade surplus with the United States. So, it can be expected that the US government will not give up using its Special 301 provisions as a sanction tool, but will continue to pay increasing attention to its trade deficit with China. The United States would like to see the trade surplus fall substantially, and would like to force China to open its markets and remove all barriers. However, the solution is usually compromise, as neither side wishes to wage a trade war.

CONCLUDING REMARKS

In the next decade, Taiwan will maintain its moderate growth, while China will continue its pattern of high growth. However, the US market will still be very important to both of them. This is particularly the case for China, because many products made in China still enjoy a comparative advantage and are highly competitive in the US market. It is inevitable that China will continue to have increasingly large trade surpluses with the United States. On the other hand, it will be almost impossible for Taiwan to again enjoy large trade surpluses with the United States, as it did before 1989.

Because of the interdependence which has gradually formed between Taiwan and China, any trade policy measures towards China taken by the US government will have an impact not only on Taiwan's investment in China but also on industrial growth in Taiwan itself. Since the United States has continued to make investments in China and also wants to penetrate China's market, the United States will be willing to make some concessions to maintain good relations with China. Particularly if using China to counter Japanese power remains an important strategy of American foreign policy, maintaining smooth relations with China is consistent with United States long-term interests.

NOTES

1. Although the United States claims to espouse free trade, the US government still prefers to make use of tariffs, quotas, anti-dumping measures and the Special 301 provisions to retaliate against its trade partners. Nevertheless, it is impossible for the US government to command private enterprises to make direct investments in certain foreign countries, or prevent them from doing so.
2. In the 1950s and the early 1960s, US aid made a remarkable contribution to Taiwan's economic development. The recovery of the agricultural sector benefited greatly from US aid, and, in its early stages, industrial development — such as of the textile industry and plastic industry — was largely attributable to the same source. In addition, Taiwan enjoyed the GSP (Generalized System of Preferences)

status offered by the United States for a long time. This helped Taiwan to expand its exports to that country.

3. Our analysis starts from 1972 and is based on consideration of the contrast between Taiwan and China. Before 1972, bilateral trade between China and the United States was negligible.

4. In the 1970s, there were a small number of incidents of smuggling in the Taiwan Straits. Most of the traded goods were foodstuffs. Once they were caught by the government, the smugglers were severely punished and the commodities were burnt.

5. In 1987, Taiwan's foreign exchange reserves rose to US$76 billion and the ratio of gross savings to GDP was as high as 38.5 percent. Since no appropriate channels were available for its use, a so-called 'financial fever' took place. The prices of stocks rose sharply and the prices of real estate skyrocketed. From 1987 to early 1990, Taiwan was in the grip of a speculative frenzy. By October 1990, this bubble economy had burst.

6. Alan Tonelson is a fellow at the Economic Strategy Institute in Washington, DC. This article was first published in The *Los Angeles Times*, and then appeared in the *China Post* (Taipei, 30 April 1995).

7. Hong Kong and Taiwan both have made major direct investments in China and most of their products are exported to the US market. So, any sanction by the United States against China would also be harmful to Hong Kong and Taiwan.

8. *Almanac of China's Economy Agency* (Beijing, 1994).

9. Direct trade between the two sides of the Taiwan Straits was not allowed by the Taiwan government, so that more than 90 percent of the trade was made through Hong Kong.

10. Between 1987 and 1994, the government in Taiwan modified its import regulations and increased the number of Chinese-origin import items many times in response to the requests of businessmen.

4

The Role of Hong Kong
in Sino-American Economic Relations

Y.Y. Kueh and Thomas Voon

INTRODUCTION: A NEW PERSPECTIVE

Hong Kong has traditionally been a very important source of China's foreign exchange earnings. Prior to the 1980s, generally about one-quarter to one-third of the country's hard foreign currency earnings were generated from exports to Hong Kong. Tiny as the British enclave may be in geographic terms, and with a population of only six million, it has nonetheless always been a very important market for China's food and food-processing industries, as well as textile and clothing manufacturers. Sales to Hong Kong have earned the Chinese government the bulk of the hard currency needed to finance her enormous import bills incurred with major western suppliers of steel, machinery and high-tech products. This specific role played by Hong Kong in financing China's industrialization programme is of course widely understood. Yet hardly any observers have come to realize that the bulk of China's food and clothing exports to Hong Kong represent none other than Hong Kong's wage outlay on labour inputs necessary for sustaining its production of exports, which are, as is well known, overwhelmingly destined for the major Western markets, the United States in particular.

An intellectually interesting point may be made on this China-Hong Kong synergy: an essential part of Hong Kong's foreign exchange earnings may itself be seen as China's indirect export to the West. Viewed this way, there is obviously something wrong with the widely held view that in the case of a complete take-over of Hong Kong by its sovereign power, China would kill the 'gold-laying goose' and loose all her direct foreign exchange earnings from Hong Kong. China has a pronounced interest in maintaining the economic status quo for Hong Kong — an interest apparent in the entire strategic design of the future Special Administrative Region under the concept of 'one country, two systems'.

The fallacy of this popular argument is clear enough. With a full-fledged socialist-style take-over, the present foreign exchange earnings as held by Hong Kong's exporters would, by implication, inevitably be entirely accruable to the government of the People's Republic of China (PRC), after allowing perhaps for certain proportion of 'transaction costs' incurred as a result of, say, impaired export incentives, reduced efficiency and loss of competent marketing and sourcing expertise. It should also be clear that under such a complete socialist takeover, the present 'direct' export earnings by China from Hong Kong would naturally become China's own liability, that is, the input costs needed for sustaining the export earnings of Hong Kong.

Interesting as the issues raised may be, intellectually speaking, we do not think it is worthwhile to pursue the matter further, because a socialist take-over of Hong Kong is clearly not on the agenda. Nonetheless, increased economic interaction and integration between Hong Kong and mainland China under the country's open-door policy in the past decade has lent some new dimension to their trade relations that seem not entirely irrelevant to the questions posed for a fully fledged political take-over of Hong Kong.

At least to the mind of many Americans, Hong Kong seems to have already become part of China proper. Any re-exports from Hong Kong of Chinese origin should thus be treated by the United States as Chinese exports, be it in terms of most-favoured-nation status (MFN) renewal, protection of intellectual property rights or otherwise. Rightly or wrongly, what is at stake is particularly the tens of thousands of Hong Kong manufacturers who prefer to have their export production contracted out, by way of what Hong Kong government statistics term as 'outward processing' (or what in official Chinese parlance is referred to as *sanlai yibu*) to the Pearl River delta basin, in order to avoid exorbitant land rental and labour cost pressures in Hong Kong.[1]

The relocation of Hong Kong's export manufacturing activities to the Pearl River hinterland is not entirely dissimilar to a socialist take-over, because in terms of trading relationship and foreign exchange accruable, it has become explicit that the land and labour inputs for Hong Kong's export product are now very much a matter of direct Chinese rather than Hong Kong contribution. Ignoring for the time being the interpretative complexities with capital contribution which very often is dominated by the Hong Kong investors' share, Hong Kong's role in this new context seems to have become very much one of export intermediary, important as this role may be.

It is obviously against this background that the familiar Sino-American dispute has arisen in recent years as to the absolute size of their trade balance with each other. To the United States, Hong Kong's exports with an 'outward-processing' element are Chinese by origin, and have helped to aggravate the US trade deficit *vis-à-vis* China. The Chinese maintain, however, that they only earn a very marginal fee for processing on behalf of Hong Kong's export manufacturers. This has in turn prompted some US government officials to argue that 'China routinely calculates exports according to value-added as opposed to internationally accepted accounting method'.[2] The dispute is clearly not just a matter of interpretative nuance. The fact that *sanlai yibu* exports have very much tilted, in the eyes of the Americans, the trade balance against their favour, already speaks for the sheer magnitude involved. *Sanlai yibu* Chinese exports may therefore be regarded as a phenomenon *sui generis*.[3]

The crux of the problem involved is obviously a matter of how one should estimate and interpret the appropriate relative shares of both the mainland Chinese and their Hong Kong counterparts in the total export margin earned from US importers. This is by no means a simple, straightforward technical matter. In addition to land and labour, capital input is involved from varying mainland Chinese and Hong Kong investors' contributions. There is also the touchy issue of how to assign weights to the different input categories. The difficulty is further compounded by the fact that apart from the voluminous 'outward processing' contracts, there is a large number of *sanzi qiye* (literally the three foreign-funded enterprises: equity joint ventures (EJV), contractual joint ventures (CJV), and *wholly foreign-owned ventures (WFV)* in China — hereafter *sanji* enterprises in this chapter). These are heavily dominated by Hong Kong capital input,[4] they are well established and engage themselves not only in output of proper Chinese origin for export, but also in 'outward processing' from Hong Kong as well.

This chapter represents a first attempt to isolate the relative contributions of Hong Kong manufacturers and exporters to the export earnings from their joint ventures based in China, be they in the form of *sanlai yibu* (outward processing) or *sanji qiye* manufacturing proper. We focus naturally on exports that are physically channelled through Hong Kong, with a view to determining the relative share of exports from China to the United States (or the rest of the world at large), which should be accounted for by Hong Kong manufacturers rather than mainland Chinese exporters. Our work is of course made against the political backdrop that there is still, and will continue to be, a line drawn between Hong Kong and China, given that post-1997 Hong Kong will retain its membership in the World Trade Organization (WTO) and many other international bodies, as a separate customs entity.

Rough as our exercise may appear to be, particularly in terms of the various assumptions made for the analysis and the statistics used (as will become apparent during the course of our discussion), we hope to at least be able to provide an innovative methodology as a basis for further verification and refinement. We hope that this will eventually contribute to solving the conflicting claims between China and the United States on their trade gains or losses against each other.

The role played by Hong Kong within the broader context of Chinese economic relations with the United States, or with the rest of the world at large, is evidently much more than a matter of facilitating and mediating Chinese trade as illustrated. Interestingly, US exports through the port of

Hong Kong to China have also experienced steady increases in the past fifteen years or so. Further, as an international financial centre, Hong Kong plays an important role in channelling overseas financial and banking resources, many of US origin, to China for financing its infrastructure projects. Hidden behind the capital and trade flows is, of course, the associated technology transfer from the West to China through Hong Kong.

Nonetheless, these are more or less familiar aspects of Hong Kong's contributions to China. They all deserve further analysis, but in this chapter we mainly concentrate on the unique phenomenon of *sanlai* or *sanji* Chinese exports, in order to isolate the possible size of the Hong Kong components as a contribution to resolving the conflicting claims between China and the United States on trade deficits against each other. In what follows, we first take stock of Hong Kong's export and import relations with both China and the United States, and give an account of its quantitative importance in linking China's dealings with the US or the rest of the world at large. This provides the necessary framework for looking at the specific issues involved in reconciling the Sino-American discrepancy.

Following the statistical reconciliation of the conflicting US and Chinese trade deficit claims, we offer an overall evaluation of the possible economic and income benefits that Hong Kong has been drawing from serving as a trade mediator between the two economic giants. This helps to highlight, from a different perspective, to what extent the US-China discrepancy is actually a matter of Hong Kong's gains. The chapter concludes with a short remark about how Hong Kong may continue to play its third-party role beyond 1997 within the broader context of Sino-US economic relations.

HONG KONG IN SINO-AMERICAN TRADE: THE NEW CONTEXT

There are two major aspects of the role played by Hong Kong as a trade facilitator or mediator. The first is that Hong Kong itself serves as an important market for China's exports. The exports have been dominated by food and clothing supplies to sustain Hong Kong's export production for the United States. From the early 1980s, industrial material, machinery and equipment have come onto the Chinese supply list as well, as the country adjusted its development strategy in favour of light industry, thus giving the heavy industry sector excess capacity to produce producer goods for export. The changes as observed over the years reflect a universal trend in export commodity composition in relation to the pace and pattern of industrialization of developing countries.

The second aspect refers to the Mainland's exports to Hong Kong that are not retained for domestic consumption but rather are re-exported to the

United States and other Western importers. This category of Hong Kong's imports from the Mainland comprises increased re-exports of truly Chinese origin, and especially the *sanlai yibu* of Chinese exports of essentially 'Hong Kong origin' by way of 'outward-processing' to the Pearl River delta. Part of the latter subcategory of Chinese exports to Hong Kong may of course be retained for local consumption,[5] but there is clear evidence that the bulk is destined for re-export to overseas markets. It is clearly the second category of Chinese exports, particularly *sanlai yibu*, that has gained an enormous importance to Hong Kong in the past decade.

Hong Kong's Imports From China and Re-exports to the United States

The figures in Table 4.1 (panel A) reveal that in 1993, 73 percent of all Hong Kong's merchandise imports from China were *sanlai yibu*, compared with 64 percent in 1991 or 58 percent in 1989, when, after nearly a decade of growth (starting the early 1980s), this type of Chinese export to Hong Kong was already entering a mature stage.

Sanlai yibu statistics are not available prior to 1989.[6] But their value for the early 1980s is virtually zero. Nonetheless, for 1989 to 1994 alone, *sanlai yibu* export from China to Hong Kong increased at a startling annual average rate of 26 percent. Amidst this spectacular growth, however, conventional Chinese exports to Hong Kong, comprised of Chinese domestic exports and re-exports proper, have also continued to thrive steadily. As is also revealed in panel A of Table 4.1, this latter category in Hong Kong's imports from China increased at an annual rate of 13 percent in 1980 to 1994, although the growth slowed down substantially to 6.9 percent per year in the more recent period of 1989 to 1994. To the extent that Chinese domestic exports constitute, in turn, the backbone of Hong Kong's own domestic exports by way of input supply for export production, the long-term growth of conventional Chinese exports to Hong Kong (at the rate 13 percent per year in 1980 from 1994), seems to be basically in line with the pace of Hong Kong's own domestic exports to the United States (at the corresponding rate of 7.4 percent), or to the world at large (9.6 percent), as shown in panel C of Table 4.1.

Likewise, to the extent that conventional Chinese exports also are comprised of re-exports via Hong Kong, the observed discrepancy in the long-term growth rate (that is, 13 percent versus 7.4 percent or 9.6 percent), may be accounted for exactly by the re-export component of truly Chinese origin. There is no doubt that amidst the massive Chinese export drive of the past fifteen years or so, a considerable proportion of increased Chinese exports proper simply has to be channelled through Hong Kong as a matter of expediency, because the Mainland could not build port facilities and export service capabilities quickly enough to cope with increased export demand.

Table 4.1 Hong Kong's Merchandise Trade With China and the United States: 1979–1994

A. Hong Kong's Imports From China and Re–export to the United States (in HK$ Millions)

	Total Import	Sanlai yibu Share		Conventional		Total Re-exported to US	
		Value	(2)/(1)*100	Value	(4)/(1)*100	Value	(6)/(1)*100
	(1)	(2)	(3)	(4)	(5)	(6)	(7)
1979	15 130	0	0.00	15 130	100.00	735	4.86
1980	21 948	0	0.00	21 948	100.00	1690	7.70
1981	29 510	0	0.00	29 510	100.00	2814	9.54
1982	32 935	–	–	–	–	3574	10.85
1983	42 821	–	–	–	–	5510	12.87
1984	55 753	–	–	–	–	8778	15.74
1985	58 963	–	–	–	–	11 256	19.09
1986	81 633	–	–	–	–	18 667	22.87
1987	117 357	–	–	–	–	27 748	23.64
1988	155 634	–	–	–	–	43 242	27.78
1989	196 676	113 581	57.75	83 095	42.25	65 993	33.55
1990	236 134	145 103	61.45	91 031	38.55	81 645	34.58
1991	293 356	187 384	63.88	95 972	32.72	103 955	35.44
1992	354 348	254 013	71.68	100 335	28.32	139 977	39.50
1993	402 161	295 203	73.40	106 958	26.60	168 331	41.86
1994	470 876	354 912	75.37	115 954	24.63	195 794	41.58
(Annual Growth %)							
1989–94	19.58	25.59	–	6.89	–	24.30	4.39
1980–94	24.48	–	–	12.63	–	40.62	12.80

Note: *Sanlai yibu* imports from China may be assumed to be zero or negligible in the early 1980s; hence 'conventional' imports are equal to imports from China for those years, comprising both retained imports and imports destined for re-export to third destinations.

Source: Census and Statistics Department, Hong Kong Government, *Hong Kong Annual Digest of Statistics*; *Hong Kong Monthly Digest of Statistics*; and *Hong Kong External Trade*, various issues.

Table 4.1 (cont'd)

B. Hong Kong's Exports and Re-export From the United States to China (HK$ Millions)

| | Total Exports | | | Sanlai yibu Share in | | | | US Share in | | | |
| | Domestic | Re-export | Total | Domestic Export | Value (4)/(1)*100 | Re-export | Value (6)/(2)*100 | Total Export | Value (8)/(3)*100 | Re-export | Value (10)/(2)*100 |
	(1)	(2)	(3)	(4)	(5)	(6)	(7)	(8)	(9)	(10)	(11)
1979	603	1315	1918	0	0	0	0	0	0	131	9.96
1980	1605	4642	6247	0	0	0	0	0	0	337	7.16
1981	2924	8044	10 968	0	0	0	0	0	0	567	7.05
1982	3806	7992	11 798	–	–	–	–	–	–	1034	12.94
1983	6223	12 183	18 406	–	–	–	–	–	–	1474	12.10
1984	11 283	28 064	39 347	–	–	–	–	–	–	2932	10.45
1985	15 189	46 023	61 212	–	–	–	–	–	–	4476	9.73
1986	18 022	40 894	58 916	–	–	–	–	–	–	4422	10.81
1987	27 871	60 170	88 041	–	–	–	–	–	–	6179	10.27
1988	38 043	94 895	132 938	–	–	–	–	–	–	9588	10.10
1989	43 272	103 492	146 764	31 962	73.86	44 906	43.39	76 868	52.38	10 265	9.92
1990	47 470	110 908	158 378	36 418	76.72	55 496	50.04	91 914	58.03	10 283	9.27
1991	54 404	153 318	207 722	40 369	74.20	73 562	47.98	113 931	57.74	13 302	8.68
1992	61 956	212 105	274 061	44 271	71.46	97 368	45.91	141 639	51.68	18 183	8.57
1993	63 367	274 561	337 928	45 141	71.24	115 037	41.90	160 178	47.40	24 601	8.96
1994	61 009	322 835	383 844	41 959	68.78	139 221	43.12	181 180	47.20	28 662	8.88
Average Growth (5)											
1989–94	7.11	25.55	21.20	9.01	–	25.39	–	18.71	–	22.80	–
1980–94	29.67	35.39	34.20	–	–	–	–	–	–	37.35	–

Note: Sanlai yibu shares in domestic exports and re-exports assumed zero or negligible in 1979–81.

Source: Census and Statistics Department, Hong Kong Government, *Hong Kong Annual Digest of Statistics* and *Hong Kong External Trade*, various issues.

Table 4.1 (cont'd)

C. Hong Kong's Exports to the United States (HK$ Millions)

	Domestic Export						Re-export				
	Value	World Total Net of sanlai yibu to China Value	Value	US Share (3)/(1)* 100	World Total (3)/(2)* 100	US Share Value	Value	(7)/(6)* 100	Chinese Origin Share (9)/(6)* Value	100	US share %
	(1)	(2)	(3)	(4)	(5)	(6)	(7)	(8)	(9)	(10)	(11)
1979	55 912	55 912	18 797	33.62	33.62	20 022	1995	9.96	5663	28.28	12.98
1980	68 171	68 171	22 591	33.14	33.14	30 072	3085	10.26	8394	27.91	20.13
1981	80 423	80 423	29 200	36.31	36.31	41 739	4785	11.46	12 834	30.75	21.93
1982	83 032	—	31 223	37.60	—	44 353	5615	12.66	14 694	33.13	24.32
1983	104 405	—	43 802	41.95	—	56 294	8028	14.26	19 680	34.96	28.00
1984	137 936	—	61 374	44.49	—	83 504	12 109	14.50	28 107	33.66	31.23
1985	129 882	—	57 687	44.41	—	105 270	14 705	13.97	34 628	32.89	32.52
1986	153 983	—	64 219	41.71	—	122 546	22 362	18.25	51 597	42.10	36.18
1987	195 254	—	72 817	37.29	—	182 780	32 456	17.76	84 266	46.10	32.93
1988	217 664	—	72 884	33.48	—	275 405	49 483	17.98	131 525	47.76	32.88
1989	224 104	192 142	72 162	32.20	37.56	346 405	72 033	20.79	188 271	54.35	35.05
1990	225 875	189 457	66 370	29.38	35.03	413 999	87 752	21.20	240 410	58.07	33.96
1991	231 045	190 676	62 870	27.21	32.97	534 841	110 800	20.72	315 689	59.02	32.93
1992	234 123	189 852	64 600	27.59	34.03	690 829	148 500	21.50	403 782	58.45	34.67
1993	223 027	177 886	60 292	27.03	33.89	823 224	180 349	21.91	474 007	57.58	35.51
1994	289 000	247 041	61 419	21.25	24.86	1 239 000	210 077	16.96	545 831	44.05	35.87
Annual Growth (%)											
1989–94	6.56	5.15	–3.9	—	—	29.03	23.87	—	23.72	—	—
1984–94	7.68	—	0.00	—	—	30.96	33.02	—	34.53	—	—
1980–94	10.87	9.63	7.40	—	—	30.42	35.19	—	34.74	—	—

Note: Outward-processing (or *sanlai yibu*) exports assumed to be zero or negligible for 1979–81; hence no distinction is made between columns (1) and (2) for these three years. The underlying HK$ figures for column (11) are given in Panel A, column (6).

Source: Census and Statistics Department, Hong Kong Government, *Hong Kong Annual Digest of Statistics*, various issues; *Hong Kong Monthly*

Unfortunately, available Hong Kong government statistics do not distinguish re-export of Chinese origin between *sanlai yibu* and re-export of conventional exports for the period under study.

Beyond our attempt to disentangle the intriguing triangular trade relationship between China, Hong Kong and the United States, however, the most noteworthy point to be made from Table 4.1 (panel A) is that a drastically increasing share of total Chinese exports to Hong Kong (comprising both the *sanlai yibu* and conventional categories), have been re-exported to the United States. The US share increased from 7.7 percent in 1980 to 19 percent in 1985 when outward-processing consignments from Hong Kong to China (especially Guangdong) started to gain momentum. By 1994, the share stood at 42 percent, representing virtually an exponential growth from the early 1980s.

In absolute value, total Chinese exports (*sanlai yibu* and exports proper combined) via Hong Kong to the United States increased at an annual rate of 24 percent from 1989 to 1994. This is higher than the growth rate of Chinese *sanlai yibu* export to Hong Kong, that is, 6 percent per year for the same period. Thus, there is no doubt that Hong Kong's outward-processing consignments to China represent very much a business conducted by Hong Kong manufacturers on behalf of their US clients.

We note also that the total volume of Hong Kong's imports from China that is re-exported to the United States has become increasingly larger than the 'conventional' type of Chinese exports to Hong Kong. In the past few years, such exports have indeed increasingly approached the value of Chinese *sanlai yibu* exports to Hong Kong in total (see panel A of Table 4.1). This clearly signifies that Hong Kong has been able to increasingly expand its export production base into the Chinese hinterland, thereby being freed from serious land and labour supply constraints encountered in Hong Kong.

Hong Kong's Exports and Re-exports From the United States to China

The economic breakthrough for Hong Kong for an accelerated integration with China is also clearly reflected in Hong Kong's exports to China. Thus, while the territory's domestic exports to China have increased at a startling annual growth rate of 30 percent from 1980 to 1994, or just 7 percent from 1989 to 1994, there is no doubt that the lion's share has been taken up by domestic exports in the form of outward-processing consignments. The share has consistently exceeded 70 percent since 1989, when the Hong Kong government began to publish such statistics (see panel B of Table 4.1).

Interestingly enough, the volume of re-exports through Hong Kong to China has been growing even faster than Hong Kong's domestic exports to China (averaging at 35 percent per year from 1980 to 1994, or 26 percent from 1989 to 1994). Re-exports have indeed remained, in absolute terms, a multiple of domestic exports. The corresponding *sanlai yibu* share in total re-exports to China has also been very substantial, ranging from 42 percent to 50 percent from 1989 to 1994. Compared with the *sanlai yibu* share in domestic exports of 69 percent to 77 percent during the same period, these percentage shares may not look as impressive. Yet in absolute terms, the *sanlai yibu* size in Hong Kong's re-exports to China (totalling HK$526 billion for the period 1989–94 taken as a whole), is in fact more than double the size of *sanlai yibu* share (HK$240 billion) of Hong Kong's domestic exports to China for the same period. More remarkably, the absolute gap between the two different *sanlai yibu* shares has widened markedly in the past few years in favour of the *sanlai yibu* share in re-exports via Hong Kong to China.

Reference should now again be made to the role played by the United States in Hong Kong's exports to China. The figures in Table 4.1 (panel B) show that as a country of origin, the US share in Hong Kong's overall re-exports to China has basically been growing in tandem with the total, with both averaging around 37 percent per year in the whole period from 1980 to 1994; or respectively 23 percent and 24 percent for the years from 1985 to 1994. However, while the declining annual growth rate for total re-exports reversed to 28 percent per year since 1989, that for the corresponding US share stagnated at 23 percent. As a result, the US share in Hong Kong's total re-exports to China declined from a high of 13 percent in 1982 (11 percent in 1986), to below 9 percent consistently for the four years from 1991 to 1994.

The decline in the US share in Hong Kong's total re-exports to China may not appear to be too remarkable, but it certainly stands in sharp contrast to the accelerated increases in the share of re-exports of Chinese origin to the United States from 5 percent in 1979, or 19 percent in 1985, to 42 percent in 1994 (panel A of Table 4.1). The implications of these divergent trends should be clear enough. US exports through Hong Kong to China probably deal mostly with finished manufactures, embodying advanced industrial technology and representing a heterogeneous mix of such producer and consumer goods as machinery and equipment, pharmaceuticals, computer software, CDs, CD-ROMs, laser discs, cassette tapes, video games and the like. These are commodities in high demand that are also prone to intellectual property rights infringement. It seems very likely that these re-exports are primarily destined to cash-rich South China, Guangdong province in particular, which customarily resorts to experienced marketing experts in Hong Kong for the necessary import sourcing overseas.

Other than customers from South China who, compared with their northern and interior counterparts, have enjoyed considerable privileges in terms of foreign exchange retention schemes, and relatively easy access to hard currency transactions, it is difficult to visualize how demand from the central authority or elsewhere in China could sustain such an impressive growth rate of imports of such 'luxurious' commodities from the United States.

At any rate, US exports via Hong Kong to China are likely to be dominated by finished manufactures, rather than raw materials or semi-manufactures, for the purpose of reprocessing for exports. By contrast, exports originating from overseas, which in the past used to be destined for Hong Kong, have in the past decade been increasingly shipped through Hong Kong and, on behalf of Hong Kong manufacturers rather than Chinese end-users, across the Shenzhen border for reprocessing for the purposes of re-exporting; hence the exponential growth of Hong Kong's re-exports of Chinese origin to the United States.

Hong Kong's Economic Relations With the United States and the World at Large

We may now turn to Hong Kong's overall exports to the United States against the backdrop of the emerging Hong Kong-Guangdong economic synergy. Several important points may be made from the data in panel C of Table 4.1.

Firstly, and most remarkably, the US share in Hong Kong's total domestic exports, discounting the *sanlai yibu* export share to China which is essentially for reprocessing for the purposes of re-export, has virtually remained constant in the past fifteen years or so, despite the entire fanfare of 'outward-processing'. The share has indeed been hovering around 35 percent from 1979 to 1994. This indicates that not only has Hong Kong continued to be heavily dependent upon the United States as a market outlet, but also that China has remained, by virtue of her overwhelming share in input supply to sustain Hong Kong's production for export, vulnerable to the vagaries of US import demand.

Secondly, both Hong Kong's domestic exports (net of *sanlai yibu* exports to China), and its US share tend to be shrinking, in absolute dollar terms, increasingly from the mid-1980s. This reflects clearly the accelerating relocation of Hong Kong's export manufacturing activities to the Chinese hinterland. The trend is also mirrored in the expanding share of Hong Kong's re-exports of Chinese origin (which covers *sanlai yibu* exports), as well as the US share therein, since the early or mid-1980s. That is to say, the increased shares have compensated exactly for the decline in Hong Kong's conventional domestic exports to the United States and the world at large.

Thirdly, taken together, the observed trends in Hong Kong's domestic exports and re-exports suggest that the Hong Kong-Guangdong synergy with respect to export-processing is to a considerable measure a matter of trade diversion (from Hong Kong to China). There is no denying, of course, that with the vast Pearl River delta hinterland being increasingly converted into a Hong Kong export production base, thereby easing Hong Kong's land and labour supply constraints, the *sanlai yibu* invention is bound to be trade-creating as well. However, the relative contributions of both aspects, trade creation versus trade diversion, deserve further examination.

We have hitherto confined our attention strictly to the triangular China-Hong Kong-US trade relationships. Looking from a broader global perspective, however, it should be noted that the share of China, as a country of origin, in Hong Kong's re-exports (outward-processing type included) to all countries has more than doubled from 28 percent in 1980, to 58 percent in 1993 at the expense of virtually all other countries. For example, in the case of Japan the share has declined from 20 percent in 1980 to only 13 percent in 1993.[7] The decline has taken place despite the fact that, among other things, a considerable proportion of Japanese car exports to China has continued to be shipped through Hong Kong.

Furthermore, the bulk of Hong Kong's global re-exports is indeed destined increasingly to the US market. The US share has increased from 10 percent in 1980 to 14 percent in 1985, and stayed at 21 percent since 1990, at the expense of almost all other countries, except China. For China as a destination for Hong Kong's re-exports, the share has, as a matter of fact, also more than doubled from some 15 percent in 1980 to 43 percent in 1985, to stabilize at between 27 percent in 1990 and 33 percent in 1993.[8] The increases should, however, be understood against the background that it has been increasingly dominated by outward-processing consignments.

These trading relationships point to the fundamental role of Hong Kong as an international 'export processing centre'. Put simply, Hong Kong has to make use of machinery and equipment imports from Japan, and increasingly China, to convert the supply of cotton yarn from Pakistan and Egypt, wool from Australia, and, say, PVC and TV tubes from Japan into textiles, fabrics, apparel, toys and sports requisites, and TV sets, with, above all, Chinese supplies of wage food and clothing to feed and clothe its workers, for exports to the huge US consumer market. And these days, the overwhelming proportions of export processing activities are indeed being subcontracted to the Pearl River delta manufacturers by way of 'outward-processing'.

It should be of interest to note that prior to 1985 when *sanlai yibu* just began to pick up momentum, the US share in Hong Kong's domestic exports still stood at around 45 percent. Thereafter, however, it declined steadily to the level of 27 percent to 29 percent between 1990 and 1993, before being further reduced to 21 percent in 1994. The relative decline in the US share is evidently very much a matter solely of accelerated increases in favour of China, from a mere 2.4 percent in 1980, to 12 percent in 1985, 21 percent in 1990, and 28 percent in 1993, as a result of increased Hong Kong 'domestic' exports to China for the very purpose of 'export-reprocessing' on behalf of import clients in the United States and other major Western markets.[9]

Taking domestic exports and re-exports together, 23 percent of Hong Kong's total merchandise exports was absorbed by the US market in 1993 or 18 percent in 1994, compared to 26 percent in 1980, or 31 percent in 1985.

Bearing in mind, however, that the bulk of Hong Kong's domestic exports are also inextricably linked to wage food and clothing supplies from China, it is clear that after China's opening up to the outside world since the late 1970s, both Hong Kong and China have continued to be substantially dependent, albeit not as markedly as before, on the US market for their export earnings. Within this context, Hong Kong in particular has actually become an adjunct to the Chinese export economy.

From an import-financing perspective, it is significant to note that Hong Kong is indeed of paramount importance to China as a source of foreign exchange earnings, direct or indirect, for financing China's massive import bills from the US, Japan or, for that matter, the world at large. The figures given in Table 4.2, which tell the Chinese story of the trade balance, reveal that for 14 years out of the total of 15 from 1979 to 1993 for which China incurred a total trade deficit to the tune of US$23 billion with the United States, the shortfall could be effectively offset by an accumulated trade surplus of US$142 billion with Hong Kong, that is, at a multiple of 6.15. For the United States and Japan combined, both being the single most important trade creditors for China, the corresponding multiple still stands at a startling high of 2.09.

That is to say, China's total export earnings from Hong Kong alone, net of the corresponding import expenditure, are more than sufficient to finance China's net import bills incurred with the United States and Japan, or the world at large, for the entire period 1979 to 1993. Even if the *sanlai yibu* component is taken out of China's exports to Hong Kong, the Chinese trade surplus with Hong Kong is still more than sufficient to cover the country's combined deficits with the United States and Japan for the 1989–93 period taken as a whole. This unequivocally speaks for the pivotal importance of Hong Kong in Sino-American, or for that matter, Sino-Japanese trade relations, or in the entire Chinese foreign trade system.

To the extent, however, that Chinese exports to Hong Kong have been increasingly dominated by *sanlai yibu* (outward processing) components, we have yet to determine whether the bulk of Chinese earnings from Hong Kong really is of Chinese or Hong Kong origin as the issue may bear on the conflict between the United States and China over the size of trade deficits.

SINO-AMERICAN TRADE BALANCE DISPUTE: THE HONG KONG LINK

Table 4.3 shows that both Chinese and American statistics consistently understate or overstate their exports or imports to or from each other. That is to say, they either overstate their bilateral trade deficits or understate their trade surplus. The discrepancy has indeed widened quite substantially since

Table 4.2 China's Trade Balance With Major Trading Partners, 1979–94 (in US$100 Millions)

Year	All Countries (1)	USA (2)	Japan (3)	Hong Kong Gross of Sanlai yibu (4)	Hong Kong Net of Sanlai yibu (5)	Ratio 1 (4)/(1)	Ratio 2 (4)/(2)	Ratio 3 (4)/[(2)+(3)]
1979	-20.10	-12.62	-11.80	33.33	—	1.66	2.64	1.36
1980	-19.00	-28.48	-11.37	40.34	—	2.12	1.42	1.01
1981	-0.10	-31.49	-13.95	40.33	—	403.30	1.28	0.89
1982	30.30	-25.23	9.07	38.67	—	—	1.53	2.39
1983	8.40	-10.45	-9.83	41.05	—	—	3.93	2.02
1984	-12.70	-16.05	-30.86	39.60	—	3.12	2.47	0.84
1985	-149.00	-27.51	-89.26	24.07	—	0.16	0.87	0.21
1986	-119.60	-20.85	-76.59	41.75	—	0.35	2.00	0.43
1987	-37.80	-17.94	-36.76	53.41	—	1.41	2.98	0.98
1988	-77.60	-32.86	-31.41	62.93	—	0.81	1.92	0.98
1989	-66.00	-34.54	-21.39	93.76	46.69	1.42	2.71	1.68
1990	87.40	-14.09	14.23	123.96	55.67	—	8.80	8.83
1991	80.50	-18.49	1.88	146.74	39.36	—	7.94	7.35
1992	43.50	-3.07	-20.04	169.79	24.61	—	55.31	2.79
1993	-121.90	-12.13	-74.74	241.95	115.91	1.918	19.95	2.79
1994	53.46	74.91	-47.48	229.08	—	—	—	-8.35
Total	-320.24	-230.89	-450.30	1420.76	282.24	4.44	6.15	2.09
Average								
1979–85	-23.17	-21.69	-22.57	36.77	—	1.59	1.70	0.83
1986–94	-17.56	-8.78	-32.48	129.26	56.45	7.36	14.72	3.13
1979–94	-20.02	-14.43	-28.14	88.80	56.45	4.44	6.15	2.09

Note:

Figures for 1981–83 are converted from RMB yuan to US Dollars by using the official annual average exchange rates. The two 1993 figures for the trade balance with Hong Kong (HK) are tentative estimates, and could be very problematic. The reasons are as follow: the year 1993 saw curiously both Chinese exports (US$22.1 billion) to and imports (US$10.5 billion) from HK being drastically curtailed from the previous year's high of US$37.5 billion and 20.5 billion respectively. A likely explanation for the precipitous drop is that the 1993 figures do not include the *sanlai yibu* components with HK. This is because HK government statistics show that both outward-processing (*sanlai yibu*) consignments (US$20.7 billion) to China and *sanlai yibu* imports (US$38.2 billion) from China in 1993 (as given in Table 4.1, panels A and B) are themselves very substantially larger than the given Chinese total exports to and imports from HK. Thus, barring any other better explanation, we simply regard the original Chinese export and import figures as net of the *sanlai yibu* component. This results therefore in the trade balance with HK of US$11.6 billion for 1993 as given for the net series. This figure is of course not directly comparable to those for 1989–92 (which are derived from HK government statistics) and seems to be biased upwards. For the 1993 trade balance (with HK) figure, we have in turn added the Hong Kong's 'outward processing' — related exports and imports to the original Chinese figures to derive the trade balance gross of the *sanlai yibu* [...] [US$20.7 billion is adjusted downwards by 10% and the comparable export figure adjusted]

1986, pointing again to the implication of the massive Chinese *sanlai yibu* exports through Hong Kong to the United States.

Part of the conflicting Chinese and American claims may be explained by the standard international statistical practice of reporting own country's exports at FOB price and taking imports from the other at CIF price. For the earlier years, say from 1979 to 1985, the discrepancy is indeed rather limited, and may therefore essentially be accounted for by the FOB/CIF difference. However, from 1985 to 1986 onwards, the Chinese *sanlai yibu* exports via Hong Kong to the United States have undoubtedly changed the relative scale of the discrepancy quite drastically, with US government statistics claiming accelerated increases in trade deficits by many times against similar but basically declining Chinese claims (see Table 4.3).

Background to the Conflicting Trade Deficit Claims

The background to the conflicting Sino-American trade deficit claims is clear enough. Both countries have differently interpreted the growth of *sanlai yibu* re-exports and, relatedly, the crucial intermediary role of Hong Kong as the port through which their exports and imports to each other flow. The Chinese recorded their direct exports to the United States in their current account, but their indirect exports to the United States through Hong Kong (*sanlai yibu* included) were regarded as Chinese exports to Hong Kong. The United States, on the other hand, claimed Chinese goods shipped through Hong Kong to be Chinese exports, but nonetheless deemed US goods transhipped to China through Hong Kong as exports to Hong Kong. Both Chinese and American statistics have therefore underreported their exports to each other and overstated their bilateral trade deficits.[10]

Given the enormous importance of *sanlai yibu* exports, it is therefore essentially a matter of how to determine Hong Kong's contribution to their total costs of production relative to the comparable Chinese share. This constitutes a good basis for accordingly apportioning the entire *sanlai yibu* export volume between the Chinese and Hong Kong shares.

Before we attempt to reconcile the Sino-American trade statistics, a few words should be said about the nature and scope of *sanlai yibu*, or outward processing (OP) activity from a Hong Kong perspective. Table 4.4 shows the Hong Kong government's statistics on the estimated value of OP-type flow of goods from China to Hong Kong by broad commodity groups from 1991 to 1994. Clearly they cover a wide range of manufactured goods which prior to the mid-1980s were traditionally produced in Hong Kong with a varying degree of labour-intensity. Note that foodstuffs and agricultural products, which are virtually non-existent in Hong Kong, are not listed as a category of OP-type imports. Of particular interest also is the fact that the OP-type flow of

Table 4.3 Conflicting Chinese Versus US Claims on Exports (X), Imports (M), and Trade Balance, 1979–94 (US$ Billions)

Year	Chinese Statistics			US Statistics			Relative Discrepancy		
	M (1)	X (2)	X - M (3)	M (4)	X (5)	X - M (6)	(1)/(5) (7)	(4)/(2) (8)	(6)+(3) (9)
1979	1.86	0.60	−1.26	0.70	1.70	1.00	1.09	1.17	−0.26
1980	3.83	0.98	−2.85	1.16	3.76	2.60	1.02	1.18	−0.25
1981	4.66	1.51	−3.15	2.06	3.60	1.54	1.29	1.36	−1.61
1982	4.28	1.76	−2.52	2.50	2.91	0.41	1.47	1.42	−2.11
1983	2.77	1.72	−1.05	2.48	2.17	−0.31	1.28	1.44	−1.36
1984	4.04	2.43	−1.61	3.38	3.00	−0.38	1.35	1.39	−1.99
1985	5.09	2.34	−2.75	4.22	3.86	−0.36	1.32	1.80	−3.11
1986	4.72	2.63	−2.09	5.24	3.11	−2.13	1.52	1.99	−4.22
1987	4.83	3.04	−1.79	6.91	3.50	−3.41	1.38	2.27	−5.20
1988	6.67	3.38	−3.29	9.26	5.02	−4.24	1.33	2.74	−7.53
1989	7.86	4.41	−3.45	11.99	5.76	−6.23	1.36	2.72	−9.68
1990	6.59	5.18	−1.41	15.24	4.81	−10.43	1.37	2.94	−11.84
1991	8.01	6.16	−1.85	18.97	6.28	−12.69	1.28	3.08	−14.54
1992	8.90	8.59	−0.31	25.73	7.42	−18.31	1.20	3.00	−18.62
1993	10.69	9.48	−1.21	31.54	8.77	−22.77	1.22	3.33	−23.98
1994	13.97	13.55	−0.42	38.00	8.80	−29.20	1.59	2.80	−29.62
Total									
1979–85	26.53	11.34	−15.19	16.50	21.00	4.50	1.26	1.40	−10.69
1986–94	72.24	56.42	−15.82	162.88	53.47	−109.41	1.36	2.76	−125.23
1979–94	98.77	67.76	−31.01	179.38	74.47	−104.91	1.32	2.17	−135.92
Average									
1979–85	3.79	1.62	−2.17	2.36	3.00	0.64	1.26	1.40	−1.53
1986–94	8.03	6.27	−1.76	18.10	5.94	−12.16	1.36	2.76	−13.91
1979–94	6.17	4.24	−1.94	11.21	4.65	−6.56	1.32	2.17	−8.50

Note: The Chinese figures for 1981–83 are converted from RMB yuan to US Dollars by using the official annual average exchange rates.
The 1993–94 Chinese export figures are adjusted values net of re-exports (including the outward processing components).

Source: Chinese statistics are from *Chinese Statistical Yearbook* various issues, except for the 1994 figures which are China's Customs Statistics from *China Trade Report* (June 1995). US statistics are from US Department of Commerce, *Statistical Abstract of the United States* (1994).

goods makes up an overwhelming share of Hong Kong's total imports from China. The overall share in 1989 when the Hong Kong government began to compile such statistics, already stood at 58.1 percent. It has increased to 76 percent in 1994 (see Table 4.4). In general, products which are based on supply of primary commodities, or those with lower value-added (for example, yarn, fabrics, and base metals and metal products), tend to exhibit smaller OP proportions. On the other hand, for manufactured products such as clothing,

Table 4.4 Values and Proportions of OP-Related Goods Flowing
From China to Hong Kong, 1991–1994

Commodity Group	Value (HK$ Millions)				OP Proportion (%)			
	1991	1992	1993	1994	1991	1992	1993	1994
Textile materials, textile articles other than textile garments	7684	8863	10 020	13 242	20.5	23.0	27.3	30.3
Articles of apparel and clothing accessories (textile garments)	51 003	59 830	67 351	70 128	86.6	84.4	83.l	83.1
Plastic articles	5641	7884	9361	11 584	84.8	89.3	90.4	87.1
Machinery and appliances; electrical equipment	23 742	32 313	36 668	48 348	78.7	81.0	76.4	82.2
Television image recorders and reproducers	26 338	31 103	37 586	50 005	89.7	92.7	91.5	94.7
Clocks and watches	8262	9682	11 331	12 724	96.4	94.3	95.8	96.4
Toys, games and sports requisites; parts and accessories	17 332	25 301	27 289	32 847	92.1	96.9	96.0	94.2
Base metals and metal products	3253	5189	6964	7965	29.6	43.6	52.3	51.2
Others (including commodities and transactions not classified according to kind)	54 129	73 848	88 633	108 069	59.5	65.9	69.3	71.5
Total	197 384	254 013	295 203	354 912	67.7	72.1	73.8	75.9

Note: The percentage figures are OP *(sanlai yibu)* shares in total exports to Hong Kong.

Source: Census and Statistics Department, Hong Kong Government.

electronic and electrical goods, watches, toys, plastic goods, ornaments, and machinery, the shares are well over 80 percent.

As a matter of fact, the bulk of *sanlai yibu* output is produced by *sanji* (*qiye*) enterprises with Hong Kong interests, or by the hundreds of thousands of small-scale township and village enterprises commissioned by Hong Kong manufacturers to do the processing in China, especially Guangdong province. The Hong Kong Trade Development Council (HKTDC) estimates that 19 000 out of 25 000 (roughly 76 percent) enterprises of Hong Kong origin in China producing for Hong Kong are involved in *sanlai yibu* activities. A Chinese source reports that over 300 000 enterprises are engaged in *sanlai yibu* activities in Guangdong province, employing more than two million local Chinese workers, earning a total processing fee (*gongjiao fei*) income of more than US$ 1.5 billion from a *sanlai yibu* exports total of US$ 15.1 billion in 1994. This presumably makes up 83 percent of the national total of *sanlai yibu* exports.[11]

The Hong Kong Trade Development Council also reported that the predominant share of Chinese *sanlai yibu* products is exported indirectly via Hong Kong to the outside world, as shown in Table 4.5. The share rose, however, by only a very small margin from 82 percent in 1988 to 86 percent in 1991. This indicates that from the very early stage it is in fact Hong Kong manufacturers who have been directly involved with, and represent the single most important clients of, Chinese *sanlai yibu* production. Needless to say, Hong Kong also commands, *vis-à-vis* other Chinese ports, absolute advantages in export shipping and related banking and insurance services to be the logical entrepôt for *sanlai yibu* exports of other sources as well. In fact, in the absence of direct navigational links with the Mainland, Taiwanese manufacturers have increasingly channelled their own outward-processing through Hong Kong to South China. And it is certainly very difficult, if not entirely impossible for Hong Kong government statistics to distinguish OP-type re-exports between Hong Kong and Taiwanese sources.

Tables 4.5 Shipping Arrangement for OP-Related Products
Made in China (% of year total)

	Indirect Exports Through Hong Kong	Direct Shipment From China
1988	82	18
1991	86	14

Note: All Chinese indirect exports through Hong Kong are customs-declared but direct shipments (termed by HKTDC as triangular trade) are not.
Source: Hong Kong Trade Development Council (1991).

Reconciliation and Implications

We may now turn to examine how Hong Kong's contribution to Chinese *sanlai yibu* exports to the United States can be reasonably separated out from the Chinese share. A number of conceptual and methodological issues should first be dealt with briefly. Firstly, in the context of *sanlai yibu* (or OP-type) re-exports, it is obviously not correct to take the conventional re-export margin earned by Hong Kong (on account of its entrepôt facilities and services), as the only stake accruable to Hong Kong as a whole. This simple method omits the important capital input and current expenditure contributed by Hong Kong investors or manufacturers towards outward-processing in the form of *sanji* enterprises for example. To rectify the downward bias, we should therefore, for the purposes of our estimates, define a 're-export margin' as a fraction of export value accruable to Hong Kong, based on Hong Kong's contribution to production and internal marketing of the *sanlai yibu* export goods.

Secondly, the FOB price of an export commodity is equivalent to the per unit cost of production, including the internal cost of marketing. This covers in our case the movement of goods within the common China-Hong Kong production zone. The unit price of a product embodies therefore: (1) the factory production cost pertaining to capital cost (for example, building, machinery and fixtures), labour, rental/rates, raw materials, fuel/electricity/water and any related fixed and variable costs of production, and (2) the marketing cost which comprises the internal costs of handling, transportation, insurance, and payments for port, financial and other trade-related services.

Thirdly, the proportional utilization of local and imported inputs by *sanlai yibu* enterprises is dependent on the type of industry. For example, the textile industry would use the domestic cotton or silk produced in China (noting, however, that chemical fibre can be more important these days), thereby raising the real cost/margin to be shared by the Chinese. In the case of Hong Kong investors contributing entirely to the production costs, the entire Chinese re-export volume may theoretically be taken as Hong Kong exports. Where an export production involves cooperating Chinese partners and the use of local labour and land resources, a proportion of the export margin should clearly accrue to them. Therefore, the production plus marketing margin as a part of the total export proceeds to be shared between the mainland Chinese and Hong Kong-based enterprises must be taken into account in adjusting the disputed trade balance statistics between China and the United States.

Fourthly, in the case of indirect exports from the United States to China via Hong Kong, it is appropriate to consider the re-export margin earned by Hong Kong just in terms of the entrepôt and brokerage fees charged by Hong Kong trade mediators. This is usally perceived to be not more than two percent of the total value of exports. However, if US export revenue registered in the

American current account is calculated using the FOB price, then adjustment of the export margin will be unnecessary since the re-export margin earned by Hong Kong has already been netted out.

The statistical process for adjusting the Sino-American trade balances comprises several steps. Firstly, we estimate the total value of Chinese *sanlai yibu* exports and the proportion of these exports which were shipped directly and indirectly via Hong Kong to the United States.[12] These values are tabulated in Table 4.6 and Table 4.7. The Chinese direct and indirect (via Hong Kong) exports to the world in total constitute, respectively, around 14 percent and 86 percent of total Chinese *sanlai yibu* exports. Chinese *sanlai yibu* exports to the United States are assumed to be similar in proportion. China's total *sanlai yibu* re-exports via Hong Kong to the United States are estimated to be HK$104.6 billion in 1993, as shown in Table 4.6. This represents 12 percent of Hong Kong's gross domestic product and 50 percent of its direct investments made in China in 1993 (see Table 4.7), pointing to the sheer importance of OP-type re-exports flowing from China via Hong Kong to the United States.

The second step involves categorizing the important production inputs, fixed and variable, used in light manufacturing into capital ($I1$),[13] rental ($I2$), labour ($I3$), raw materials ($I4$), fuels/charges ($I5$), and distribution ($I6$), and then estimating the expected percentage use of each category of inputs relative to total usage of inputs. The estimates are based on actual cost data obtained during our survey of five (5) enterprises in Shenzhen specializing in *sanlai yibu* activities. The estimated percentage shares for the various input cost categories are tabulated in Table 4.8. On the average, Hong Kong contributed 71.5 percent, and China 28.5 percent, to the aggregate production costs.[14]

Finally, the adjustment of the bilateral balance of trade figures between China and the United States may be made by resorting to the estimated re-export margin earned by Hong Kong (0.715) and China (0.285). We first deduct the OP-related re-export value (OP-RX) from the unadjusted Chinese value of indirect exports to the United States to derive China's exports proper to the United States. We then add to China's exports proper the Chinese share of OP-RX (that is, 0.285 (OP-RX)) to obtain total Chinese real (actual) exports to the United States (that is, exports of truly Chinese origin). China's adjusted trade balance with the United States is Chinese total real exports to the United States less Chinese imports from the United States.[15] The adjusted figures for 1991 to 1993 are shown in Table 4.9.

The adjusted estimates show that the flows of real Chinese production (exports of 100 percent Chinese origin) to the United States are substantially smaller than those originally recorded in US statistics, after netting away the re-export margin earned by Hong Kong. Overall, the unadjusted US deficits with China were approximately overstated by 93.65 percent, 90.03 percent and 132.98 percent in 1991, 1992 and 1993, respectively. As a matter of fact, the adjusted US trade deficits for the three years, 1991 to 1993 have turned out to

Table 4.6   Chinese Trade With the United States via Hong Kong, 1978–94 (HK$ Billions)

	All products (1)	Chinese Re-exports to the US		Direct exports (4)	US Exports to China Re-exports via Hong Kong (5)	(%s)/[(4)+(5)]*100 (6)
		OP-type only (2)	(2)/(1)*100 (3)			
1978	0.3730	0.0003	0.1	8.5051	0.3199	3.6
1979	0.7353	0.0079	1.1	18.7098	0.1307	0.7
1980	1.6899	0.0685	4.1	20.1636	0.3368	1.6
1981	2.8136	0.1644	5.8	17.7015	0.5669	3.1
1982	3.5739	0.2575	7.2	15.7998	1.0337	6.1
1983	5.5099	0.4441	8.1	23.4810	1.4735	5.9
1984	8.7781	1.2101	13.8	30.1080	2.9316	8.9
1985	11.2558	1.9150	17.0	24.2704	4.4759	15.6
1986	18.6668	3.2918	17.6	27.2930	4.4221	13.9
1987	27.7480	4.6564	16.8	27.3210	6.1786	18.4
1988	43.2419	9.2742	21.4	39.1861	9.5883	19.7
1989	65.9928	20.7779	31.5	44.9280	10.2652	18.6
1990	81.6445	33.9013	41.5	37.4699	10.2832	21.5
1991	103.9551	47.2561	45.5	48.8082	13.3016	21.4
1992	139.9767	70.2564	50.2	57.4382	18.1827	24.0
1993	168.3313	104.5966	62.1	67.8447	24.6010	26.6
1994	195.7943	127.6630	65.2	68.0064	28.6615	29.6

Note: Column (2) figures are indirectly estimated using OP (*sanlai yibu*) plus *sanlai qiye* outputs from Guangdong, considering the growth rate of OP in Guangdong (bearing in mind that Guangdong produces more than 85% of all OP-type outputs in China) and the compositon of Chinese re-exports to the United States via Hong Kong as a basis of exercising judgement. For instance, there was a negligible quantity of OP production in Guangdong in 1978. As a result we expect little Chinese OP-related exports to the United States. On the other hand, there was a tremendous increase in OP-type outputs (both from *sanji* and township enterprises) in 1993, constituting about 62% of Guangdong's total exports. This percentage is smaller than the figure listed in Table 4.4 which shows that 76% of the goods flowing from China to Hong Kong in 1994 is OP-related. Besides, we also observe that about 86% of Chinese total re-exports to the United States is manufactured products in 1993, a large percentage of which is believed to be OP-related.

Source: Census and Statistics Department, Hong Kong Government.

Table 4.7 Percentages and Values of Direct and Indirect OP-Related
Exports From China to the United States in 1993

	% of OP-XV	OP-XV (HK$ billion)	OP-XV as % FDI	OP-XV as % GDP
Direct	14	14.6435	6.94	1.65
Indirect	86	89.9531	42.60	10.13
Total	100	104.5699	49.54	11.78

Note: OP-X denotes outward-processing-related export value. GDP and FDI stand respectively for Hong Kong's gross domestic products (HK$887.614 billion in 1993) and realized foreign direct investment in China (HK$211.1364 billion).

Table 4.8 Hong Kong's Average Proportional Contribution of Each
Input to Total Production Value, According to 1995/96
Survey of Eight Different Industries in Guangdong

	I_1	I_2	I_3	I_4	I_5	I_6	π	Total
Hong Kong	0.094	0.021	0.027	0.326	0.016	0.131	0.113	0.728
China	0.010	0.029	0.078	0.068	0.045	0.030	0.012	0.272
Total	0.104	0.050	0.105	0.394	0.061	0.161	0.125	1.000

Note: I denotes input and subscripts 1, 2, 3, 4, 5 and 6 denote, respectively, capital, rental, labour, raw materials, fuels/charges, and distribution (refer to Appendix 1). π denotes the profit margin earned by the surveyed firms. The figures are computed using survey data collected from eight different Guangdong-based joint-ventures engaging in various outward-processing activities. The labour cost was estimated to be about 10.5% of the total export value, using the sample data. This figure is lower than that quoted by *Hong Kong Industrialist*, 'Hong Kong investment in China: Riding high', monthly magazine published by The Federation of Hong Kong Iindustries, (May 1995).

be very close to the adjusted Chinese trade balances which now show a surplus instead of a deficits against the United States. They are HK$50.3 billion (US deficit) versus HK$56.4 billion (Chinese surplus) for 1991; and respectively HK$71.2 billion versus HK$87.4 billion in 1992, HK$74.7 billion versus HK$84.8 billion in 1993; and HK$105.7 billion versus HK$89.0 billion. The relative discrepancy for the three years stands respectively at only 12 percent, 23 percent, 14 percent and 16 percent, using the US deficits as the base measure.

Rough as our adjusted estimates may appear to be, they reveal nonetheless that US trade deficits with China have continued to persist through the recent

Table 4.9 Trade Balance: American and Chinese Statistics 1991–1994 (HK$ Billions)

Year	US			Chinese		
	X	M	X-M	X	M	X-M
1991	48.3039 (13.3016) –	145.6785 – {111.2761}	–97.3746 (–84.0730) {–49.6706}	47.5372 (103.9551) [69.5527]	61.3383 – –	–13.8011 (90.1542) [55.75161]
1992	57.5513 (18.1837) –	197.2090 – {146.0623}	–139.6577 (–121.4750) {–70.3283}	65.9921 (139.9767) [88.8302]	68.2942 – –	–2.3021 (137.6746) [86.5279]
1993	67.5030 (24.6010) –	241.6032 – {165.4569}	–174.1272 (–149.5262) {–73.3529}	73.2989 (168.3313) [92.1850]	82.0776 – –	–8.7787 (159.5526) [83.4063]
1994	68.0064 (28.6615) –	293.6640 – {200.7253}	–225.6576 (–196.9961) {–104.0574}	92.4825 (195.7943) [102.8556]	107.9602 – –	–15.4777 (180.3166) [87.3779]

Note: Figures in round brackets include the indirect US-China trade in the form of HK re-exports. Figures in square brackets show the OP-adjusted exports, denoting total re-exports minus OP-related re-exports (which is equal to China's traditional domestic exports) plus China's share of OP-related re-exports, imports from China minus the re-export margin earned by Hong Kong. Figures in { } indicate the flow of real Chinese production to the US, denoting US total imports from China minus the re-export margin earned by Hong Kong.

years. This is clearly related to a discernible shift in the direction of China's trade, particularly on the export side, with the United States becoming an increasingly important market for its manufactured goods. China's exports to the US, including the entire OP proportion through Hong Kong, have increased, as a share in US global imports, from 6 percent in 1979 to 14 percent in 1985 and 26 percent in 1992.[16] Such a shift can primarily be explained by China's evolving competitiveness, coupled in particular with the emerging comparative advantage associated with the China-Hong Kong economic synergy in light manufacturing and outward processing. Put differently, the increased Sino-American trade imbalances should essentially be seen 'as a result of the catching-up industrialization of China following the flying geese pattern of development' of other Asian newly industrialized countries.[17]

A more fundamental point which emerges from our reconciliation of the conflicting Sino-US trade deficit claims is that the size of China's surplus as claimed by the United States can now be scaled down very substantially and that the netted-out balances clearly imply that the overwhelming proportion of China's trade surplus with the United States really represents none other than the fact that Hong Kong, or for that matter Taiwan as well, have been able to successfully export (by way of outward-processing) the US trade deficits incurred with them to the Chinese hinterland. As we have noted elsewhere, the China's increasing trade surplus with the United States since the mid-1980s is clearly a mirror image of the comparable but consistently shrinking trade balances of both Hong Kong and Taiwan *vis-à-vis* the United States.[18]

It should also be of interest to note that China's favourable trade balance with the United States is occasionally explained as being brought about by the Chinese ability to manipulate the RMB/US$ exchange rate for promoting exports. There is of course a good case for such an argument, bearing in mind that the RMB/US$ rate has been rising steadily, and at times quite drastically, in nominal or real terms, ever since the early 1980s. However, a regression analysis for the years 1978 to 1993 based on the unadjusted China trade balance figures reveals that changes in the RMB exchange rate in real terms do not really bear to any significant extent on the growth of China's trade surplus with the United States.[19] A possible explanation is that the bulk of OP-type export and import flows between Hong Kong and China is, by the nature of the transactions, not at all vulnerable to fluctuations in the RMB/HKD exchange rate, let alone that the Hong Kong dollar has been pegged to the US dollar ever since late 1983.

THE STAKE OF HONG KONG IN A SINO-AMERICAN CROSSFIRE

By virtue of the highly enhanced symbiotic relationship between Hong Kong and China, it is clear that any US-initiated trade sanctions against China will seriously affect Hong Kong as well. In the past several years, the Hong Kong government, wary of an abrupt withdrawal by the United States of China's MFN status, has painstakingly estimated each year, ahead of the June deadline for MFN renewal, the possible impact on the Hong Kong economy in terms of trade, income and job losses.

As shown in Table 4.10, Hong Kong's exports of Chinese origin to the United States could be easily slashed by up to nearly 50 percent or a minimum of one-third, in case of MFN withdrawal. It is not clear how exactly the statistics are compiled. But given that US demand for the export commodities involved are all highly price-elastic, the estimated magnitude of re-export losses seems to be quite reasonable. At any rate, according to the same Hong Kong government estimates, if MFN sanctions were implemented, the multiplier effect of a shortfall in re-exports to the US would have led to the expected Hong Kong GDP growth rate of around 5.5 percent for both 1993 and 1994 to be curtailed by 2.2 percent to 3.1 percent, and employment reduced by a massive component of up to 69 000 and 75 000 persons respectively in the

Table 4.10 Economic Impact on Hong Kong of a Withdrawal by the US of the MFN Status for China: Hong Kong Estimates of Trade and GDP Losses, 1991–94

	1991	1992	1993	1994	1995
Losses in RXc					
%	–	35 – 47	34 – 47	–	2.3
Value (HK$ b)	–	36 – 49	47 – 66	55 – 77	4.5
Losses in Related Trade					
As % of total trade	–	6 – 8	6 – 9	–	–
	35	91 – 123	118 – 166	133 – 187	–
GDP Losses					
Growth %	0.7	1.8 – 2.5	2.2 – 3.1	2.2 – 3.1	0.14
Value (HK$b)	–	12 – 16	16 – 23	19 – 26	–
Job Losses (1000 Persons)	16.6	44 – 60	49 – 69	54 – 75	4.7

Note: RXc stands for re-exports of Chinese origin. The 1995 figures are not comparable to the 1991–94 ones. They refer to the possible impact of a US trade retaliation against China on account of Chinese 'infringement' of US intellectual property rights. The scope of sanctions by way of imposing punitive tariffs on selected target commodities is much more limited, compared to a blanket denial of MFN status. The 'hitlist', which amounted to US$1.08 billion in total, as announced in early 1995 covers such OP-type products as electrical and plastic products, telephone answering machines, wireless telephones, furniture, ceramic products, footware and sporting goods.

Source: Hong Kong Government Trade Department.

two years involved. This is indeed nothing short of a doomsday forecast for Hong Kong.

An independent estimate of the possible magnitude of GDP losses in Hong Kong, as a result of a US withdrawal of MFN status for China, may also roughly be made on the basis of the adjustments we have made to Chinese re-exports through Hong Kong to the United States. Take the year 1993 for example, for which Chinese *sanlai yibu* or OP-type exports to the United States are given to be HK$105 billion in total (see Table 4.6). With an estimated Hong Kong share of 71.5 percent (relative to its contribution to capital input and current expenditure on *sanlai yibu* production; see Table 4.8), the figure of HK$105 billion translates into an absolute share of HK$75.1 billion to the credit of Hong Kong, as compared to HK$29.9 billion for the Chinese counterparts involved with *sanlai yibu* production.

Assuming that MFN withdrawal would, in line with Hong Kong government's elasticity estimates, curtail the OP-type exports on account of the Hong Kong share, by 34 percent to 47 percent (see Table 4.10), this would give an effective export loss of HK$25.5 to HK$35.3 billion. If we further assume that for every Hong Kong dollar of OP-type exports, Hong Kong earns an value-added of say, HK$0.5, then the net GDP losses will stand at a total of HK$10.2 billion to HK$12.8 billion or alternatively HK$14.1 billion to HK$17.7 billion respectively. These estimated losses fall behind the Hong Kong government estimates of HK$16 billion to HK$23 billion for 1993, but if the multiplier income effect is taken into consideration in our independent estimate, the two sets of outcomes would probably come quite close to each other.[20]

The estimated dollar-by-dollar losses should be placed in the broader context of the Hong Kong-China economic synergy, if one is to understand the full scale of economic losses which could incur to Hong Kong in the case of MFN non-renewal. There are two aspects to the economic synergy. The first is that with the massive relocation of Hong Kong's manufacturing undertakings to the Pearl River delta, Hong Kong's industrial structure has basically been hollowed out in the past decade, so much so that one may rightly speak of a 'Manhattanization' of Hong Kong in terms of its changing economic function. Specifically similar to New York City proper, Hong Kong has these days become very much an international centre of banking, finance, shipping, insurance and global communications, serving increasingly and linking the vast industrial Chinese hinterland to the outside world.[21]

The second related aspect of the Hong Kong-China synergy is that in the past ten years or so, Hong Kong has also increasingly been transformed from an important manufacturing centre into an entrepôt of world scale. This has occurred not only on account of the increasing share of Chinese re-exports of OP-type outputs, (in relation to Hong Kong's shrinking domestic exports per se), but also more importantly, a substantial and rising proportion of Chinese imports and re-exports of Chinese origin proper has continued to be channelled through Hong Kong. Note especially that US exports via Hong Kong to China alone have increased, as a share of total China-bound US exports, from 1.6 percent in 1980 to 16 percent in 1985, and then further to a most impressive high of 30 percent in 1994 (see Table 4.6). This speaks for the very importance of Hong Kong as an international hub of marketing, sourcing, financing and shipping services. In addition, Hong Kong also provides well-established and excellent port facilities.

Perhaps the most important point which should be made in this context is that contrary to the narrower perception of the Hong Kong-China synergy being more a matter of 'trade diversion' (from Hong Kong to China for exports to the US) than anything else, the Hong Kong economy has, as a matter of fact, been growing at a rate (generally 5 percent per year) significantly faster than that of any established industrialized country in the past decade or so. This has taken place against the backdrop of a labour supply in Hong Kong which could increase at the rate of only around one percent per year; hence, until recently, mounting pressure from a labour shortage in the territory. Clearly, the Chinese industrial backbone is more than strong enough to support the now predominantly service-based, Manhattan-type economy of Hong Kong. Viewed against this new context, it should also be clear that the China factor will play a increasingly crucial role in the economic prosperity of Hong Kong towards and beyond 1997, and that any crossfire between the two economic giants, China and the United States would have a wounding effect on the fortunes of Hong Kong.

CONCLUSION — BEYOND 1997

Any speculation to be made about the economic fate of Hong Kong beyond 1997 is bound to be more a matter of academic exercise in political science rather than economics. In economic terms, any adaptations and adjustments made are necessarily marginal in scale. Clearly the source of any significant disturbance will be political in nature. What the political balance between China and the United States will hold for the Hong Kong economy is beyond the realm of economic analysis. However, given that MFN renewal has been delinked from the human rights issue since 1994, it seems that an important stage has already been set in the depoliticization of Sino-American economic relations. It is of course far too early for anyone to predict that Sino-American economic relations, and with it the prosperity and stability of Hong Kong, will be free from further political influence. But given the sheer size of the present-day Chinese economy, and of its enhanced international linkages, as well as the importance of Hong Kong as an international economic phenomenon, it appears more difficult for any US decision-makers to take policy measures, which would exert severe economic consequences.

One should nonetheless be prudent enough to remain a realist in that initiatives of a political nature from the US government will probably come to disturb the equilibrium from time to time with varying scale of damage, whether for reasons of trade imbalances with China, China's market inaccessibility or otherwise. There is a critical example of side evidence to sustain such a perception: the US has incurred, for more than two decades now, persistent and massive trade deficits with Japan, and with South Korea and Taiwan as well, but never really have their trade frictions assumed such a political tone as in the case of the US dispute with China. Perhaps, given the important stake both the United States and China are perceived to have in Hong Kong either in economic or, more importantly, political terms, Hong Kong could hopefully serve as a stabilizer in Sino-American relations.

NOTES

1. The Chinese acronym *sanlai yibu* refers literally to the 'three (3) comings' *(sanlai)* or supplies; that is, processing of materials supplied (from outside), assembling of parts supplied and manufacturing on specification; and 'one (1) compensation' *(yibu)*, that is, compensation trade. The latter refers to the contractual arrangements whereby the Hong Kong partners, supply old or new manufacturing machinery and the Chinese side provide labour for processing materials supplied by the former with a view to having the finished products shipped back to Hong Kong for export or other uses. The Hong Kong partners 'compensate' the Chinese collaborators for processing costs by agreeing eventually to transfer ownership of the machine and equipment used. Hereafter we will use the term 'outward-processing' and *sanlai yibu* interchangeably depending on whether it is looked at from the mainland Chinese or Hong Kong perspective. In short, in outward-processing, all or part of the raw materials or semi-manufactures are exported from or through Hong Kong to China for processing/reprocessing with a contractual arrangement for subsequent re-importation of the processed goods into Hong Kong. Export proper is common to the world's export trade but *sanlai yibu* is peculiar to the China-Hong Kong common production region.

2. United States Information Service (USIS-Hong Kong), *Economic Backgrounder*, (11 April 1994), p. 2. This appears to be a grossly inaccurate generalization. Apart perhaps from the *sanlai yibu* type of exports, in the early 1980s, regular Chinese exports are normally priced with gross output value rather than value-added. And from 1985, *sanlai yibu* exports have been assumed into official Chinese customs statistics at full value, instead of just the 'processing' fee *(gongjiao fei)*.

3. Since *sanlai yibu* involves essentially small-scale, labour-intensive manufacturing activities and their outputs are virtually all destined for export, the phenomenon stands in sharp contrast to investments by multinational corporations in third countries that are primarily for import-substitution and deal with large-scale, capital-intensive technology. Another difference is that, where possible, MNCs normally make use of locally available materials rather than semi-manufactured products brought in from home countries, and where their outputs are destined for third countries, they are often exported directly from the countries in which funds were invested rather than being shipped back to home countries for re-export, as is the case with *sanlai yibu* within the Hong Kong-Guangdong context.

4. Hong Kong generally accounted for 50 percent to 70 percent of China's realized foreign direct investment (FDI) intake since 1984; see Y.Y. Kueh, 'Foreign investment and economic change in China', *The China Quarterly*, No. 131 (September 1992), p. 674. The latest available figure for 1995 is given as 61 percent by a senior Chinese official from the Ministry of Foreign Trade and Economic Cooperation (see *Ta-Kung Pao* (TKP), May 1995). For Guangdong province alone, Hong Kong's FDI share ranges generally from 70 to 90 percent; see Y.Y. Kueh and Robert Ash, 'The fifth dragon: economic development', in Brian Hook (ed.), *Guangdong: China's Promised Land* (Hong Kong: Oxford University Press, 1996).

5. A good example is curtain supplies in Hong Kong. In the past, the tens of thousands of small curtain shops normally did their own cutting and sewing at the back of the shops. But these days, the processing is all done on specifications across the border in Shenzhen by regular weekly or daily consignments on behalf of Hong Kong clients rather than overseas customers.

6. The Hong Kong Census and Statistics Department only began to compile statistics on domestic exports and re-exports to China for outward-processing purposes in the third quarter of 1988, and the statistics on imports from China related to outward processing in the first quarter of 1989.

7. Y.P. Ho and Y.Y. Kueh, 'Whither Hong Kong in an open-door, reforming Chinese

Economy', *The Pacific Review*, Vol. 6, No. 4 (December 1993), p. 340 for 1980, 1985, 1990, and same sources as given therein for 1993.

8. Ibid, p. 341, the spectacular increase in 1985 to 43 percent of China's share in Hong Kong's total re-exports was probably caused by two factors. The first is the so-called Hainan 'car scandal' when the island's government made use of its special privileges in foreign trade autonomy to import, 'illicitly' through Hong Kong, a large consignment of Japanese cars (with foreign currencies obtained from the black market in exchange for a special renminbi development grant from the central government) for resale in the inland market for profiteering. The second factor is that the central government had to spend a large amount of its precious foreign exchange reserves (totalling some US$2 million) to import relatively luxurious commodities in order to soak up excessive renminbi supply which was brought about in late 1984 as a result of misconceived wage and banking policies. A large proportion of the imports was probably hastily channelled through Hong Kong as an efficient trade mediator. See Y.Y. Kueh, 'Economic reforms in China: Approach, vision, and constraints', in Dieter Cassel (ed.), *Wirtschaftssysteme im Umbruch: Sowjetunion, China und industrialisierte Marktwirtschaften zwischen internationalen Anpassungszwang und nationalen Reformbedarf* (Munich: Franz Vahlen Press, 1990).

9. See Table 4.1 (panel C) and Y.P. Ho and Y.Y. Kueh, 1993, *The Pacific Review*, op. cit., p. 342.

10. See Y.W. Sung, 'Foreign trade and investment', *China Review* (Hong Kong: The Chinese University Press, 1991), pp. 15.1–21.

11. See *Ta-Kung Pao*, 5 April 1995. However, the implied national total of US$18.2 billion (=US$15.1 billion/0.83) for *sanlai yibu* exports in 1994 is substantially lower than the HK$ equivalent of US$ 46 billion (= HK$ 355 billion) given by the Census and Statistics Department (CSD) , Hong Kong Government (HKG) as cited in Table 4.1, panel A, column (2). Comparable statistics for 1992 also reveal a similar discrepancy, with a CSD survey showing that Guangdong province alone accounted for 93 percent of total Chinese *sanlai yibu* exports to Hong Kong in 1992. It is difficult to reconcile the discrepancy. One possible explanation is that the HKG figure (US$46 billion), which is 60 percent higher than the Chinese one (US$18.2 billion), may, FOB/CIF gap apart, represent exactly the margin earned by Hong Kong manufacturers. If correct, then the margin may indeed loom larger, to the extent that the Chinese figure refers to their *sanlai yibu* exports at large, including those exported directly from China. Another possible explanation for the discrepancy is that the lower Chinese figure represents some kind of estimate made by the Chinese authorities of their own share in total *sanlai yibu* exports, in a way perhaps similar to the attempt to be made in the following section of this chapter. We really do not know for sure how the Chinese figure is calculated.

12. A fraction of *sanlai yibu* exports by Hong Kong and Taiwan based investors in provinces other than Guangdong is directly exported to the United States; see Q. Luo and C. Howe, 'Direct investment and economic integration in the Asia Pacific: The case of Taiwanese investment in Xiamen', *The China Quarterly,* No. 137 (December 1993), p. 746. However, detailed statistics are not available. We therefore will only estimate the 're-export margin' earned by Hong Kong.

13. If capital is borrowed, we estimate the capital cost in terms of interest repayment plus the costs of maintaining and replacing building, machinery and fixtures.

14. The average profit margin for the five surveyed companies (see Appendix 1) is 10 percent, which is lower than that (15 percent) estimated by HKTDC in 1991 , indicating that profit could have fallen in recent years. We attribute the 10 percent profit margin to the Hong Kong share to make it a total of 71.5 percent as a basis for apportioning the total *sanlai yibu* exports to the total China versus Hong Kong shares (see Appendix 1 for explanation). Note, however, that the validity of our

surveyed results may be weakened by the small sample size used and by the limited range of company types chosen, which could, collectively, give rise to the limiting nature of our estimates. Nevertheless, pending a more comprehensive and rigorous survey, we propose to estimate the OP-related export margin earned by Hong Kong for both the direct and indirect export enterprises using the preliminary survey results.

15. In the case of US exports to China, we do not net out the re-export margin for two main reasons. Firstly, little production in the United States has an outward processing origin. Secondly, the redistribution margin earned by Hong Kong in the case of US indirect exports to China via Hong Kong has been netted out since US FOB prices were made use of in compiling the US statistics.

16. Nicholas R. Lardy, 'Re-defining US-China economic relations', *Analysis Monograph Series*, No. 5 (Seattle, Washington: National Bureau of Asian and Soviet Research, June 1993).

17. Joseph C.H. Chai, 'US-China trade conflict and its implication for Australia's agricultural trade'. See Chapter 11.

18. *Financial Times* (London), 22 May 1993, (Interview with Y.Y. Kueh); see also Robert Ash and Y.Y. Kueh, 'Economic integration with greater China: Trade and investment flows between China, Hong Kong and Taiwan', *The China Quarterly*, No. 136 (December 1993), p. 727.

19. Note that in our estimates we have also ignored the parallel curtailment in the Chinese share of OP-type exports through Hong Kong, and the possible impact of a Chinese retaliation on US re-exports via Hong Kong to China.

20. For an excellent, full-scale study of industrial changes in Hong Kong, see Y.P. Ho, *Trade, Industrial Restructuring and Development in Hong Kong* (London/Honolulu: MacMillan Press/University of Hawaii Press, 1992).

Appendix 4.1(a) Percentage Input Contribution to Production by China and Hong Kong for the Eight Surveyed OP-Related Firms in Guangdong

Survey Companies

	A		B		C		D		E		F		G		H	
	HK	CN	HK	CN	HK	CN	HK	CN	HK	CN	HK	CN	HK	CN	HK	CN
Capital	13.0	0	13.0	0	13.0	0	11.5	0	9.0	0	6.8	3.2	8.8	2.2	0	2.4
Rental	2.0	5.0	3.0	5.0	1.5	0	1.5	0.5	5.0	10.0	2.4	0	1.0	0.8	0	1.5
Labour	2.5	5.0	4.0	8.0	2.0	15.0	2.0	1.0	6.0	6.0	2.3	6.5	0.5	2.8	2.0	18.0
Raw Material	45.0	0	16.0	16.0	30.0	0	40.0	0	0	-20.0	39.7	10.6	51.4	5.7	38.6	3.3
Fuel/Charges	1.5	2.0	2.0	3.5	2.0	12.0	1.5	12.0	2.5	2.5	2.7	2.0	0.5	1.5	0.3	0.5
Distribution	10.0	1.5	15.0	3.5	15.5	3.0	20.0	2.5	17.0	8.0	6.0	2.5	9.5	1.8	12.0	0
Total	74.0	13.5	53.0	36.0	64.0	30.0	76.5	16.0	39.5	46.5	59.9	24.8	71.2	14.8	52.6	25.7

Note: (1) HK and CN denote Hong Kong and China's share of imput contribution. Companies A,B,C, and D related, respectively, to printing, electronics, textile and household goods production.

(2) Companies E, F and G, relate, respectively, to production of processed food, spectacle frames, and watches. Company H is a village enterprise, specializing in exports of clothes and household curtains. Each entry represents the percentage of the respective company's turnover (gross margin). Profit margin for each company can be derived from the last row of the table. For example, company A's profit margin is 12.5%, that is, (100-74-13.5)%.

Appendix 4.1(b) Average Percentage Input Contribution by China and Hong Kong and the Profit Margin of the Surveyed Companies

Hong Kong	China	Profit Margin (HK)	Profit Margin (CN)	Total
61.5	26.0	11.3	1.2	100

Note: Capital includes interest repayment, depreciation and bank fees/charges. Rental includes land and warehouse charges. Labour includes salary and wages. Raw materials and semi-manufactured products imported from ROW and subsequently brought into China are treated as costs incurred by Hong Kong. Fuel/charges include heating, electricity, water, insurance and sundry expenses. Distribution includes advertising, handling, transportation, travelling, postage, telecommunications, packaging and quality control.

5

The United States Versus Japan in Market Shares in Hong Kong and Taiwan

Kai-cheong Lei

INTRODUCTION

The increasing importance of the Asia-Pacific rim countries, the East Asia countries in particular, in the world economy has been recognized by economists and governments all over the world. Many countries, both inside and outside Asia, have reset their economic policies accordingly in order to maximize their national interests through trading or investing in this prosperous region. As a result, the relationships between the East Asian economies and some major powers have turned down new avenues. Take the cases of Japan and the United States as an example. According to some estimates,[1] the United States has since 1992 already shifted her centre of gravity in trading from Europe to the Asia-Pacific region since 1992. During 1993, total trade between the United States and that region amounted to US$361 billion, which was higher by more than 50 percent than the corresponding figure with Europe (US$239 billion). In the same year, the Asia-Pacific region absorbed 30 percent of US total exports and supplied 41 percent of US total imports. Japan, at the same time, has also shifted her focus back to Asia. During 1992, Japan's exports to the Asia-Pacific region went up by 14 percent while those to the United States increased only 7 percent. In that same year, 31 percent of Japan's exports went to this region, which was not only larger than the 18 percent to Europe but also larger than the 29 percent to the United States. What is more important, these changes are expected to continue in the future. Therefore it becomes obvious that the battlefield of trade competition is once again located in Asia.

This chapter concentrates on a study of the price competition between the United States and Japan in two important Asian markets: Hong Kong and Taiwan. A study on Hong Kong and Taiwan is not only important for its own sake but is also important for an integrated understanding of China's development within the 'Greater China' framework. China is no doubt the single most important market within the Asia-Pacific region and her development has contributed to the growth of other countries both inside and outside the region. China's own economic development, on the other hand, is closely related to the development of other parts of 'Greater China', namely Hong Kong and Taiwan. To the extent that the United States, as a resource supplier, has been contributing significantly to the successful development in Hong Kong and Taiwan and to the extent that Hong Kong and Taiwan have been acting as two major supporting partners to China's economic growth since the late 1970s, the US factor's contribution to China's economic development can only be properly assessed when both the direct and indirect supply of US resources to China are taken into account. This chapter, therefore, can also be viewed as a partial contribution to the understanding of the whole picture.

The United States, on the other hand, has a strong foreign competitor in both the Hong Kong and Taiwan markets, namely Japan. As indicated in the next section, the competition and substitution between the United States and Japan is both obvious and significant. Competition can be performed in many ways, either through prices or through other instruments. For instance, non-price factors such as trade credit allowance as well as inward foreign direct investment may be quite important. Yet, the key and basic element of competition is price competition and price elasticity is the most important parameter concerning competition. A model with an explicit measure for the price elasticity of substitution is therefore set up for this purpose in this chapter following the discussions on market structure in the next section. Other factors that may also contribute to our understanding of the competition mechanism are also incorporated into the basic model. Empirical analysis is then performed for Hong Kong and Taiwan in the fourth section of this chapter. After detailed discussions of the results and implications, a concluding section follows.

THE UNITED STATES AND JAPAN IN THE TAIWAN AND HONG KONG MARKETS SINCE THE 1970s

That both Hong Kong and Taiwan are rapidly growing economies over the past four decades is well known to the world. Indeed, their performances are so remarkable that each of them has been crowned as a so-called Newly-Industrializing Economy (NIE) by the OECD in the 1970s. There were only ten economies in the whole world given this honour at that time.[2]

One of the three criteria adopted by the OECD for identifying a developing country as NIE is a rising share of world exports of manufactures.[3] As resource-poor (except for human resources) economies, the way by which Hong Kong and Taiwan manage to accomplish the requirements set by that criteria is to make use efficiently of the resources imported from other countries. Resources in the form of industrial materials and semi-manufactures are especially crucial for their export industries. In this respect, Japan and the United States, as main suppliers of the required resources, have been contributing their shares to the successful development in Hong Kong and Taiwan. The following table summarizes some relevant information.

Table 5.1 Japan and US Market Shares in Nominal Imports of Taiwan and Hong Kong, 1971–1993

Period	Taiwan				Hong Kong			
	JM %	UM %	(JM+UM) %	(JM/UM)	JM %	UM %	(JM+UM) %	(JM/UM)
1971–75	37.3	24.1	61.4	1.57	21.9	12.5	34.4	1.76
1976–80	31.0	23.0	54.0	1.35	22.7	12.1	34.5	1.88
1981–85	27.5	23.2	50.7	1.19	23.0	10.5	33.5	2.19
1986–90	31.5	23.3	54.8	1.36	18.1	8.3	26.4	2.18
1991–93	30.1	22.0	52.1	1.37	16.8	7.5	24.5	2.25
1971–93	31.6	23.2	54.8	1.37	20.8	10.4	31.2	2.03

Note: JM and UM stand for Japan's market share and the United States market share respectively.

Source: (1) *Taiwan Statistical Data Book*, various issues.
(2) Census and Statistics Department, Hong Kong Government, *Hong Kong Annual Digest of Statistics*, various issues.

Table 5.1 offers several important observations. Firstly, Japan and the United States together have supplied more than 50 percent of total imports to Taiwan during 1971–93; the corresponding figure for Hong Kong is 31 percent. Secondly, judging from the sub-period figures, the US-Japan combined share in Taiwan fluctuates only within a rather narrow range from 51 percent to 55 percent during 1976–93; but in Hong Kong such a combined share presents a significant downward trend from 34 percent to 25 percent during 1971–93. Thirdly, the US share in the Taiwan market, which is about 23 percent on the average, is rather stable while the Japanese share declines from 37 percent to 30 percent during 1971–93; in the Hong Kong market, both the US share and the Japan share tend to decline over time. Lastly, and perhaps most importantly, as a result of changing market shares with different patterns, the relative market share of Japan to the United States in the Taiwan market has declined with some fluctuations from 1.57 in 1971–75 to 1.37 in 1991–93. The pattern of change in Hong Kong is again different: the relative shares increase rather than decrease from 1.76 to 2.25 almost persistently from period to period. These patterns indicate that competition and substitution between the United States and Japan must have been quite active in both Hong Kong and Taiwan.

One additional point, which is related to the China factor in the Hong Kong market, deserves attention. In the 1970s the degree of importance of China as a supplier to Hong Kong falls between that of Japan and of the United States; but it has overtaken the importance of Japan since China opened its door to the world economy in the early 1980s. If imports from China are put aside, then the average Japan share and US share in the Hong Kong market should be adjusted upward by 7 percent and 3.5 percent respectively. The adjusted shares also present different patterns of change from the unadjusted patterns: the Japan share now becomes rather stable while the US share declines.[4] But since the China factor is not our target in this chapter, the Hong Kong analysis in the following sections will still use the unadjusted figures.

Similarly, the real importance of Japan and the United States in the Taiwan market is also greater than is implied in Table 5.1, because there has not been a single other country in the whole world whose market share in Taiwan has exceeded 5 percent on the average during 1971–93. Even for the two major oil suppliers, Saudi Arabia and Kuwait, the respective shares are only 4.7 percent and 4.4 percent in that period. Japan and the United States, in other words, have faced no real competitors except each other in the Taiwan market. Their positions are not only strong but are overwhelmingly strong. Such market structure provides us with a rationale for concentrating our competition study on only the two major suppliers, namely the United States and Japan.

BASIC THEORETICAL MODEL

The starting point is the import function. Two separate functions are specified for imports from Japan (JA) and imports from the United States (US) as follows:

$$(JA) = \alpha_0 (PJ)^{\alpha_1}(PU)^{\alpha_2}(PD)^{\alpha_3}(Y)^{\alpha_4} \exp\{e_1\} \tag{1}$$

$$\alpha_0 > 0, \alpha_1 < 0, \alpha_2 > 0, \alpha_3 > 0, \alpha_4 > 0$$

$$(US) = \beta_0 (PJ)^{\beta_1}(PU)^{\beta_2}(PD)^{\beta_3}(Y)^{\beta_4} \exp\{e_2\} \tag{2}$$

$$\beta_0 > 0, \beta_1 > 0, \beta_2 < 0, \beta_3 > 0, \beta_4 > 0$$

Both JA and US are measured in real terms. Export prices of Japan and US are denoted by PJ and PU respectively. Two factors associated with the domestic economy, either Taiwan or Hong Kong, are also introduced: namely, domestic price (PD) and the scale of the economy (Y) which may be represented by GDP or by other measures such as the total volume of trade. All prices are measured in terms of US dollars. Error terms are expressed by $\exp\{e_1\}$ and $\exp\{e_2\}$ respectively.

As far as price competition is concerned, the traditional specification of import demand emphasizes only the price competition between the exporters and the domestic producers. Such a specification tends to ignore the competition between the various suppliers for a country's imports. The specification of (1) and (2), on the contrary, differentiates between the various competitive suppliers.[5]

The next step is to combine (1) and (2) to form a ratio function so as to provide a direct way to study the changes in relative market shares (RMS), that is, (JA/US).

$$(JA/US) = \gamma_0 \, (PJ)^{\gamma 1}(PU)^{\gamma 2}(PD)^{\gamma 3}(Y)^{\gamma 4} \, \exp\{e\} \tag{3}$$

$$\begin{aligned}
\text{Where} \quad \gamma_0 &= (\alpha_0 / \beta_0) > 0, \\
\gamma_1 &= (\alpha_1 \_ \beta_1) < 0, \\
\gamma_2 &= (\alpha_2 \_ \beta_2) > 0, \\
\gamma_3 &= (\alpha_3 \_ \beta_3), \\
\gamma_4 &= (\alpha_4 \_ \beta_4), \\
e &= (e_1 - e_2) \sim N(0, \sigma^2)
\end{aligned}$$

In order to obtain an explicit measure for the price of substitution, a restriction $\gamma_1 = -\gamma_2 = \gamma$ is then imposed on (3) so that it becomes

$$(JA/US) = \gamma_0 (PJ/PU)^p (PD)^{p3}(Y)^{p4} \, \exp\{e\} \tag{4}$$

The parameter γ is nothing but the elasticity of substitution. Notice that equation (4) is basicly equivalent to the equations derived by Armington, Hickman, and Hickman and Lau which are based on a cost minimization approach.[6]

In addition to γ, there are two important parameters, γ_3 and γ_4. The former represents the difference in the cross elasticity of demand for the Japanese products and for the US products. As a measurement of difference, γ_3 can either be positive, negative or even zero. If the value is zero, it means that price inflation in the domestic economy has a neutral effect on RMS. On the other hand, a positive value implies a bias in favour of Japan while a negative value implies a bias in favour of US. Similar meanings can be attached to γ_4, which is a measurement of the difference in scale elasticity, a positive (negative) γ_4 implies a favourable (unfavourable) bias towards Japan relative to the United States.

MAIN EMPIRICAL FINDINGS

Equation (4) is the basis of the present analysis and is estimated for both Hong Kong and Taiwan in this study by using annual data from 1971 to 1993 by the method of Ordinary Least Squares (OLS). Each regression is in log-linear form. Empirical results obtained from the Taiwan market and the Hong Kong market are reported separately below. The elasticity of substitution will be our major concern.

Elasticity of Substitution Between Japan and the United States in the Taiwan Market

In the Taiwan study, the scale variable is represented by real GDP, while domestic price is measured by the wholesale price index (PW). When equation (4) is estimated for the overall imports market, the following results are obtained.

For total imports

$$\log(JA/US) = 2.9795 - 0.6380 \log(PJ/PU)$$
$$(3.12)$$
$$+ 0.4058 \log(GDP) - 0.6770 \log(PW)$$
$$(3.62) \qquad\qquad (-4.34) \qquad\qquad (5)$$
$$DW = 2.34, \quad \bar{R}^2 = 0.46, SEE = 0.10$$

Figures in parentheses are the estimated t-values. $\bar{R}^2$ is the adjusted coefficient of determination, DW is the Durbin-Watson statistic, and SEE stands for the standard error of the estimate. The t-value in equation (5) indicates that each variable in the regression is statistically significant at the 95 percent confidence level.[7]

Equation (5) implies that the estimated elasticity of substitution is about 0.64, which is inelastic. Price competition between the United States and Japan in the Taiwan market as a whole is therefore not so strong. One plausible explanation is that Taiwan's imports from the United States include some agricultural products such as raw cotton and wheat, and such US products face virtually no competition, let alone substitution, from Japan. The overall elasticity of substitution is consequently on the low side. Further investigation in this respect is given in a later section.

Another interesting result is revealed by the scale bias, which is positive (0.41). Japan, in other words, has benefited more from Taiwan's economic development than has the United States. This finding may be helpful in providing a partial explanation of why Japan could enjoy an increasing surplus from their Taiwan trade year after year ever since the early 1960s. As Taiwan's economy grows, not only have Japan's exports to Taiwan grown but Japan's relative market share in Taiwan has also grown. The United States, on the other hand, could enjoy an increasing share but not an increasing relative share in Taiwan.

The domestic price (inflation) bias, on the contrary, is negative (–0.68). Taiwan's inflation is revealed as a more favourable factor for the US exporters than for Japan's exporters. It also means that Taiwan's cross price elasticity of demand for Japanese products (α_3) is smaller than the corresponding elasticity for US products (β_3).

For heavy-industry manufactured goods

As explained before, the United States exports certain agricultural products to Taiwan that are not substitutable by imports from Japan. The major items include soybeans, wheat and raw cotton. As percentages of total imports from the United States, these three items together take up 23.7 percent in the 1970s, 10.5 percent in the 1980s and 5 percent in the period 1991–1993. Although an obvious downward trend is observed, their importance in the overall assessment of the substitution elasticity should not be overlooked.

In order to eliminate possible distortion due to the inclusion of agricultural goods, a new estimation is made with agricultural goods, textile products, and miscellaneous products excluded. Textile products are unimportant for both Japan and the United States in their Taiwan sales; the weights in total sales for the former are less than 4 percent over the sample period while for the latter nearly zero. The new group of commodities includes as components the following items: machinery and electrical equipment, transportation equipment, basic metal and articles thereof and chemicals.

In the absence of a better term, the new commodity grouping will be called the heavy-industry manufactured goods, or simply as h-manufactured goods in the present study. Table 5.2 summarizes the development pattern of this market.

Table 5.2 Taiwan's Shares of H-Manufactured Imports in Total
Imports From Japan and the United States

Period	From Japan (%)	From US (%)	Relative market shares: Japan to US
1971–75	78.5	52.3	2.39
1976–80	81.3	54.1	2.05
1981–85	82.8	51.4	1.92
1986–90	83.0	58.1	1.98
1991–93	78.9	57.3	1.88
1971–93	81.1	54.4	2.06

Source: Taiwan Statistical Data Book.

As seen from Table 5.2, for both Japan and the United States, more and more of their exports to Taiwan belong to this group of goods. Meanwhile, the figures in relative market shares indicate that Japan's position relative to that of the United States is much stronger in this market than in the overall market (compared with Table 5.1). On the other hand, as agricultural goods are excluded, the degree of competition between the United States and Japan is expected to be higher in this market.

$$\log(JA/US) = 6.1645 - 1.1496 \log(PJ/PU)$$
$$(-4.37)$$
$$+ 0.4897 \log(GDP) - 0.9272 \log(PW)$$
$$(3.40) \qquad (-4.63) \qquad\qquad (6)$$
$$DW = 2.16, \ \bar{R}^2 = 0.56, \ SSE = 0.13$$

Equation (6) indicates that, as fully expected, the elasticity of substitution is much larger (in absolute terms) in this market. It is not only elastic (−1.15) but is about two times higher as in the overall market (−0.64). Price competition between the two suppliers has therefore evidently been strong for the h-manufacturing goods in Taiwan.

The scale effect is again in favour of Japan. Actually, the scale bias is not only positive (0.49) but also larger than the corresponding figure in the overall market (0.41).

This bias result also implies that Taiwan's scale (income) elasticity of demand for Japanese h-manufacturing products (α_4) is greater than that for the US counterpart products (β_4). There may be a deep structural explanation for this. As has been pointed out by many development economists, the Taiwan economy was composed of many small to medium-sized firms right from the start of industrialization, and these firms have remained as the majority of producers even today. Large conglomerates in Taiwan, unlike their counterparts in South Korea, have never had a chance to dominate the economy.[8] Given this structural composition in production scales, it implies that so far as imported machinery and equipment are concerned, capital goods in small to medium sizes are much more welcomed by the Taiwan producers. If, at the same time, it is also true that Japan, as compared with the United States, is the one who produces more of the small to medium-sized capital goods, then it is only natural to discover that Taiwan's scale elasticity for Japanese products is larger than the corresponding elasticity for US products.[9] The value of (α_4) is therefore greater than (β_4).

Equation (6) also indicates that there is a price bias in favour of the United States' position relative to Japan's position in the Taiwan h-manufacturing goods market.

Elasticity of Substitution Between Japan and the United States in the Hong Kong Market

In the study for Hong Kong, the scale variable is also represented by real GDP, but in the absence of a published wholesale price index, price is measured by the consumer price index (PC) instead. Equation (4) is also estimated for both the overall market and a sub-market.

For total imports

As is generally understood, the Hong Kong market is much closer to the free market model than is the Taiwan market. While the Taiwan economy is heavily guided by various growth-promotion policies implemented by the government, the Hong Kong economy is relatively free from governmental intervention. The price mechanism is therefore expected to be more effective in Hong Kong than in Taiwan. As a consequence, the price elasticity of substitution should also be higher in Hong Kong. This expectation is indeed fully supported by the empirical findings presented below.

$$\log(JA/US)= 3.5524 - 1.1958 \log(PJ/PU)$$
$$(-8.22)$$
$$+ 0.3472 \log(GDP) - 0.3465 \log(PC)$$
$$(3.76\,) \qquad\qquad (-2.55) \qquad\qquad (7)$$
$$DW = 1.63, \quad \overline{R}^2 = 0.90, \ SSE = 0.07$$

The overall elasticity of substitution in Hong Kong, unlike in Taiwan, is elastic (−1.20), signifying that the Hong Kong economy is much more flexible than the Taiwan economy is in making choices between the two imports suppliers, Japan versus the United States, whenever there is a change in relative prices for imported goods. Putting it another way, as far as the response to price changes is concerned, the structure of import demand in Taiwan is much more rigid than in Hong Kong. Whenever there is a one percent increase in Japan's export prices relative to the US export prices, Japan's market share will drop only by 0.64 percent relative to the US share in the Taiwan market, while it will drop by 1.2 percent relative to the US share in the Hong Kong market. As our findings suggest, the price mechanism is much more effective and market forces are much more powerful in Hong Kong than in Taiwan.

Turning to the scale effect and the domestic price effect, the Taiwan pattern appears in the Hong Kong market too. The scale effect (0.35) is in favour of Japan while the domestic price effect is in favour of the United States. In the process of industrial development, small-scale enterprises are also important in Hong Kong.[10] The same explanation given for a positive scale effect for Taiwan therefore also applies to Hong Kong. On the other hand, in terms of magnitudes, both the scale effect and the domestic price effect seem to be smaller in Hong Kong than in Taiwan. To be sure, a straight comparison is impossible since the price variable is measured differently in the two studies. Yet, as far as a rough comparison is admissible, the results may represent a manifestation of the fact that the Hong Kong market is more diversified in terms of import sources than is the Taiwan market . As imports have more choices, the elasticity with respect to a particular supplier is smaller. Also it just happens that the difference in elasticity between the Japanese products and the US products turns out to be smaller too.

For consumer goods and producer goods

The sub-market in this section refers to the market that combines together the following groups of goods: consumer goods, capital goods, and raw materials and semi-manufactures. Foodstuffs and fuels are therefore excluded in the following analysis.[11]

$$\log(JA/US) = 4.3481 - 1.2865 \log(PJ/PU)$$
$$(-8.68)$$
$$+ 0.3184 \log(GDP) - 0.3291 \log (PC)$$
$$(3.38) \qquad\qquad (-2.38) \qquad\qquad (8)$$
$$DW = 1.70, \ \overline{R}^2 = 0.90, \ SSE = 0.07$$

The foodstuffs market in Hong Kong, like the agricultural market in Taiwan, is more important for US exporters than for Japanese exporters. On average, the ratio of nominal market shares (Japan versus the United States) is just slightly below 0.5 during the sample period, and there is also a trend which is in favour of the United States. Fuels, on the other hand, are imported mainly from Singapore and China. When these groups of goods are excluded, the elasticity of substitution becomes –1.29, which is about 7.5 percent higher than the overall substitution elasticity (–1.2).

The scale effect is again in favour of Japan and the domestic price effect is in favour of the United States in this sub-market.

CONCLUSIONS AND REMARKS

In this chapter, I have set up a model to measure the price competition between the United States and Japan in two important Asian markets: Hong Kong and Taiwan. The findings are both interesting and illuminating.

With respect to price competition, the estimated elasticity of substitution indicates that, as far as the whole market is concerned, price competition is stronger in Hong Kong. This finding is consistent with our general understanding that the market mechanism is more effective in Hong Kong than in Taiwan due to the former's *laissez-faire* environment. The general picture is presented in Table 5.3.

Table 5.3 Elasticity of Substitution Between US and Japanese Imports

	In Taiwan	In Hong Kong
Total imports	-0.64	-1.19
Manufacturing imports*	-1.15	-1.29

*   Manufacturing imports has different meaning in the Taiwan study and in the Hong Kong study. For exact definitions, see the text on pp. 97–102.

In addition to substitution elasticity, the model also provides measures of scale and domestic price effects. The scale effects in the four regression analyses all point to a bias in favour of Japan, meaning that Japan has benefited more from the importing country's economic development than has the United States. This finding may serve as a partial answer to why Japan could enjoy a persistent and increasing surplus in her Taiwan and Hong Kong trade. Japan's market shares have grown with the domestic economy's economic growth. Rapid growth in Taiwan and Hong Kong leads to rapid growth in Japan's market shares.

The domestic price effect, on the contrary, is in favour of United States exporters. Inflation in Taiwan seems to have stimulated more imports from the United States than from Japan.

There are several ways that the empirical part of this chapter could be improved. Firstly, some finer price indices for imported goods are perhaps more desirable than the export prices for the measuring of the elasticity of substitution. Import prices differentiated between sources, for example, may be better for studies focusing on a particular country. Yet, given our intention to make comparisons between different economies, namely Hong Kong and Taiwan, using a uniform set of export prices instead still has its own merit. Secondly, price indices differentiated between commodity groupings are no doubt more suitable for industry-by-industry analysis. But data as such are usually not available in published form. Special efforts must be made to accomplish this requirement. Thirdly, non-price factors may also have an important role to play in the game of market competition. While the difficulties associated with the measuring of non-price competition should not be underestimated, additional variables representing trade credit allowance as well as inward foreign direct investments may be worth considering. Finally, so far as the dynamics of competition could be also important, estimations based on some distributed-lag models may be more meaningful. But the above would involve much more technical complexity than a paper addressed to the general reader can incorporate. In terms of econometrics, the present framework is indeed quite simple. But the findings are by no means negligible. Our estimates of the price elasticity of substitution are both significant and plausible. What is perhaps more important, so far as the United States-Greater China economic relations are concerned, is that any attempt which may lead to a better understanding of the American position in the former markets is worth trying. The price elasticity of substitution is no doubt an important parameter one should look at for both marketing and policy considerations.

NOTES

1. *Ming Pao Daily News*, 5 June 1995.
2. For more information, see N. Grimwade, *International Trade: New Patterns of Trade. Production and Investment* (London: Routledge, 1989), especially pp. 311–33.
3. Ibid, p. 312.
4. Detailed information can be founded in Hong Kong Census and Statistics Department, *Annual Digest of Statistics*.
5. V.A. Muscatelli and A.A. Stevenson, 'Intra-NIE competition in exports of manufactures', *Journal of International Economics*, No. 37 (1994), pp. 29–47, have used a similar approach to study export functions for the Asian NIEs.
6. P.S. Armington, 'A theory of demand for products distinguished by place of production', *IMF Staff Papers,* Vol. 16, No.1 (1969), pp. 159–76; B. Hickman, 'A general linear model of world trade', in R.J. Ball (ed.), *The International Linkage of National Economic Models* (North-Holland, 1973), and B. Hickman and L.J. Lau, 'Elasticities of substitution and export demands in a world trade model', *European Economic Review,* Vol. 4 (1973), pp. 347–80.
7. The required t-ratio for 19 degree of freedom is 1.729. See D.N. Gujarati, *Basic Econometrics* (3rd edition) (New York: McGraw-Hill, 1995), p. 809.
8. See, for example, D. Dollar, and K. Sokoloff, 'Industrial policy, productivity growth, and structural change in the manufacturing industries: A comparison of Taiwan and South Korea', in J.D. Aberbach, D. Dollar and K.L. Sokoloff (eds.), *The Role of the State in Taiwan's Development* (New York: M.E. Sharpe, 1994), pp. 8–11, and H. Pack, 'New perspectives of industrial growth in Taiwan', in G. Ranis (ed.), *Taiwan: from Developing to Mature Economy* (New York: Westview Press, 1992), pp.103–6. C.J. Lee, 'An analysis of the international factors that influence the development of small and medium enterprises: The case of Taiwan', *Conference on Global Interdependence and Asia-Pacific Cooperation,* Conference Series No. 24, (Chung-Hua Institution for Economic Research, Taipei: CIER Press, 1992), pp. 279–319, has a more detailed analysis on the importance of small-scale enterprises for Taiwan.
9. Since the 1960s, Japan's exports have shifted away from labour-intensive, light manufactures towards more capital-intensive goods. See N. Grimwade, 1989, op. cit., pp. 283–4.
10. Y.P. Ho, *Trade, Industrial Restructuring and Development in Hong Kong* (London: Macmillan, 1992).
11. The Hong Kong government classifies imports by end-use category as consumer goods, raw materials and semi-manufactures, capital goods, foodstuffs, and fuels. See Hong Kong Census and Statistics Department, *Annual Digest of Statistics*.

6

United States Direct Investment in China: Basic Facts and Some Policy Issues

Leonard K. Cheng

INTRODUCTION

In this chapter, I shall focus on the investment relation between China and the United States. A description and analysis of the statistics of US direct investment (DI) in China will be presented,[1] to be followed by a discussion of some policy issues and areas of disagreements between the two sides in the investment arena.

It is useful to point out at the outset that investment and trade relations are closely related and are different facets of the overall economic relations between the two countries. As we shall see, as a source country of foreign direct investment (FDI) in China, the United States is less important compared with its role as China's trading partner.

Up to the end of 1993, the US cumulative DI accounted for 6.5 percent of all contracted FDI and 8.6 percent of all realized FDI in China, making it a distant second to Hong Kong and Macau.[2] Its shares of contracted DI and realized DI in 1992 were 5.4 percent and 4.6 percent, respectively.[3]

According to Chinese statistics, in 1992 about 10 percent of Chinese exports went to the United States, making the US market the third largest export market for Chinese products. In the same year China bought about 11 percent of its imports from the United States. However, a substantial portion of China's exports to Hong Kong was ultimately bound for the United States,[4] making the US market much more important than Chinese statistics has indicated. The US market has been an important factor behind the export-oriented FDI in China, regardless of whether the investment was made by US firms or firms from other areas such as Hong Kong and Taiwan. Indeed, according to US statistics imports from China in 1992 were about three times the Chinese figure. US exports to China as recorded in Chinese statistics were only slightly larger than as recorded by the US. This is consistent with the fact that a much smaller percentage of US exports to Hong Kong ended up as re-exports to China.[5]

STATISTICS ON US DIRECT INVESTMENT IN CHINA

Data Sources

The data on US direct investment used in this chapter are obtained from the *Almanac of China's Foreign Economic Relations and Trade* (*Almanac* for short) published by the Ministry of Foreign Trade and Economic Cooperation (MOFTEC), *China Foreign Economic Statistics 1979–91* published by the Statistical Bureau of China, *US Investment in China* published by the US-China Business Council, and *China Economic News*, 25 July 1994. Additional statistics are provided by MOFTEC.

Like other sources of FDI in China, three kinds of statistics are provided for US direct investment in China. They are the number of approved agreements (contracts); the amount of investment approved (often referred to as 'contracted investment'); and the utilized amount of investment (often referred to as 'realized investment'). Since direct investment takes time to implement, contracted investment in any particular year gives an indication of investment plans in future years instead of actual investment in the same year. For the same reason, much of the investment realized in a particular year is the result of contracts approved in previous years.

Thus, when contracted investment experiences a strong upward trend, the ratio of realized to contracted investment is expected to be substantially below unity. In addition, some approved projects have not been followed through by any investment activities. In the period from 1984 (the first time when investment data were classified according to source of investment) to 1992, the total realized US investment was 39 percent of its total contracted investment, higher than the 31 percent for all FDI.

To the extent that statistics are available, US direct investment in China can be broken down according to geographical regions, economic sectors, and modes of investment, namely, 'contractual joint ventures' or 'cooperative joint ventures' (CJV), 'equity joint ventures' (EJV), 'wholly foreign owned enterprises' (WFOE), and 'joint development' (JD).

In an equity joint venture, the partners would share profits, losses and any other risks in accordance with their respective shares of the venture. In contrast, in a CJV a contract would spell out what each of the partners will bring to and get from the venture. It was not unusual that the risks associated with cooperation were skewed towards one of the partners. Wholly foreign-owned enterprises are self-explanatory. 'Joint development' ventures were set up predominantly between a corporation or ministry under the Chinese central government and one or more foreign partners for the purpose of exploring and developing natural resources such as coal, oil and natural gas. In general no legal entity was created for JDs.

Annual Flows and Cumulative Stocks of US Direct Investment

The number of US DI projects in China from 1983 to 1992 and the cumulative number of investment projects since 1983 are given in Table 6.1. The number of contracts has increased without interruption in every year during the period, even though the total number of projects by all foreign investors fell drastically in 1986 and again in 1989.[6] In terms of the number of contracts, the US share of the cumulative number of projects after 1983 remained below 5 percent until 1992, in which year it reached 5.8 percent.

Table 6.1 Number of US Direct Investment Contracts

	1983	1984	1985	1986	1987	1988	1989	1990	1991	1992
Number of US contracts	32	62	100	102	104	269	276	357	694	3265
Total number by all countries/ regions	638	2166	3073	1498	2233	5945	5779	7273	12 978	48 764
% of projects by US	5.02	2.86	3.25	6.81	4.66	4.52	4.78	4.91	5.35	6.70
Cumulative number of US contracts since 1983	32	94	194	296	400	669	945	1302	1996	5261
Total number by all countries/ regions	638	2804	5877	7375	9608	15 553	21 332	28 605	41 583	90 347
% of projects by US	5.02	3.35	3.30	4.01	4.16	4.30	4.43	4.55	4.80	5.82

The amount of contracted investment each year and the amount of cumulative contracted investment since 1983 are given in Table 6.2 and depicted in Figure 6.1. US contracted investment in 1983 was very large, accounting for about one quarter of all contracted FDI in that year. The amount fluctuated but declined in 1986 due to a general worsening of the investment environment in China. The recovery in 1988 and 1989 was short-lived due to the student movement in the latter year. Following an overall surge in FDI in China, US contracted investment in 1992 was record-breaking. In terms of cumulative contracted investment since 1983, the share by US investors dropped from 25 percent in 1983 to 7.3 percent in 1992, and further to 6.5 percent in 1993.[7]

Table 6.2 Contracted Amount of US Direct Investment (US$10 000)

	1983	1984	1985	1986	1987	1988	1989	1990	1991	1992
Amount of US investment	47 752	16 518	115 202	52 735	34 219	37 040	64 052	35 782	54 808	312 125
Total investment by all countries/ regions	191 690	287 494	633 321	283 434	370 884	529 706	559 976	659 611	1 197 682	5 812 351
% of investment by US	24.91	5.75	18.19	18.61	9.23	6.99	11.44	5.42	4.58	5.37
Cumulative investment since 1983	47 752	64 270	179 472	232 207	266 426	303 466	367 518	403 300	458 108	770 233
Total cumulative investment by all countries/ regions since 1983	191 690	479 184	1 112 505	1 395 939	1 766 823	2 296 529	2 856 505	3 516 116	4 713 798	10 526 149
% of cumulative investment by US	24.91	13.41	16.13	16.63	15.08	13.21	12.87	11.47	9.72	7.32

Note: All the figures shown in 1983, 1984 and 1985 include compensation trade and others because they cannot be flushed from US figures.

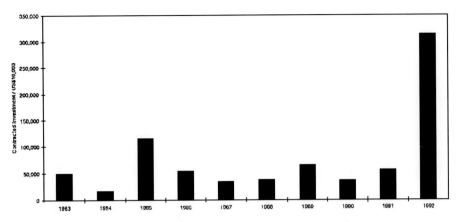

Figure 6.1 Contracted Amount of US Direct Investment, 1983–1992

The amount of realized investment since 1984 is given in Table 6.3 and depicted in Figure 6.2. While realized investment for all countries continued to grow in the second half of the 1980s, realized US DI fell in 1987 and 1988 and did not recover fully until 1990. The June Fourth Incident in 1989 had a significant negative impact on contracted investment but a smaller impact on realized investment, again in contrast to the continued upward surge of both contracted and realized FDI in the post-1989 period. Basically, as US investors stayed away from China in the aftermath of the military crackdown, investors from other areas moved in. US contracted investment in 1990 and 1991 were below the 1989 level but US realized investment in these same years was above the 1989 level. As China returned to the path of reform following Deng Xiaoping's tour of South China in early 1992, US contracted investment exploded like all FDI but the increase in realized investment was less dramatic.

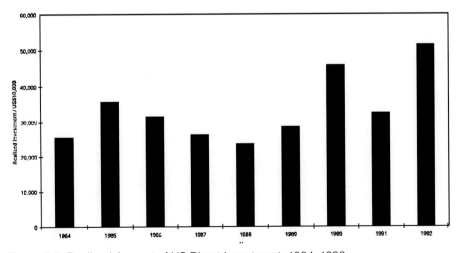

Figure 6.2 Realized Amount of US Direct Investment, 1984–1992

Table 6.3 Realized Amount of US Direct Investment (US$10 000)

	1984	1985	1986	1987	1988	1989	1990	1991	1992
Amount of US investment	25 625	35 719	31 490	26 280	23 596	28 427	45 599	32 320	51 105
Total investment by all countries/regions since 1983	141 885	195 615	187 489	231 353	319 368	339 257	348 711	436 634	1 100 751
% of investment by US	18.06	18.26	16.80	11.36	7.39	8.38	13.08	7.40	4.64
Cumulative investment since 1984	25 625	61 344	92 834	119 114	142 710	171 137	216 736	249 056	300 161
Total cumulative investment by all countries/regions since 1984	141 885	337 500	524 989	756 342	1 075 710	1 414 967	1 763 678	2 200 312	3 301 063
% of cumulative investment by US	18.06	18.18	17.68	15.75	13.27	12.09	12.29	11.32	9.09

Note: All the figures shown in 1984 and 1985 include the compensation trade & others because they cannot be flushed from US figures.

Up to the end of 1993, US investors had 12 000 approved investment agreements, pledged $14.6 billion of investment funds, and actually made US$5.2 billion of investment. As a percentage of the total FDI in China, US investment accounted for 6.9 percent of the number of agreements, 6.5 percent of the total contracted investment and 8.56 percent of the total realized investment. Surprisingly, the average size per US investment contract ($1.2m) was slightly below the average size of all FDI ($1.25m).

Tables 6.4 and 6.5 show the US cumulative contracted and realized investment in China since 1983 and 1984, respectively, by measuring investment in 1990 US producer prices.[8]

A comparison of Table 6.4 with Table 6.2 and of Table 6.5 with Table 6.3 shows that as far as the share of cumulative investment in China is concerned, the measurement of investment in constant 1990 dollars has not produced any major difference. Whether cumulative investment is measured in current dollars or constant dollars, the US share of contracted direct investment fell from 25 percent in 1983 to 15 percent in 1987, to about 10 percent in 1991, and then to somewhat above 7 percent in 1992.

The decline in US share of realized investment was, in contrast, less drastic given the same starting year. It fell from 18 percent in 1984 to below 16 percent in 1987, above 11 percent in 1991 and over 9 percent in 1992. Thus, the decline in realized investment by the United States was smaller than its contracted investment.

Geographical Distribution of US Investment

Two sets of data about the geographical distribution of US investment are used. The first set comes from *China Foreign Economic Statistics 1979–91*, which gives a breakdown of US investment according to China's administrative regions (that is, provinces, municipalities and autonomous regions) for five consecutive years (1987–91). The second comes from the US-China Business Council's US Investment Database, which covered a total of 517 US-funded enterprises.

To get a broad view of the geographical distribution of US FDI, the 30 administrative regions are combined into three groups: the coastal regions; the inland and northern regions; and the western regions. Using this classification, Table 6.6 shows the shares of contracted FDI in these regions based on the first data set while Table 6.7 shows the shares based on the second. A comparison of these two tables shows that the US Investment Database contained a larger percentage of US investment in the western and inland and northern regions but a smaller percentage in the coastal regions than the first data set.

In Tables 6.8 and 6.9, the administrative regions are grouped according to the US-China Business Council study. The first data set shows more investment

Table 6.4 Cumulative Contracted US Direct Investment
Measured at 1990 Prices (US$10 000)

	1983	1984	1985	1986	1987	1988	1989	1990	1991	1992
Cumulative investment since 1983	57 088.72	76 385.89	208 091.25	267 171.76	304 821.05	344 648.76	410 911.31	446 693.31	499 857.50	796 992.76
Total cumulative investment by all countries/ regions since 1983	229 170.24	566 745.70	1 290 793.62	1 608 332.71	2 016 404.72	2 585 966.12	3 165 267.89	3 824 878.89	4 936 639.88	10 519 853.96
% of cumulative investment by US	24.91	13.48	16.12	16.61	15.12	13.33	12.98	11.68	10.02	7.58

Note: All the figures shown in 1983, 1984 and 1985 include the compensation trade and others because they cannot be flushed from US figures.

Table 6.5 Cumulative Realized US Direct Investment
Measured at 1990 Prices (US$10 000)

	1984	1985	1986	1987	1988	1989	1990	1991	1992
Cumulative investment since 1984	29 936.43	70 772.38	106 051.51	134 966.57	160 337.95	189 746.02	235 345.02	266 695.68	315 346.3
Total cumulative investment by all countries/ regions since 1984	165 757.29	389 395.28	599 444.49	853 994.93	1 197 392.37	1 548 357.73	1 897 068.73	2 320 607.16	3 368 494.83
% of cumulative investment by US	18.06	18.17	17.69	15.80	13.39	12.25	12.41	11.49	9.36

Note: All the figures shown in 1984 and 1985 include the compensation trade and others because they cannot be flushed from US figures.

in the coastal, near inland and far inland regions but less investment in the metropolitan areas than the second data set.

A comparison of the last column of Table 6.6 with our 1991 figures indicates that relative to all foreign investment in China, the United States seemed to have focused less on the western regions but more on the coastal regions.[9] Within the coastal regions, US investors tended to have invested relatively more heavily in the north and middle, but substantially less heavily in the south. As pointed out by the US-China Business Council (1991), US investors have focused more on major cities and the north, in contrast with investors from Hong Kong, Macau and Taiwan, who have invested relatively more heavily in the south.[10]

Table 6.6 Percentage of Amount of US Direct Investment, 1987–91

Regions	1987	1988	1989	1990	1991	Total
Coastal regions	93.33	93.20	97.02	93.99	89.99	93.55
North:	*46.19*	*11.77*	*9.12*	*17.97*	*24.77*	*21.25*
Liaoning	10.68	0.76	4.76	6.50	4.66	5.42
Beijing	28.56	6.92	1.45	3.39	10.62	9.54
Tianjin	0.26	1.58	0.93	5.81	6.68	3.15
Hebei	6.69	2.52	1.99	2.27	2.82	3.13
Middle:	*27.99*	*32.03*	*24.20*	*51.39*	*42.02*	*35.05*
Shandong	0.69	2.47	6.72	6.72	17.85	7.73
Jiangsu	8.94	3.60	1.74	16.19	9.94	7.72
Shanghai	16.45	18.78	8.28	26.41	10.39	14.93
Zhejiang	1.91	7.19	7.46	2.07	3.83	4.66
South:	*19.15*	*49.40*	*63.70*	*24.63*	*23.19*	*37.26*
Fujian	0.95	4.98	0.99	4.90	3.42	2.87
Guangdong	18.00	41.75	60.46	18.45	13.35	31.58
Guangxi	0.21	0.26	0.16	0.65	1.01	0.47
Hainan	0.00	2.41	2.08	0.63	5.41	2.34
Western regions	0.13	2.22	0.68	0.79	4.70	1.83
Xinjiang	0.00	0.97	0.00	0.00	0.00	0.15
Gansu	0.00	0.00	0.00	0.00	0.13	0.03
Ningxia	0.00	0.00	0.08	0.00	0.11	0.05
Shaanxi	0.10	0.00	0.07	0.12	0.29	0.13
Yunnan	0.00	0.68	0.11	0.03	0.00	0.14
Guizhou	0.00	0.40	0.00	0.04	1.06	0.33
Sichuan	0.03	0.17	0.43	0.60	3.10	1.00
Inland and northern regions	6.54	4.58	2.30	5.22	5.31	4.62
Shanxi	0.00	0.25	0.07	0.45	0.56	0.27
Inner Mongolia	4.41	0.00	0.00	0.01	0.05	0.78
Jilin	0.00	0.46	0.40	1.24	1.38	0.72
Heilongjiang	0.07	1.14	0.46	0.73	1.41	0.78
Anhui	0.06	0.27	0.11	0.11	0.35	0.18
Jiangxi	0.32	1.77	0.00	0.00	0.50	0.45
Henan	0.21	0.20	0.49	0.88	0.50	0.46
Hubei	1.00	0.04	0.56	0.10	0.42	0.44
Hunan	0.46	0.45	0.21	1.70	0.15	0.53
% Total	100.00	100.00	100.00	100.00	100.00	100.00

Table 6.7 Regional Distribution of US FIEs in China

Region	% of number of FIE	% of Total Investment (US$ million)
Coastal regions	85.11	82.47
North:	*29.79*	*23.58*
Liaoning	4.84	4.41
Beijing	16.83	15.32
Tianjin	6.19	2.40
Hebei	1.93	1.45
Middle:	*27.66*	*25.73*
Shandong	2.71	1.01
Jiangsu	7.54	2.84
Shanghai	14.51	19.61
Zhejiang	2.90	2.27
South:	*27.66*	*33.17*
Fujian	4.06	1.32
Guangdong	23.02	31.59
Guangxi	0.39	0.06
Hainan	0.19	0.19
Western regions	6.19	3.28
Xinjiang	0.39	0.44
Gansu	0.19	0.06
Ningxia	0.39	0.19
Shaanxi	2.13	1.77
Yunnan	0.39	0.00
Guizhou	0.77	0.25
Sichuan	1.93	0.57
Inland and Northern Regions	8.70	14.25
Shanxi	0.19	11.03
Inner Mongolia	0.19	0.95
Jilin	0.39	0.06
Heilongjiang	1.55	0.50
Anhui	1.55	0.25
Jiangxi	0.58	0.32
Henan	0.97	0.06
Hubei	1.74	0.63
Hunan	1.55	0.44
% Total	100.00	100.00

Note: FIE denotes foreign-invested enterprises.

At this point, the only data about the sectoral and modal distribution of US investment in China are contained in the US-China Business Council's US Investment Database. The following two sections summarize results provided in *US Investment in China* based on this database.

Table 6.8 Percentage of Amount of US Direct Investment, 1987–1991

Regions	1987	1988	1989	1990	1991	Total
Metropolitan	45.27	27.28	10.66	35.61	27.69	27.62
Beijing	28.56	6.92	1.45	3.39	10.62	9.54
Shanghai	16.45	18.78	8.28	26.41	10.39	14.93
Tianjin	0.26	1.58	0.93	5.81	6.68	3.15
Coastal	47.86	65.66	86.21	57.73	61.29	65.46
Guangdong	18.00	41.75	60.46	18.45	13.35	31.58
Jiangsu	8.94	3.60	1.74	16.19	9.94	7.72
Liaoning	10.68	0.76	4.76	6.50	4.66	5.42
Fujian	0.95	4.98	0.99	4.90	3.42	2.87
Zhejiang	1.91	7.19	7.46	2.07	3.83	4.66
Shandong	0.69	2.47	6.72	6.72	17.85	7.73
Hebei	6.69	2.52	1.99	2.27	2.82	3.13
Hainan	0.00	2.41	2.08	0.63	5.41	2.34
Near inland	2.27	3.69	2.00	5.13	4.87	3.54
Hubei	1.00	0.04	0.56	0.10	0.42	0.44
Anhui	0.06	0.27	0.11	0.11	0.35	0.18
Hunan	0.46	0.45	0.21	1.70	0.15	0.53
Henan	0.21	0.20	0.4 9	0.88	0.50	0.46
Jiangxi	0.32	1.77	0.00	0.00	0.50	0.45
Guangxi	0.21	0.26	0.16	0.65	1.01	0.47
Jilin	0.00	0.46	0.40	1.24	1.38	0.72
Shanxi	0.00	0.25	0.07	0.45	0.56	0.27
Far inland	4.61	3.36	1.14	1.53	6.16	3.38
Shaanxi	0.10	0.00	0.07	0.12	0.29	0.13
Sichuan	0.03	0.17	0.43	0.60	3.10	1.00
Heilonajiang	0.07	1.14	0.46	0.73	1.41	0.78
Guizhou	0.00	0.40	0.00	0.04	1.06	0.33
Ningxia	0.00	0.00	0.08	0.00	0.11	0.05
Xinjiang	0.00	0.97	0.00	0.00	0.00	0.15
Yunnan	0.00	0.68	0.11	0.03	0.00	0.14
Gansu	0.00	0.00	0.00	0.00	0.13	0.03
Inner Mongolia	4.41	0.00	0.00	0.01	0.05	0.78
% Total	100.00	100.00	100.00	100.00	100.00	100.00

Sectoral and Size Distribution of US Investment

In terms of the number of investment projects, the top five industries are, in descending order, electronics, miscellaneous light industry, food and agriculture, services and chemicals. However, in terms of the total amount of investment, the top five industries, again in descending order, are tourism, natural resources, food and agriculture, chemicals and transportation.

The changes in the sectoral composition of US investment in China during the sample period were similar to those of all foreign investment, namely from

Table 6.9 Regional Distribution of US FIEs in China

Regions	% of number of FIE	% of Total Investment
Metropolitan	37.52	37.33
Beijing	16.83	15.32
Shanghai	14.51	19.61
Tianjin	6.19	2.40
Coastal	47.20	45.08
Guangdong	23.02	31.59
Jiangsu	7.54	2.84
Liaoning	4.84	4.41
Fujian	4.06	1.32
Zhejiang	2.90	2.27
Shandong	2.71	1.01
Hebei	1.93	1.45
Hainan	0.19	0.19
Near inland	7.35	12.86
Hubei	1.74	0.63
Anhui	1.55	0.25
Hunan	1.55	0.44
Henan	0.97	0.06
Jianoxi	0.58	0.32
Guangxi	0.39	0.06
Jilin	0.39	0.06
Shanxi	0.19	11.03
Far inland	7.93	4.73
Shaanxi	2.13	1.77
Sichuan	1.93	0.57
Heilongjiang	1.55	0.50
Guizhou	0.77	0.25
Ningxia	0.39	0.19
Xinjiang	0.39	0.44
Yunnan	0.39	0.00
Gansu	0.19	0.06
Inner Mongolia	0.19	0.95
% Total	100.00	100.00

Note: FIEs denotes foreign-invested enterprises.

natural resources and tourism in the early 1980s to manufacturing in the second half of the 1980s (the surge in real estate investment after 1992 was too recent to be captured by the database).

The average investment is US$3.27 million per project (which contrasts with the average of $1.2 million per project based on data provided in the *Almanac*). The largest average investment is found in tourism ($12.47m), to be followed by natural resources ($7.27m), transportation ($6m), chemicals ($5.92m) and food and agriculture ($3.4m). In contrast, the smaller ones are found in services ($0.54m), consulting ($0.67m) and miscellaneous light industry ($0.88m).

Modal Distribution of US Investment

In terms of numbers of investment projects, EJVs account for over three-quarters, to be followed by 13 percent of CJVs, 7 percent of WFEs, and 4 percent of JDs. In terms of total investment, EJVs account for only about 30 percent because of their small size ($1.64m). CJVs account for 32 percent since they are much bigger ($9.9m). JDs, by far the biggest ($30.6m), account for 29 percent of the total investment, while WFOE's with a medium size ($3.4m) account for 8.6 percent.

What Have the Data Revealed?

From the description in the above sections, we see that overall US investors in China followed a similar trend to other foreign investors in terms of changes in the amount of contracted and realized investment. For instance, we see the concentration in natural resources and tourism in the early period, and a shift to manufacturing since the mid-1980s. However, US investment from 1987 to 1991 was more sensitive to deterioration in China's investment environment and to the June Fourth Incident.

US firms were strong in natural resources, energy, transportation, high technology and specific manufacturing industries such as chemicals. Given their emphasis on long-term development of manufacturing capability rather than short-term export-processing activities, US DI in China tended to favour EJV over CJV as a mode of investment when compared with investors from other countries and areas. This suggests that US investors would be more concerned about the protection of foreign investment provided by China's legal system. The emphasis on the domestic market and sophisticated technology has accounted for the relatively high concentration of US DI in the municipalities, in particular Shanghai. Among others, intellectual property rights protection would be of great importance to US investors.

Although there are many US multinational enterprises that have invested in China, there are far more small investors from the US than from Europe, Australia and Japan. The small US investors are mainly in services and light manufacturing.

Finally, it is helpful to reiterate that the US market for Chinese products is an important factor for the export-processing type of FDI in China, whether or not the foreign investors are from the United States. China's high degree of trade dependence on the United States implies that the United States might flex its trade muscle to influence its investment relations with China, and the bilateral trade balance in China's favour could generate pressure on the United States government to open up the Chinese market for US goods and services, whether they are produced in the United States or China.

US INVESTORS AND POTENTIAL POLICY

Disagreements

China has entered into bilateral investment agreements with over fifty countries, including Japan, Germany, the United Kingdom, and France. However, it does not have a bilateral investment agreement with the United States because the two sides disagree on issues such as arbitration and compensation for expropriation.[11]

Political and Social Stability

A common concern among foreign investors, including US investors, is China's potential political instability and the possibility of social chaos. Will the government after Deng be too weak to implement the painful yet necessary reforms? Will there be a political breakup of the type observed in the former Soviet Union? Will there be social turmoil as inflation remains in double digits and corruption reaches unacceptable proportions? Will the various factions within the ruling party engage in a destabilizing power struggle?

No one can answer the above questions with certainty, but China and the United States will remain at odds over the state of human rights and the pace of democratization in China. China will regard US criticism as meddling in China's internal affairs while the United States will continue to argue for their universality. In the area of democratization, there is not much the United States can do short of overt or covert hostility towards the Chinese government. In the area of human rights, the trade linkage has been broken in the United States' own economic interest. While US firms operating in foreign countries are asked to observe certain guidelines voluntarily, China has not been singled out as a target.[12] As for corruption, it will add to the difficulties and costs of doing business in China, but its adverse consequences for the Chinese government are far more serious. The Chinese government needs to keep corruption under control to ensure its own survival.

In any case, the extent of conflict arising in the areas of democratization and human rights will depend on the mood of the legislative and executive branches of the US government as much as events taking place in China. But one thing is certain. The two sides will continue to have skirmishes over them. The issue of corruption depends mostly upon the Chinese government's own will to stamp it out, and US influences will be minimal.

Economic Environment

External trade and investment environment

China's accession to GATT and membership of the WTO would be a milestone in its integration with the world economy. Stability in economic relations between China and the major economic powers is a key determinant of foreign investment in China. For example, China's most-favoured-nation (MFN) status has been an annual worry for the United States and other foreign investors in China who sell their products to the US market. Any serious deterioration in US-China relations might lead to retaliation against US investors.

The US position on China's accession to GATT and membership in the WTO can well be regarded as a litmus test of the two countries' economic relations. Under what conditions will the United States support China's WTO membership drive? Will the US invoke Article XXXV (the 'non-application' clause) if China does become a contracting party to GATT? Will the US Congress revise its laws to eliminate the annual review of China's MFN status after China's admission to the WTO?

In any case, both US firms with investment in China and the US administration have set the following conditions for China's membership in WTO: further concessions in the areas of market access (that is, reduction or elimination of tariff and non-tariff barriers), improvements in intellectual property rights protection; and transparency of its trade and investment policies. As we shall see below, the extent and timing of market access and application of international rules on trade and investment are areas of major disagreement and tough negotiation.

Macroeconomic stability

Foreign investors are concerned about the risk of inflation and the damaging effects of cycles of boom and bust, as macroeconomic instability could lead to business difficulties and even failures. The government is no less concerned about macroeconomic instability, as it is most concerned about the political fall-out. Thus, there does not seem to be any disagreement about the need to maintain macroeconomic stability. The real difficulty is that monetary policy is still a hostage to the inefficient state-owned enterprises and local demand for investment credit. Ideological prejudice against the non-state sector and the fear of large-scale unemployment continue to be stumbling blocks in China's effort to improve the efficiency of its state-owned enterprises.

Legal Environment

The United States as a society is more legalistic than most other countries. Compared with investors from Hong Kong and Taiwan, US investors are at a disadvantage in developing the connections (*guanxi*) that are needed to strike deals in the absence of a well-defined and transparent legal system. Thus, it is natural that US investors would press the Chinese govenment to put in place a predictable and transparent legal system to protect their interest.

The legal system

Most of the complaints about China's legal system with regard to the protection of foreign investment have to do with deficiencies in the country's legal system. They include the legal framework, enforcement of laws and regulations, transparency and uniform application of the law in different territorial subdivisions.

According to Chinese officials, by the end of 1993 China had promulgated over 500 laws related to FDI at various administrative levels, and it had signed over 50 bilateral agreements on the protection of foreign investment. It is also a participant in the Convention Establishing the Multilateral Investment Guarantee Agency and a signatory country to the Convention on the Settlement of Investment Disputes. Several laws on the protection of intellectual property rights have been promulgated, for example the Patent Law. China has codes on property rights and has also signed several international treaties on the protection of property rights. Even some critics of China over the lack of investment protection measures admit that China has made 'admirable progress in creating a **legal framework** for copyright, patent, and trademark protection'.

What really counts, of course, is the **enforcement** of the laws and regulations on the statute books. The major differences in opinions are about the extent of effective enforcement of Chinese laws, including the ability of the Chinese courts to enforce their rulings. Issues about the rule of law and sanctity of contracts arise because of widespread corruption and the difficulties of enforcing judgment against businesses that belong to local governments and the army. The extent to which contracts are enforced also raises questions about the depth of commitment and behaviour of Chinese firms, in particular state-owned enterprises, when they form joint ventures with foreign partners.

There are lots of complaints about the lack of **transparency** in the Chinese legal system.[13] One reason is that circulars, rules and internal directives are not well-known to foreign investors. According to Chinese officials, all the promulgated rules and regulations on FDI have been announced and published. They are available to potential foreign investors. Despite such assurances, there are still complaints that many trade regulations remain unpublished for 'security' reasons, and officials consistently refuse to state unambiguously how many goods and services are still subject to tariff and quota restrictions.

China has made progress in cleaning up its numerous internal directives and regulations, but more work is needed to clean them up completely and to publicize them to foreign investors and traders if they are still in effect. To meet the continued criticism that China fails to announce import quotas and trade regulations and their cancellation (or relaxation) despite claims by Chinese officials to the contrary, China has expressed willingness to publish all investment laws, regulations, administrative guidelines and policies in an official journal and to designate enquiry points to provide information and texts. This is part of its effort to join GATT and the WTO.[14]

The fact that there are over 500 laws related to foreign investment is in itself a source of confusion. Many of the laws were improvised in reaction to new developments in the global and domestic investment environment. It would be desirable for the sake of transparency and for streamlining the investment regime if the existing laws could be replaced by a small number of more general investment laws. Of special interest to foreign investors is increased transparency with regard to proper procedures and determination of compensation in case of appropriation.

Even if hidden rules and regulations are either eliminated or publicized, the lack of a legal tradition means that the same national law might be interpreted and enforced in significantly different ways in different parts of the country. The lack of **uniform application** of the law in different regions and cities is an important reason for the confusion and inconsistencies in the Chinese legal system. For example, some local officials, in order to attract FDI to their own districts, have tried to stretch the law to, or even beyond, the limit. As another example, customs levies may vary from port to port. These practices have created a perception among foreign investors of a lack of transparency and fair competition. As we shall see below, this is a problem that the Chinese government will have to deal with in its efforts to grant national treatment and most-favoured treatment to foreign investors. Along with the investment rules themselves, the lack of a uniform application of rules between the central government and provincial governments are regarded by US investors in China as a significant problem.

With regard to China's legal system, disagreement between the Chinese and US governments is found less in long-term goals but more in terms of what has been accomplished and the speed for necessary additional reform. To avoid unnecessary confrontation, the line between technical assistance to improve China's legal system and infringement upon China's sovereignty needs to be drawn clearly.

Protection of foreign investment and investors

A key concern of the United States with regard to its investment and trade interests is the protection of intellectual property rights. Because a major competitive advantage of US firms is their advanced technologies and well-received brand names, insistence on protection of these intangible assets makes good sense. By threatening trade sanctions, it succeeded in forcing the

Chinese government into accepting a Sino-American agreement on intellectual property protection in February 1995.

Given the Chinese government's objectives to stimulate invention and innovation in its emerging market economy, its long-term goal of protecting intellectual property rights is not incompatible with the demands of the United States. The main differences between the two sides were about the speed with which the long-term measures could be implemented, given the perceived short-term costs of speedy implementation. In the end, China agreed in February 1995 not only to close down factories which pirated US intellectual property and investigate others which were accused of doing so, but also to make periodic reports to the United States about the enforcement of intellectual property rights laws and to open its domestic market for US investment in music, software and so on.

The US-China agreement on intellectual property protection has helped to smooth bilateral trade and investment relations, and has also signalled China's commitment to fulfilling GATT's Agreement on Trade Related Aspects of Intellectual Property Rights.[15] The danger of potential conflicts between China and the United States, however, remains and will depend on the implementation of the bilateral agreement.

Another area that the United States attaches importance to is expropriation and compensation. The United States insists that China accept international standards on expropriation and compensation and give investors access to binding international arbitration for settlement of disputes with the state.[16] It is hard to see why China would not follow widely accepted international practices in these areas,[17] but given the lack of experience on the part of China, disagreements on the details of implementation cannot be ruled out.

The incident of the McDonald's restaurant in Beijing's Wangfujing Street has attracted worldwide attention to questions about the validity of contracts in China and the kind of compensation provided when contracts are broken. Under the international limelight, McDonald's seemed to have got a very favourable deal by working with the Beijing City government for a mutually acceptable solution.

Foreign investors, especially small investors, complain that they are often subject to unreasonable and unlawful harassment by local officials. For instance, meddling by officials in the hiring and firing of workers. Purely commercial disputes might turn into criminal cases. Government officials are perceived as having unlimited investigative power in matters such as valuation of assets and tax evasion. This is an area of concern to the United States as well, because, while many US investors are major multinational companies which are, presumably, relatively immune to harassment by local and low level officials, a large number of investors from the US are small.

Until recently, the concern about personal protection of foreign investors has been confined mainly to Chinese investors from Hong Kong, and Macau and Taiwan as well as investors of Chinese origin from other countries. The case of the Australian Chinese investor James Peng in Shenzhen has stirred up concerns about the personal protection of foreign investors under Chinese law. The incident involving Miami businessman Troy McBride in Hefei means that personal protection is not just a problem for investors of Chinese ethnicity.[18] Although the number of such incidents is small relative to the cases which have been resolved quietly and legally, the negative publicity has brought attention to the issue of personal protection. Differences in legal systems might lead to disagreements and even diplomatic rows.

Rights and Restrictions

Administrative approval

In setting up enterprises in China, foreign investors as a rule have to go through protracted contract negotiation and a long process of multi-level approval by government officials. Government bureaucracy, no doubt, often results in delays and irrational decision making, and has added to the cost of doing business in China.[19]

It does not appear likely that at least for many years to come, China will switch from its current practice of authorization to that of notification, under which foreign investors are only required to notify the government about their investment, and under which they can proceed with their plans unless explicit government disapproval is received within a certain time limit. Until the markets for key inputs such as land, raw materials and utilities have become sufficiently well developed, the terms of getting critical inputs will continue to be decided on a case-by-case basis and thus a switch to notification does not seem plausible.

Trading rights

Under the present arrangement, foreign-funded enterprises can only export goods produced by themselves and import equipment and raw materials needed for their own production. The United States is quite persistent in pressing China to grant trading rights (rights to import and rights to export) to domestic and foreign-funded enterprises.[20]

Do foreign-funded enterprises have trading rights under GATT rules? If one can interpret China's restrictions on the enterprises' trading rights as an extreme form of trading formality, then these restrictions violate Article VIII: 'Fees and Formalities connected with Importation and Exportation.' One might perhaps argue that such restrictions directly violate Article XI: 'General

Elimination of Quantitative Restrictions'.[21] If one were to examine directly the 'Agreement on Trade-Related Investment Measures' (TRIMs), however, trading rights are not explicitly stated.

China has granted trading rights to a small fraction of Chinese firms that meet the government's criteria, so it is not an issue about national treatment. One may argue that China's reluctance to grant trading rights to every enterprise has to do with the monopoly position of the foreign-trade corporations. However, on a practical level, China is also reluctant to allow every firm to engage in foreign trade because it is concerned that the resulting competition among Chinese firms in the global market will lead to cut-throat pricing and a deluge of anti-dumping cases filed by foreign governments against Chinese firms. Like many developing countries whose exports have increasingly run against US anti-dumping laws, China feels that these laws are a veil of protectionism. Feeling that it is disadvantaged by the lack of such laws, China has moved to legislate its own anti-dumping laws, and the result can be a 'lose-lose' situation for everyone involved.

In any event, some US officials have argued that trading rights are fundamental to free trade regardless of the lack of clear reference in GATT rules. In addition, given the bilateral trade imbalances, insisting on unrestricted trading rights would seem an important strategic move in opening up the Chinese market for US products and in reducing the US bilateral trade deficit. China, in its recent GATT negotiation, has offered to phase out restrictions on trading rights over a period of seven or eight years. However, the United States has not agreed to the inclusion of this concession in the draft protocol on China's accession to GATT.

Foreign exchange

When China first introduced its open-door policy, foreign-funded enterprises were required to export enough to meet their own foreign exchange needs arising from the need to import inputs, unless special arrangements were approved by the central government. This 'trade balancing requirement' was clearly in violation of GATT's Agreement on TRIMs.[22] To soften the foreign exchange requirements on individual firms, China introduced the foreign exchange swap markets in 1988.

Beginning on 1 January 1994, China replaced its dual exchange rate system (that is, the official rate plus the swap rates) by a unified exchange rate determined by the interbank market for foreign exchange. Under this system, domestic enterprises are now required to sell their foreign exchange receipts (except receipts on the capital account) to designated banks on the spot, while purchases of foreign exchange require approval. Unlike domestic firms, foreign-funded enterprises are not required to surrender their foreign exchange receipts, but up to now they must trade only in the swap markets.[23]

One disadvantage of the swap markets is that it takes longer to settle transactions through them than through the interbank market. Thus, there has been pressure to make the interbank foreign exchange market available to foreign-funded enterprises as well. There is rumour that these foreign enterprises might be allowed to trade on the interbank market in Shanghai later in 1995.[24] There were charges that foreign-funded enterprises would only be allowed to do so by surrendering all their foreign exchange to the Bank of China,[25] but the vice-governor of the People's Bank confirmed that no such condition would be imposed.

More generally, the United States has been criticizing China's policy of restricting foreign exchange transactions. Given the recent Mexican foreign exchange crisis, restrictions on short-term capital movement will undoubtedly continue.

Judged by the development of its foreign exchange system, China has come a long way towards the objective of making the renminbi a convertible currency. The policymakers do not hesitate to adopt the principles of convertibility and the removal of barriers to capital exports as long-term goals. But free convertibility beyond the current account and the removal of barriers to capital exports are unlikely to be implemented in the foreseeable future. Implementation will depend upon the country's ability to deal with external imbalances, and sizeable foreign reserves (which stood at US$60 billion by the middle of 1995) is only one of the necessary conditions.

In the above sections, all the disagreements between China and the United States with the exception of human rights and democratization, are disagreements about the speed of moving towards the agreed objectives, not about the objectives themselves. I should also point out that their differences in timing are about five years or less in most cases, so it would be far-fetched to suggest that they raise questions about China's sincerity in addressing the various issues, as some critics have charged.

CONFLICTS BETWEEN NATIONAL ASPIRATIONS AND INTERNATIONAL RULES

Some disagreements between China and the United States seem more fundamental in the sense that their long-term goals are in conflict. For instance, should China attempt to influence its industrial structure (key industries) and its technological capabilities? To what extent and with what timetable should China abide by GATT/WTO rules with regard to market access and technology transfer? In what way and at what speed could national treatment be achieved?

Industrial Policy: China's New Approach Towards FDI

In response to the regional imbalances aggravated by an FDI policy that up until recently had been based on geographical location, China has started to gradually replace it with an industrial policy that not only will eliminate differential treatment on the basis of geographical location, thereby encouraging FDI to move to the inland and western regions, but also may achieve a more desirable sectoral composition than that which has been attained so far.

The government would work to create conditions that are favourable to extending national treatment to foreign firms, attracting large MNEs, and the conversion and upgrading of existing enterprises through foreign participation. Through the use of its industrial policy, which will rely increasingly on policy loans and financial subsidies rather than fiscal benefits, it will direct FDI into infrastructure, basic and key industries, high and new technology industries, and into agriculture and related industries.

According to two guidelines approved by the State Council in 1994 and scheduled for promulgation later in 1995, infrastructure includes transportation; basic industries include energy and raw materials; key industries include electronics, machinery, petrochemicals, automobiles and building and construction; high and new technology industries include civilian airplanes, and energy-saving and materials-saving technologies. FDI will also be encouraged in export-oriented industries and industries that utilize the resources and labour of the interior regions of China.[26]

Since the industrial policy has yet to take shape, it is not clear to what extent it will be in conflict with the various provisions of the GATT Uruguay Round agreements. In addition, it is not clear whether the degree of protection given to Chinese enterprises during the transition period will be in conflict with the same agreements, and how long it will take to achieve transparency in the law and regulations. However, the United States has already criticized China for its announcement to subsidize its automobile industry, claiming that the action has raised doubts about China's commitment to WTO rules and obligations. The United States has also expressed concern that the industrial policy for automobiles might be extended to other industries.[27]

Indeed, MOFTEC has given notice that it 'will continue to protect its infant industries, including telecommunications, steel, energy, transportation, textiles, pharmaceuticals and financial services'.[28] China's basic position is that it must develop its own key industries and sectors, but will welcome the participation of foreign firms because their capital, technology and managerial skills can play an important role in rationalizing and modernizing these industries. However, 'China will not let [GATT] re-entry be used to cripple its infant industries', according to Long Yongtu, deputy minister of MOFTEC.[29] It seems that China is cautious about not turning a good thing into a nightmare, but its insistence on protecting infant industries will not please its critics or help its efforts to join the GATT/WTO.

China's industrial policy does not necessarily discourage foreign investors. On the contrary, it intends to let foreign firms in to increase competitive pressure on domestic firms and to upgrade its industries to world standards. For instance, foreign oil companies are invited to cooperate with China in the development of oil and natural gas fields in the Tarim Basin in the Xinjiang Autonomous Region and in the South China Sea. Other examples include the automobile industry, transportation, and the financial sector which will be opened to foreign firms on a trial basis and in a controlled manner.

By pointing out that China plans to set up more high-grade pharmaceutical joint ventures to manufacture substitutes for imported products and to export a large proportion of the product, a US official has complained that China continues to use restrictive investment practices. But what is wrong with its plans unless import tariffs and export subsidies are introduced? It is ironic that the United States should take such a strong stand against China's industrial policy, when the United States under the Clinton administration is indeed advocating some form of industrial policy for itself in order to compete against the Japanese in high technology industries.

It may help to keep things in perspective to point out that OECD member countries 'continue to use a wide variety of instruments to stimulate investment'.[30] The incentives provided for and constraints imposed on foreign investors by China are very similar to those practised by other developing countries. Nor are they generally different in kind from those found in some of the OECD member countries, although the magnitudes of China's policy incentives and restrictions tend to be larger and their scope wider.

Market Access, National Treatment, Discrimination, and Unfair Competition

Market access

The 'General Agreement on Trade in Services' (GATS) contains a provision on market access. As a specific commitment with country-specific concessions, the market access provision's purpose is to progressively eliminate restrictions on the number of service providers, the kind of joint ventures through which services are provided, and limitations on the level of foreign participation.

According to the two guidelines mentioned in the above section, foreign investment in the following industries will be restricted but not banned: banking, retailing, real estate, light industry (such as televisions, refrigerators and washing machines), coal mining and medicine. Foreign investment will be prohibited in telecommunications services, media, education, security-related sectors such as weapons, and industries that damage the environment.

Since the United States is strong in banking, insurance, retailing, medicine, transportation and telecommunications services, restriction and prohibition of foreign investment in these areas will be an important source of friction in Sino-American economic relations. To promote its economic interests, the United States can be expected to attempt to pry open the relevant Chinese markets with GATT/WTO rules and other international agreements such as a yet-to-be developed multilateral investment agreement. Specifically, to prevent vague promises about market opening, US negotiators would be looking for a timetable for market access, that is, a timetable for the elimination or reduction of trade and investment barriers.

National treatment and discrimination against foreign-funded enterprises

The GATS contains a provision on national treatment, which contains the obligation that either foreign service suppliers are treated no less favourably than domestic suppliers or, failing that, that the conditions of competition should not be modified in favour of domestic suppliers.

More directly, the *OECD Declaration and Decisions on International Investment and Multinational Enterprises* (*IIME* for short) contains the principle of National Treatment as follows: 'Member countries should . . . accord to enterprises operating in their territories and owned or controlled directly or indirectly by nationals of another Member country treatment . . . no less favourable than that accorded . . . to domestic enterprises' and 'will endeavour to ensure that their territorial subdivisions apply 'National Treatment'.[31]

US investors have complained about China's discrimination against foreign-funded enterprises *vis-à-vis* Chinese state-owned enterprises in terms of unequal market access, provision of bank loans and inputs such as energy and raw materials, and performance requirements such as local content and trade-balancing requirements, not to mention higher prices for airline tickets. They also complain about provincial barriers used to protect local industries.[32] Thus, they have argued that China should accord them the better of national or MFN treatment, including the right of establishment with limited exception (that is, China adopts a 'notification' instead of the present 'authorization' system).

On the question of national treatment, Chinese officials and foreign investors often do not see eye to eye. From China's point of view, the question is not about discrimination against foreign investors, but about discrimination in their favour, that is, that China has given foreign investors better than national treatment. Whether the benefits of preferential tax treatment outweigh the costs of discrimination mentioned above is an empirical question, but the emergence of bogus foreign enterprises in response to the differential treatment tends to reinforce both the belief and stance of the officials.

Despite differences in opinion on whether foreign investors get a better or worse deal than their Chinese counterparts, the Chinese government has repeatedly stated that national treatment is its long-term objective.[33] As with many other policy changes, China wants to reach that objective gradually rather than abruptly. If China joins the WTO as a developing country, then many of the performance requirements will have to be phased out within a five-year period.

To keep things in perspective, let me point out that China's concerns about and arguments for protecting banking, insurance, finance, energy, transportation, telecommunications and so on, from competition posed by FDI, and the way it wishes to open up these sectors, are similar to those in some OECD member countries where these sectors are, or were, protected. To wit, according to the 1991 Review of the IIME,[34] 'the vast majority of exceptions to National Treatment are sector-specific and these tend to concentrate on areas such as natural resources, transportation and financial services . . . In broad terms, measures are mostly geared to managing the way in which certain areas are opened up to foreign investment and to taking account of specific preoccupations (such as to ensure a degree of protection to specific domestic activities or cultural interests) and not to prevent international direct investment except in specific areas, for example, where a country's public order and essential security interests are prevalent.' In addition, 'it is not uncommon to find such restrictions in natural resources and energy as well as in the services sectors, particularly in areas such as banking, insurance, transportation and the media.'[35]

Despite the observed similarities, disagreements with the US will likely continue with regard to the timetable of granting national treatment to foreign investors.

State monopolies and unfair competition

US investors have complained about the difficulty of getting into markets that are dominated by state monopolies, now the only kind of monopoly in China. They also raise questions about fair competition when the state regulates industries and at the same time controls firms which compete in the industries. Furthermore, they argue that the ban on foreign provision of telecommunications and insurance services is due primarily to the fact that these two industries are dominated by monopolies.

In transportation, telecommunications, other public utilities and insurance, the Chinese government has chosen to create a state duopoly or oligopoly to increase competition before it considers opening the industry to foreign investors and private competitors.[36] The principle of National Treatment as contained in the IIME states that in case monopolies are open up, 'access to move into these areas should . . . be provided on a non-discriminatory basis as between **private** (emphasis my own) domestic and foreign-controlled enterprises already established in the country in question.'[37] Thus, this approach does not violate the OECD principle of National Treatment because the new entrants are also state-owned enterprises. Nonetheless, not opening up industries that are dominated by state monopolies and oligopolies will be a sore point between the two countries as China bids for membership in the WTO.[38]

Performance Requirements

The United States has criticized China for using GATT-illegal trade-related investment measures, including local content requirements, performance requirements (export requirements and forced transfer of technology) and foreign currency balancing requirements.[39] An example is its recent automobile policy, which allegedly contains several measures inconsistent with GATT/WTO: linkages of tariff cuts to local content requirements,[40] foreign currency balancing requirements and implicit import substitution targets.

Given China's interest in promoting technology- and knowledge-intensive industries, some commentators point out that China should strengthen the protection of intellectual property rights to attract investment by US high technology firms. However, the problem is much deeper because China wishes to seek technology transfer from foreign firms to Chinese firms or to joint ventures with Chinese partners, not just local production by foreign firms. The desire to exchange market for technologies has been criticized by the United States as '**forced transfer of technology**'.

Again, to keep things in perspective, let me point out that while TRIMs are 'used widely in developing countries, they are also to be found in some (OECD) Member countries'. Interestingly enough, technology transfer as a performance requirement is not explicitly included in the 'Illustrative List' of TRIMs. Regardless, this might be another hot spot in the US-China tension.

CONCLUSIONS

In this chapter, I have provided some basic facts of US direct investment in China and identified some potential Sino-American disagreements and conflicts in their bilateral investment relations, which are intertwined with their bilateral trade relations.

In the areas of legal environment (the legal system and protection of foreign investment and investors), administrative approval, trading rights and foreign exchange, disagreements will be less about long-term objectives but more about the speed of reform. I believe the two sides are more likely to reach agreement after negotiation.

In contrast, in the areas of industrial policy, infant industry protection and the exchange of markets for technology, I believe there are fundamental disagreements. These issues are part and parcel of China's bid for WTO membership, so the two sides are expected to be tough negotiators, and negotiated solutions are harder to achieve.

In spite of the above disagreements, US investment in China will continue. The Chinese market is too important for US firms to hold back from until all the wrinkles are ironed out. Despite all the drawbacks and risks, the Chinese market holds promise for good returns to US investors.

NOTES

1. No statistics on China's investment in the United States is available, but the amount is believed to be very small.
2. Leonard K. Cheng, 'Foreign direct investment in China', Report prepared for OECD, COM/DAFF/IME/TD(94)129/REV1, January 1995, Tables 7a and 7b.
3. See Table 6.2 below.
4. In 1992, 58 percent of China exports to Hong Kong were re-exported, and 21.5 percent of Hong Kong's total re-exports went to the United States, see Leonard K. Cheng, 'Hong Kong's trade and industry: 1997 and beyond', in Joseph Y.S. Cheng and Sonny Shiu Hing Lo (eds.), *From Colony to Special Administrative Region: Hong Kong's Challenge Ahead* (Hong Kong: The Chinese University Press, 1996). More directly, in the same year 39.5 percent of China's exports to Hong Kong were exported to the United States, see Y.Y. Kueh and Thomas Voon, 'The role of Hong Kong in Sino-American economic relations'. See Chapter 4, Table 4.1.
5. The figure for 1992 was 8.57 percent, see Y.Y. Kueh and Thomas Voon, 1997, op. cit., Table 1.
6. The total number of projects by all foreign investors did not recover to the 1985 level until 1988.
7. The 1993 figure, taken from *China Economic News,* 25 July 1994, includes investment from 1979 to 1982. Therefore, we cannot obtain the flow figure for 1993 by taking the difference between the 1993 and 1992 cumulative investment figures, since the 1992 figure does not include investment in the period before 1983.
8. The US producer price index of capital equipment was used to obtain real investment measured in 1990 US dollars.
9. See Leonard K. Cheng, 'Foreign direct investment in China', 1995, op. cit., Table 4(a).
10. US-China Business Council, *US Investment in China,* 1991.
11. US Embassy (Beijing), IMI-China 1994 Investment Climate Statement (26 July 1994).
12. *Asian Wall Street Journal*, 27 March 1995.
13. The 'General Agreement on Trade in Services' (GATS) contains transparency requirements which include (a) prompt publication of all relevant laws and regulations, (b) reasonable, objective and impartial administration of measures of general application that affect trade in services and (c) qualification recognition through the adoption of internationally agreed criteria. *The OECD Declaration and*

Decisions on International Investment and Multinational Enterprises states that member countries 'recognise the need to give due weight to the interests of Member countries affected by specific laws, regulations and administrative practices in this field providing official incentives and disincentives to international direct investment . . . and will endeavour to make such measures as transparent as possible'. China is not a member of the OECD, but as a major recipient of FDI in the world, it will be increasingly expected to share responsibilities and abide by internationally accepted rules in the arena of international direct investment.

14. According to the US Embassy (1994), op.cit., the United States and China signed a memorandum of understanding which commits China to publicize all laws related to trade and refrain from enforcing unpublished laws.

15. This agreement covers copyright, trademarks, industrial designs, patents, and trade secrets. It requires signatory countries to provide procedures and remedies under their national law for effective protection of each category of intellectual property rights, including criminal procedures and penalties in cases of 'wilful trademark counterfeiting or copyright piracy on a commercial scale'.

16. According to US Embassy (1994), op. cit., the Beijing Conciliation Centre, an organization affiliated with the China Council for the Promotion of International Trade, signed an agreement with the American Arbitration Association in 1992. Under this agreement, the two sides will work together in joint conciliation to resolve US and Chinese trade and investment disputes.

17. Chinese law requires compensation of expropriated foreign investment, but the terms of compensation are not clearly spelt out. So far there has not been any case of expropriation of foreign investment since China's opening to the outside world in 1979, and indeed its joint venture law generally forbids nationalization.

18. *Far Eastern Economic Review,* (6 April 1995), p. 22.

19. The United States regards the right to establish business enterprises as a necessary step for China's accession to the GATT. US Embassy (1994), op. cit.

20. Richard Mueller, 'China should open its markets to gain accession to GATT' (in Chinese), *Hong Kong Economic Journal,* 31 October 1994 and the comments of the US Delegate to OECD on my 'Foreign direct investment in China', op. cit., and its earlier version, 29 December 1994 and 13 March 1995.

21. The article states that 'no prohibitions or restrictions other than duties, taxes or other charges, whether made effective through quotas, import or export licenses or other measures, shall be instituted or maintained by any contracting party on the importation of *any* (my emphasis) product of the territory of any other contracting party or on the exportation or sale for export of *any* (my emphasis) product destined for the territory of any other contracting party'.

22. See 'Performance Requirements' on pp. 131 below.

23. Since the renminbi is traded in Hong Kong, foreign-funded enterprises can obtain foreign exchange in Hong Kong if they can move large sums of renminbi out of China, which also requires approval and is not normally allowed.

24. *Eastern Express,* 12 April 1995.

25. US Delegate to OECD, op. cit.

26. *South China Morning Post*, 21 March 1995 and *Hong Kong Economic Journal*, 7 June 1995. The two guidelines are 'Provisional regulations on directing the orientation of foreign investment' and 'The list of industries targeted for foreign investment'.

27. *Asian Wall Street Journal,* 8 November 1994.

28. Protection of 'infant' industries can in principle be legitimized under Article XVIII of the GATT, 'Government assistance to economic development'. But it is not clear whether and to what extent existing WTO members will accept the protection of these industries.

29. *South China Morning Post,* 7 November 1994.

30. Organization for Economic Co-operation and Development, *The OECD Declaration and Decisions on International Investment and Multinational Enterprises,* Basic Texts and 1991 Review, (OECD: Paris, 1992), p. 75.
31. Ibid.
32. For example, see American Chamber of Commerce, 'Chairman's memo: Gerry Murdock on China, IPR and GATT', *AmCham,* (Hong Kong: August 1994), p. 27.
33. Article 6 of China's Foreign Trade Law (adopted by the National People's Congress on 12 May 1994) grants most-favoured-nation treatment and national treatment in foreign trade on a reciprocal basis. Article 23 of the same law extends market access and national treatment to international trade in services.
34. Organization for Economic Co-operation and Development, *The OECD Declaration and Decisions,* op.cit.
35. Leonard K. Cheng, 'Foreign direct investment in China', op.cit., pp. 27–28 and p. 31.
36. In the telecommunications industry, the existing monopoly is the Ministry of Posts and Telecommunications. Unicom, firm established by the Ministry of Railways, the Ministry of Electronics Industry and the Ministry of Electricity with investment from some other state enterprises will compete against the existing monopoly. In the case of insurance, the industry is dominated by the People's Insurance Company of China, and the government intends to break it up into several divisions to compete in commercial insurance.
37. Organisation for Economic Co-operation and Development, *The OECD Declaration and Decisions*, op.cit., p. 27.
38. *Hong Kong Economic Journal*, 31 October 1994.
39. The TRIMs states that, among others, 'local content requirements' and 'trade-balancing requirements' are inconsistent with Article III (national treatment) and Article XI (prohibition of quantitative restrictions) of the GATT. The agreement requires mandatory elimination of all such FDI measures within two years for developed countries and within five years for developing countries.
40. According to US Embassy, op. cit., no joint venture will be approved unless it provides for at least 40 percent local content.

7

Double-Edged Trade Effects of Foreign Direct Investment and Firm-Specific Assets: Evidence From the Chinese Trio

Chin Chung

INTRODUCTION

It has been hotly debated in the literature whether foreign direct investment (FDI) is trade-reducing or trade-enhancing. Citing Japanese FDI towards Asian developing countries as an example, Kojima contended that while the traditional oligopolistic FDI (for example, US investment in Europe in chemicals and electronics during the 1950s) works to reduce trade between the home and host countries, the new form of 'labour-oriented' FDI (For example, Japanese investment in Asian low wage countries in the 1960s) tends to increase trade.[1] The rationale behind this argument is essentially that FDI originating in the oligopolistic industries of the Western world was largely carried out by prestigious firms with specific technological know-how that was highly competitive in export markets and much too sophisticated for local industries to emulate. As a result, FDI worked against the structure of comparative advantage between the home and host economies and engendered a trade reduction effect. By contrast, the cost-conscious, labour-seeking Japanese FDI was conducted with a view to achieving competitive costs in the standard-skill industries, which conformed better with the structure of comparative advantage between the two economies and, therefore, resulted in a trade augmenting effect.

Kojima used these differential trade effects as a welfare criterion for the investing country, contending that the oligopolistic (or market-oriented) type of FDI is *detrimental* to the home country because 'it causes loss of export markets and later reverse imports, generates employment problems for the investing country and consequent protectionist barriers to exports manufacturing capacity in developing countries which plays a harmonious role for both sides because the industries chosen, such as textiles and other labor-intensive consumer goods industries, are those in which the investing country is losing its comparative advantage while the developing countries are gaining it.'[2]

To stretch this argument one step further, Lee contended that labour-oriented FDI is *beneficial* to the home country because it makes it possible for the affected firms to maintain the value of the industry-specific capital, thereby facilitating the contraction of industries losing comparative advantage at a lesser cost than if foreign investment was not possible.[3] He argued that in the absence of FDI domestic structural adjustment can be made only by transferring industry-specific capital in the declining industries to another industry. Such a transfer, however, entails a cost to society as the capital either becomes scrapped or less productive if used in another industry. It follows that the country gains from foreign investment by avoiding this loss. He further portrays, in the spirit of Akamatsu,[4] a picture of three countries moving forward in an orderly 'Flying Geese' pattern, where firms in the transition (intermediate) country losing comparative advantage in labour-intensive industries will invest abroad as they experience falling or low profit rates at home, whereas those in capital- and knowledge-intensive industries which are gaining comparative advantage will invest at home as they experience rising or high profit rates. The latter industries will also receive FDI from the developed country which is in turn losing comparative advantage in some of its capital- and knowledge-intensive industries. During this process FDI nicely facilitates domestic structural adjustment by bringing about an intercountry, intracountry, inter-industry transfer or scrapping, which is, according to Lee, the only feasible alternatives in the absence of FDI.[5]

The purpose of this chapter is to give an example of a contrary case, showing that the Kojima-cum-Lee argument may have erred in a fundamental sense. It will be argued that any capital movement in the form of direct investment entails a reorganization of production activities across national borders and therefore will have double-edged effects on the original pattern of trade. Different types of FDI do not seem to differ in this regard. However, the amount of firm-specific assets a FDI firm possesses will exert a lasting impact on the trade prospects between the host and home economies. Market-oriented FDI substitutes local production for cross-border trade while generating investment-induced trade in intermediate goods and owner-specific components and parts. Labour-oriented FDI, on the other hand, utilizes local production to satisfy third market demand, again generating trade in semi-products between the home and the host. Both types of FDI entail a substitution effect (target product) and an augmentation effect (logistic supply). In both cases, trade in the FDI target product is *shifted* from the FDI home to the FDI host, although in the market-oriented case it succumbs to the form of local production and exchange. The real difference between an expansionary act and a defensive act, therefore, does not lie in their differential trade effects in a static sense but rather in their dynamic prospect in maintaining the strength of logistic supply in the face of market competition and in creating new competitive edges in a whole array of new products for domestic production and trade. These capabilities are key factors determining the pace of domestic restructuring and the ultimate pattern of trade between the two economies. They are also dividing features by which one may judge, if one must, whether an outward FDI is *beneficial* or *detrimental* to the home economy.

A conceptual cornerstone of the oligopolistic theory of FDI is that the firm making a direct investment abroad must possess some kind of intangible assets to offset disadvantages inherent in operating in a foreign land.[6] Intangible assets may take the form of firm-specific advantages in production, management, and/or marketing. Since such intangible assets are often possessed by firms producing differentiated products, FDI is said to be associated with industries characterized by product differentiation.[7] Furthermore, as investing abroad entails a large burden on the FDI firm in terms of managerial, technical and financial resources, FDI is often carried out by large, integrated firms. This is the standard theoretical framework against which the Western countries' FDI is put to examination.

Theoretical considerations notwithstanding, there has been contrary evidence of FDI by small, specialized firms producing products that are not highly differentiated.[8] FDI from Japan in the 1960s, and from Taiwan, Korea and Hong Kong in the 1980s are prominent examples. Unlike their Western predecessors, these countries in their respective times have invested more heavily in labour-intensive, standard-skilled industries in developing countries. What, then, are the 'intangible assets' possessed by these smaller FDI firms? In particular, what enables them to venture abroad in an act of FDI and how does this behaviour affect the long-term trade pattern between the home and the host economies?

As Mason suggested in the Japanese case, marketing channels may be a key. He argued that Japanese firms may have specific assets in the form of marketing know-how and superior technology in the labour-intensive industries *vis-à-vis* the other developing countries.[9] Chen and Wang also found that manufacturing technology may have been the firm-specific advantage that underlaid Taiwanese FDI in the electronics industry. In other words, an ability to produce reasonably good-quality products at low cost was what distinguished these smaller FDI firms from their potential competitors. Thus, its seems that labour-oriented FDI conducted by small and medium enterprises (SMEs) can also be explained by the intangible asset theory originally proposed to explain the behaviour of oligopolistic firms.[10] As Lee himself puts it, in other than a long-run equilibrium, firms producing non-differentiated products also possess intangible assets. The only difference between a firm producing a differentiated product and a firm producing a non-differentiated product is that the former may be able to keep its intangible assets for a longer period of time than the latter.[11]

Here lies the crux of the matter. Japanese industries in the 1960s and Taiwanese and Hong Kong industries in the 1980s were, for the most part, receivers of Western technologies. They had not introduced any significant innovations which would invite massive imitation overseas as envisaged in the product cycle model.[12] The type of technology they relied on was mature and standardized and often embodied in the machinery and equipment they used. Compared with the first generation of the product cycle, which had pitted technology inventors against cost savers, they belonged to the second or third generation of the product cycle, which pitted cost savers against cost savers. The essence of their intangible assets, then, may be thought of as an 'early entry advantage' based on manufacturing experience (that is, movements up the learning curve in a general sense) which gave them an edge over latecomers. However, a comparative advantage based on past experience is, in the nature of the case, temporary, inevitably undermined sooner or later by imitators and rivals. As a result, these intangible assets may be too 'thin' to render a FDI successful if not substantiated by additional sources of advantage. Chung argues that Taiwanese investments in China by export-oriented SMEs are aided by a peculiar 'locational advantage' deep-rooted in their linguistic and cultural proximity to China which effectively lowers the transaction costs of operating in a foreign land.[13] Ozawa also conceded that Japan's escape from domestic macroeconomic calamities was engendered by a 'collective will' (that is to say, the government) and that without the help from the government the capacity of small labour-intensive Japanese firms to go overseas would have been very limited.[14]

Aside from being relatively meagre in technological capability, the majority of Taiwanese and Hong Kong SMEs are also rather specialized in their respective fields, each producing only a narrow range of similar products (apparel, footwear, toys and the like). As a result, they usually do not possess sufficient managerial, technological, and financial resources to spread them evenly between overseas and domestic operations. When they invest abroad in an attempt to salvage their sector-specific capital, they often have to hold back on domestic restructuring for a considerable amount of time (until they are firmly rooted in the overseas operations). As a result, the home country not only sees its comparative *disadvantage* industries quickly evaporate as a result of outward FDI, but also witnesses its comparative *advantage* industries slow because not enough entrepreneurial talent is left at home to cultivate domestic potential. The larger the size of this SME-dominated, cost-driven sector in the home economy, the more likely the latter is going to be haunted by the potential process of 'industrial hollowing-out' as a result of inadequate entrepreneurial attention (and physical resources) devoted to domestic restructuring at a time of urgent need. It is in this sense that the smooth industrial transmission process suggested by Lee may be incomplete and that, contrary to Kojima's contention, labour-oriented FDI with insufficient intangible assets may actually be detrimental to the home country despite the fact that it saves the industry-specific capital for individual FDI firms.[15]

The recent surge of FDI by Taiwan and Hong Kong in China is very relevant to the discussion above. We will show, by referring to the experience of the Chinese trio, that FDI, albeit labour-oriented, works as a double-edged sword on the trade performance of the home country. On the one hand, FDI serves as an engine for vertical trade from the home to the host economy which, in turn, helps fuel the FDI operations overseas. On the other hand, it tends to reduce home exports (and later to increase home imports) of the FDI-targeted products, as the latter are being transplanted overseas. The derived demand for machinery and intermediate products will only partially offset the decline in exports of the FDI-targeted products, as part of the value-added generated overseas must accrue to the host country. The imbalance will be greater if the FDI firms do not possess sufficient intangible assets or if these assets are short-lived. In particular, the speed with which domestic restructuring takes place will hinge upon the ability of these and other firms to develop new competitive edges in different products to be produced and traded, which in turn hinges upon the inherent competitiveness of these firms in terms of technological capability, human resources and cross-border production strategies.

In the next section, the intensified trade flows and FDI movements within the trio are examined to give a proper background for subsequent discussions. The third section looks at the FDI-induced logistic supply conducted by Taiwanese and Hong Kong firms in support of their mainland operations. The fourth section illustrates the other edge of the FDI trade effect, namely, the 'export shift' from the FDI home to the FDI host, and the imbalance problems that emerge along with it. The fifth section of this chapter discusses the implications for the home economy in terms of GDP growth, export performance and domestic capital formation within the manufacturing sector. A simple statistical test is also conducted to substantiate the argument made in this chapter for the case of Taiwan. Finally, the last section concludes this chapter.

Economic Interactions Among the Trio

Both Hong Kong and Taiwan have enhanced their trade links with China significantly since the mid-1980s. Trade with China grew at an average annual rate of 25.5 percent for Hong Kong and 20 percent for Taiwan from 1986 to 1994, compared with the overall trade growth of 7.7 percent for Hong Kong and 10.6 percent for Taiwan over the same period. Moreover, China has become the foremost trading partner with Hong Kong since 1986, accounting for more than one-third of its total imports and over 40 percent of its re-export activities from that time on (Table 7.1). While Hong Kong's domestic exports in recent years seem to have come to a standstill, its imports and re-exports sectors continue to boom as a result of close ties with China. The situation with Taiwan is similar. From 1986 to 1994, the importance of Hong Kong and China together as an export market for Taiwan increased substantially from 7.3 percent to 22.9 percent, and in 1995 they overtook the United States and became the most important export market for Taiwan. This rapid growth in trade can be attributed to a number of factors, foremost among which is the relocation of Hong Kong and Taiwanese manufacturing industries across the border to Chinese provinces.[16] As is well known, Hong Kong has been the primary source of outside direct investment for China ever since China adopted its open-door policy in 1979. As of the end of 1993, Hong Kong's cumulative contractual investment in China had reached US$150 billion, accounting for over 68 percent of the total FDI China received between 1979 and 1993. Currently it is estimated that there are over 50 000 Hong Kong factories in Guandong province alone, directly or indirectly employing 5 to 6 million people (equal to the size of the population of Hong Kong itself).[17] The relocation of industries has resulted in a rapid increase in the volume of goods moving between Hong Kong and China. According to Tuan and Ng, in 1993, 72 percent to 74 percent of Hong Kong's exports to China and Hong Kong's imports from China were outward-processing related.[18]

In addition to Hong Kong's own processing activities in Guandong, a second important factor contributing to the tremendous increase in Hong Kong's trade links with China is, in fact, Taiwan's FDI towards the Mainland. During the same period, Taiwan has also come under the pressure of increasing domestic production costs. Like Hong Kong entrepreneurs, Taiwanese manufacturers have responded by relocating a major part of their labour-intensive production processes overseas, and the most popular site for such production transplantation is without doubt China. Taiwanese FDI to China took off quickly after 1987 when, coincidentally, the Taiwan government decided to lift the ban on visits to family members on the Mainland after a forty-year freeze. By the end of 1994, its cumulative investment in China amounted to US$2.63 billion with over 27 000 investment projects. Taiwan's share in China's total foreign investment was 8.3 percent in terms of contracted value and 11.8 percent in terms of the number of cases contracted, which made Taiwan the second largest investor on the Mainland next only to Hong Kong.

As a result of the Taiwan government's persistent refusal to allow direct shipping links with China, most of the trade flows generated from such foreign production have to go indirectly through an entrepôt like Hong Kong. Taiwan-China trade thus showed up in Hong Kong's trade record as part of the re-export trade. This has done much to foster Hong Kong's entrepôt trade

Table ... Taiwan and Hong Kong External Trade by Major Partners

	Taiwan						Hong Kong					
	(Share %)			(avg. growth rate %)			(Share %)			(avg. growth rate %)		
	1980	1986	1994	1950-86	1986-90	1990-94	1980	1986	1994	1980-86	1986-90	1990-94
Exports to:	100.0	100.0	100.0	15.0	13.9	7.1	100.0	100.0	100.0	14.5	10.1	-0.4
US	34.1	47.7	26.2	18.8	3.4	5.8	33.1	41.7	28.5	19.0	0.8	-1.9
Hong Kong (incl. China)	7.8	7.3	22.9	11.1	30.8	25.2	—	—	—	—	—	—
China	—	—	—	—	—	—	2.4	11.7	27.7	49.6	27.4	6.5
Japan	11.0	11.4	11.0	13.1	16.3	2.8	3.4	4.0	4.7	17.8	18.1	-3.5
Germany	5.4	3.2	3.5	2.9	25.7	12.5	10.8	7.2	5.8	7.0	12.9	-8.3
Singapore	2.8	2.3	3.6	9.3	24.1	11.3	2.6	1.8	5.5	7.7	29.2	11.9
UK	2.4	2.4	2.3	12.7	19.6	2.4	10.0	6.4	4.6	6.5	8.0	-6.6
Rest of World	36.5	25.7	30.5	—	18.6	7.2	37.7	27.2	23.2	18.7	8.7	-10.9
Imports from:	100.0	100.0	100.0	3.4	17.7	10.4	100.0	100.0	100.0	16.3	23.5	18.1
Japan	27.1	34.1	29.0	7.5	18.0	9.3	23.0	20.4	15.6	14.0	16.4	17.2
US	23.7	22.5	21.1	2.5	18.3	8.5	11.8	8.4	7.1	9.8	22.2	14.6
Germany	3.7	4.7	5.6	7.9	21.5	13.7	2.6	1.2	2.3	19.2	15.8	17.9
Hong Kong (incl. China)	1.3	1.6	1.8	7.3	30.7	4.5	—	—	—	—	—	—
China	—	—	—	—	—	—	19.7	29.6	37.6	24.5	30.4	18.8
Taiwan	—	—	—	—	—	—	7.5	8.9	8.6	20.2	24.8	16.6
Singapore	1.1	1.4	2.8	8.1	32.9	14.9	6.6	3.9	5.0	6.7	24.5	24.1
S. Korea	1.1	1.4	3.5	7.9	32.6	22.7	—	4.0	4.6	—	26.6	19.6
Rest of World	42.0	34.3	36.2	3.6	23.5	12.9	29.2	23.6	19.2	12.0	17.3	18.1
Re-exports to:	—	—	—	—	—	—	100.0	100.0	100.0	26.4	35.6	23.0
US	—	—	—	—	—	—	10.3	8.5	22.2	22.5	70.4	24.4
China	—	—	—	—	—	—	15.4	42.1	34.1	49.4	21.1	30.6
Japan	—	—	—	—	—	—	7.3	15.2	5.8	42.7	7.0	22.4
Germany	—	—	—	—	—	—	0.2	2.1	4.4	25.3	74.3	15.5
Singapore	—	—	—	—	—	—	8.3	0.9	2.1	-13.1	84.7	12.8
Taiwan	—	—	—	—	—	—	7.4	7.1	2.4	25.4	21.7	10.8
UK	—	—	—	—	—	—	—	1.6	2.9	—	58.5	22.6
Rest of World	—	—	—	—	—	—	51.1	22.5	26.1	10.2	44.9	25.5

Source: Calculated from *Monthly Statistics on Taiwan's Export-Import Trade; Hong Kong Monthly Digest of Statistics*, various issues.

during this period. In fact, almost 17.5 percent of Hong Kong's entrepôt trade in 1994 was due to Taiwan's 'indirect trade' with China through Hong Kong (including transhipment), which accounted for at least 5 percent of Hong Kong's total trade volume in that year. As a result of Taiwan's persistent refusal to establish direct shipping links with China, the role of Hong Kong as an entrepôt has been strengthened significantly during the past ten years.

Table 7.2 presents the results of a recent report on the industrial distribution of Taiwan's and Hong Kong's FDI in China. The figures are obtained from an official survey of all FDI operations in China as of the end of 1992.[19] Compared with FDI from advanced countries, Taiwans and Hong Kong's FDI concentrated more on such labour-intensive sectors as apparel, plastic products, metal

Table 7.2 Industrial Distribution of FDI in China: 1992 Survey Data

Unit: %

FDI Source Industry	Total	Hong Kong	Taiwan	United States	Japan	Sing- apore	Others
Agriculture & forestry	1.80	1.62	0.80	1.33	2.07	1.53	4.35
Manufacturing	62.12	59.13	76.72	73.71	33.93	61.61	72.34
Processed foods	4.13	2.72	8.09	7.71	1.43	15.64	7.56
Beverages & tobacco	1.33	1.18	0.86	5.77	0.07	I.32	1.57
Textiles	7.95	9.59	7.92	3.23	1.15	4.41	4.92
Wearing apparel	5.14	5.98	5.12	2.24	4.12	2.29	1.82
Leather products	1.91	2.15	1.78	1.46	0.74	0.46	1.82
Wood & bamboo products	1.85	1.25	3.31	1.11	2.84	3.45	3.68
Paper products	1.75	1.93	1.39	1.74	0.32	0.54	2.41
Chemicals	2.31	1.88	1.72	8.72	0.74	2.13	1.79
Chemical products	2.44	2.01	3.64	4.75	1.32	7.43	2.60
Petroleum & coal	0.20	0.15	0.05	0.39	0.00	1.38	0.68
Rubber	0.51	0.41	1.43	0.69	0.05	0.05	0.54
Plastic products	5.59	5.44	9.35	2.23	0.69	4.36	8.40
Non-ferrous mineral products	4.68	5.22	2.51	5.82	1.36	6.39	5.29
Base metals	1.24	1.18	0.85	0.66	1.85	0.45	2.21
Metal products	3.13	2.83	5.25	6.94	1.07	1.09	2.62
Machinery	1.75	1.10	3.59	3.13	2.34	1.54	2.99
Electrical appliances	9.40	9.47	9.37	9.42	3.87	6.75	9.23
Transportation equipment	1.91	1.07	1.86	3.00	3.11	0.21	7.17
Precision instruments	0.80	0.83	0.81	0.59	0.39	0.63	1.11
Miscellaneous products	3.27	2.71	7.82	3.57	0.95	1.10	3.93
Services & construction	37.09	39.25	22.48	25.50	64.01	36.86	23.13
Total	100.00	100.00	100.00	100.00	100.00	100.00	100.00

Source: Adapted from Gao, Charng et al., *A Comparative Study of Foreign Investment in Mainland China* (in Chinese), project report commissioned by the Investment Commission, Taipei, 1994, Appendix Tables 5–3, p. 261.

products, electrical appliances and miscellaneous products. In total, Taiwanese businessmen have poured over US$2.63 billion into their Mainland operations as of early 1993 as realized (not just contracted) FDI. Together, Hong Kong and Taiwan accounted for 76.3 percent of all the FDI received by China during this fourteen-year span.

INVESTMENT AS AN ENGINE FOR VERTICAL TRADE (LOGISTIC SUPPLY)

It is well-documented in the literature that Taiwan's indirect exports to China over the past decade have been characterized by large flows of intermediate products such as plastic materials, cotton cloth, synthetic fibre and yarn, and electronic components and parts.[20] The share of these intermediate products remained as high as 74 percent of the entire indirect exports to China as of 1995. Statistical analysis of Taiwan's trade with China in recent years also supports the hypothesis that trade in both directions is positively correlated with Taiwan's outward investment in China. More specifically, several studies have tried to empirically divide Taiwan's indirect trade with China into an 'investment-induced' part and an 'autonomous' part. Using input-output linkage analysis, Chung and Chung et al. first estimated the investment-induced exports from Taiwan to the mainland to be roughly 40 percent–45 percent of the total actual exports in 1991[21] and the remaining 55 percent–60 percent was deemed 'autonomous' exports aimed at local demand in the Chinese market (Table 7.3). The implication is that without the derived demand from Taiwanese FDI on the Mainland, the commodity exports to the Mainland

Table 7.3 Estimated Contribution of Investment-Induced Trade to Actual Trade Between Taiwan and China (1991)

	Actual volume of indirect trade in 1991 (US$ bil.)	Estimated contribution of DFI-induced trade to total trade			
		(A) Estimates from Gao et al. (1992)		(B) Estimates from Chung et al. (1993)	
		(US$ bil.)	(%)	(US$ bil.)	(%)
1. Taiwan's indirect exports	4.67	2.13	45.6%	1.91	40.8%
2. Taiwan's indirect imports	1.13	0.86	76.2%	0.72	63.9%
3. Total bilateral trade	5.79	2.99	51.6%	2.63	33.0%
4. Taiwan's bilateral surplus	3.54	1.27	35.9%	1.19	33.6%

Source: Chung et al., *Mainland China's Export Promotion Policy and Its Impact on Taiwan's Trade Performance,* Chung-Hua Institution for Economic Research, 1993, Chapter 4, Tables 4–9, p. 154.

in 1991 would have been 40 percent to 45 percent less than observed. Gao, Lee and Lin arrived at similar estimates based on survey data.[22] On the import side, the same studies estimated that investment-induced indirect imports from China (that is, return sales to the home country by FDI firms) were as high as 64 percent–76 percent of the actual indirect imports from China. Taken together, the investment-related trade flows accounted for 33 percent–51 percent of the actual indirect trade between the two economies, resulting in an investment-induced trade surplus for Taiwan equalling one-third of the total trade surplus with China in 1991.[23]

In the case of Hong Kong, various authors have also documented the importance of semi-finished products such as apparel, shoes and toys in the trade flows between Hong Kong and China. For example, Tuan and Ng find that, in 1993, the proportion of outward-processing trade as a percentage of total trade with China was 72 percent for imports (finished or semi-finished products), 74 percent for domestic exports (raw materials, components and parts), and 78 percent for re-exports (including both types). Combining the experiences of Taiwan and Hong Kong FDI operations, it seems clear that trade among the Chinese trio has been characterized by investment-induced trade, that is exports of raw materials, components and parts to China in exchange for imports (or re-exports) of processed or assembled goods from China.[24]

The reason why FDI firms resort to overseas sourcing of intermediate inputs has been examined in the literature from different angles. In the case of FDI in mainland China, a first important factor at work until very recently has been the lack of a proper indigenous supply base.[25] The Chinese official policy of encouraging outward processing activities (*liangtou zaiwai*) further reinforced this tendency towards outward sourcing. Under this policy, foreign investors were obliged to provide their own materials and semi-finished products such that the internal market of China was not disturbed by additional demands from foreign operations. Chung describes this phenomenon as an inadvertently self-imposed 'enclave' economy.[26]

A second, and more general, motive for FDI firms to hold on to their original supply sources is their need to control product quality, especially at the earlier stages of a FDI operation.[27] Being newly situated in the host country and lacking adequate knowledge of local supply sources, the FDI firm may choose to use exactly the same components and parts as in domestic production so as to avoid the possibility of product failure. This is particularly important for export-oriented firms because their implicit assets are nothing but production credentials, which are key to sustaining their export orders. Even for domestic market-oriented FDI firms, retaining long-standing customer-supplier relationships seems a better way to uphold product quality, the supply schedule and thus corporate image in the market-place.

The above two types of overseas sourcing usually generate what we call inter-industry or intra-industry trade, by which we mean, for example, domestic supply of shoe soles and polished leather to overseas shoemakers (intra-industry trade), or the exports of steel rods and plastic materials for manufacturing sporting goods (inter-industry trade). Both of these lead to commodity flows in which the exporting and importing firms are not necessarily related in equity terms. A third type of overseas sourcing, however, is what we call intra-firm trade, where the parent at home and the subsidiary abroad are linked by trade in semi-finished products across national borders. An important function of intra-firm trade is transfer pricing which allows the parent firm to extract economic rent from the subsidiary.[28] In order to do this, however, the parent firm must achieve a significant degree of vertical integration prior to FDI such that the owner-specific economic rent embodied in, for example, key components and parts may be captured through transfer pricing. Japan, for example, has been known to establish automobile assembly lines in the United States while importing large quantities of components and engines from Japan at high costs as a way of circumventing the Voluntary Export Restraints (VERs) imposed by the US government. Lack of vertical integration in the parent firm leaves little room for division of labour between overseas and home production and, as a result, dispossesses the necessary means by which economic rent may be transferred from the subsidiary to the parent firm (that is, other than the trivial case of remittance of financial profits, which may itself be limited by a variety of circumstances). Furthermore, not only is a considerable degree of internal linkage essential, the intermediate products which are a manifestation of the parent firm's intangible assets must also be competitive enough such that the parent-subsidiary trade arrangement may be substantiated without sacrificing total profit rates. In other words, intra-firm transactions are preferred to inter-firm transactions only when the parent firm is able to provide world-competitive components and parts for its subsidiaries.

As commented on previously, however, manufacturing firms from Hong Kong and Taiwan alike are among the least vertically integrated producers in the world. They are mostly SMEs working closely together in a regional production network, each specializing in the manufacturing of a few items and parts thereof.[29] The scope for trade enhancement between the parent and the subsidiary is therefore greatly limited. Also important are the characteristics of the industries involved: for most labour-intensive, low-technology products, the inherent levels of technology and production processes do not entail much possibility for intra-firm division of labour. Most of the processes may be labour-intensive, or it may be too costly to divide the knowledge-intensive parts from the labour-intensive parts of the entire production process (such as footwear and apparel design, cutting, sewing and finishing). Because a large number of Taiwanese and Hong Kong firms are engaged in such industries, the scope for intra-firm division of labour is further limited.[30]

It is thus clear that the investment-induced trade among the trio has by and large consisted of inter- and intra-industry trade (rather than intra-firm trade) in which upstream producers at home furnish raw materials, components and parts for downstream FDI firms who have a presence in China. Compared with intra-firm trade, which has a strong internal motivation due to a need to appropriate rent, the momentum for inter- and intra-industry trade is likely to taper off over time as local supply capacity gradually builds up either through indigenous effort or through second-tier FDI firms who follow in the footsteps of first-tier end-product manufacturers. In the case of Taiwan, for example, it has been widely documented that investments made by large-scale bicycle assemblers such as Merida (in Longhua, Guangdong) and Giant (in Kunshan near Shanghai) attracted numerous component and parts suppliers to establish production networks nearby to serve local demand generated by these firms.[31] In other words, one expects to see a gradual decline of FDI-related exports from home and a concomitant increase in the importance of local shipments. According to a 1992 survey of 431 Taiwanese firms from different manufacturing sectors, 71.4 percent of the raw materials, components and parts necessary for their FDI operations in China were purchased from Taiwan (including parent and other firms) while only 20.8 percent were acquired from local sources (including indigenous firms and local FDI firms). A similar survey conducted among 285 firms in January 1995 indicates, however, that sourcing from Taiwan has declined to a mere 36.2 percent while local procurement has soared to 40.2 percent (Table 7.4). Figures for the procurement of machinery and equipment were 85.7 percent from Taiwan versus 7.4 percent from local sources in 1992, as compared with 68.5 percent from Taiwan versus 18.3 percent from local sources in January 1995.

INVESTMENT AS A SUBSTITUTE FOR HORIZONTAL TRADE (EXPORT SHIFT)

Linking the host country to the international market has been an important contribution of FDI to developing countries. In the past, Taiwan and Hong Kong both benefited substantially from export-oriented FDIs originating in advanced countries, in particular Japan and the United States. These FDIs consisted mostly of foreign-local joint ventures and original equipment manufacturing (OEM) contracts for various labour-intensive products such as apparel, bicycles, electronic appliances, and miscellaneous items, in which Taiwanese and Hong Kong firms quickly mastered the production technology and became leading exporters in the world. Two decades later, Taiwanese and Hong Kong firms under macroeconomic pressures have turned into labour-

Table 7.4 Changes in the Sourcing Behaviour of
Taiwanese FDI in China: 1992–1995

Sourcing Behaviour	Study and Sample Size		
	Yen, Lin, & Chung (1992)* (n=431)	Industrial Federation (Nov. 1994)** (n=317)	Industrial Federation (Jan. 1995)*** (n=285)
Purchases of raw material, components, and parts (%)			
from Taiwanese (or parent) firm	71.4	47.2	36.2
from local Chinese firms	16.0	29.8	40.2
from local foreign firms	4.8	11.4	10.0
from a third country	7.2	11.6	13.6
Purchases of machinery and equipment (%):			
from Taiwanese (or parent) firm	85.7	73.0	68.5
from local Chinese firms			
from local foreign firms	7.4	17.0	18.3
from a third country	6.2	10.0	13.2

Source: *   Yen, Lin and Chung (1992), *A Study of Investment and Trade Relations between Taiwan and Mainland China*, Chung-Hua Institution for Economic Research.
      ** Industrial Federation, Taiwan (1994).
     *** Industrial Federation, Taiwan (1995).

seeking FDI firms themselves and, in so doing, have found that access to the international market to be one of their most valuable assets *vis-à-vis* emerging competitors. It is important to note within this context, however, that the essence of such labour-oriented FDI is precisely to transplant production activities to a low-cost base and, as a result, an export shift lies at the heart of such a move.[32] One therefore expects to see production reshuffling between high-cost and low-cost locations and ensuing export substitution between the home and host economies. The extent of this export substitution in the case of Hong Kong is shown in Table 7.5 below. It is estimated that out of the total of manufacturing exports by Hong Kong firms, 95.4 percent of the travel goods and handbags were produced in and exported from Guangdong and only 4.6 percent were processed and exported from Hong Kong. Similar figures for the manufacture of toys are 94 percent (Guangdong) and 6 percent (Hong Kong), and for miscellaneous products are 80.5 percent (Guangdong) and 19.5 percent (Hong Kong).[33] On average, more than 60 percent of Hong Kong's previous production and exports have already been transferred to the Mainland. This helps explain the observed decline of Hong Kong's domestic exports in recent years in most of these export sectors.

Table 7.5 Exports from Hong Kong and Guangdong by Hong Kong Firms, 1993, in HK$ Millions (and Percentage Share)

Unit: HK$ Millions

SITC	Commodity	Exports of Hong Kong firms producing in:		
		Hong Kong*	Guangdong**	Total
83	Travel goods & handbags	104 (4.6)	2170 (95.4)	2274 (100)
894	Toys	431 (6.0)	6724 (94.0)	7155 (100)
899	Miscellaneous manufactures	327 (19.5)	1347 (80.5)	1674 (100)
76	Telecommunications & sound recording equipment	1716 (22.1)	6041 (77. 9)	7757 (100)
69	Metal manufactures n.e.s.	600 (37.8)	988 (62.2)	1588 (100)
65	Textiles	2 092 (40.6)	3057 (59.4)	5149 (100)
84	Clothing	9289 (51.3)	8826 (48.7)	18 115 (100)
77	Electrical machinery & appliances	2930 (51.4)	2774 (48.6)	5740 (100)
75	Office machines & automatic data processing machines	2229 (63.5)	1279 (36.5)	3508 (100)
885	Watches & clocks	1701 (66.8)	847 (33.2)	2548 (100)
	Subtotal	21 419 (38.6)	34 053 (61.4)	55 472 (100)
	All commodities	28 815 (39.6)	43 965 (60.4)	72 780 (100)

Note: percentage share in parenthesis.
  *   Hong Kong's domestic exports.
  **   Re-exports of Guangdong origin involving outward processing (taken to be 93.3% of re-exports of China origin involving outward processing).
Source: Sung, Yun-Wing (1994), 'The Economic Integration of the China Circle: Implications for the World Trading System', Table 5. Original data are from Hong Kong Census and Statistics Department.

The situation for Taiwan is similar. For example, more than 70 percent of Taiwan's shoe-making industry and over 95 percent of Taiwan's umbrella industry have been transplanted to China since the mid-1980s. As a result, in 1994, shoes made in mainland China captured 45 percent of the US market, a share enjoyed by products from Taiwan in 1986. Table 7.6 reports a set of

Table 7.6 Estimated Contribution of Taiwan's FDI to
China's Export Performance (1992)

Sector	Estimated Sectoral DFI* (US$ mil.)		Estimated Export Shift** (US$ mil.)		As % of China's Exports (1992)		
					China's Exports (US$ mil.)	Taiwan's Contribution (%)	
	(A)	(B)	(A)	(B)		(A)	(B)
Textiles	85~208		223~546		7749	2.88~7.05	
Apparel	125~134		325~348		16 469	1.97~2.11	
Leather goods	19~47		93~242		2329	3.99~9.88	
Wood products	69~87		192~242		1820	10.55~13.30	
Miscellaneous	263~205		995~776		5516	18.04~14.07	
Rubber & plastics	335~283		814~688		1830	44.48~37.60	
Non-ferrous minerals	64~66		88~91		1299	6.77~7.00	
Metal products	85~138		98~159		1600	6.13~9.94	
Electrical & electronics	338~246		1537~1119		8176	18.80~13.69	
Transportation equipment	215~49		505~115		2202	22.93~5.22	
Others	402~550		455~622		32 834	1.39~1.89	
Manufacturing total	2013		5325~4936		67 553	7.88~7.31	

Note: *   Sectoral FDI is estimated from two alternative series of FDI distribution across manufacturing sectors. Distribution (A) is adopted from the Investment Commission, Taiwan, based on investment registration data of US$735 million as of April 1991, with the assumption that the same industrial distribution is applicable as of end of 1992, when total investment reached US$2 billion; distribution (B) is based on Chinese official survey results reported in Table 7.2 above. Estimates derived from each are reported side by side (connected by the symbol '~') in this table.

       **   Estimates of 'export shift' are derived from multiplying sectoral FDI by the overseas capital productivity, which is assumed to be 1.2 times that of domestic output-capital ration based on survey results reported in Chung et al. (1993).

Source: Domestic output-capital ratio: *Census of Industry and Commerce of Taiwan*, 1992.
China's manufacturing exports: *China's Customs Statistics*, 1993. Original data is classified by SITC (revision 3). We have re-classified the data into 20 manufacturing sectors as shown in Table 7.2.

estimates for Taiwan's 'contribution' towards China's manufacturing exports by way of FDI. For the manufacturing sector as a whole, Taiwanese FDI of US$2 billion in 1992 had generated an estimated sum of exports of between US$4936 and 5325 million, which accounts for 7.5 percent to 7.9 percent of China's total manufacturing exports in that year.[34] In some of the sectors where Taiwanese FDI was particularly concentrated, the share of Taiwan's contribution towards China's sectoral exports went as high as the 37.6 percent to 44.5 percent range for rubber and plastic products, 5.2 percent to 22.9 percent for transportation equipment (in particular bicycles), 13.7 percent to 18.8 percent for electrical and electronics products (telephone sets, colour TV sets, tape recorders and so on).

The transplant of export manufacturing bases has an immediate impact on the export market shares enjoyed by Taiwan and Hong Kong in the United States and Japanese markets and on their respective trade balance position *vis-à-vis* these latter economies. Between 1989 and 1994, both Taiwan and Hong Kong suffered a serious deterioration in their export market shares in Japanese and US markets for such labour-intensive items as travel goods, apparel, footwear, umbrellas, furniture and miscellaneous products (Table 7.7). A resultant transfer of trade surpluses from Taiwan and Hong Kong to China has made China the nation with the second largest trade surplus with the United States (after Japan) and has helped trigger Sino-American trade conflicts in recent years (Table 7.8). The degree of Taiwanese involvement in China's manufacturing exports to the United States has been such that the recent US threat to impose trade sanctions upon China spelled disaster for Taiwanese investors. According to one estimate it is projected that US$1 billion worth of tariff sanctions imposed on Chinese exports (as proposed by the US government in February 1995) would have rendered an immediate loss of US$274 million for Taiwanese investors in the form of lost orders, which was about 27 percent of China's total exports to the US affected by the proposed sanction (Table 7.9).[35]

There is no consensus, however, as to whether these export substitutions should be regarded as a positive or negative development for the home economy. One argument advanced in the literature is that they are a result of free market forces (that is, shifting comparative advantage between different countries) and therefore should not be a cause for policy concern. Furthermore, the argument goes, since the FDI firms are in a position to control more production bases and therefore bigger export market shares, their actions are beneficial to the home country because they generate greater GNP.[36]

Opponents of this view, however, point to the fact that governments around the world are more concerned with GDP generation rather than with GNP generation because the latter may prove illusory for the home economy. Profits earned from overseas operations may be used for expansionary purposes in the host country or simply lie idle in some Swiss bank rather than being ploughed back to benefit home employment and public taxation. More importantly, there are different *types* of FDI, all generating the same phenomenon of export substitution, some of which lead to mutually beneficial division of labour between home and host economies, while others simply transplant domestic production overseas. In other words, the welfare implications of export substitution are difficult to assess *a priori* as they hinge

Table 7.7 Percentage Changes in Export Market Shares for Taiwan, Hong Kong and China in Selected Product Groups in the US and Japanese Markets: 1989–1994

Product Category	The US Market			The Japanese Market		
	Taiwan	Hong Kong	China	Taiwan	Hong Kong	China
HS 42 Handbags & travel goods	–9.12	–1.38	+30.95	–1.56	–4.42	+21.99
HS 46 Woven baskets	–4.49	–1.60	+14.81	–26.02	–0.77	+37.08
HS 61 Knitted apparel & accessories	–6.17	–2.77	+0.52	–10.96	–4.40	+24.07
HS 62 Non-knitted apparel & accessories	–5.08	–5.29	+4.91	–5.23	–1.93	+29.86
HS 64 Footwear & accessories	–20.03	–0.42	+36.27	–17.92	–0.18	+35.68
HS 65 Hats & accessories	–6.28	–0.56	+3.78	–8.16	–0.59	+2.77
HS 66 Umbrellas, sticks, & stages	–27.5 4	–3.08	+27.98	–65.23	–2.46	+72.46
HS 67 Feather goods, man-made flower, etc.	–4.77	–0.76	+29.76	–9.29	–2.41	+9.44
HS 94 Furniture & lighting	–11.44	– 0.44	+13.85	–11.52	–0.20	+8.85
HS 95 Toys, games, & sporting goods	–8.73	–3.07	+24.35	–7.96	–1.34	+19.09
HS 96 Miscellaneous products	–4.67	–6.14	+10.50	–2.53	–3.72	+11.12
Manufacturing total	–1.13	–0.60	+3.33	–0.33	–0.27	+4.71

Note: '–' means a decrease in import market share (in percentage points) during the period 1989–94, while '+' indicates an increase.

Source: The export market shares for Taiwan, Hong Kong and China are calculated from the customs statistics of the US and Japan (on tape).

primarily on a contemporaneous restructuring effort in the home economy as well as the degree of success it is able to achieve. The point is that industrial realignment is not a guaranteed process and that characteristics of the FDI firms (and domestic firms in general) are among the crucial factors determining

Table 7.8 Shifting Trade Surpluses With the United States Among the Trio

Year	(A) Taiwan	(B) Hong Kong	(C) China	(A)+(B)+(C) The Trio
1987	16.04	4.06	3.40	26.48
1990	9.13	1.87	11.49	22.49
1992	7.80	−0.77	19.94	26.97
1994	6.30	−2.42	19.80	33.68

Source: United States Customs Statistics.

Table 7.9 Potential Impact on Taiwanese FDI of US Sanctions Against China (1995)

Sector affected by US sanctions	Sectoral sanction (US$ 10 000)	Taiwan DFI's export contribution (%)	Potential impact (US$ 10 000)
Processed foods	3097.5	1.39~1.89	43.1~58.5
Wearing apparel	6876.2	1.97~2.11	261.4~145.1
Wood products	5632.4	10.55~13.30	594.2~749.1
Paper products	6452.9	1.39~1.89	89.7~122.0
Plastic products	45 615.3	44.48~37.60	20 289.7~17 151.4
Rubber products	1626.3	44.48~37.60	723.4~611.5
Metal products	4562.1	6.13~9.94	279.7~453.5
Electronics	10 583.7	18.80~13.69	994.9~1448.9
Transport equip.	1925.6	22.93~5.22	220.8~100.5
Miscellaneous	21 682.0	18.04~14.07	−3901.7~3050.7
Total sanctions	108 000.0 (100.0%)	− −	27 398.6~23 891.2 (25.4%~22.1%)

Source: Sanctions data are from the US Trade Representative's Office as reported in *United Daily News* (in Chinese), 21 February 1995. Estimates for Taiwanese FDI's export contributions are adapted from Table 7.6.

whether a successful upgrading at home will indeed take place.[37] In the case of Taiwan and Hong Kong, it seems that the odds are generally against a quick and successful restructuring at home. Lack of enduring firm-specific assets make FDI firms (especially SMEs) from these economies more migrators than diversifiers in their overseas operations. The lure of a vast Chinese market coupled with a key dose of cultural advantage further intensify these firms' tendency to relocate rather than to diversify. Even in the case of horizontal and/or vertical division of labour between the home and host economies, there is a higher risk that overseas operations will supplant domestic production as technological differences between the two economies lessen and therefore cost calculations become more important over time. Last, but not least, the fact that these firms constitute a considerable part of their home countries' economic strengths further blemishes the prospect of a successful and problem-free transformation as conjectured by Lee.[38]

EMPIRICAL EVIDENCE ON DOMESTIC RESTRUCTURING

To sum up the above discussions, investment-induced trade largely consists of logistic supply of intermediate products, machinery and equipment in support of overseas FDI operations, while the ensuing 'export shift' signifies a horizontal substitution of export performance from the FDI home to the FDI host country. In the terminology of the 'Flying Geese' pattern of industrial development, the FDI home economy must now endeavour to gain competitiveness in an entire range of new products so as not to be left out of the flock. We argue that the lack of solid firm-specific assets on the part of Taiwanese and Hong Kong FDI firms results in a delay of industrial restructuring at home because not enough economic resources and entrepreneurial talent are left to facilitate a smooth intra- and/or inter-industry restructuring. In this section we turn to look at the actual economic performance of Hong Kong and Taiwan in recent years to see if the arguments presented above can be substantiated by empirical evidence.

With the relocation of manufacturing activities to Guangdong, the share of manufacturing in Hong Kong's total GDP has shrunk substantially within a fifteen-year span, from 23.9 percent in 1980 to 9.3 percent in 1995 (Table 7.10). This phenomenon has struck some as a textbook case of industrial hollowing-out.[39] The average GDP growth rate has also come down from 7.7 percent during the 1980 to 1987 to a mere 5.1 percent from 1987 to 1994, which was the lowest among the Four Asian Dragons in that latter period. Nevertheless, Hong Kong has been fortunate in that it benefited substantially from reassuming the important entrepôt role it once played decades ago. Along with the decline to the manufacturing sector, it has developed a booming service and transport

Table 7.10 Percentage Changes in the Sectoral Composition
of Hong Kong's and Taiwan's GDP

	Hong Kong			Taiwan		
	1980	1986	1994	1980	1986	1994
GDP Share in:						
Agriculture and fishing	0.9	0.5	0.2	7.8	7.8	3.6
Manufacturing	23.9	22.3	9.3	41.5	43.6	29.0
Mining, electricity & construction	8.2	7.9	7.5	9.9	8.7	8.2
Services	67.0	69.3	83.0	40.8	39.9	59.2
Average real GDP growth						
1980–1987		7.7			8.3	
1987–1994		5.1			6.9	

Source: *Hong Kong Monthly Digest of Statistics*, Census and Statistics Department, Hong Kong, various issues; *Economic Yearbook of the Republic of China* (1994), Directorate-General of Budget, Accounting and Statistics, Executive Yuan, Taiwan.

sector due to its increased economic ties with China. Being a city-economy and a free port, Hong Kong is currently moving along an inter-sectoral restructuring path to become a regional financial and transportation centre, drifting further away from its traditional manufacturing activities.

On the other hand, Taiwan's restructuring process may prove to be more arduous. Compared with Hong Kong, Taiwan has a stronger manufacturing base which, however, needs to be stepped up technologically in almost every line of activity. As the bulk of Taiwanese SMEs venture into the vast Chinese market, however, the Taiwan economy itself is left with little impetus to move forward as strongly as in the recent past. As with Hong Kong, Taiwan's share of manufacturing in Taiwan's GDP has fallen sharply from 43.6 percent in 1986 to 29.0 percent in 1994, dropping 14.6 percentage points in less than ten years. Average GDP growth registered 6.9 percent from 1987 to 1994 (compared with 8.3 percent from 1980 to 1987) and was the second lowest growth rate achieved by the Four Asian Dragons (only slightly better than Hong Kong but much lower than the 7.9 percent in South Korea and 8.8 percent in Singapore). Table 7.11 presents a quick comparison of Taiwan's industrial development in the two periods 1980–87 and 1987–93 in terms of export performance, real GDP growth and domestic capital formation within the manufacturing sector. It can be seen that out of the twenty manufacturing sectors in total, only seven sectors (those with asterisks) have shown increased real GDP growth, six show accelerated export expansion, and only three show hastened capital formation in the second period. Among the faster-growing sectors, especially in terms of GDP performance, two are dominated by public enterprises (the petroleum and coal industry and the tobacco industry), indicating that the private sector has been slow in making realignment efforts during this latter period. Manufacturing GDP growth for the second period averaged 4.7 percent compared with 8.5 percent in the first period, while total exports grow only 1.5 percent compared with 12.5 percent previously, and real capital formation was 6.5 percent compared with 6.6 percent before. All in all, one does not see any serious signs of *spontaneous* structural change but more of a passive adjustment as a result of the exodus of labour-intensive industries which tilted the balance towards what is left on the island.

It is interesting to note that some of these sectors have shown a faster growth in exports but not in real GDP or capital formation (such as textiles, paper products, chemicals and chemical products, and basic metals), and some have shown faster growth in capital formation but not in real GDP or exports (such as precision instruments). The former industries have exhibited this peculiar pattern primarily because they had been the main suppliers of raw materials and semi-finished products to downstream producers of apparel, electronics devices and miscellaneous products. Now that their downstream customers have migrated to the Mainland, the original supply relationship must assume the new form of cross-border trade with little or no corresponding gains in domestic production. Nor is it necessary, or so it seems, for these firms to step up capital formation because total sales have remained more or less constant. Alternatively, these industries have not been able to enhance their competitiveness and increase relative market shares over this period of presumably intense restructuring.[40] For the latter group of products, with higher levels of investment but a laggard output performance, it obviously takes time for them to form new competitive edges as older products and equipment become obsolete. In other words, they will have to keep up the investment level for a sustained period of time before the current downward trend in output and exports changes course and turns up again.[41]

Table 7.11 Industrial Restructuring in Taiwan: 1980–1987 Versus 1987–93

Unit: avg. %

Industry	RGDP Growth		Export Growth		Real K Capital	
	1980–87	1987–93	1980–87	1987–93	1980–87	1987–93
1. Processed foods	4.4	2.6*	6.7	-1.9	11.8	4.1
2. Beverages & tobacco	3.5	5.3*	-8.0	-1.9	12.4	3.1
3. Textiles	4.3	-1.2	8.3	8.7*	9.3	3.5
4. Apparel	5.0	-5.6	8.6	-7.6	4.1	-2.7
5. Leather products	25.8	-6.9	24.9	-12.4	18.7	3.4
6. Wood & bamboo products	7.2	-3.3	6.9	-16.7	-0.2	2.7
7. Paper products	7.2	-1.8	9.0	13.4*	11.5	9.6
8. Chemicals	12.3	6.8	13.5	16.0*	8.8	8.5
9. Chemical products	11.6	8.3	7.8	8.7*	9.1	–
10. Petroleum & coal	1.9	6.8*	–	–	15.7	14.4
11. Rubber products	10.5	1.2	14.3	-3.2	10.1	2.8
12. Plastic products	12.6	1.1	–	–	9.1	–
13. Non-ferrous mineral products	4.5	8.4*	12.8	–4.3	13.4	3.5
14. Basic metals	9.2	8.8	10.0	11.8*	15.1	5.3
15. Metal products	7.4	9.4*	18.3	6.3	14.2	10.1
16. Machinery	5.7	10.3*	13.6	13.8*	5.8	6.4*
17. Electrical & electronics	16.1	10.9	16.3	9.6	5.8	8.8*
18. Transportation equipment	5.6	8.4*	18.1	7.3	12.2	4.9
19. Precision instruments	8.8	1.6	9.6	4.6	7.9	8.8*
20. Miscellaneous products	11.7	-4.1	12.0	-9.1	2.3	–1.2
Manufacturing Total	8.5	4.7	12.5	1.5	9.7	6.5

Note: Sectors with asterisks are the ones showing better performance in the second period compared with the first period.

Source: *Statistics of Industrial Production Monthly, Taiwan Area* (1994); *Monthly Statistics of Exports and Imports, Taiwan Area*, various issues; *The Trends of Multifactor Productivity* (1995).

According to our argument, it is the relative strength of domestic capital formation, compared with outward FDI, which may be thought of as an embodiment of firm-specific assets on the part of FDI firms, that determines the speed and content of domestic restructuring. If sectoral investment in the comparatively advantaged sectors do not show obvious signs of speeding up, one may then say that domestic restructuring has not been proceeding smoothly. In what follows, a simple correlation analysis will be conducted between the following variables: FDIINTENS (Taiwanese cumulative FDI towards China by sector as a share of domestic capital formation in that sector from 1987 to 1993); RGDPG (average growth rate of sectoral real GDP from 1987 to 1993); XG8793 (average growth rate of sectoral exports from 1987 to 1993); and RKG (average growth rate of sectoral real capital formation). It is expected that a high value of FDIINTENS, meaning insufficient domestic investment in the face of capital outflows, will tend to hurt domestic performance not only in exports, but also in sectoral GDP and further incentives for capital accumulation. On the other hand, lower levels of FDIINTENS signifies more vigorous attention to industrial realignment has been given to domestic sectors and that, as a result, domestic performance in terms of exports, GDP, and sectoral capital formation will be on track. The results are tabulated in Table 7.12. It is obvious that the four key variables are negatively correlated as expected and are statistically significant at the one percent level.

Table 7.12 Pearson Correlation Coefficients Between Taiwan's (China-bound) FDI-Intensity, Export Performance, Real GDP Growth, and Domestic Capital Formation

(n=18)

	DFIINTENS	XG 8793	RGDPG	RKG
DFIINTENS	1.00000	−0.6475*** (0.0037)	−0.7079*** (0.0010)	−0.6727*** (0.0022)
XG8793		1.0000	0.6736 (0.0022)	0.7260*** (0.0006)
RGDPG			1.0000	0.6137*** (0.0068)
RKG				1.0000

Note: *** refers to 1 % significance level; figures in parenthesis are α-values.
Source: DFIINTENS: Cumulative realized DFI to China at the end of 1993 are adopted from Gao et al. (1994), Appendix Table 5.2, p. 260; domestic investment data are from *The Trends in Multifactor Productivity* (1995), Directorate-General of Budget, Accounting and Statistics, Executive Yuan, ROC.
XG 8793: *Monthly Statistics on Taiwan's Export-Import Trade, Taiwan Area*, ibid.
RGDPG: *Statistics of Industrial Production Monthly, Taiwan Area* (1994), ibid.
RKG: *The Trends in Multifactor Productivity* (1995), ibid.

CONCLUDING REMARKS

Against the background of intense direct investment and trade flows among the Chinese Trio, this chapter deals with the divergence between private interests and social benefits in an act of FDI, particularly that of a labour-seeking nature. As Arndt noted in an excellent discussion of technology transfer as a result of FDI, scope for trade continues provided technological advance (in the home country) reopens the gap as fast as it is closed.[42] In the same vein, we argue that outward FDI from newly-industrializing economies such as Taiwan and Hong Kong runs the risk of depriving the home economy of the necessary means to embark on successful domestic transformation. This is particularly true for FDI firms with meagre firm-specific assets in the form of technological superiority, R and D capability, marketing skills or managerial capacities. These labour-intensive, small-scale manufacturers are able to engage in outward FDI only because they are assisted by other sources of advantage, that is, government coordination and facilitation in the case of Japan in the 1960s, and cultural proximity in the case of Taiwan and Hong Kong in recent years. Since they lack a sufficient degree of in-house production integration, investment-induced exports tend to taper off while export substitutions become the norm as a result of the transplant of production activities. More importantly, FDI by small, specialized firms drains resources away from domestic restructuring and leaves the home economy hungry for new capital as well as adequate entrepreneurial attention. Put differently, although individual FDI firms get to keep their industry-specific capital by relocating production overseas, society loses in terms of foregone chances for intra-firm upgrading and/or intra- and inter-industry restructuring. Contrary to Kojima's view, then, it seems that FDI from these economies should be in line with their *own* comparative advantage rather than with the comparative advantage of the host country so as to make it beneficial for domestic restructuring.

An important distinction needs to be made here, however, between coordinated and uncoordinated acts of FDI with meagre firm-specific assets. In the case of FDI by small- and medium-sized Japanese firms in the 1960s, government or the 'collective will' assumed an important role in guiding investment activities not only in these firms' outward FDI but also in their domestic restructuring. The fact that these FDI firms often constituted the outer ring of industrial *keiretsu* further implied that they could upgrade at home under the technological, financial and managerial umbrella of the *keiretsu* to which they belonged. In other words, a crucial dose of intangible assets was injected from outside which helped these firms maintain a healthy division of labour across national borders over time. The stories of Taiwanese and Hong Kong FDI firms may be quite different, however, as the role of government is not clear and SMEs are usually independent exporters. With the exodus of these firms, their connection with the home economies may dwindle over time. This implies a need for government intervention both at the industry and at the firm level, providing more infrastructure and inter-firm coordination to help generate the necessary momentum for domestic restructuring so that these FDI firms may find new ways to make domestic operations profitable and so that the home economy may thrive along with the success of individual firms' FDI.

NOTES

1. Kiyoshi Kojima, 'A macroeconomic approach to foreign direct investment', *Hitotsubashi Journal of Economics*, Vol. 14 (1973), pp. 1–21, and Kiyoshi Kojima, *Foreign direct investment: A Japanese Model of Multinational Business Operations* (New York: Praeger, 1978).
2. Kiyoshi Kojima (1973), op. cit., p. 4 and Kiyoshi Kojima (1978), op. cit., p. 115.
3. Chung H. Lee, 'On Japanese macroeconomic theories of foreign direct investment', *Economic Development and Cultural Change*, Vol. 32 (1984), pp. 713–723, and 'Foreign direct investment, structural adjustment, and international division of labour: A dynamic macroeconomic theory of foreign direct investment', *Hitotsubashi Journal of Economics,* Vol. 31 (1990), p. 69.
4. Kaname Akamatsu, 'A historical pattern of economic growth in developing countries', *Developing Economics,* No. 1 (1962), pp. 3–25.
5. Chung H. Lee, (1984, 1990), op. cit., seemed to have played down the possibility of selling off the industry-specific capital (perhaps in a turn-key fashion) here. Although this may yield less present value to the capital owner in the absence of a perfect future market, it may however keep the owner's human capital within the home economy for intra- and/or inter-industry upgrading and/or diversification.
6. See for instance, Stephen Hymer, *The International Operations of National Firms: A Study of Foreign Direct Investment,* Ph.D. thesis, (1960), Department of Economics, MIT (Cambridge Mass.: MIT Press, 1976); Richard Caves, 'International corporations: The industrial economics of foreign investment', *Economica*, Vol. 38 (1971), pp. 1–27; F.T. Knikerbocker, *Oligopolistic Reaction and the Multinational Enterprise*, Ph.D. thesis, Graduation School of Business Administration, Harvard University, Boston, MA, 1973; Peter Buckley and Mark Casson, *The Future of Multinational Enterprise* (London: Macmillan, 1976); and J.H. Dunning, *International Production and Multinational Enterprise* (London: George Allen and Unwin, 1981).
7. Richard Caves (1971), op. cit.
8. For a pioneering discussion of the small-firm FDI originated from the third-world countries, see Louis Wells, *Third World Multinationals* (Cambridge: MIT Press, 1983).
9. R. Hal Mason, 'A comment on Professor Kojima's Japanese type versus American type of technological transfer', *Hitotsubashi Journal of Economics*, February 1980, pp. 42–52. It must be noted, however, that the advantage of market access was accorded to these firms under the umbrella of giant trading companies (or *sogo shosha*) which served as providers of marketing and technology infrastructure for their smaller, satellite firms.
10. Tain-jy Chen and Wen-thuen Wang, 'Globalization of Taiwan's electronics industry', in Chien-nan Wang (ed.), *Globalization, Regionalization, and Taiwan's Economy* (Taipei: Chung-Hua Institution for Economic Research, 1994), pp. 199–214.
11. Chung H. Lee (1984), op. cit., p. 715.

12. Raymond Vernon, 'International investment and international trade in the product cycle', *Quarterly Journal of Economic,* Vol. 80 (1966), pp. 190–207.
13. Chin Chung, 'The changing pattern of division of labour across the Taiwan Strait: Macro overview and the sectoral analysis of the electronics industry', paper presented at the International Conference on the *China Circle,* sponsored by the Institute for Global Conflict and Cooperation, University of California at San Diego, Hong Kong, December 1994. Similar considerations apply to Hong Kong investors operating in the Pearl River Delta region, but perhaps not in other areas of mainland China.
14. Terutomo Ozawa, 'Japan's new resource diplomacy: Government-backed group investment', *Journal of World Trade Law,* Jan.–Feb. 1979, p. 84.
15. Chung H. Lee (1990), op. cit., pp. 61–72.
16. Chyau Tuan and Linda F.F. Ng, 'Microeconomic foundations of Hong Kong's investment towards mainland China in the integration process of the South China growth triangle', paper presented at the International Conference on the *Emergence of the South China Growth Triangle,* Chung-Hua Institution for Economic Research, Taipei, 5–6 May, 1995; Chyau Tuan and Linda F.F. Ng, 'Hong Kong's outward investment and regional economic integration with Guangdong: Process and impliations', *Journal of Asian Economics,* Vol. 6, No. 3, 1995, pp. 385–405 and Tsung-ta Yen, Y.C. Lin and Chin Chung, *A Study of Taiwan's Investment and Trade Relations with Mainland China* (in Chinese), research project report commissioned by the Council for Economic Planning and Development (Taipei: Chung-Hua Institution for Economic Research, 1992).
17. See, for example, Yun-wing Sung, 'The economic integration of the China circle: Implications for the world trading system', paper presented at the conference on the *China Circle,* sponsored by the Institute for Global Conflict and Cooperation, University of California at San Diego, (Hong Kong, December, 1994), and Chyau Tuan and Linda F.F. Ng (1995) for a detailed discussion of this phenomenon.
18. Chyau Tuan and Linda F.F. Ng (1995), op. cit.
19. For details of the method used to compile these data, see S. Gao, Joseph S. Lee and Chu Chia Steve Lin, *An Empirical Study of Taiwanese Firms' Mainland Investment on Industrial Upgrading in Taiwan and on the Vertical Division of Labour across the Taiwan Strait* (in Chinese), research project report commissioned by the Ministry of Economic Affairs, 1993.
20. See, for example, Chin Chung, 'Taiwan's FDI in Mainland China: Impact on the domestic and host economies', paper presented at the Third Annual Conference of the Chinese Economic Association (UK), December 1991, London; later published in Thomas Lyons and Victor Nee (eds.), *The Economic Transformation of South China: Reform and Development in the Post-Mao Era* (Ithaca: Cornell East Asian Series, 1995), pp. 215–242; Chen Lee-in Chiu and Chin Chung, 'An assessment of Taiwan's indirect investment toward Mainland China', *Asian Economic Journal,* Vol. 7, No. 1 (1993), pp. 41–60; and Charng Gao et al., *A Comparative Study of Foreign Investment in Mainland China* (in Chinese), Research project report commissioned by the Investment Commission, Taiwan (Taipei: Chung-Hua Institution for Economic Research, 1994).
21. Because earlier Taiwanese FDI was more concentrated in export-oriented sectors, which had to meet a 70% export ratio decreed by the Chinese authorities, it is reasonable to use the input-output table method in deriving the correspondence estimates. For later years, however, especially after 1992 when domestic market-oriented FDI started to boom, the same methodology should be used more carefully so as not to exaggerate the results. See Chung (1991, 1995) and Chung et al., (1993), op. cit.
22. S. Gao, Joseph S. Lee, and Chu-chia Steve Lin (1993), op. cit.
23. The imbalance was in part due to the Taiwan government's imposing import

restrictions on Chinese commodities while allowing free exports from Taiwan to China via a third country, as explicated in Chin Chung (1991, 1995), op. cit.

24. Chyau Tuan and Linda F.F. Ng (1995), op. cit.
25. Chen Lee-in Chiu and Chin Chung (1993), op. cit., and Yu-Shan Wu, 'Shifting dependency: Taiwan's new growth pattern', paper prepared for the American Enterprise Institute's project, unpublished manuscript, 1994.
26. Chen Lee-in Chiu and Chin Chung (1993), op. cit.
27. Donald Lecraw ,'Choice of technology in low wage countries: A non-neoclassical approach', *Quarterly Journal of Economics,* Vol. 53 (1979), pp. 631–654.
28. R. Hal Mason (1980) and Mark C. Casson and G. Norman, 'Pricing and sourcing strategies in a multinational oligopoly', in M.C. Casson (ed.), *The Growth of International Business* (London: George Allen and Urwin, 1983).
29. This is especially true in the export sector as opposed to the domestic market-oriented sector in these economies. See, for example, Tein-chen Chou, *Industrial Organization in the Process of Economic Development: The Case of Taiwan* (Chicago: Louvain-la-Neuve, 1985) and Gary G. Hamilton (ed.), *Business Networks and Economic Development in East and Southeast Asia* (Hong Kong: Centre of Asian Studies, University of Hong Kong, 1991).
30. In this respect Hong Kong may have benefited more from geographical proximity to China than Taiwan has in that goods can be swapped back and forth within a day's time without incurring large transportation costs.
31. Tsung-ta Yen, Y.C. Lin and Chin Chung (1992), op. cit.
32. Chin Chung (1991, 1995), op. cit.
33. See Yun-wing Sung (1994), op. cit.
34. These estimates were obtained using input/output analysis combined with survey data for relevant parameters such as export propensities for each individual sector. See Chen Lee-in Chiu and Chin Chung (1993), op. cit.
35. From Table 7.7 it is clear that China's export booms in these sectors more than offset the combined losses of Taiwan and Hong Kong, indicating that the Chinese export drive in these labour-intensive products may have been supported by multilateral interests (including township and village enterprises in the rural areas of China). However, we have reason to believe that economies of scale of Taiwanese and Hong Kong FDI played an important part in augmenting China's exports in these sectors. In fact, many Taiwanese firms have been documented to enlarge their scale of operations after the initial profit was made, ibid.
36. See, for example, Chi Shive, 'Foreign direct investment and industrial adjustment in Taiwan', in Jien-nan Wang (ed.), *Globalization, Regionalization, and Taiwan's Economy* (Taipei: Chung Hua Institution for Economic Research, 1995), pp. 171–197, and Steve Chu-jia Lin, 'Parent-subsidiary division of labour and industrial upgrading of Taiwanese FDI firms: Comparison between electronics and footware industries', in M.J. Rao (ed.) *Economic Cooperation in the Greater South China: Industrial Interactions among Taiwan, Hong Kong, Macao and South China* (in Chinese) (Hong Kong: World Wide Publications, 1995), pp. 176–200.
37. For a discussion of the different types of FDI strategies in mainland China pursued by Taiwanese firms, see Chin Chung, 'Firm characteristics and FDI strategy: A three-way typology of Taiwanese investment in Mainland China', paper presented in the International Conference on the South China Growth Triangle, co-sponsored by International Center for Economic Growth and Chung-Hua Institution for Economic Research, June 1995, Taipei.
38. Chung H. Lee (1990), op. cit.
39. For an in-depth discussion of Hong Kong's industrial hollowing-out, see Jiang Lin, 'Hong Kong's industrial structure towards the twenty-first century', (in Chinese), in M.J. Rao (ed.), *Economic Cooperation in the Greater South China: Industrial Interactions among Taiwan, Hong Kong, Macao, and South China* (in Chinese) (Hong Kong: World Wide Publications, 1995), pp. 220–256.

40. Indeed we have seen various upstream producers establishing additional capacities on the mainland to serve local Taiwanese FDI firms as well as potential local demand. Again, domestic upgrading efforts are, to some extent, diverted through these second-tier outward FDIs.
41. There is yet a third class of industries which have shown faster growth in GDP but not in exports or capital formation (such as beverages and tobacco, petroleum and coal, non-ferrous mineral products metal products, and transportation equipment). The explanation seems to lie in the fact that these industries traditionally cater for more domestic consumption, and are somewhat segregated from competitive export markets due either to tariff protection (that is, automobiles) or transportation costs (that is, basic metals and non-ferrous mineral products).
42. H.W. Arndt, 'Professor Kojima on the macroeconomics of foreign direct investment', *Hitotsubashi Journal of Economics,* Vol. 15, No. 1 (1974), pp. 26–35.

8

The Impact of Renminbi Devaluation on Hong Kong and China Trade

Kui-yin Cheung

INTRODUCTION

Since China launched its economic reforms and adopted the open-door policy in the late 1970s, it has become a significant factor in world trade. From 1979 to 1993, China's exports increased from US$13.7 billion to US$91.8 billion at more than 16 percent per year, a rate that would have been inconceivable before the adoption of the open-door strategy. As in other centrally planned economies, the price of foreign exchange had little effect on the volume of either imports or exports. In the pre-reform era, China's exports were used to earn enough hard currency to import goods for industrialization and self dependence. Thus, the exchange rate was largely a passive policy instrument in the formulation of its trade policy. In addition, China's exchange rate was highly overvalued and the resulting excess demand for foreign exchange was handled through a rigid system of exchange control. Even in the post-reform era, the domestic currency cost of earning foreign exchange was continually and persistently higher than the official exchange rate, making most exports financially unprofitable, particularly manufacturing goods which were usually sold at a financial loss.[1,2]

Since 1980, the renminbi (RMB) has experienced substantial depreciation against major currencies. From 1980 to 1992, the renminbi devalued by 74 percent versus the US dollar, 85 percent versus the Japanese yen, 71 percent versus the ECU (European Currency Unit) and 60 percent versus the Hong Kong dollar.[3] The devaluation of China's exchange rate was, without doubt, intended to promote exports and to restrain imports so as to improve China's current account position. This includes the RMB devaluation of 13.6 percent in July 1986,[4] 21.2 percent in December 1989, 9.57 percent in November 1990[5] and 33.4 percent in January 1994.[6] In particular, the RMB devaluation in 1989 and 1990 helped China to move from a current account deficit of US$ 6.6 billion in 1989 to a current account surplus of US$ 8.12 billion in 1991.

China's open-door policy has not only intensified the trade relationship between Hong Kong and China, but also revitalized Hong Kong's traditional entrepôt trade which was once active some thirty years ago. Since 1980, Hong Kong and China have become each other's most important trade partner. Table 8.1 shows the estimates of the average annual rate of growth in bilateral trade between Hong Kong and China from 1980 to 1991. From 1979 to 1993, Hong Kong's domestic exports to China grew 66 times and in 1993 were estimated to have reached US$8116 million. During the same period, Hong Kong's imports from China grew drastically as well and in 1993 were 17 times those in 1979. The majority of these imports from China, however, are for re-export and are of outward-processing in nature. The re-export portion of imports grew rapidly and exceeded the retained portion by 1986. The share of imports of Chinese products re-exported via Hong Kong to total imports from China rose from 24.7 percent in 1977 to 87.1 percent in 1993. This highlights the growing importance of the outward-processing trade between Hong Kong and China. In fact, exports of *sanzi* enterprises in China, particular in the Pearl River delta region of, Guangdong, through Hong Kong have indeed become so substantial that in the last few years they have been the focal point of US-China trade disputes, with the Chinese arguing that when calculating its trade surplus with the United States these 'outward processing' activities[7] from Hong Kong should not be taken into account since the Chinese partners earn only a minimal share of the processing fees.

Table 8.1 The Average Annual Growth Rate (%) of Hong Kong and China Trade

		HK imports from China			HK exports to China	
Period	Total	Retained in Hong Kong	Re–exported elsewhere	Total	Hong Kong goods	Hong Kong Re–exports
1980–91	23.57	8.96	28.76	31.86	32.03	31.79
1980–85	19.76	14.38	28.34	45.65	44.95	45.88
1985–91	26.74	4.44	31.83	20.36	21.26	20.06

Source: Hong Kong Census and Statistics Department, *Hong Kong Monthly Digest of Statistics*, various issues.

The organization of this chapter is as follows. Following this introductory section, on pp. 165–167 examines the impact of the devaluation of the RMB on Hong Kong and China trade. This includes the retained imports from China and domestic exports to China. Since China is the predominant supplier of fresh vegetables and of many specialty foodstuffs to Hong Kong, its demand elasticity for imports is believed to be low. Thus the devaluation of the RMB might have an adverse effect on Hong Kong's imports of traditional Chinese products. Section three on pp. 170–174 investigates the possible impact of devaluation on Hong Kong's re-exports from China and its investment in China particularly in the Pearl River delta region of Guangdong. Section four on pp. 174–176 summarizes the empirical results of the estimation of the effects of real exchange rate changes of the RMB relative to the Hong Kong dollar on Hong Kong and China trade. Section five on pp. 176–177 concludes the study.

THE IMPACT OF THE DEVALUATION OF THE RENMINBI ON HONG KONG AND CHINA TRADE

To examine the impact of RMB devaluation on Hong Kong and China trade it is important to examine the real exchange rate changes relative to the US and Hong Kong dollars because nominal exchange rate changes do not necessarily mean real exchange rate changes. By definition, the change in real exchange rate is the change in the nominal exchange rate net of the difference in the inflation rate between the home and the trading partners. In relative form:

$$RS = S - (P_d - P_f)$$

where RS is the change in real exchange rates, S is the change in nominal exchange rates, P_d and P_f are respectively, the inflation rate of the home and the trading partners. Based on the above equation, a nominal devaluation will only be effective in increasing the real exchange rate (RS) if the inflation rate at home (P_d) goes up at a rate which is less than the rise in inflation of the trading partner, P_f. In addition, a change in RS is a necessary, but not sufficient condition for the balance of trade adjustment in the short run. Whether a rise in RS can stimulate the export of tradable goods depends, among other factors, on the supply elasticity of the traded goods sector in the home country. Countries with high supply elasticity seem more sensitive to positive changes in the real exchange rate than those with low supply elasticity.

The average official exchange rates of the RMB versus the US and Hong Kong dollar prevailing from 1978 to 1993 are shown in Table 8.2. In China's case, the changes in the real exchange rates play a significant role in the balance of trade adjustments. Table 8.2 shows the real RMB exchange rate movements relative to the US and Hong Kong dollars as well. The result indicated that the repeated devaluations from 1980 to 1987 have succeeded in increasing the real RMB exchange rate versus the USD (that is, real depreciation). In fact, China has been able to maintain its inflation at a rate lower than nominal devaluation during the period. From 1992 to 1993, China's trade competitiveness with the United States appeared to come from the outcome of Hong Kong-China economic integration and comparative advantage in labour-intensive manufacturing as the real exchange rate of RMB was revalued relative to the US dollar.

Table 8.2 Changes in RMB Exchange Rates, Inflation Rates and
Real Exchange Rates, 1978–1993

Year	RMB/US$	RMB/HK$	IN$_{HK}$ (%)	IN$_{CN}$ (%)	IN$_{US}$ (%)	R$_{CU}$ (%)	R$_{CH}$ (%)
1978	1.5771 (−9.17)	0.3370 (−10.96)	5.72	0.90	7.54	−2.53	−6.14
1979	1.4962 (−5.13)	0.3049 (−9.42)	11.69	2.00	11.42	4.29	0.27
1980	1.5303 (2.28)	0.3011 (−1.25)	14.92	7.41	13.49	8.36	6.26
1981	1.7455 (14.06)	0.3080 (2.30)	13.83	2.43	10.78	22.41	13.69
1982	1.9227 (10.15)	0.2980 (−3.25)	10.52	1.98	5.72	13.89	5.29
1983	1.9809 (3.03)	0.2530 (−15.10)	9.92	1.94	3.11	4.20	−7.12
1984	2.5755 (30.02)	0.3549 (41.90)	8.42	2.67	4.33	31.68	47.65
1985	3.2015 (24.31)	0.4079 (13.62)	4.16	11.87	3.65	16.09	5.91
1986	3.7221 (16.26)	0.4768 (16.89)	4.02	7.13	1.82	10.95	13.78
1987	3.7221 (0.00)	0.4790 (0.46)	5.26	8.67	3.69	−4.98	−2.95
1988	3.7221 (0.00)	0.4761 (−0.61)	7.4	20.80	4.02	−16.78	−14.01
1989	4.7221 (26.87)	0.6048 (27.03)	9.68	16.27	4.86	15.46	20.44
1990	5.2221 (10.59)	0.6699 (10.76)	9.76	1.42	5.37	14.54	19.1
1991	5.4121 (3.64)	0.6943 (3.64)	10.98	5.10	4.20	2.74	9.52
1992	5.7553 (6.34)	0.7431 (7.03)	9.63	8.56	3.07	0.85	8.1
1993	5.8382 (1.44)	0.7509 (1.05)	8.79	17.00	2.98	−12.58	−7.16
Average	(8.42)	(5.26)	9.04	7.26	5.63	6.79	7.04

Note: IN$_i$ denotes inflation rate of country i.
R$_{CU}$ and R$_{CH}$ denote real exchange rate changes in China relative to the United States and Hong Kong dollars. The negative sign represents RMB revaluation. Figures in brackets denote percentage change in exchange rate.

Source: Exchange rate data (year-end) were taken from State Statistical Bureau, *Statistical Year Book of China,* various issues. Inflation rate data were obtained from International Monetary Fund (1994).

The real RMB exchange rate changes relative to the Hong Kong dollar are positive for most of the time during the study period, except for 1983, 1987, 1988 and 1993. That means that the RMB exchange rate has a real depreciation versus the Hong Kong dollar. This appears to be a contributory factor prompting many Hong Kong manufacturers to move their production process to the Mainland in an attempt to reduce their production costs and maintain their competitiveness internationally.

Retained Imports From China

Hong Kong is a tiny place with a dense population of over 6 million. To meet the needs of this population and the requirements of its diverse industries, Hong Kong is almost entirely dependent on imported resources. Because of Hong Kong's geographical proximity to China, it is natural to rely on China as a major source of imports.[8] From the mid–1950s, Hong Kong became a prominent market for exports from China and most of China's exports were consumed in Hong Kong. In 1966, retained imports from China accounted for 82 percent of Hong Kong's imports from China and 25.9 percent of Hong Kong's total retained imports. Since then, Japan has taken over the role of top supplier of Hong Kong's retained imports. As Table 8.3 shows, China's exports retained in Hong Kong have been stagnant since 1987. The ratio of Hong Kong's retained imports from China to Hong Kong's total imports from China has declined drastically from 41.4 percent in 1986 to 12.9 percent in 1993. One of the contributory factors has been the decline in food exports from the Mainland, despite rising per capita income in Hong Kong. The proportion of total Chinese food exports retained in Hong Kong fell by more than 50 percent during the 1980s. In addition, China has been unable to capture the higher end of Hong Kong's market, which is dominated by Japan, the United States and Taiwan. Besides, Hong Kong consumers, in general, have a perception of Chinese goods as cheap, but inferior in quality and design, especially in manufacturing products. This has shifted the demand for these goods to other overseas countries, like Taiwan and South Korea. Recently, Taiwan and South Korea have emerged as important sources of supply to Hong Kong.[9] Given the increasing affluence of Hong Kong and the Japanese dominance in motor vehicles, quality electrical appliances, and fashionable consumer goods, the future of Chinese products, especially manufacturing products, in the Hong Kong market will not be optimistic.[10]

Since China is the predominant supplier of foodstuffs and agricultural products to Hong Kong, China has closely monitored price conditions for these products in the Hong Kong market and uses export licences to control the volume of exports so as to maximize commodity export income generated from this market. Indeed the importance of the Hong Kong market largely

Table 8.3 Hong Kong and China Trade (US$ Millions)

	HK imports from China			HK exports to China		
Year	Total	Retained in Hong Kong	Re-exported elsewhere	Total	Hong Kong goods	Hong Kong re-exports
1966	487	399	88 (18.1)	13	3	10 (83.3)
1970	467	376	9.1 (19.5)	11	5	6 (54.5)
1975	1378	1096	282 (20.5)	33	6	28 (84.8)
1977	1734	1306	428 (24.7)	44	7	38 (86.4)
1979	3044	2139	905 (29.7)	383	121	263 (68.7)
1981	5315	3479	1836 (34.5)	1961	523	1438 (73.3)
1983	5890	3725	2165 (36.8)	2531	856	1675 (66.2)
1984	7100	4224	2876 (40.5)	5033	1443	3590 (71.3)
1985	7449	3893	3556 (47.7)	7857	1950	5907 (75.2)
1986	10252	4963	5289 (51.6)	7550	2310	5241 (69.4)
1987	14776	6131	8645 (58.5)	11290	3574	7716 (68.3)
1988	19406	5926	13480 (69.5)	17030	4874	12157 (71.4)
1989	24431	5127	19310 (79.0)	18816	5548	13268 (70.5)
1990	29482	4825	24657 (83.6)	20305	6086	14219 (70.0)
1991	37615	5435	32180 (85.6)	26631	6974	19656 (73.8)
1992	45423	5513	39910 (87.9)	35141	7949	27192 (77.4)
1993	51564	6654	44910 (87.1)	43321	8116	35205 (81.3)

Note: Figures in parenthesis represent percentage of total exports (imports).
Source: Census and Statistics Department, Hong Kong Government, *Hong Kong Review of Overseas Trade*, various issues.

explained why the number of licenced export goods exceeded the number of licenced import goods in the 1980s.[11] As mentioned before, these goods are of inferior quality in nature and the volume of import demand for these goods declines with the affluence of Hong Kong people. In addition, most of the supplies of foodstuffs from China are quoted in Hong Kong dollars and some of the collective farms in Shenzhen exporting fresh vegetables and livestock to Hong Kong are run by Hong Kong investors. Together with the fact that other manufacturing products imported from China are primary in nature with low value-added (for example, yarn, fabrics, metals and metal products and fuels), the devaluation of the RMB has only a negligible effect on Hong Kong's retained imports from China.

Domestic Exports to China

Hong Kong's role as a direct supplier of goods to China has grown dramatically since 1978. In 1977, the share of Hong Kong domestic exports in China's total imports was only about 0.1 percent. In 1989, for the first time, domestic exports exceeded China's exports retained in Hong Kong, and since then Hong Kong's visible trade has had a direct trade surplus with China. However, it is important to note that, although an increasing proportion of Hong Kong domestic exports to China are of finished goods and for final consumption, the majority of these exports consisted of raw materials, parts, semi-manufactures, machinery and electrical equipment and were related to outward-processing activities commissioned by Hong Kong enterprises, amidst the tight labour market and high rent situation in Hong Kong. This reflects the growing importance of outward-processing activities in southern China. Analysed by broad commodity categories, as shown in Table 8.4, watches and clocks, toys and sports equipment, stereo and video equipment have the highest share in domestic exports to China during the period from 1989 to 1992.[12] The same commodity categories were found to have the highest share in imports from China as well. Machinery and electrical appliances had the lowest proportion in both domestic exports to China and re-exports from China. The percentage of outward-processing trade with respect to most individual commodity groups was close to their import equivalents, except the ratio for machinery and electrical equipment which were somewhat lower than the others. In a large measure, we might expect that this is due to the existence of a strong demand for such Hong Kong products in China. The same was true for re-exports as there was a large market in China for foreign machinery, electrical equipment, consumer electronics such as television sets and sound recorders, as well as metals and metal products.[13]

The devaluation of the RMB would increase the import price and lower the import demand for these goods. However the positive income effect due to the growth of per capita income in China has outweighed the adverse price effect of devaluation; thus we continue to observe a strong demand for these goods.

Table 8.4 Percentage Share of Trade of Outward-Processing Nature to
Total With China by Commodity Groups, 1989 and 1992

Commodity group	Domestic exports		Re-exports		Imports	
	1989	1992	1989	1992	1989	1992
Textiles	84.8	87.4	71.5	81.9	12.8	23.0
Clothing	85.1	93.2	87.3	76.0	84.5	84.4
Plastic products	83.9	77.5	58.0	64.5	73.4	89.3
Machinery and electrical appliances	56.7	59.7	24.9	27.3	77.8	81.0
Electronic products	94.6	92.7	43.1	41.4	85.2	92.7
Watches and clocks	98.5	98.6	92.5	97.7	94.6	94.3
Toys, games and sports goods	96.4	91.9	60.1	80.1	94.1	96.9
Metals and metal products	64.2	69.0	37.8	34.8	30.2	43.6
All commodities	76.0	74.3	43.6	46.2	58.1	72.1

Source: Census and Statistics Department, Hong Kong Government, *Hong Kong External Trade*, various issues.

THE RE-EXPORT AND OUTWARD-PROCESSING TRADE WITH CHINA

Since the adoption of an open-door policy by China in the late 1970s, one of the significant impacts on the Hong Kong economy has been the change in trade structure. The obvious evidence is the rise of re-exporting from the territory and the increasing economic integration with southern China, particularly Guangdong. In 1988, for the first time, the value of re-exports exceeded domestic exports (see Table 8.5). In 1993, 78.7 percent of Hong Kong's total export were re-exports. The share of re-exports of Chinese products via Hong Kong in total imports from China rose from 24.7 percent in 1977 to 87.1 percent in 1993. Since 1980, China has become the largest source of, as well as the largest market for, Hong Kong's re-exports. In 1992, China accounted for 58.4 percent of Hong Kong's re-exports by origin and 30.7 percent by destination. The re-export trade involving China reached US$80,115 million in 1993 and accounted for 76 percent of Hong Kong's total re-export in that year. Due to robust growth in outward processing activities, as well as continued trade expansion in China, it is envisioned that the share of re-exports will completely outweigh that of domestic exports in the foreseeable future.

As mentioned above, the most dramatic manifestation of China's economic reform and open-door policy was to attract foreign direct investment (FDI). Together with continuous import and export expansion, FDI has not only increased exposure of the Chinese economy to the outside world, but also

Table 8.5 Hong Kong's Visible Trade (HK$ Millions)

Year	Domestic exports	Percentage change	Re-exports	Percentage change	Total exports	Total imports	Percentage change
1974	22 911	17.6	7124	9.2	30 035	34 120	17.6
1975	22 859	−0.2	6973	−2.1	29 832	33 472	−1.9
1976	32 629	42.7	8928	28.0	41 557	43 293	−29.3
1977	35 004	7.3	9829	10.1	44 833	48 701	12.5
1978	40 711	16.3	13 197	34.3	53 908	63 056	29.5
1979	55 912	37.3	20 022	51.7	75 934	85 837	36.1
1980	68 171	21.9	30 072	50.2	98 243	111 651	30.1
1981	80 423	18.0	41 739	38.8	122 162	138 375	23.9
1982	83 032	3.2	44 353	6.3	127 385	142 893	3.3
1983	104 405	25.7	56 294	26.9	160 699	175 442	22.8
1984	137 936	32.1	83 504	48.3	221 440	223 370	27.3
1985	129 882	−5.8	105 270	26.1	235 152	231 420	3.6
1986	153 983	18.6	122 546	16.4	276 529	275 955	19.2
1987	195 254	26.8	182 780	49.2	378 034	377 948	37.0
1988	217 664	11.5	275 405	50.7	493 069	498 798	32.0
1989	224 104	3.0	346 405	25.8	570 509	562 781	12.8
1990	225 875	0.8	413 999	19.5	639 874	642 530	14.2
1991	231 045	2.3	534 841	29.2	765 886	778 982	21.2
1992	234 123	1.3	690 829	29.2	924 952	955 295	22.6
1993	223 027	−4.7	823 224	19.2	1 046 251	1 072 597	12.3

Source: Census and Statistics Department, Hong Kong Government, *Hong Kong Annual Digest of Statistics*, (1978–1994).

caused a drastic change in the trade structure of Hong Kong, thus having a significant impact on the economic structure of Hong Kong. With this policy, Hong Kong enterprises started to invest in China in order to take advantage of the abundant cheap labour and land supply by moving their labour-intensive manufacturing base to the open coastal area of southern China.[14] Through this spatial division of labour, Hong Kong's manufacturing industry has been able to maintain its international competitiveness.[15] This development gives rise to a large volume of what is called 'outward-processing trade' between Hong Kong and China.

In this outward-processing trade, there are both exports and imports. As regards exports, it included both domestic exports and re-exports of raw materials, parts and semi-manufactures from and through Hong Kong to China, normally with import duties exempted, for processing with a contractual arrangement for subsequent reshipment of the processed goods either to Hong Kong for final packaging and further processing if necessary or elsewhere via Hong Kong. On the other hand, there were imports from China of which all or part of the raw materials and semi-manufactures, including near-finished products, were under contractual arrangement previously exported to China from or through Hong Kong for further processing if necessary in Hong Kong before export to third countries. In the last decade, the continued shift of production facilities or part of the production processes to the Pearl River delta region, which is situated just next to Hong Kong, has effectively enlarged Hong Kong's productive capacity. It is estimated that almost four-fifths of Hong Kong's manufacturers have transferred their production base to the Mainland and around 25 000 to 30 000 factories just in the Pearl River delta region alone are engaged in outward-processing for Hong Kong companies, while between three and four million local Chinese workers are directly or indirectly employed by these firms.[16] In the late 1980s, the manufacturing sector has been able to release a good portion of its labour resources to other sectors which are likewise faced with the problem of labour recruitment in an overall very tight labour market. The service sector in general, and trading, finance and business services in particular have been absorbing these labour resources and their relative contributions to the domestic economy have been rising as a result. It was estimated, on a conservative assumption, that the processing/assembly fees, including transport costs, that China earns from such operations constituted no more than 20 percent of the value of the exports, and the average re-export mark-up margin for these finished products of Chinese origin for the period 1990 to 1993 was as high as 21.7 percent.[17] In 1992, 68 percent of China's exports to the United States went through Hong Kong in the form of re-exports.

Since the exports of raw materials, parts and semi-manufactures for outward-processing activities in China are exempted from import duties and, under the contractual arrangement, the finished product has to be exported to Hong Kong for final packaging and further processing if necessary before re-export to third countries, the RMB devaluation relative to the Hong Kong dollar helps reduce production costs (since wages and land cost are paid in RMB) and thus offsets rising production costs due to inflation in the Pearl River delta region (and China in general). Moreover, as a large portion of their exports consists of consumer goods such as clothing, footwear, toys, and watches and clocks, which are price sensitive to currency fluctuations, any RMB depreciation would make such goods more competitive in foreign markets, leading to a significant increase in demand. Alternatively, the profit margins will be higher if Hong Kong manufacturers choose not to lower the price of their exports. Thus, other than the push and pull factors suggested in most of the literature, the continued RMB depreciation versus the US and Hong Kong dollars in real terms since the mid-1980s has been a contributory factor prompting many Hong Kong companies, including non-manufacturers, to move to the Mainland in an attempt to reduce their costs and increase their profits. The recent more stringent government legislation to control industrial pollution has further accelerated this trend. It is believed that a closer economic integration between Hong Kong and Guangdong will result. As this trend continues to develop, there will be a rapid development of the service sector (trade, transport, finance and communications) and a fading manufacturing industry, thus confirming the change in the industrial structure of Hong Kong.

By contrast, investors in China's retail industry will be adversely affected by the devaluation as their earnings will be eroded. The situation, however, is not as bad as expected because the RMB devaluation would only raise the nominal price of imports, but not their scarce price, and thus this does not add to inflation. After devaluation, the usual inflationary effects would only be in the short run for, under exchange control, devaluation has significant deflationary effects.[18] In the short run, export earnings might decrease due to the J-curve effect. If export earnings can be increased, the bottleneck on production can be overcome and output can be increased. Therefore devaluation of the RMB exchange rate is deflationary rather than inflationary. Thus demand for imports might not be decreased.

As mentioned above, domestic exports to China consist of two types: one for final consumption and the other for outward-processing purposes. The two portions are rather unequal in terms of value. In 1992, the outward-processing portion accounts for 72 percent of total domestic exports (see Table 8.6). The portion for final consumption depends on prevailing economic conditions in China; while the outward-processing portion is affected by the economic conditions of the global economy, as the finished products are eventually shipped via Hong Kong to industrial countries, such as the United

Table 8.6 Hong Kong's Domestic Exports to China: Estimated Value and Share Involving Outward Processing (*sanlai yibu*)

Quarter	Estimated value of outward processing (HK$ million)	Estimated proportion of outward processing (percentage of total)	Estimated proportion of conventional trade (percentage of total)
1989	31 392	73.9	26.1
1990	36 418 (13.04)	76.7	23.3
1991	40 369 (10.85)	74.2	25.8
1992	44 271 (9.67)	71.8	28.2
1993	45 141 (1.97)	71.3	28.7
1994	41 959 (−7.05)	68.8	31.2

Note: Estimated value of *sanlai yibu* are not available before 1989.
           Figures in brackets denote percentage change.
Source: Census and Statistics Department, Hong Kong Government, *Hong Kong Monthly Digest*, (1991–95), various issues.

States, Japan and Western European countries. In the first quarter of 1993, domestic exports for final consumption rose 21.7 percent, while those for outward-processing increased by 18.7 percent. Such a performance was mainly the result of China's robust economic growth. With the steady growth in household income, despite the devaluation of the RMB in November 1991, a strong demand for imports was observed before the government introduced macroeconomic and administrative measures to cool its overheated economy.

THE EMPIRICAL EVIDENCE

Our estimation of the growth rate of Hong Kong's domestic exports to China (HKDXC), re-exports to China (HKRXC) and imports from China (HKMC) on the real exchange rate changes of RMB relative to the Hong Kong dollar (R_{CH}) for the period 1979 to 1993 is shown in Table 8.7. For domestic exports, the estimated coefficient of R_{CH} is 0.327, which is as expected. This implies that a one-percent increase in the real exchange rate changes of the RMB relative to the Hong Kong dollar (that is, depreciation) will increase the growth of domestic exports to China by 0.33 percent. As mentioned before, domestic exports to China consist of two portions: those for outward processing and those for final consumption. The former, which accounted for 72 percent of total domestic exports in 1992, depends on economic conditions in Western economies, while the latter is affected by economic conditions in China. As a result of China's robust economic growth and steady growth in household

Table 8.7 The Estimation of the Growth Rate of Hong Kong Domestic Exports, Re-exports to China and Imports From China, 1979–1993

Dependent variable	β_0	β_1	R^2	SSE	DW	rho
HKDXC	28.05	0.327 (0.824)	0.773	5639.6	1.573	0.23
HKRXC	31.0	0.465 (0.658)	0.656	20074	1.972	0.384
HKMC	25.38	0.2718 (0.680)	0.428	5079.3	I.773	0.379

Note: For all equations, the explanatory variable is the rate of change in real RMB exchange rates relative to Hong Kong dollar. Therefore β_0 and β_1 are the coefficients of the intercept term and the explanatory variable respectively. Figures in parentheses are t-ratio. Since there existed autocorrelation in all of the original equations, the transformed equations were re-estimated by the Cochrane-Orcutt Iteration Method.

income, we expected to see an increase in domestic exports, despite devaluation of the RMB relative to the Hong Kong dollar. The estimated coefficient of R_{CH} is not statistically significantly different from zero. $R^2 = 0.773$, however, shows that 77.3 perent of the variation of the growth in domestic exports to China can be explained by the variations of changes in real RMB exchange rates relative to the HK dollar, R_{CH} , alone.

Similar results were obtained for the growth rate of re-exports to China. The estimated coefficient of R_{CH} is 0.465, which is as expected. This implies that a 1 percent increase in the real exchange rate changes of the RMB relative to the Hong Kong dollar will increase the growth rate of re-exports to China by 0.47 percent. The rationale behind this is similar to that of domestic exports. The estimated value involving outward-processing in re-exports to China is 46 percent in 1992 (see Table 8.8). The estimated proportion of re-exports for China's own consumption and those for outward processing are roughly equal in value. Following a similar argument, we expect to have a positive relationship between the growth rate of re-exports to China and the real exchange rate changes of the RMB relative to the Hong Kong dollar. The estimated coefficient of R_{CH}, again, is statistically insignificant. R^2, 0.656, shows that 66 percent of the variations of the growth rate of re-exports to China can be explained by the variations of the change in real RMB exchange rates relative to the Hong Kong dollar, R_{CH} , alone.

Table 8.8 Hong Kong's Re-exports to China: Estimated Value and Share Involving Outward Processing (*sanlai yibu*)

Quarter	Estimated value of outward processing (HK$ millions)	Estimated proportion of outward processing (percentage of total)	Estimated proportion of conventional trade (percentage of total)
1989	44 906	43.4	56.6
1990	55 496 (23.58)	50.0	50.0
1991	735 626 (32.55)	48.0	52.0
1992	97 368 (32.36)	45.9	54.1
1993	115 037 (18.15)	41.9	58.1
1994	139 221 (21.02)	43.1	56.9

Note: Estimated value of *sanlai yibu* are not available before 1989.
Figures in brackets denote percentage change.
Source: Census and Statistics Department, Hong Kong Government, *Hong Kong Monthly Digest*, (1991–95), various issues.

For the growth rate of imports from China, the estimated coefficient of R_{CH} is 0.27, which is as expected. This implies that a one-percent increase in the real exchange rate changes of the RMB relative to the Hong Kong dollar will increase the growth rate of imports from China by 0.27 percent. Again most of the imports from China, 72 percent of total imports in 1992 (see Table 8.9), are the reshipment of the processed goods to Hong Kong for final packaging and further processing, if necessary, before exporting to Western countries. The estimated coefficient, again, is not statistically significantly different from zero. The F statistics, which is 2.243, is not significant at the five-percent level. This confirms that the changes in real RMB exchange rates relative to the Hong Kong dollar, R_{CH}, alone cannot explain the variations of the growth rate in imports from China. Other variables, like the growth rate of real GNP in the United States and the real exchange rate changes of the RMB relative to the US dollar, might need to be incorporated in the model in future research. The simple model, with only one explanatory variable, has been used in this chapter to investigate if there exists any impact on Hong Kong and China trade upon the devaluation of the RMB relative to the Hong Kong dollar. Basically the model works reasonably well and confirms our analysis in previous sections.

Table 8.9 Hong Kong's imports from China: Estimated Value and Share Involving Outward Processing *(sanlai yibu)*

Quarter	Estimated value of outward processing (HK$ millions)	Estimated proportion of outward processing (percentage of total)	Estimated proportion of conventional trade (percentage of total)
1989	113 581	57.7	42.3
1990	145 103 (27.75)	61.5	38.5
1991	197 384 (36.03)	67.3	32.7
1992	254 013 (28.69)	71.7	29.3
1993	295 203 (16.22)	73.4	26.6
1994	354 912 (20.23)	75.4	24.6

Note: Estimated value of *sanlai yibu* are not available before 1989. Figures in brackets denote percentage change.
Source: Census and Statistics Department, Hong Kong Government, *Hong Kong Monthly Digest*, (1991–95), various issues.

CONCLUSION

As China continues to launch its economic reform and adopt its open-door policy and becomes more market-oriented, the country will slowly move towards its goal of full convertibility of the RMB on the current account by the year 2000. The 33 percent depreciation of the RMB in January 1994 and the unification of China's dual exchange rate was the first step in making the RMB convertible for trade and trade-related transactions. To comply with the Memorandum of Understanding (MOU) and GATT/WTO in its bid to become a founding member of the WTO, the Chinese government has committed itself to reform its trade regime in the context of market access and its foreign exchange system.

As part of the reform of its trade regime and market access, in December 1993, China reduced the import tariffs on 2898 items. As a result, China's current average tariff rate is reduced to 36.4 percent. At the same time, the import licensing requirement was lifted on 283 items. In addition, import quotas on 195 items were abolished in May 1994. To meet the requirements of the GATT/WTO, China has promised to phase out all import licences and quotas by 1999. It has also set up a committee to draft a proposal for comprehensive tariff reductions for the country's accession to the GATT/WTO.

As part of the foreign exchange reform, in April 1994, the interbank foreign exchange market — the Shanghai Foreign Exchange Trading Center (FETC) — which links with 25 other Chinese cities, including Beijing, Tianjin, Shenzhen, Hangzhou and Xiamen, began to operate in Shanghai. The principal dealers are authorized foreign exchange banks which set the buying and selling prices of foreign exchange against the RMB within a prescribed range. The exchange rate of the RMB will then be determined primarily by market forces. Furthermore, China has already partially liberalized its current account by allowing domestic firms to obtain foreign exchange from designated banks for merchandise trade purposes upon presentation of either an import contract or import licence (if required). Given that the Chinese economy is still in a state of transition, further reform of the foreign exchange system including eliminating the requirement for the surrender of foreign exchange, liberalizing access to the swap centres, and making the system more transparent can only be achieved at later stage.

In the long term, the new exchange rate system will be beneficial to China and Hong Kong. It will stimulate FDI in China and speed up the country's reform and the process of induction to GATT/WTO. As China's external trade continues to expand, the intermediary role of Hong Kong will also be enhanced. Even though there might be more direct trade between China and the rest of the world, Hong Kong is likely to maintain its role as entrepôt and gateway to China, as Hong Kong continues to have the edge over China in infrastructure, banking and insurance, communication facilities, marketing, financing, quality control, product design and production management. Thus Hong Kong will become more important as an entrepôt as well as a control base for China in the future.

NOTES

1. Since the 1980s, China has operated a dual exchange rate system. The official exchange rate is set daily and generally applies to priority imports for state enterprises under the State Plan. The 'swap' rate, China's second rate, is determined at foreign exchange adjustment centres (FEAC). Joint ventures, foreign invested enterprises and domestic trading firms with access to foreign exchange may buy and sell foreign exchange quoted at the swap centres. Swap centre rates are established through an open bidding system (in 15 centres) or as the State Administration of Exchange Control (SAEC) matches applications for foreign exchange (in approximately 85 centres).

    From 1980 to 1992, China continued to maintain extensive restrictions on access to foreign exchange. For goods on the restricted list, an enterprise must receive a licence from the Ministry of Foreign Trade and Economic Cooperation (MOFTEC) before it can buy foreign exchange in the swap centres. For those goods that do not require MOFTEC approval, access is based on a priority list of uses of foreign exchange drawn up in conformity with state industrial policy. The authorities generally discourage purchases of foreign exchange to finance imports of goods not formally approved by the government. In April 1992, the authorities issued new guidelines outlining priorities for access to foreign exchange in the swap centres. Preferred access was given to those purchasing foreign exchange for agricultural inputs and products, interest payments and remittances, technology imports, and inputs to key construction projects. Access to swap centres was also granted for purchases of foreign exchange for industrial inputs, educational materials and some spare parts. Purchases of foreign exchange for a wide range of consumer and luxury goods, such as cigarettes, wine, clothing, household appliances, and photographic film etc. are prohibited (USIS, 27 March 1993).

    On 1 January 1994, China unified its dual exchange rates at the more depreciated swap centre rate and announced it would abolish swap centres in favour of an interbank market for foreign exchange. The new, unified exchange operates as a managed float, with the People's Bank of China (PBOC) setting each day's exchange rate according to market conditions and relative to the price for foreign exchange on the previous day. While domestic firms are still required to surrender their foreign exchange, with effect from 1 April 1994, government approval would no longer be required for purchases of foreign exchange for trade and trade-related current account transactions. Moreover, companies are allowed to purchase foreign exchange automatically from designated banks upon presentation of: an import contract; a request for payment from a foreign institution; and an import licence (if required).

    The new regulations on 26 March 1994 maintained the requirement that foreign-funded firms must use the existing swap centres and may trade their surplus or deficit of foreign exchange in the swap centres but only with other foreign-funded enterprises. The State Administration of Exchange Control must approve individual foreign exchange transactions and has the authority to deny access to foreign exchange for purposes that do not accord with national policy (USIS, 25 July 1994).

2. In 1978, the average domestic currency cost of earning US$1 in export sales is 2.53 yuan, while the average official exchange rate is 1.68 Yuan. The situation has not much improved in the post-reform era. In 1988, the average domestic currency cost of earning US$1 in export sales was 5.80 yuan, while the average official exchange rate was 3.78 Yuan.

3. The RMB exchange rates for all other foreign currencies are calculated according to their respective prevailing exchange rates with the US dollar.

4. Trade liberalization in 1984 triggered a rush for imports, doubling China's expenditure

on foreign merchandise from US$21.4 billion in 1983 to US$42.2 billion in 1985. As exports rose just 23 percent, the result was an unacceptably large trade deficit of US$14.9 billion. To narrow this gap, the Chinese government mobilized trade policy as well as the administrative devices at its disposal. In July 1986, the RMB was devalued to US$1=3.72 yuan.

5. At year end 1988, the average exchange rate at adjustment centres was almost 7 yuan per US dollar compared with the official rate of 3.72 yuan per US dollar. Subsequently, the official rate was devalued twice (in December 1989 and November 1990) and in late 1990 it stood at 5.2 yuan per US dollar, compared with the average rate of about 5.7 Yuan per US dollar.

6. On 1 January 1994 China's dual exchange rates were unified at the rate of 8.72 yuan per US dollar. The unification represents an effective depreciation of 31 percent.

7. Hong Kong accounts for 68.2 percent of China's foreign direct investment (FDI), and in Guangdong province 82.5 percent of contractual FDI and 76.4 percent of the realized FDI come from Hong Kong in 1993.

8. Aside from the usual merchandise imports, around 75 to 80 percent of fresh water now consumed in Hong Kong is imported from China.

9. Not only has Taiwan surpassed the United Kingdom as Hong Kong's major supplier since the mid-1970s, it has also replaced the United States since 1987, and become Hong Kong's third target import source.

10. In the 1980s, even though the quantity of China's exports to Hong Kong — of consumer goods, capital goods, raw materials and semi-manufactures and other commodities — as a whole grew faster than those from other exporting countries, the unit value indices of Hong Kong imports from China rose slower than the indices for other exporting economies in all end-use categories except fuels. The overall unit index of imports from China in 1989 was 129, lower than that of Hong Kong's imports from all sources, which was 151. For consumer goods, it was 138 from China and 163 from all supply sources. Such differentials in price movements should reflect that retained imports from China or at least their commodity composition were not so welcome in Hong Kong. See Tien-tung Hsueh and Tun-oy Woo, 'The development of China's foreign trade and the role of Hong Kong, 1979–1989', in Edward K.Y. Chen and T. Maruya (eds.), *Guangdong 'Open Door' Economic Development Strategy,* Centre of Asian Studies, The University of Hong Kong, 1992, p.81.

11. In 1989, only 45 imports were licensed but 212 commodities were subjected to export licensing; 175 were required only when they were sold to Hong Kong, only 37 were required for all international markets. See Nicholas Lardy, *Foreign Trade and Economic Reform in China, 1979–1990* (Cambridge: Cambridge University Press, 1992).

12. Because of the rapid expansion of the outward-processing trade with China since 1980s, the Hong Kong Census and Statistics Department began to compile statistics on domestic exports and re-exports to China for outward-processing purposes in the third quarter of 1988; and statistics on imports from China related to outward-processing in the first quarter of 1989.

13. Y.P. Ho and Y.Y. Kueh, 'Whither Hong Kong in an open-door, reforming Chinese economy?' *The Pacific Review,* Vol. 6, No. 4 (1993).

14. The rising production costs from high wages, the soaring prices and rentals of industrial and commercial premises eroded profit margins and competitiveness in international markets. These are the main pushing factors of Hong Kong's outward investment, while abundant labour supply, abundant land supply and market potential are the main pulling factors.

15. According to the Hang Seng Economic Monthly Survey in 1989, the monthly wage level of unskilled labour was US$412 in Hong Kong, while that in Shenzhen was

US$75 (HK$585) making Hong Kong's labour at least five times as expensive as that in Shenzhen. Moreover, the monthly industrial rental cost per square foot was HK$8 (New Kowloon) compared to around HK$0.8–1.50 in Shenzhen, which was about one-tenth to one-fifth of the Hong Kong's rental cost.

16. In fact, the report of the Hong Kong Government Industry Department shows that the manufacturing sector's contribution to Hong Kong's GDP has dropped from 20.8 percent in 1982 to 13.7 percent in 1992. The number of persons engaged in manufacturing industry declined only from 892 140 in 1982 to 508 133 in 1993. The magnitude of the outward-processing component was about five to seven times as large as Hong Kong manufacturing workforce.

17. According to Hongkong Bank, 'Recent developments in Hong Kong — China export patterns', *Economic Report,* September 1994, the average re-export margins on Hong Kong's re-export of China origin:

Year	1990	1991	1992	1993	1994(H1)
%	17.4	20.5	22.9	26.1	26.5

18. Yun-wing Sung, 'The impact of the devaluation of the Renminbi on China's trade', in T.T. Hsueh, Y.W. Sung and J. Yu, (eds.), *Studies on Economic Reforms and Development in the People's Republic of China* (Hong Kong: The Chinese University Press, 1993).

9

The Implications of China's Admission to the WTO for Greater China

Yun-wing Sung

INTRODUCTION

The opening of China coincided with the emergence of severe labour shortages in Hong Kong and Taiwan and the need for the latter two economies to restructure. The export-oriented, labour-intensive industries of Hong Kong and Taiwan have moved to Guangdong and Fujian on a large scale. The economic integration of Greater China has been largely market-driven, and occurred without a multilateral institutional framework. The very intense trade and investment flows among the trio (China, Taiwan and Hong Kong) has led to the emergence of Greater China, which in turn has had dramatic impacts on world trade and investment.

Hong Kong accounted for around 60 percent of the total inward foreign direct investment (FDI) in China and Taiwan was a distant second with a share of 8 percent. Such investments have generated huge trade flows. In 1994, enterprises with foreign investment (including processing operations and foreign invested enterprises), mostly operated by investors from Hong Kong and Taiwan, accounted for 44 percent of China's exports. In the same year, Hong Kong's re-exports of goods made in Guangdong under outward-processing contracts were US$51.6 billion, vastly exceeding the domestic exports of Hong Kong (that is, exports of goods made in Hong Kong) of US$28.7 billion and also Thailand exports of US$45 billion. It is no exaggeration to say that the synergy of China's cheap labour with Hong Kong and Taiwan know-how and capital is the main factor behind China's spectacular export drive.

In terms of the degree of economic integration, there are three concentric layers in the China Circle, with the Hong Kong-Guangdong economic nexus or Greater Hong Kong as the core; Greater South China (GSC) covering Hong Kong, Guangdong, Fujian and Taiwan as the inner layer; and Greater China covering Hong Kong, Taiwan and China as the outer layer. Within GSC, Hong Kong and South China are much more tightly integrated than Taiwan and South China. This is a result of both geography (there is no land bridge connecting Taiwan with the Mainland) and Taiwan's policy of no direct business links with China. Hong Kong is the pivot for the integration of the China Circle as most Taiwan-Mainland transactions occur via Hong Kong.

Table 9.1 shows the basic economic indicators of Greater China. Guangdong's 1994 exports of US$50.2 billion surpassed Hong Kong domestic exports of US$28.7 billion and also exports from Thailand of US$45 billion. Fujian was a distant second to Guangdong in terms of economic strength. Macau's economy is much smaller than that of Hong Kong and can be regarded as an appendage of the Hong Kong economy.

Table 9.1 Basic Indicators of Greater China, 1994 and 1995

Indicators	Hong Kong 1994	1995	Taiwan 1994	1995	Macau 1994	China 1994	1995	Guangdong 1994	1995	Fujian 1994
Area (sq.km)	1068	–	35961	–	19	960 000	–	177 901	–	121 400
Population (million)	6.01	6.19	21.13	21.30	0.41	1199	1211	66.91	–	31.8
GDP (US$bn)	130.3	142.0	243.7	257.2	6.5	522.3	691.4	49.2	65.1	19.6
Per Capita (US$)	21 501	23 019	11 520	12 490	15 878	436	571	736	–	614
GDP growth rate (%)	+5.4	+4.6	+6.1	+6.3	+4.0	+11.8	+10.2	+18	+15	+21
Exports (US$bn)	151.4[a] 28.7[b]	172.3 30.0	93. 0 –	111.7 –	1.87 –	121.7 –	148.8 –	50.2[c] 47.0[d]	– 56.6[d]	– 8.1

Note: a Total exports (including re-exports)
       b Domestic exports
       c China Customs Statistics
       d MOFERT (Ministry of Foreign Economic Relations and Trade) statistics
Source: *Statistical Yearbook*, various issues; *Hong Kong Monthly Digest of Statistics; Monthly Bulletin of Statistics of Republic of China*; Far Eastern Economic Review: *Asia Yearbook.*

Taiwan should be able to join the World Trade Organizaton (WTO) after China's entry. The entry of China and Taiwan into the WTO would promote the integration of the trio in many ways. To qualify for WTO membership, China must radically reform its trading system and Taiwan has to further liberalize its trade. This would allow greater scope for market forces to strengthen the integration of the trio. WTO membership would also give China and Taiwan some recourse against protectionism. This would facilitate the relocation of the labour-intensive, export-oriented industries of Hong

Kong and Taiwan to the Mainland. WTO membership for both the Mainland and Taiwan would also strengthen the reformers in the Mainland as well as strengthen the international position of Taiwan. Taipei can thus afford to allow its ties with the Mainland to grow further.

This chapter will examine the impact of China's entry into the WTO on Greater China and beyond. After the introduction, the second section on pp. 183–188 will briefly describe the pattern of trade and investment among the trio. The third section on pp. 188–192 will analyse the characteristics of the economic integration of the trio. The impact of China's entry into the WTO will then be analysed, including the effects on economic reforms in China (pp. 192–193), on macrostability in China (pp. 192–193), on commodity trade (pp. 194–195), on services trade (p. 196), and on Taiwan's relationship with China (pp. 197–198). The ninth section (pp. 198–201) examines the proposals to strengthen the integration of Greater China. The tenth section (pp. 201–202) examines the impacts of APEC (Asian Pacific Economic Community) on China's admission to the WTO.

TRADE AND INVESTMENT AMONG THE TRIO

Table 9.2 shows China's contracted inward investment by source. Hong Kong is by far the largest investor in China and Taiwan is a distant second while the United States and Japan are in third and fourth places. The large share of Hong

Table 9.2 Contracted Foreign Investment in China by Source, 1979–94 (US$ Millions)

	1979–90	1991	1992	1993	1994*	1979–94
National Total	45 244 (100)	12 422 (100)	58 736 (100)	111 967 (100)	82 680 (100)	311 049 –
Hong Kong	26 480 (58.5)	7531 (60.6)	40 502 (69.0)	74 264 (66.3)	47 158 (57.0)	195 935 (63.0)
Taiwan	2000 (4.4)	1392 (11.2)	5548 (9.4)	9,970 (8.9)	5384 (6.5)	24 322 (7.8)
US	4476 (9.9)	555 (4.5)	3142 (5.3)	6879 (6.1)	6054 (7.3)	21 096 (6.8)
Japan	3662 (8.1)	886 (7.1)	2200 (3.7)	3015 (2.7)	4070 (4.9)	13 833 (4.4)

Note: *   Preliminary data on foreign direct investment from *South China Morning Post*, 8 April 1995.
    Figures in brackets indicate percentage share of the national total.
Source: *Almanac of China's Foreign Relations and Trade*, various issues.

Kong in China's investment conceals an important middleman role of Hong Kong. In China's statistics, investment from Hong Kong includes the investment of the subsidiaries of foreign companies incorporated in Hong Kong. Many multinational companies like to test the Chinese investment environment through investments from their Hong Kong subsidiaries because Hong Kong has the required expertise and is the foremost centre for China's trade and investment. Chinese enterprises also invest in China from their Hong Kong subsidiaries to take advantage of the preferences given to foreign investors. There is no reliable estimate on the amount of Chinese capital 'round-tripping' via Hong Kong.

China-Hong Kong Investment Links

Hong Kong and China are each other's foremost partner in investment. Hong Kong's cumulative utilized FDI in China from 1978 to 1994 totalled US$60 billion. Guangdong accounted for 40 percent of Hong Kong's investment in China and a third of total FDI in China.

Hong Kong's industrial investment in Guangdong has transformed Hong Kong manufacturing as well as the entire Hong Kong economy. It is often reported that Hong Kong manufacturing firms employ up to 3 million workers in Guangdong, almost seven times the manufacturing labour force in Hong Kong. By moving the labour-intensive processes to Guangdong, Hong Kong can concentrate on the more skill-intensive processes such as product design, sourcing, production management, quality control, marketing, shipping, insurance, and business and financial services. Hong Kong has become the service centre of an industrialized Guangdong.

Hong Kong has also become the major funding centre for Chinese firms. A number of China investment funds were established which invested in industries and shares in China's stock markets. In 1992, China approved the public listing of selective state enterprises in the Hong Kong stock market and their shares are popularly called H-shares. By the end of 1994, H-shares and Red Chips (Hong Kong listed companies controlled by China) have a total capitalization of US$13.3 billion or 4 percent of the market capitalization of the Hong Kong stock market.[1]

Hong Kong is the prime destination for China's outward investment. Although precise data is lacking, it appears that China's cumulative investment reached US$20 billion in 1994 and that China has surpassed Japan to become the foremost investor in Hong Kong. China's investment strengthens the ties of Hong Kong to China and enhances the position of Hong Kong as the gateway to China. It is natural for Chinese enterprises and investors to move their capital to Hong Kong, as Hong Kong has stricter protection of property rights than China and the funds can also be used much more flexibly in Hong Kong.

China's Trade With Hong Kong

It is often said that Hong Kong and China are the foremost trading partners of each other. While the statement is technically true, it is misleading because it lumps together China's trade with third countries via Hong Kong (Hong Kong's entrepôt trade) and China's trade with Hong Kong itself.

As a large proportion of China's trade is conducted via Hong Kong in the form of entrepôt trade, China's statistics on its trade by country is very misleading, as evidenced by the well-known Sino-American dispute on the size of their bilateral deficits. Hong Kong's imports of Chinese goods in 1994 totalled US$58.7 billion or 49 percent of China's exports. Of Hong Kong's imports from China, 90 percent was re-exported to third countries and only 10 percent was retained in Hong Kong. Though China was by far the foremost supplier of Hong Kong's re-exports, with a share of 58 percent, China supplied only 9.5 percent of Hong Kong's retained imports. China was in the third place after Japan and the United States. Hong Kong's retained imports from China have been stagnating since 1987 and their share of Hong Kong's retained imports has declined sharply. China has been unable to capture the higher end of Hong Kong's market, which is dominated by Japan.

Hong Kong was the largest final market (that is, excluding Chinese exports via Hong Kong) for Chinese exports in the late 1960s and early 1970s, but the Hong Kong market was overtaken by the Japanese market and the US market in 1973 and 1987 respectively. Hong Kong consumed only 4.7 percent of China's exports in 1994.

Hong Kong's exports to China have increased extremely rapidly since 1978. China imported increasing quantities of Hong Kong goods, mostly components and semi-manufactures, as a result of the relocation of Hong Kong's manufacturing operations to China. Hong Kong's domestic exports to China in 1995 were US$8.2 billion or 6.2 percent of China's imports. Hong Kong was the fourth supplier of China after Japan, Taiwan and the United States. In 1995, Hong Kong's re-exports of third country goods to China were US$49.6 billion or 37.6 percent of China's imports. Hong Kong's total exports (domestic exports plus re-exports) to China accounted for 43.8 percent of China's imports in 1995.

Since China's opening in 1979, Hong Kong's role as China's entrepôt has been greatly enhanced by the decentralization of China's system of foreign trade. Decentralization vastly increased the number of trading partners and raised the cost of searching for a suitable trade partner. Intermediation emerged to economize on search costs, and this demand was channelled to Hong Kong due to its efficiency in trading.[2] Though China has established many more direct links with the outside world since 1978, the share of China's foreign trade handled via Hong Kong rose sharply. From 1979 to 1993, the share in

China's total exports of Chinese goods re-exported via Hong Kong rose from 6.6 percent to a peak of 51 percent,[3] and the share in China's total imports of Hong Kong's re-exports of third country goods to China rose from 1.7 percent to 34 percent.

Taiwan's Investment in China

Taiwan's initial investment in China was largely in small-scale, labour-intensive operations producing light manufactures for export. The industries involved include textiles, footwear, umbrellas, travel accessories and electronics. The projects were concentrated in Fujian, Guangdong and particularly in the Xiamen region of Fujian. However, Taiwanese investment was increasing in size and sophistication, with an increasing number of more technology-intensive projects such as chemicals, building materials, automobiles and electronic products and components. The fields of investment have diversified from manufacturing into real estate, finance, tourism and agriculture. The location of investment had spread inland from the coast.

The surge in Taiwanese investment in the Mainland raised fears that such investment would lead to the 'hollowing out' of Taiwan industry and also pose security concerns. The Taiwan government tried to cool down the Mainland investment boom by improving the investment environment in Taiwan and steering investment away from the Mainland to ASEAN Countries. To control the Mainland investment boom, Taiwan authorized 3319 products for indirect investment in September 1990. These were mostly labour-intensive products with a low level of processing. Authorization was not granted for investment in industries that were still competitive in Taiwan, including naphtha, catalysts, knitwear, synthetic leather, sheet glass and glass fibre.

China's Trade With Taiwan

The explosive growth of Taiwan's trade with the Mainland in the form of Hong Kong re-exports is well known and is regularly reported. Hong Kong statistics on re-exports of Taiwanese (Chinese) origin to China (Taiwan) have often been used by researchers to gauge the magnitude of Taiwan-Mainland trade. What is not well known is that there is a very substantial direct trade between Taiwan and the Mainland. Due to Taiwan's ban on direct trade with the mainland, this direct trade usually involves the switching of trade documents. Taiwanese exporters claim that their goods are destined for Hong Kong when the goods left Taiwan. However, on arrival in Hong Kong, the trade documents are switched, claiming that the goods are destined for the Mainland. As the goods are consigned to a buyer in the Mainland, they do not go through Hong Kong customs and are not recorded as part of Hong Kong's trade. Such trade is called 'direct trade' in this chapter because it looks like indirect trade in terms of trade documentation, involving two separate sets of trade documents, but is direct trade in reality because no third party buys the goods involved for resale. By switching trade documents, the Taiwanese exporters save on the expenses associated with going through Hong Kong customs and also preserve confidentiality of the transaction because Hong Kong customs keep no records of the trade.

In Taiwan's 'direct exports' to China, Taiwan usually records the exports as destined for Hong Kong. However, the goods are not imported into Hong Kong as they are shipped to the Mainland. Taiwan's 'direct exports' to the Mainland should be equal to the difference between Taiwan's exports to Hong Kong and Hong Kong's imports from Taiwan after adjusting for the cost of insurance and freight, that is, the difference between CIF and FOB prices. This represents an application of the trade-partners statistics technique. [4]

In 1994, Taiwan's 'direct exports' to the Mainland were US$8203 million, exceeding Taiwan's indirect exports to the Mainland via Hong Kong of US$7476 million. Taiwan's 1994 exports to the Mainland via Hong Kong (including direct and indirect exports) should thus be US$15 679 million or 16.8 percent of Taiwan's total exports. After adjusting for Hong Kong's re-export margin and the cost of insurance and freight, 1994 mainland imports from Taiwan should be US$17 995 million, or 15.6 percent of the Mainland's imports.

In 1994, Taiwan's 'direct imports' from China were US$2564 million while Taiwan's indirect imports from China via Hong Kong were only US$1361 million. Taiwan's total 1994 imports should thus be US$3925 million or 4.6 percent of Taiwan's imports. After adjusting for Hong Kong's re-export margin and the cost of insurance and freight, 1994 Mainland exports to Taiwan should be US$3569 million or 2.9 percent of the Mainland's total exports. By 1992, the Mainland had become the fourth largest supplier of Taiwan after Japan (30.2 percent), the United States (21.9 percent), and Germany (5.4 percent) just surpassing South Korea (3.2 percent). Taiwan has also become a significant market for the Mainland.

Taiwan has a massive surplus in its commodity trade with the Mainland, partly because of Taiwan's policy of only importing selective commodity items from the Mainland, and partly because of the lack of the Mainland's competitiveness in producing items demanded in Taiwan. However, Taiwan has large deficits with the Mainland in tourism, gifts and remittances, and in investment. The payments balance across the Taiwan straits is thus more even. Moreover, intra-industry trade is expected to develop rapidly with the surge in Taiwanese investment on the Mainland and the further liberalization of Taiwan's controls on imports from the Mainland.

It must be stressed that Taiwan-Mainland trade has grown extremely fast and is now very substantial. In 1992, the Mainland surpassed Japan to become the second largest market for Taiwan after the United States, which has a market share of 28.9 percent. In 1994, the market shares of the top four markets of Taiwan, namely, US, China, Japan, and Hong Kong (excluding re-exports elsewhere) in Taiwan's exports were 26.2 percent, 16.8 percent, 11.0 percent and 5.4 percent respectively. From 1986 to 1994, Taiwan's total exports to the Mainland increased 21.5 times, and the average annual rate of growth was 47 percent. Taiwan's exports to the United States has declined in absolute terms since 1987, and the Mainland, together with Hong Kong, may soon become Taiwan's largest market. By 1991, the Mainland's imports from Taiwan constituted 13 percent of the Mainland's total imports, and Taiwan has surpassed Hong Kong and the United States to become the Mainland's second largest supplier after Japan, which has a share of 20 percent.

As the potential size of the Mainland's economy is much bigger than that of Taiwan, the Mainland may become Taiwan's top market in the long term, but Taiwan is unlikely to be the Mainland's top supplier. Taiwan's manufacturing base is quite narrow and cannot produce the large variety of products demanded by the Mainland. When China liberalizes its imports, China's imports of final goods will increase relative to its imports of semi-manufactures, and it is likely to shift its imports to Japan and the West.

GREATER CHINA: CHARACTERISTICS OF ITS ECONOMIC INTEGRATION

Greater China differs in two crucial aspects from traditional trade blocs such as the European Union. Firstly, the economic integration of Greater China has developed naturally and spontaneously without a formal multilateral institutional arrangement such as discriminatory tariff preferences in the form of a free trade area or a customs union. Secondly, Greater China is an outward-looking instead of inward-looking economic area.

Greater Hong Kong was the first and most successful subregional economic zone in East Asia. As East Asian countries liberalize their economies in the 1980s, numerous subregional economic zones emerged due to the operation of geographic and market forces. Intense trade and investment flows grew among geographically contiguous but politically separated border areas, taking advantage of the complementarities in factor endowment and technological capacity among countries at different stages of economic development.[5] These subregional economic zones are variously called transnational export processing zones, natural economic territories[6] and growth triangles (ASEAN terminology). These zones include the **Tumen River area development project** in north-east Asia involving the Russian Far East, Mongolia, north-east China, the Korean peninsula and Japan; the **baht economic zone** encompassing Thailand and the contiguous border areas of southwest China, Myanmar, Laos, Cambodia and

Vietnam; the **Mekong River Basin Project** involving the riparian countries of Thailand, Myanmar, Vietnam, Laos, Cambodia and south-west China; and three growth triangles of ASEAN, namely, the **Southern Growth Triangle** involving Singapore, the Johore state in Malaysia, and Batam island in Indonesia, the proposed **Northern Growth Triangle** encompassing western Indonesia, northern Malaysia, and southern Thailand, and the proposed **Eastern Growth Triangle** involving Brunei, eastern Indonesia, the southern Philippines, and Sabah and Sarawak in Eastern Malaysia.[7] The success of the GSC was one of the factors that stimulated the formation of the **Southern Growth Triangle** of ASEAN in 1989.

Integration via Cultural Affinity

Despite the intense trade and investment flows among the trio, there is an obvious lack of institutional integration among them. Due to Taiwan's ban on direct business deals with the Mainland, China and Taiwan are institutionally more closely integrated with most economies than with each other.

Even though China will resume sovereignty over Hong Kong in 1997, it is specified in the Sino-British Agreement on Hong Kong that Hong Kong will remain a separate customs territory and will continue to have its own currency. Migration from China to Hong Kong will be strictly controlled. It can be argued, therefore, that, even after 1997, Hong Kong and the Mainland will be less institutionally integrated than Greece and Ireland, which are both members of the European Union (EU) with freedom of movement of goods and factors between the two countries. As China is not a member of the WTO and the Chinese currency is not convertible, Hong Kong is institutionally more closely integrated with most of the economies of the free world than with China.

Though economic theory concentrates on tariffs, controls on migration, and exchange integration, the effect of geographical and cultural distances may be even more important. Hong Kong is only half-an-hour's train ride from China, and Taiwan is quite close to China in terms of geography. The importance of cultural affinity is quite evident. People in Hong Kong have their ancestral roots in Guangdong, and Guangdong is the prime site of Hong Kong's investment in China. Taiwan has also accounted for the bulk of investment in Fujian. It should be noted that geographic and cultural proximity can enable businessmen to evade the formal barriers to trade and investment. Tariffs can be evaded through smuggling, and there is rampant smuggling from Hong Kong and Taiwan to China. The movement of people from Hong Kong and Taiwan to China is relatively free though movement in the other direction is highly controlled. However, illegal immigrants from the Mainland are quite common in Hong Kong and Taiwan, as the labour markets in the two economies are extremely tight. Though the Chinese *yuan* (renminbi) is not convertible, the Hong Kong currency has circulated widely (and unofficially) in Guangdong, especially in the Shenzhen Special Economic Zone. The Hong Kong government estimated that the amount of Hong Kong dollars circulating in China amounts to between 22 percent and 25 percent of the total supply of the Hong Kong currency, or roughly HK$17 billion (US$2.2 billion).[8] A grey market for *yuan* has also existed in Hong Kong for some time. The grey market was turned into an open market in 1993 when China officially permitted visitors to bring 6000 *yuan* out of or into China. Many Hong Kong tourist shops also accept payment in *yuan*.

Unilateral Policy Changes

Unilateral policy changes are also important in the integration of the trio. As mentioned earlier, China has tailored its open-door policy to build closer links with Hong Kong and Taiwan. Of the four SEZs (Special Economic Zones) established in 1979 with special autonomy in managing foreign trade and investment, Shenzhen and Zhuhai in Guangdong were adjacent to Hong Kong and Macau respectively; Fujian operates the Xiamen SEZ which is opposite to Taiwan. The Shantou SEZ in Guangdong has close links to overseas Chinese populations, including a community in Hong Kong that originated in Shantou.

Taiwanese businesses enjoy special concessions in China over all other overseas businesses. Taiwanese goods face lower taxes in China and the import controls on Taiwanese goods are less stringent. A 1988 State Council decree also gave Taiwanese investors favourable treatment over other foreign investors. Local authorities also tend to give Taiwanese investors more favourable treatment in terms of faster approval process or better supporting services.

Though the Mainland is more open to Taiwan than to any other economy, Taiwan is less open to the Mainland than to other economies. Taiwan's import controls on Mainland products have been gradually liberalized since 1987. The number of items allowed to be indirectly imported has increased from 29 items (in July 1987), to 90 items (in January 1989), to 155 items (in early 1990), and then to 1654 items by the end of 1993.[9] In July 1987, Taiwan eased its foreign exchange controls, and Taiwanese businesses started to invest indirectly on the Mainland via subsidiaries established in Hong Kong or elsewhere. In November that year, Taiwan allowed its citizens to visit their mainland relatives and Taiwanese visitors to the Mainland soared. In October 1989, Taiwan promulgated regulations sanctioning indirect trade, investment and technical cooperation with China. Taiwan's policy requires that all trade, investment and visits have to be conducted indirectly, that is via Hong Kong or third places. Taiwan still prohibits investment from the Mainland, though it is reported that the Mainland has invested in Taiwan through its overseas subsidiaries.

China is planning to abolish the special favours for Taiwanese and overseas Chinese investors as part of the reform package to gain entry into the WTO. However, Hong Kong residents and Taiwanese will continue to enjoy simpler border formalities and probably special informal treatment from local authorities in Guangdong and in Fujian.

Greater China as an Outward-Looking Economic Group

Though the economies of the trio are tightly linked, it must be stressed that Greater China is not an inward looking trade bloc. The picture given by trade statistics, that the trio trade largely among themselves, is misleading. Though China and Hong Kong are each other's foremost trading partner, close to 90 percent of the trade flow represents China's trade with third countries via Hong Kong. Statistics on China-Hong Kong investment is similarly misleading as they include the investment in China from subsidiaries of multinationals incorporated in Hong Kong. Moreover, the 'round-tripping' of Chinese capital via Hong Kong to be invested back in China skews upwards both China's investment in Hong Kong and Hong Kong's investment in China.

China surpassed the United States to become the top market for Hong Kong's domestic exports in 1993, taking 28 percent of domestic exports. From 1978 to 1993, the market share of China in Hong Kong's domestic exports rose from an insignificant 0.2 percent to 28.4 percent while the market share of the United States declined sharply from 37.2 percent to 27.7 percent. However, over 70 percent of Hong Kong's domestic exports to China consist of semi-manufactures supplied to the outward-processing operations of Hong Kong investors in China. If we exclude the trade in semi-manufactures and just look at Hong Kong's domestic exports of final goods in 1993, China's 1993 share would be 10.6 percent instead of 28.4 percent, and the United States would still be by far the largest market with a share of 33.9 percent. As mentioned before, if we net out the imports for Hong Kong's re-exports, Japan is by far the largest supplier of Hong Kong's retained imports. Semi-manufactures also account for the bulk of the Taiwan-Mainland trade flow because of the substantial investment by Taiwan in processing operations on the Mainland. Even if we do not net out the trade in semi-manufactures in the Taiwan-Mainland trade, the United States is still Taiwan's foremost market and Japan is by far the foremost supplier. The same is true of the Mainland. The economic reality of the trio is that the United States is their largest market, and Japan is their largest supplier of capital goods and technology. Though the Mainland may become an important consumer market in the long run, the industrial base in Hong Kong and Taiwan is too narrow to meet the demands of the Mainland. Greater China looks outward for its capital goods, technology and market.

The Prospect of Further Integration

Due to the many differences in the political, legal and economic systems between the Mainland on the one hand, and capitalist China (Hong Kong and Taiwan) on the other, the economic integration of the Mainland with capitalist China will be highly uneven. Integration will proceed rapidly in some areas but slowly in others. Between the Mainland and capitalist China, controls on movements of goods are relatively liberal whereas controls on capital and foreign exchange are more strict and controls on migration are the most strict. Integration of the commodity market between the Mainland and capitalist China will proceed rapidly due to the relatively mild controls on the flow of goods. However, even for the commodity market, one should distinguish between export-processing industries and import-competing industries. The outward-processing operations of capitalist China located on the Mainland have developed extremely rapidly because their products are exported and they are not hampered by China's foreign exchange controls. The growth of external investment in China's import-competing industries will necessarily be slower due to China's foreign exchange controls.

The integration of service industries between the Mainland and capitalist China will similarly be slow because most services cannot be exported and are sold in the domestic market. Moreover, services are performed on people and require people-to-people contacts. The controls of capitalist China on migration from the Mainland will hamper the full integration of services.

The integration of financial markets between the Mainland and capitalist China will also be quite slow as China's foreign exchange controls on the capital account are likely to be quite strict even in the medium term. The integration of the labour markets between the Mainland and capitalist China will probably be very slow due to controls on migration.

JOINING THE WTO AND CREDIBILITY OF REFORM POLICIES IN CHINA

After fifteen years of partial economic reforms in China, the need for thorough economic reforms is widely recognized, especially reforms of state-owned enterprises, of the banking and monetary system, and also of the fiscal system. However, further reforms are difficult as China has implemented most of the easy reforms. China has already gone through four cycles of liberalization and recentralization, and the credibility of the government has suffered heavily. Policies that lack credibility seldom succeed. For instance, the experiences of many developing countries have demonstrated that credibility is crucial to successful trade liberalization. The standard way to liberalize trade is through devaluation and dismantling import controls. However, investment in export-oriented industries is costly and takes time to bear fruit. Investors must be convinced that benefits to exports that arise from devaluation will be sustained and the benefits will not be eroded by inflation. Otherwise, investors will not respond to devaluation by investing in export-oriented industries. Importers will go on an import binge if they expect a reversal of import liberalization. In short, a trade liberalization package that lacks credibility will result in an unsustainable trade deficit, leading to reimposition of import controls.

China's entry into the WTO will enhance the credibility of China's reform package because it represents a commitment to the international community to carry through wide-ranging reforms involving import liberalization, reform of the exchange rate regime and also reform of the monetary and fiscal systems. Though reforms are still going to be difficult, without credibility they are next to impossible.

It must be stressed that the remnant of central administrative economic planning in China is the biggest obstacle in the economic integration of Greater China. Central administrative controls inhibit the market forces which drive economic integration. Successful economic reforms will greatly facilitate the economic integration of Greater China.

FAVOURABLE IMPACTS ON MACROSTABILITY

Fighting inflation and macrostability is recognized to be the number-one problem in China. China's entry into the WTO will have a significant anti-inflationary impact, and the taming of inflation in China will have highly favourable effects on the economic integration of Greater China.

China's entry into the WTO will have the following anti-inflationary effects: lowering the price of imports through tariff reduction; increasing supply via the increase in imports; lowering the growth of the money supply via the decrease in China's trade surplus; and enhancing the credibility of China's anti-inflationary measures.

Until 1995, China has had huge surpluses in both commodity trade and capital flows, and there has been pressure on the renminbi to appreciate. To prevent appreciation, the People's Bank has bought the excess foreign currency with renminbi and this has contributed to the increase in money supply and inflationary pressures. China could have avoided the inflationary consequence of a balance of payments surplus by appreciation, but appreciation is the wrong move in view of China's impending entry into the WTO which will imply lower tariffs, increased import, and pressures of depreciation.

It should be noted that China can unilaterally liberalize imports and thereby cut down its huge trade surplus without joining the WTO. However, such a policy has less credibility as it is not part of an international agreement, and credibility is crucial to the success of both trade liberalization and macrostabilization. As China has already gone through four stop-go/reform-recentralization cycles in the reform era, Chinese government policies are not noted for their credibility. China's entry into the WTO will enhance the credibility of China's anti-inflationary policies because inflation will imply reimposition of import controls and suspension of currency convertibility which violate China's commitment to the WTO.

THE IMPACT ON THE COMMODITY TRADE

China's entry into the WTO will expand both China's imports and exports. Imports will expand with import liberalization, and exports will expand as China will gain some recourse against protectionism. Given the efficiency of Hong Kong as a trading centre, the expansion of Chinese trade will imply a greater demand for Hong Kong services.

The WTO will only give moderate recourse against protectionism. It is highly unlikely that the United States will repeal the Jackson-Vanik amendment on granting MFN status to 'countries under the control of international communism'. The annual debate on the renewal of China's MFN status will thus continue. However, the supporters of China will have stronger arguments on their side after China's entry to the WTO.

China will also gain some protection against anti-dumping duties that are getting more and more prevalent. Since 1979, there have been over 180 charges of anti-dumping against China, involving exports worth over US$2 billion. The WTO has clear procedures on anti-dumping duties. A country that intends to levy anti-dumping duties has to notify the affected country beforehand and can only impose such duties after a process of consultation and investigation that establishes injury for the industry concerned. As China is not a member of the WTO, some anti-dumping duties are levied on China even without prior notification. In early 1993, Mexico levied anti-dumping duties on China without notification. The average duty was a huge 300 percent, with the highest rate exceeding 1000 percent! Mexico admitted that such a course of action would not have been taken if China were a member of WTO.

China's entry into the WTO will reinforce the spectacular expansion of Chinese exports and boost the relocation of the labour-intensive industries of Hong Kong and Taiwan to the Mainland. Such industrial relocation will again accelerate the structural transformation of Hong Kong into the service hub of China.

With the rise of wages and land prices in Guangdong and rising world protectionism, there is concern that the outward-oriented, labour-intensive processing operations of Southern China might have no future. The concern is premature. Though wages have risen rapidly in Guangdong, the renminbi has also depreciated rapidly, and wages have also risen rapidly in Hong Kong and Taiwan. The wages gap between Hong Kong and Guangdong has not shrunk.[10] Though land prices have risen rapidly in Shenzhen and other cities, there are vast areas near Hong Kong where land is still cheap. As Guangdong and Fujian have a population of nearly 100 million, and the supply of out-of-province labour is more or less unlimited, the supply bottlenecks are lack of roads, ports, power and infrastructure rather than the availability of cheap labour and land.

Protectionism is certainly a problem. The WTO provides only weak recourse against anti-dumping duties. China is exhausting its export quotas on textiles and clothing and the number of anti-dumping charges against China is increasing very fast. However, the problem on the demand side is exaggerated. Take the case of the United States, the largest market for China and for Greater China. Though China's exports to the United States have increased very rapidly, exports from Hong Kong and Taiwan to the United States have declined as a result of the relocation of Hong Kong and Taiwan industries to China. US exports to Greater China have also increased very rapidly due to the economic prosperity of Greater China and also trade liberalization in Taiwan and in China. The absolute size of the US trade deficit with Greater China has been roughly constant since 1987[11] and its size relative to US exports has shrunk markedly.

Though China is running up against quota constraints in its clothing exports, the possibility of quality upgrading should not be ignored. Moreover, China has a large import market and thereby has considerable bargaining power in world trade. The growing opposition in the United States to revoking China's MFN status shows that even the United States has to reckon with China's power in world trade.

According to a World Bank study, the world market has ample room for China's exports as long as China can avoid undue concentration in sensitive markets and products.[12] For instance, China's penetration of European Free Trade Association (EFTA) markets is negligible. Considerable opportunities still exist for China to upgrade the quality of its present exports as the average price for China's major exports are substantially below those of the four Asian Dragons. Many opportunities also exist for China to diversify into other labour-intensive products where developing countries have not yet made significant inroads into OECD markets. Such products worth more than US$220 billion in 1990 OECD imports were identified in the World Bank study.[13]

THE IMPACT ON THE SERVICE TRADE

With the signing of the General Agreement on Trade in Services (GATS) in the Uruguay Round, China would be bound by the Agreement upon its entry into the WTO. China has already promised to open up its banking, insurance, accounting and shipping sectors. As Hong Kong has a strong comparative advantage in services, China's entry to WTO will strengthen the position of Hong Kong as the service hub of China.

The United States has repeatedly pressured China to open its services sector with threats of unilateral action under the Special 301 Act. After entry into the WTO, China's bargaining position would be strengthened as its negotiations with the United States would come under the due process of the multilateral system of the GATS. Moreover, concessions given to the US would also be given to other members of the GATS.

As mentioned before, the integration of services in Greater China is not going to proceed as rapidly as the integration of export-processing industries due to China's foreign exchange controls and the controls on migration in Hong Kong and Taiwan. Moreover, services are more dependent on the regulatory regime and there are many differences in the political, legal and economic systems between the Mainland and capitalist China (Hong Kong and Taiwan). China's entry to the WTO will help to overcome some of the obstacles in the integration of services. China will have to adopt international practices in regulating its service sector. Moreover, China has to be committed to a convertible renminbi, at least for current account transactions. This will remove a major obstacle in investment in the services sector.

When China opens its services sector, Hong Kong is in a strong position to capture a substantial portion of the business. Services require people-to-people contacts. Geographical and cultural proximity are thus very important assets in the services trade. Hong Kong residents do not need a visa to visit China.

Hong Kong already has a head start in the services sector in China. Hong Kong banks, including the Hong Kong and Shanghai Bank, the Bank of China Group with its thirteen sister banks and the Bank of East Asia have long-established branches in China. As mentioned above, an offshore renminbi market exists in Hong Kong. On 19 June 1993, a Memorandum of Regulatory Cooperation was signed between the securities authorities in China and Hong Kong, regulating the listing of Chinese firms in the Hong Kong stock market. By the end of 1994, fifteen such stocks (commonly called H-shares) were listed in Hong Kong.

THE RELATIONSHIP WITH TAIWAN

Taiwan will be able to join the WTO after the entry of China. Taiwan-China business relationships will come under the multilateral framework of the WTO and Taiwan's investment in China will be protected. Taiwan's international status will be strengthened. Confident of its international status, it is probable that Taiwan will allow its economic ties with the Mainland to develop further. This will of course strengthen the integration of Greater China.

The prospect of Taiwan-Mainland trade is undoubtedly bright as the two economies are complementary as well as dynamic. Taiwan has made clear that it will not sanction direct economic links with the Mainland unless Beijing renounces the use of force in the Taiwan Straits, an option which Beijing is so far unwilling to give up. However, a breakthrough cannot be ruled out in the post-Deng era.

The prohibition of direct economic links is quite costly as Taiwan is very close to the Mainland and taking the route via Hong Kong is much more time-consuming, especially for business travellers. It was estimated that Hong Kong would lose one billion US dollars (US) from the opening of direct links due to losses in transportation, trade, telecommunications and tourism. The gain for Taiwan would probably be much greater because direct links save a lot of travelling and transportation time and open up many new economic opportunities.

However, the impact of the official opening of direct trade between the two economies may not be as dramatic as expected because half of the existing trade is already 'direct'. Though official direct trade is not allowed, Taiwan has increasingly softened the interpretation of its ban. This has decreased the cost of 'direct trade' and should lead to the substitution of 'direct' for indirect trade. On the other hand, the Mainland has continued to decentralize its trading system which leads to an increase in search costs and an increase in reliance on intermediation, especially on the extensive trading networks of Hong Kong.

As China is likely to further decentralize its foreign trade and investment, the prospect of Hong Kong as a middleman is very bright. There are significant economies of scale and economies of agglomeration in trading activity and it is very difficult for other cities such as Taipei, Singapore and Shanghai to compete with Hong Kong because Hong Kong is the established centre for China's trade. The existence of economies of scale in intermediation would enhance the demand for the middleman as small firms will not be able to trade efficiently.

Traders tend to agglomerate in a city, suggesting that there are significant external economies involved. This implies that once a city acquires a comparative advantage in trade, the advantage feeds upon itself, and more trading firms will come to the city, making the city even more efficient in trade.[14]

In China's trade with its major partners (including the United States, Canada, Japan, Singapore, Germany, the United Kingdom, Australia, France and Italy), the effect of China's trade decentralization has overwhelmed the decrease in the costs of establishing direct trade links, and China relies more and more on indirect trade via Hong Kong.[15]

Taiwan-Mainland trade provides a very interesting case for studying the impact of direct trade on indirect trade because the relative advantage of direct to indirect trade is particularly significant for Taiwan. The savings in direct-trade of transportation costs are large as Taiwan is close to the Mainland. Moreover, the search cost of direct trade is comparatively low for Taiwan because of cultural proximity. Taiwanese firms also have large trading networks on the Mainland. However, around half of Taiwan-Mainland trade is still taking the form of indirect trade via Hong Kong despite the availability of 'direct trade'. This confirms the efficiency of Hong Kong in intermediation. In the recent case of the opening of direct trade with South Korea, a substantial portion of China-South Korean trade continues to go through Hong Kong. The case of the opening of direct Taiwan-Mainland trade may prove to be the same.

Even if Taiwan decides to initiate direct links today, it should be noted that the negotiation of direct air or sea links is often very time-consuming in the best of circumstances. With political mistrust on both sides, the negotiations will probably be protracted. The impact of the opening of direct Taiwan-Mainland trade will very likely be gradual. Though Taipei aspires to become a regional financial, corporate and transportation centre, Taipei will not be a serious threat to Hong Kong in the medium term due to the economies of agglomeration in trading and financial activities.

STRENGTHENING THE INTEGRATION OF GREATER CHINA

There have been a lot of proposals for promoting the integration of the trio through institutional arrangements such as the formation of a free trade area. Most of these proposals are utopian and counterproductive. The reality is that there are very real political differences dividing the Mainland and Taiwan, and such differences are not going to disappear overnight with economic integration. While the economy of Hong Kong is irrevocably tied up with that of the Mainland, Taiwan will not allow its economy to be too dependent on the Mainland unless the Mainland is willing to give up the use of force in the Taiwan Straits.

The economic reality of the trio is that the United States is their largest market and Japan is their largest supplier of capital goods and technology. An inward-looking bloc of the trio excluding the United States and Japan would thus not be in the long term interest of the trio.

Though Hong Kong is irrevocably integrated with the Mainland, it must be remembered that Hong Kong can function as the bridge linking the Mainland and the world only because Hong Kong is also irrevocably integrated with the world economy. An inward-looking bloc involving Hong Kong and the Mainland would be detrimental to both.

Hong Kong is traditionally a free port and the freedom of movement of goods and capital in Hong Kong is enshrined in the Sino-British agreement on the future of Hong Kong as well as the Basic Law because all parties involved recognized that such freedoms are essential to the future prosperity of Hong Kong. As the free port status of Hong Kong is guaranteed by constitution and by international agreement, the only way that the Mainland and Hong Kong can form a trade bloc is for the Mainland to abolish all its tariffs. This is obviously ludicrous and utopian.

Shenzhen has built a 'second line' managing the flow of goods and people between its SEZ and the rest of China, and Shenzhen has plans to become a free trade zone. However, even if Shenzhen were to become a free trade zone, Hong Kong and Shenzhen would still be separate entities in trade. Trade between Hong Kong and Shenzhen would be like trade between Hong Kong and any other free trade zone, such as Singapore or the Kaohsiung export processing zone. Moreover, Hong Kong has to maintain its border controls against Shenzhen and the Mainland. To qualify for WTO membership, Hong Kong must be able to effectively distinguish between goods made in Hong Kong and those that are made in Shenzhen and elsewhere. The abolition of Hong Kong border controls on Shenzhen would jeopardize Hong Kong's WTO membership and Hong Kong's textile and clothing quotas. As China is applying for WTO membership, the abolition of Shenzhen's border controls on Hong Kong goods would also pose complications for China's WTO membership and China's textiles and clothing quotas. Theoretically, Hong Kong and Shenzhen can enter WTO as a single customs territory. However, this poses many political and technical complications. It will infringe on Hong Kong's autonomy as Shenzhen will then have a say over Hong Kong's trade policy as well as textile and clothing quotas. China is also unlikely to give up control on Shenzhen's external economic affairs. It will require amendments to the Sino-British agreement on the future of Hong Kong as well as the Basic Law. A trading bloc involving Hong Kong and Shenzhen is thus also utopian.

The Mainland's unilateral tariff and investment preferences for Taiwan are 'unGATTable', economically inefficient, politically counterproductive, and detrimental to the long-term integration of the trio. Taiwanese businessmen are given special concessions over others on the grounds that they are Chinese and Taiwan is a part of China. However, Hong Kong businessmen are not entitled to the same treatment even though Hong Kong is also a part of China, and the mainland Chinese themselves receive the worst treatment of all. The logical conclusion is that Taiwanese businessmen receive the best treatment only because Taiwan's reunification with the Mainland is not assured, and there is no need to give special treatment to Hong Kong businessmen because Hong Kong's return to the Mainland is already assured. Taiwanese businessmen will thus try to maintain Taiwan's political separation from the Mainland in order to keep their concessions. The policy of the Mainland is time-inconsistent and runs contrary to the goal of national reunification.

Beijing's tariff exemption for Taiwanese goods in 1980 was largely reversed in 1981 to stem the flood in the Mainland market of Taiwanese goods and Hong Kong goods with fake Taiwanese certificates of origin. The episode illustrated the economic and political dangers of favouritism and discrimination. However, Beijing has yet to learn the lesson in full. Special concessions were given to Taiwanese investors in 1989 and Beijing has problems with investors putting on a Taiwanese disguise. There were also complaints of unfair competition from domestic producers in the Mainland whose exports have been displaced by the exports of Taiwanese investors in the Mainland.

In 1991, some Hong Kong businessmen lobbied for tariff preferences from the Mainland. Such preferences, if granted, would be detrimental not only to the Mainland but also to Hong Kong. Free competition has long been the source of strength and dynamism of the Hong Kong economy. Such preferences would entice Hong Kong businessmen to spend their energy on lobbying for favouritism instead of concentrating their resources on improving productivity. Moreover, there is 'no free lunch' and Hong Kong's seeking of favouritism from the Mainland would invite the Mainland to ask for reciprocal favouritism from Hong Kong. Given Chinese sovereignty and Beijing's intervention-prone record, Hong Kong would have a hard time preserving the autonomy promised in the Basic Law. The seeking of favouritism from Beijing would further compromise Hong Kong's ability to manage its own affairs. It should be stressed that the erosion of Hong Kong's autonomy and dynamism would also be detrimental to China's long-term interests.

It should be noted that Hong Kong and Taiwanese businessmen already have a tremendous advantage in the Mainland market due to geographic proximity and cultural affinity. If Hong Kong and Taiwanese businessmen cannot compete against foreigners in the Mainland market, they must be highly inefficient and they deserve to lose in competition.

It is often not realized that tariff preferences and institutional arrangements may not be important for economic integration. Economic integration means the lowering of transaction costs, and tariffs are often only a small part of transaction costs. Other factors such as transportation costs, cultural affinity, foreign exchange controls, and government regulations may be much more important. According to Ulrich Heimenz of the Kiel Institute of Economics, tariff preferences did not play a significant role in ASEAN's integration, and . . . '[I]n the ASEAN group, transaction costs were lowered through the emergence of Singapore as a regional trading and services centre and [through] software cooperation among member countries. In the North-Pacific it was unilateral policy action such as the partial liberalisation of [the] goods and services trade which served the same purpose of reducing transaction costs and thereby stimulating trade integration. These findings contain the important lesson that trade expansion depends on a wide range of interlinked influences and not just on discriminatory trade preferences. This should be taken into account when designing foreign economic policies in the Asian-Pacific region.'[16]

In the case of the integration of the trio, the pivotal role of Hong Kong as an efficient middleman and the importance of the unilateral trade liberalization of the Mainland and Taiwan were clearly important. The integration of the trio will continue to be largely market-driven, though consultation through APEC, through semi-official organizations such as the Straits Foundation in Taiwan, or through privately sponsored forums to improve information flow and to discuss possible policy coordination will be useful. WTO membership for both the Mainland and Taiwan would give a tremendous boost to the integration of the trio. Institutional discriminatory preferences are utopian and counterproductive, and unilateral discriminatory preferences are 'unGATTable' and detrimental.

APEC AND THE WTO

Formed in 1989 as a low profile forum, APEC reflected the spontaneous, market-driven integration in the Asia-Pacific Area. China, Taiwan and Hong Kong were admitted to APEC in November 1991. The transformation of APEC from a talk-shop to a more serious economic community occurred in November 1993 at the Seattle Summit. The United States tried to demonstrate that the United States could turn to East Asia should the GATT fail, and other members saw an enhanced APEC as a way of keeping US interests engaged in the region. APEC leaders thus agreed to annual summits.

In the 1994 Bogor summit in Indonesia, APEC agreed to the goal of comprehensive liberalization. Developed and developing members should achieve the goal by 2010 and 2020 respectively. In the Osaka summit of November 1995, APEC members committed themselves to various liberalization packages. China reportedly accepted a 'road map' provided by the United States, proposing to overhaul China's trade regime. Moreover,

China promised to slash tariffs on 4000 of its 6000 import items by 30 percent in 1996. China's average tariffs would be lowered from 35.9 percent to around 22 percent (the actual effect would be less dramatic as China's actual 1994 tariff revenue was only 3.3 percent of the value of its imports due to widespread exemptions and tariff evasion). The resulting revenue would be recouped by gradual elimination of tax exemptions given to foreign investors. Specifically, tariff-free imports of capital equipment by foreign-invested enterprises would be annulled by 1 April 1996. This promotes national treatment, which is a norm of the WTO. China also promised to eliminate quota, licensing and other import controls on about 170 tariff categories, representing 30 percent of the imports subject to import controls. Early convertibility of the renminbi on the current account was also promised.

The momentum set up in the Osaka summit was derailed by China's military exercises in the Taiwan Straits in late 1995 and early 1996. Sino-American relationships became tense and China lost the chance of entering the WTO in 1996. Despite such setbacks, China adhered to the promises made in the Osaka summit and cut tariffs on 1 April 1996.

For China, APEC can be a partial substitute for the WTO as China's commitments to APEC would enhance the credibility of China's policies of reform and trade liberalization. APEC opens the markets of its members to Chinese exports and also provides a forum for interactions among the trio.

However, APEC is at best an imperfect substitute for the WTO. APEC cannot give China recourse to the protectionist actions of non-APEC members. Moreover, the APEC process is fuzzy and less rule-based in comparison to that of the WTO. For enhancing the credibility of trade liberalization, APEC membership counts much less than WTO membership because APEC allows its members to make vague and fuzzy committments.

The advantage of the APEC process is its flexibility. As China's trade regime is far from 'GATTable', it is rash for China to jump into the rule-based WTO system. To use the imagery of Deng Xiaoping, the APEC process provides the stepping stones for China to cross the treacherous river of economic reforms into the land of the WTO.

NOTES

1. Nick Ni, *Asian Perspectives: China's Expanding Economic Interests in Hong Kong*, Nomura Research Institute Hong Kong Limited, Vol. 11, no. 6 (December, 1994), p. 4.
2. Yun Wing Sung, *The China-Hong Kong Connection: The Key to China's Open Door Policy* (Cambridge: Cambrige University Press, 1991), pp. 28–43.
3. The share of Chinese exports re-exported via Hong Kong has fallen to 45 percent and 42.5 percent in 1994 and 1995 respectively. This may not imply a decline in Hong Kong's role as China's entrepôt as China's exports have been increasingly

transhipped via Hong Kong instead of re-exported via Hong Kong (see Hong Kong Trade Development Council, *Hong Kong's Trade and Trade Supporting Services,* Hong Kong, April 1996). The change is partly due to China's liberalization of shipping services.

4. Yun Wing Sung, 'Subregional economic integration: Hong Kong, Taiwan, South China and beyond', in Edward K.Y. Chen and Peter Drysdale (eds.), *Corporate Links and Foreign Direct Investment in Asia and the Pacific* (Australia, Harper Educational, 1995), pp. 75–79.

5. Siow Yue Chia, 'Motivating forces in subregional economic zones', Pacific Forum/ CSIS occasional papers, Honolulu, (December 1993).

6. Robert A. Scalapino, 'The United States and Asia: future prospects', *Foreign Affairs,* (Winter 1991/92), pp. 19–40.

7. Siow Yue Chia, op. cit., (1993).

8. *Hong Kong Economic Journal* (in Chinese), 5 May 1994.

9. Milton Yeh, 'Ask a tiger for its hide? Taiwan's approach to economic transaction across the Straits', paper prepared for the conference on *Economic Interdependence and Challenges to the Nation State: The Emergence of National Economic Territories in the Asia-Pacific* sponsored by the Pacific Forum/CSIS in Hong Kong on 17–19 April, 1994, p. 42.

10. Yun-Wing Sung, Pak-Wai Liu, Yue-Chim Richard Wong and Pui-King Lau, *The Fifth Dragon: The Emergence of the Pearl River Delta* (Singapore: Addison Wesley, 1995), p. 112.

11. Yin-Ping Ho, 'China's foreign trade and the reform of the foreign trade system', in Joseph Yu-shek Cheng and Maurice Brosseau (eds.), *China Review* (Hong Kong: Chinese University Press, 1993), pp. 17–32.

12. World Bank, *China-Foreign Trade Reform,* Washington DC, (1994), pp. 163–165.

13. Ibid.

14. Yun-Wing Sung (1991), op.cit., pp. 28–42.

15. Yun-Wing Sung (1991), op.cit., pp. 141–143.

16. Ulrich Heimenz, 'Asian-Pacific leadership: Implications for foreign policy of Japan and the US', paper presented at the 19th Pacific Trade and Development Conference on *Economic Reforms and Internationalization: China and the Pacific Region,* Beijing, (May 27–30, 1991), mimeo, p. 14.

10

SINO-JAPANESE ECONOMIC RELATIONS AND THEIR IMPLICATIONS FOR SINO-AMERICAN RELATIONS

Hiromi Yamamoto

INTRODUCTION

Sino-Japanese relations have developed significantly though not always smoothly since the establishment of diplomatic relations in 1972. In the next section, the basic patterns of the development process of Sino-Japanese economic relations are analysed in terms of trade, direct investment, official development assistance, and other flows. Following that, the present and future of Sino-Japanese relations are analysed by paying particular attention to perceptions on both sides. In the third section, the triangular relationship of Japan, China and the United States is examined. The fourth section follows the way that Sino-Japanese relations are linked with Japanese-American relations in order to show that Japanese-American relations are a key factor for Sino-American relations.

THE DEVELOPMENT OF SINO-JAPANESE ECONOMIC RELATIONS

Japan's Trade With China

According to Table 10.1 Japan's trade with China has been increasing rapidly since the opening of diplomatic relations between the two countries in 1972. In 1994 the total value of Japan's exports amounted to US$18.7 billion while that of imports had risen to US$27.6 billion. So the total value of trade amounted to US$46.2 billion. After a set-back in 1990, in the aftermath of the Tiananmen Square incident, the total value of trade between the two countries has continuously set new records every year since 1991 (Table 10.1). In 1993 Japan took second place as a trade partner with China after the United States; this status quo was maintained in 1994.

According to Japanese figures, Japan's trade deficit with China reached its highest record of US$8.9 billion in 1994. There are three reasons why it reached such a high level: firstly, Japan increased re-imports of manufactured goods

Table 10.1 Japan's Trade With China, 1972–1994

(Unit: US$ Millions)

Year	Exports	Growth rate %	Imports	Growth rate %	Total trade	Growth rate %	Balance of trade
1972	608.9	5.3	491.1	52.0	1100.0	22.0	117.8
1973	1039.5	70.7	974.0	98.3	2013.5	83.0	65.5
1974	1984.5	90.9	1304.8	23.0	3289.2	63.4	679.7
1975	2258.6	13.8	1531.1	17.3	3789.6	15.2	727.5
1976	1662.6	-26.3	1380.9	-10.5	3033.4	-20.0	281.7
1977	1938.6	16.6	1546.9	12.8	3485.5	14.9	391.7
1978	3048.7	57.3	2030.3	31.2	5079.0	45.7	1018.5
1979	3698.7	21.3	2954.8	45.5	6653.5	31.0	743.9
1980	5078.3	37.3	4323.4	46.3	9401.7	41.3	755.0
1981	5095.5	0.3	5291.8	22.4	10 387.3	10.5	-196.4
1982	3510.8	-31.1	5352.4	1.1	8863.2	-14.7	-1841.6
1983	4912.3	39.9	5087.4	-5.0	9999.7	12.8	-175.0
1984	7216.7	46.9	5957.6	17.1	13 173.3	31.7	1259.1
1985	12 477.4	72.9	6482.7	8.8	18 960.1	43.9	5994.8
1986	9856.2	-21.0	5652.4	-12.8	15 508.6	-18.2	4203.8
1987	8249.8	-16.3	7401.4	30.9	15 651.2	0.9	848.4
1988	9476.0	14.9	9858.8	33.2	19 334.8	23.5	-382.8
1989	8515.9	-10.1	11 145.8	13.1	19 661.7	1.7	-2629.9
1990	6129.5	-28.0	12 053.6	8.1	18 183.0	-7.5	-5924.0
1991	8593.1	40.2	14 215.8	17.9	22 809.0	25.4	-5622.7
1992	11 949.1	39.1	16 952.8	19.3	28 901.9	26.7	-5003.8
1993	17 273.1	44.6	20 564.8	21.3	37 837.8	30.9	-3291.7
1994	18 681.6	8.2	27 566.0	34.0	46 247.6	22.2	-8884.4

Source: Japan's Ministry of Finance.

and intermediate goods from China because it had invested so much in China. Secondly, China cooled its economy so that its imports decreased, and thirdly, the appreciation of the yen against the dollar weakened the international competitiveness of Japanese exports.

On the other hand, according to China's customs statistics, China's trade balance with Japan had a deficit of US$2.0 billion in 1992, US$7.5 billion in 1993, and US$4.1 billion in 1994. The reason why the two countries each claim a trade deficit with each other is that neither customs statistics takes re-exports via Hong Kong into account.

According to the *Annual Review of Hong Kong External Trade*, Japan's re-exports to China via Hong Kong increased from US$3.2 billion in 1990 to US$10.0 billion in 1993 and then dropped to US$7.7 billion in 1994. On the other hand, China's re-exports to Japan increased from US$2.1 billion in 1990 to US$4.6 billion in 1993 and then dropped to US$3.4 billion in 1994. As a result Japan's indirect trade with China via Hong Kong always had a surplus. Japan's surplus increased from US$1.1 billion in 1990 to US$5.4 billion and then dropped to US$4.2 billion in 1994.

So Japan's total trade balance with China, including direct and indirect trade with China, had a deficit of US$4.8 billion in 1990, US$3.7 billion in 1991, and US$1.5 billion in 1992, but a surplus of US$2.1 billion in 1993 and US$133 million in 1994.

Since 1991 China has faced an investment boom of historic proportions as many countries and regions in addition to Japan began to invest in China. Japan's increased imports from China include products not just from Japanese plants in China but also from companies from the Asian NIEs and ASEAN countries which have increased their investments in China very much. One effect has been that along with the increase in investment in China, Japan has increased its imports of manufactured goods from China at an average annual growth rate of 34 percent during the 1991–4 period. Japan's imports of manufactured goods represented only 27 percent of total Japanese imports from China in 1985, but the share had risen to 70 percent by 1994. Textile products had a share of more than half of the imports of manufactured goods. On the other hand, machinery was only a small share, although the imports of machinery are increasing rapidly. The imports of processed food increased because Japanese firms promoted the development of such imports.

Japan's exports to China have had ups and downs because of the economic policy cycles of the Chinese government, namely, the government sometimes imposed import restrictions owing to the current account deficit. Recently Japan increased exports such as machinery and equipment (see Table 10.2), but the growth rate of these exports now has become stagnant because Japanese firms in China sold their products primarily on the domestic market and the appreciation of the yen has cut the international competitiveness of Japanese goods. As a result, the growth rate of Japan's exports to China is quite stagnant compared with that of imports.

Looking at Japan's exports to China by item, machinery ranks the first, sharing about 60 percent of total exports in 1994. In particular, the export of electrical equipment and accessories has increased rapidly (Table 10.2). Among them the exports of electronics such as integrated circuits increased swiftly. On the other hand, exports of vehicles decreased by 60 percent owing to the abolition of preferential treatment for foreign companies in 1994.

In 1972 iron and steel accounted for more than half of Japan's exports to China while Japan's major imports from China were textile materials and crude oil (see Table 10.3). Since then the commodity composition of exports has changed drastically. Exports to China often suffer from changes in economic policies, such as tight monetary policy, which brings about delays in issuing letters of credit. It is true that in the early stages of direct investment an investing country can export capital goods. But once production gets on the right track, the investing country might have a trade deficit because of an increase in re-imports.

Japanese Investment in China

In 1994 foreign direct investment on a contract basis in China decreased owing to the rapid decrease in investment from Hong Kong and Taiwan. However, Japanese investment was actually increasing from January to September 1994. According to Chinese statistics, the amount of investment through signed contracts from Japan reached US$2.86 billion, an increase of 27 percent compared with the previous year. On the other hand, the amount of investment actually used reached US$1.39 billion, an increase of 50 percent compared with the previous year.

According to statistics prepared by the Ministry of Finance, Japan's investment in China has increased steadily since 1991 (Table 10.4). In the fiscal year 1993, China became the largest host country in terms of Japanese investment in Asia, surpassing Indonesia. In the first half of 1994 China was the second largest host country after the United States in terms of Japanese investment.

Two reasons can be pointed out as to why Japanese investment in China increased very rapidly. Firstly, the underlying rapid appreciation of the yen led many Japanese companies to move their factories out of Japan. Secondly, China is becoming a large attractive market for the world.

Taking an overall look at Japanese investment in China, the following characteristics can be seen: to begin with, firms have a tendency to invest in China not as a single investor but in the form of a business group, including subcontractors. Secondly, firms which have already invested in China increase

Table 10.2 Japan's Major Exports to China, 1988–1994

(Units: US$ Millions %)

Item	1988	1989	1990	1991	1992	1993	1994	%
Foods	25.0	25.0	25.4	27.6	32.6	29.5	53.6	0.3
Textile materials and products	586.7	554.5	609.3	926.5	1223.0	1384.1	1804.5	9.7
Chemicals	941.4	788.1	751.0	1071.6	1073.5	1054.8	1359.9	7.3
Nonmetalic minerals	133.6	171.5	140.6	189.4	171.8	173.5	247.0	1.3
Base metals and related products	2736.1	2540.9	1193.1	1554.3	1734.5	3366.9	2713.4	14.5
Iron and steel	2471.4	2323.2	1058.6	1364.2	1472.3	2965.7	2250.7	12.0
Machinery	4564.5	3956.4	2834.1	4094.0	6613.0	9937.2	11 027.4	59.0
General industrial machinery	1683.7	1528.7	1026.4	1484.9	2850.3	4589.6	4676.7	25.0
Electric equipment	2059.8	1811.9	1269.3	1779.2	2204.4	3137.6	4077.8	21.8
Ship and transportation equipment	531.4	372.2	317.1	550.5	1166.2	1959.3	1977.7	10.6
Precision instruments	289.5	243.6	221.7	279.6	392.1	250.6	295.3	1.6
Other	4886.0	479.2	575.5	729.6	1100.2	1326.7	1473.8	7.9
Total	9475.9	8515.8	6129.5	8593.1	11 949.0	17 273.0	18 679.9	100.0

Source: JETRO, Gaikoku Boeki Gaikyo (Outlook of Foreign Trade), various issues.

Table 10.3 Japan's Major Imports From China, 1988–1994

(Units: US$ Millions %)

Item	1988	1989	1990	1991	1992	1993	1994	%
Foods	1781.1	1953.6	1935.4	2446.0	2787.0	3224.9	4731.7	17.2
Textile materials	581.0	485.9	315.5	334.4	221.3	195.8	30.6	0.1
Metals	56.3	75.7	38.6	37.0	30.3	23.8	25.9	0.1
Other materials	680.8	789.4	732.8	773.6	821.8	825.9	1231.7	4.5
Mineral fuels	2118.5	2097.8	2911.5	2363.2	2286.2	2090.0	1929.9	7.0
Crude oil	1601.5	1531.2	2277.8	1767.4	1789.1	1676.8	1485.9	5.4
Chemicals	619.4	708.8	652.0	742.7	702.5	741.0	941.0	3.4
Machinery	149.5	340.7	514.7	824.0	1112.0	1794.7	2816.4	10.2
Others	3871.8	4693.5	4952.8	6694.5	8991.4	11 668.2	15 857.8	57.5
Total	9858.8	11 145.7	12 053.5	14 215.8	16 952.8	20 564.7	27 565.0	100.0

Source: Table 10.2.

Table 10.4 Japan's Investment in China, 1979–1994

(Unit: US$ Millions)

	Japan's Statistics		China's Statistics		Number of JV
	Number of commitments	Amount	Number of Commitments	Amount	Establishments
1979	3	14	–	–	6
1980	6	12	–	–	20
1981	9	26	27	950	28
1982	4	18	–	–	29
1983	5	3	–	–	107
1984	66	114	138	203	741
1985	118	100	127	471	1412
1986	85	226	94	210	892
1987	101	1226	110	301	1365
1988	171	296	237	276	3909
1989	126	438	294	440	3659
1990	165	349	341	460	4093
1991	246	579	599	812	8359
1992	490	1070	1805	2172	34 354
1993	700	1691	3488	2960	53 891
1994	289	1136	2228	3516	27 858
79–93	1595	4472	7182	8934	112 895
79–94	2584	7299	9410	12 450	140 753

Note: 1. Japan's fiscal year data are based on the statistics of the Ministry of Finance.
2. China's calendar year data are based on the statistics of the Ministry of Foreign Trade.
3. Data about the number of establishments of joint ventures by calendar year in the whole country are based on the data of the Ministry of Foreign Trade.
4. 1994 data, except for the number of joint-venture establishments, refer to January to June only.

the number of their factories there. Thirdly, many holding companies are established. Fourthly, Japanese firms in China increase sales in the domestic market. Fifthly, Japanese investments begin to cover many industries ranging from processing and assembling industries to materials and tertiary industries. And finally, firms are thinking of investing in the inland areas, although the large-scale Japanese investments concentrate on Shanghai.

In the past two or three years Japanese big businesses have increased their investments so swiftly that the average amount of investment per Japanese firm increased from US$2.42 million in 1993 to US$3.93 million in the first half of 1994. For example, in 1994 the Toyoda Tsusho group invested US$44 million in establishing a factory for aluminum products in Kunshan and the Yaohan group put more than US$10 million into setting up an international wholesale centre in Shanghai.

Yet, according to a survey by the *Japan-China Investment Promotion Organization in the Autumn of 1994*, out of 230 Japanese firms in China, 97 companies evaluated an improvement in the managerial environment in China while 201 companies pointed out a change for the worse in the managerial environment (plural answers were permitted). Good points in the improvement in the managerial environment were as follows: improvement in infrastructure; the increase in demand and sales in the domestic market; enacting new economic laws; and the improvement in obtaining industrial materials. However, there were some answers saying that the infrastructure and supply of industrial materials had deteriorated. It may be said that the reason why we find mixed answers about these problems is the different situation in different areas in China.

On the other hand, the bad points listed were as follows: increases in prices and costs; too many changes in economic laws; the difficulty of employing good staff and workers and frequent occurrence of job-hopping and head-hunting; tight monetary policy; and, finally, corruption and the deterioration of social security.

In the survey, one in four Japanese firms in China complained of the increases in prices and costs. In particular, labour costs and prices of materials were said to have increased rapidly. Most firms say that labour costs and prices of materials increased 10 to 20 percent while about 10 percent of the firms say that they had increased 50 percent. Japanese small-scale firms, which were driven into China by the appreciation of the yen, are facing an unexpected situation of severe inflation and sudden changes in economic laws and are worried about their future.

As a result, the objective of Japan's investors is changing from aiming at the *liangtou zaiwai* to aiming at the domestic market. The term *liangtou zaiwai* means that investors import materials and sell their products to international markets. As a result more and more Japanese firms are in a position in which China's economic policy influences them very much.

Japan's Financial Cooperation With China

Official Development Assistance (ODA)

Japan's ODA during the 1979–93 period amounted to US$7796.4 million including the total of bilateral grants and ODA loans, as is shown in Table 10.5. However, traditionally, Japanese aid to China has been predominantly in the form of loans rather than grants.

Japan's ODA loans to China in total, as of 31 March 1994, amounted to 1399.12 billion yen and the total number of commitments to 162. In terms of ODA to China by sector, loans to transportation amounted to 742.24 billion yen (91 commitments), sharing 53.1 percent of the total; those to electric power and gas to 192.95 billion yen (23 commitments), 13.8 percent; commodity loans 130 billion yen, 9.3 percent; loans to agriculture, forestry and fishery 102.25 billion yen (17 commitments), 7.3 percent; loans to telecommunications 96.804 billion yen (13 commitments), 6.9 percent; financial-intermediary loans 70 billion yen (1 commitment), 5.0 percent; loans to social services 60.84 billion yen (11 commitments), 4.3 percent; and loans to irrigation and flood control 4.02 billion yen (1 commitment), 0.3 percent.

Japan's ODA loans to China, which started in April 1980, have been divided into four 'rounds'. The First Round loans (1980–84) amounted to 330.90 billion yen. The number of commitments was five. The Second Round loans (1984–90) for 16 projects amounted to 470 billion yen. The Third Round loans (1990–95) for 42 projects amounted to 810 billion yen, including 40 billion yen under the Financial Recycling System.

In December 1994 the Japanese government decided to give the first part of the Fourth Round loans (1996–98) to China. The total amount of the loans is 580 billion yen, involving 44 commitments over the three years. The average annual amount of the loans amounts to 193.3 billion yen, an increase of 43 percent compared with that of the Third Round loans, thereby exceeding the amount of loans given to Indonesia. It follows, therefore, that China will become the largest beneficiary of Japanese ODA thanks to the Fourth Round loans. This time it should be noted that among the current projects there are six projects for environmental control such as a project to control acid rain in Liuzhou, and 27 projects in the inner region, including the *Nansui beitiao zhongyanxian* (water-way from Danjiangkou, Hebei, to Beijing).

Japan Export-Import Bank loans

In general, because it carries out a division of labour with the OECF, Japan Export-Import Bank loans are used mainly for energy development. China has accepted a total amount of 1700 billion yen for 49 projects since 1979. The terms of the loan are not as good as for the ODA, but it is true that they have played a very important part in the development of the energy sector in China.

Private sector financial cooperation

The financial cooperation of the private sector includes direct investment and export by the deferred payment method. As Japan's direct investment in China has been mentioned above, it is necessary to have a look here at exports by the deferred payment method. Plant exports by the deferred payment method increased from US$81.10 million in 1990 to US$1083.96 million in 1993. In terms of the share of Japan's plant exports by country, in 1993 China took 22.8 percent of the total plant exports, with a total of 36.9 percent for Asia, including South-east Asia and the Middle East.

Table 10.5 Japan's ODA to China, 1979–1993

(Unit: US$ Millions)

	1979	1980	1981	1982	1983	1984	1985	1986
Total Bilateral Grants	2.6	3.4	12.1	38.6	51.1	41.5	42.7	86.9
Grant Assistance	–	–	2.5	25.5	30.6	14.2	11.5	25.7
Technical Assistance	2.6	3.4	9.6	13.5	20.5	27.3	31.2	61.2
Bilateral ODA Loans	–	0.9	15.6	330.2	299.1	347.9	345.2	410.1
Total	2.6	4.3	27.7	368.8	350.2	389.4	387.9	497.0

	1987	1988	1989	1990	1991	1992	1993	Total
Total Bilateral Grants	130.3	154.7	164.1	201.3	194.1	259.3	299.5	1682.3
Grant Assistance	54.3	52.0	58.0	37.8	56.6	72.1	54.4	495.0
Technical Assistance	76.0	102.7	106.1	163.5	137.5	187.5	245.1	1187.3
Bilateral ODA Loans	422.8	519.0	668.1	521.7	391.2	791.2	1051.2	6114.1
Total	553.1	673.7	832.2	723.0	585.3	1050.6	1350.7	7796.4

Source: Ministry of Foreign Affairs, *Waga Kuni No Seihu Kaihatsu Enjo (Japan's ODA)*, various issues.

PRESENT AND FUTURE OF SINO-JAPANESE ECONOMIC RELATIONS

The Japanese View of the Chinese Economy

A recent joint survey[1] of 303 industrialists by the *Japan Economic Journal, the Economic Daily* of South Korea, and the *Jingji Cankao Bao* of China gave us the following interesting results.
1. China's annual economic growth rate during the 1995–2000 period is estimated at 7 to 10 percent.
2. About 57 percent of the Japanese industrialists and 82 percent of the Korean industrialists surveyed have their own plans for investing in China.
3. More than 30 percent of the industrialists in Japan and South Korea expect that China will lead the world economy in the year 2001.
4. Crucial points concerning the Chinese economy are the incompleteness of the national market, frequent changes of economic policy, and severe inflation.
5. Japan's annual economic growth rate is estimated to be between zero to three percent up to the year 2000.

These points should be examined in more detail. Firstly, concerning the first point, 49 percent of Japanese industrialists say so. Concerning the third point, most Japanese industrialists think it is the large size of the Chinese market that will make China the leader in the world economy. Concerning the fourth point, the Japanese industrialists think that the most important problem for the Chinese economy is the acceleration of inflation, the second-ranking problem being changes in economic policy, and the third-ranking problem increases in income differentials between the coastal and the inner regions.

The Japanese Way of Thinking About China

A Japanese who has stayed in China for many years has written that Sino-Japanese relations faced the age of destruction in the first half of twentieth century, faced that of remaking in the second half of this century, and will enter into the age of mutual prosperity in coexistence in the next century.[2]

Japan has had a long tradition of *Datsu A Nyu O* (Japan should go out of Asia and join Western Europe) since the Meiji Restoration in the mid-nineteenth century. Yukichi Fukuzawa, the educationist who founded Keio University, was the first to stress *Datsu A Nyu O* in the Meiji era.[3] Some people emphasize *Datsu O Nyu A* (Japan should get out of Western Europe and join Asia). However, I think the course Japan should take is *Nyu O Nyu A* (Japan should enter into both Western Europe and Asia).

In other words, in order to maintain and strengthen Japan's position in world politics and economy, Japan should take a 'general equilibrium' approach instead of a 'partial equilibrium' approach in term of economics. Here I mean something like the 'Fukuda doctrine' in the late 1970s that stressed omnidirectional diplomacy through the 'general equilibrium' approach.

The Chinese View of the Japanese Economy

According to the survey by the three newspapers mentioned above, most Chinese industrialists think that Japan will open its market sooner or later. However, few Chinese firms have any plans to invest in Japan.

Concerning the Japanese economy in the future, about 37 percent of the Chinese industrialists surveyed predicted that the Japanese economy will grow at an average annual rate of from zero to three percent up to the year 2000. About 23 percent of the Chinese industrialists think that the rapid appreciation of the yen will lead to a hollowing of the Japanese economy in which Japanese firms will increasingly move their factories abroad.

Concerning the faults of Japanese firms, the Chinese industrialists point out three problems: exclusiveness in favouring subcontracting firms; cautiousness over technology transfer; and high wages.

THE TRIANGULAR RELATIONS OF CHINA, JAPAN, AND THE UNITED STATES

East Asia as the Emerging Market

Now everyone knows that the Asia-Pacific region is going to be the economic growth centre of the world economy in the next century. Clear evidence can be provided from the strong growth rates for trade in the region. In particular, as shown in Tables 10.6 and 10.7, the exports of East Asia, that is the Asian NIEs, ASEAN (the Association of South-east Asian Nations) and China, amounted to US$598.3 billion in 1993, increasing by 10.2 percent. Its imports amounted to US$626.5 billion, increasing by 13.2 percent over the 1990s figures. East Asia's share of world imports was 13.28 percent in 1990 and 17.66 percent in 1993. It is an astonishing fact that this share exceeded that of the United States by 1.47 percent in 1990 and 5.29 percent in 1993. This is due to the fact that the incomes of East Asian countries, mainly the Asian NIEs, increased rapidly and that imports of capital goods, that is, machinery including parts and semi-manufactured goods, increased as overseas Chinese businessmen invested in China. So it is not too much to say that East Asia has emerged as a large demand absorber in the world.

Table 10.6 World Trade by Country and Region in 1993

(Unit: US$ Millions)

Export \ Import	USA	Japan	East Asia	Asian NIEs	ASEAN	China	EU	The World
USA	–	47 999	76 300	50 256	16 209	9 836	96 044	462 171
Japan	105 405	–	133 128	81 283	32 571	19 274	57 153	363 108
East Asia	139 946	77 314	222 547	130 933	37 214	54 401	87 707	659 619
Asian NIEs	80 497	29 922	130 670	51 688	28 002	50 980	48 372	365 323
ASEAN	26 911	25 818	31 061	21 642	5 998	3 421	20 650	138 896
China	32 539	21 574	60 816	57 602	3 214	–	18 684	155 400
EU	93 845	25 952	71 776	40 553	17 077	14 146	745 652	1 319 792
The World	568 800	214 200	580 976	334 776	119 400	126 800	1 292 700	3 730 700

Source: JETRO, *JETRO Boeki Hakusho 1994 (JETRO White Papers on Trade 1994)*, p. 16, Table 1–1–8.

Table 10.7 Shares of Trade by Country and Region, 1985–1993

(Unit: %)

Export	Import	USA	Japan	East Asia	Asian NIEs	ASEAN	China	EU	The World
USA	85	–	1.25	1.40	0.93	0.25	0.21	2.70	11.76
	90	–	1.46	1.69	1.23	0.32	0.14	2.94	11.81
	93	–	1.29	2.05	1.35	0.43	0.26	2.57	12.39
Japan	85	3.68	–	2.35	1.25	0.41	0.69	1.17	9.77
	90	2.74	–	2.56	1.71	0.67	0.18	1.62	8.64
	93	2.83	–	3.57	2.18	0.87	0.52	1.53	9.73
East Asia	85	2.92	1.77	2.69	1.61	0.60	0.48	1.13	10.51
	90	3.16	1.90	4.08	2.54	0.85	0.69	2.02	13.28
	93	3.75	2.07	5.97	3.51	1.00	1.46	2.35	17.68
Asian NIEs	85	2.19	0.63	1.44	0.56	0.43	0.45	0.67	6.29
	90	2.17	0.91	2.30	1.00	0.67	0.63	1.23	8.02
	93	2.16	0.80	3.50	1.39	0.75	1.37	1.30	9.79
ASEAN	85	0.50	0.78	0.65	0.50	0.11	0.03	0.30	2.52
	90	0.50	0.63	0.73	0.57	0.11	0.05	0.42	2.59
	93	0.72	0.69	0.83	0.58	0.16	0.09	0.55	3.72
China	85	0.23	0.36	0.60	0.54	0.06	–	0.16	1.70
	90	0.49	0.38	1.05	0.97	0.08	–	0.37	2.66
	93	0.87	0.58	1.63	1.54	0.09	–	0.50	4.17
EU	85	3.61	0.44	1.12	0.56	0.26	0.30	19.48	35.84
	90	2.90	0.86	1.46	0.88	0.38	0.20	24.87	41.04
	93	2.52	0.70	1.92	1.09	0.46	0.38	19.99	35.38
The World	85	18.07	6.08	9.16	5.22	1.83	2.11	35.09	100.00
	90	14.76	6.22	11.46	7.37	2.61	1.47	40.77	100.00
	93	15.25	5.74	15.57	8.97	3.20	3.40	34.65	100.00

Source: JETRO, JETRO Hakusho Boeki Hen (JETRO White Papers on Trade), p. 17, Table 1–1–9.

Japan's Shift to East Asia

Although the United States has been the major trading partner of Japan throughout the post-war period, in the 1990s a noticeable shift to East Asian partners can be seen in Japan's trading patterns. According to Table 10.7, in terms of Japan's exports in 1993 the first trading partner was East Asia, the second the United States and the third the European Union (EU). Apart from East Asia the first trading partner was the United States, the second the Asian NIEs, the third the EU, the fourth ASEAN, and the fifth China. It is worth noting that the United States' share fell from 1.46 percent in 1990 to 1.29 percent in 1993.

According to Table 10.7 in terms of Japan's imports in 1993, the first trading partner was East Asia, the second the United States, and the third the EU. Apart from East Asia the first trading partner was the United States, the second the Asian NIEs, the third the EU, the fourth ASEAN, and the fifth China. It should be noted that the US share fell from 3.68 percent in 1985 to 2.83 percent in 1933.

China as Trading Partner

Within this dynamically growing region, how is the Chinese role developing? According to Table 10.7, China's share of exports in the total exports of the world increased from 2.11 percent in 1985 to 3.40 percent in 1993. China's share of exports to the world in 1993 exceeded that of ASEAN. In terms of China's exports in 1993 the first trading partner was East Asia, the second Japan, the third the EU, and the fourth the United States. It is worth nothing that apart from East Asia as a whole the Asian NIEs are China's largest trading partner.

On the other hand, according to Table 10.7, China's share of imports out of the world total increased from 1.70 percent in 1985 to 4.17 percent in 1993. Thus, as with exports, China's share of world imports in 1993 exceeded that of ASEAN. In terms of China's exports in 1993 the first trading partner is East Asia, the second the United States, the third Japan, and the fourth the EU. It should be noted that the Asian NIEs are again the largest trading partner apart from East Asia.

These facts show that China is growing in importance as a trade partner in the world. It might be said that the growth of exports contributes to the growth of China's economy, so that China is flying on the 'flying geese' course.

Comparing Japan-China and US-China Economic Relations

According to Table 10.8, Japan's total trade with China was larger than that of the United States with China throughout the 1979–89 period except in 1986. During the 1990–93 period Japan's total trade was smaller than that of the United States. However, in 1994 the situation reversed so that Japan became China's larger trading partner.

However, in terms of direct investment on approval basis in China, Japan lagged behind the United States, according to Table 10.8. Japan's investment in China increased from US$579 million in 1991 to US$1691 million in 1993, so that China ranked first in terms of Japan's investment destinations in Asia. Even though Japanese investment in China has been strong in recent years, US investment in China in cumulative total still exceeds Japanese investment in China (Table 10.8).

According to Table 10.7 in terms of US imports in 1993 the first trading partner was the EU, the second East Asia, and the third Japan. Apart from East Asia the first trading partner was the EU, the second the Asian NIEs, the third Japan, the fourth ASEAN, and the fifth China. The US share of exports to China increased from 0.23 percent in 1985 to 0.87 percent in 1993, even though the US share of exports in the world's total exports decreased from 18.07 percent in 1985 to 15.25 percent in 1993.

CONCLUSION

Up to now it is not too much to say that Japanese-American relations have determined the course of Sino-Japanese relations. In the light of its own China problems Japan has followed US policy. It is true that Japan had trade with China through the famous Liao-Takasaki agreement for unofficial Sino-Japanese trade during the 1960s before the opening of the diplomatic relationship. But it is well-known that prime minister Eisuke Sato (1964–72) was always worried about when the United States would approve the recognition of China. Concern about the US attitude to China, therefore, has remained a factor of importance to Japan.

However, in recent years it has been possible to detect some slight differences of emphasis between Japan and the United States. For example, at the Houston G–7 Economic Summit in 1990, Japanese prime minister Toshiki Kaifu put emphasis on resuming ODA to China in order not to leave China standing alone after the Tiananmen incident in 1989. Nicholas Lardy says that since then the United States has been far behind Japan in terms of trade with and investment in China.[4] Besides, the appreciation of the yen against the dollar has forced not only large Japanese firms but also small and medium firms to move their factories to Asia, especially China.

Of course, over the years Japan has had many trade conflicts with the United States. The difficult trade talks between the two countries early in 1995 suggests that US-Japan relations may follow one scenario suggested by Glen Fukushima, who worked for the US trade representative for many years — namely that after the Republican electoral victories in November 1994 a new styled 'economic nationalism' may be at work.[5] However, numerical trade targets are not accepted by Japan. Of course now most Japanese are beginning to think of the quality of life by getting rid of price differentials between the domestic and international markets. The trend will undoubtedly affect Japan's external economic relations with both the United States and China.

Also important is the state of politics in Japan which are now in disarray. In 1993 the Miyazawa administration of the Liberal Democratic Party collapsed. The Hosokawa and the Hata coalition administrations tried to open the market for trade liberalization; the present Murayama administration is doing the same thing. It seems that Japan could form a relatively strong stable government which has the ability to control the bureaucrats and to carry out trade liberalization only after two or three general elections under the new election system.

According to a recent joint survey[6] by the *Yomiuri Shimbun* newspaper and Gallup in Japan, China and South Korea, 59.4 percent of the Chinese people say that the most important country to the Chinese economy is the United States, while 19.9 percent of those say that the second is Japan. Here Japan faces a dilemma even if it becomes the largest trading partner after the United States. The Japanese make much of the Chinese while the Chinese make much of the Americans; the Americans too make much of the Chinese. This is a triangular relationship.

As a result it seems to me that in order to cope with this dilemma Japan should become a leader of the Asia Pacific Economic Cooperation (APEC) forum which includes both China and the United States as members. APEC should not be a closed but an open economic community and through APEC Japan could realize the 'general equilibrium' approach. Shigeharu Matsumoto, a famous journalist and the director of the International House in Tokyo, once said, 'Sino-Japanese problems are truly Japan-US problems. This is true in the pre-war and post-war period.'[7] Even now this saying is very valuable in thinking about Sino-American relations.

NOTES

1. *Japan Economic Journal*, 24 May 1995.
2. M. Watanabe, *Chugoku deno Bijinesu* (Doing Business in China) (Tokyo: The Simul Press, 1992).
3. Y. Fukuzawa, 'Datsu A Ron (On getting out of Asia)', *Jiji Simpo*, 1885.
4. N.R. Lardy, *China in the World Economy* (Washington, DC: Institute for International Economics, 1994).

5. G.S. Fukushima, '*Beikoku ga Nihon ni Nozomu noha Keizaimen deno "Futsuu no Kuni"* (What the United States wants is an economically ordinary country, Japan)', *Nihon Keizai Kenkyu Senta-Kaiho*, No. 723 (March 1995), pp. 4–8.
6. *The Yomiuri Shimbun,* 1 June 1995.
7. S. Matsumoto, *Shanghai Jidai* (The Age of Shanghai) (Tokyo: Chuo Koron Sha, 1975).

11

US-China Trade Conflict and Its Implications for Australia's Agricultural Trade

Joseph C.H. Chai*

The US-China trade conflict is characterized by persistent bilateral trade imbalances in China's favour since the early 1980s (see Table 11.1). According to US statistics, during the 1984–94 period, US exports to China rose at an annual average rate of only 6.2 percent, whereas Chinese exports to the United States grew at an annual average rate of 8.9 percent. As a result the US trade balance with China turned from surplus into deficit in the early 1980s and by 1993 China had become the country with which the United States had the largest deficit after Japan.[1]

The US-Japan trade imbalance has its origin in the underlying macroeconomics or, more specifically, in the discrepancy between Japanese and US savings and investment rates.[2] On the other hand, the US-China trade imbalance factor is partly a result of China's catching-up industrialization following the 'flying geese' pattern of development. It is also a result of the strategy of Asian NICs to relocate their labour-intensive manufacturing export base to China in response to rising labour costs and land prices, the appreciation of their currencies, and the increased pressure to reduce their trade surplus with the United States. Consequently, part of the Asian NIC-US merchandise trade imbalance has been exported to China.

To reduce its deficit with China, the United States has employed a wide range of mechanisms including bilateral negotiations with and unilateral measures imposed on China. China was criticized by the United States for seeking to export its goods aggressively in foreign markets while limiting access of its trading partners to its own market. In 1992 the United States successfully negotiated two trade agreements with China. The first was the Memorandum of Understanding (MOU) on intellectual property rights (IPR) which committed China to strengthen its IPR protection, and a second MOU on market access committed China to a significant liberalization of some key

* Research assisted by James Laurenceson and data provided by Professor Y.Y. Kueh are gratefully acknowledged.

Table 11.1 US-China Trade Trends Using the US
System of Accounting, 1980–1994 (in US$ Billions)

	US exports to China	US imports from China	Trade balance
1980	3.8	1.2	2.6
1981	3.6	2.1	1.5
1982	2.9	2.5	0.4
1983	2.2	2.5	−0.3
1984	3.0	3.1	−0.1
1985	3.9	3.9	0.0
1986	3.1	4.8	−1.7
1987	3.5	6.3	−2.8
1988	5.0	8.5	−3.5
1989	5.8	12.0	−6.2
1990	4.8	15.2	−10.4
1991	6.2	18.9	−12.7
1992	7.4	25.7	−18.3
1993	8.8	31.5	−22.7
1994	8.8	38.0	−29.2

Source: 1980–1992: D.A. Rondinelli, *Expanding Sino-American Business* (Westport: Quorum Books, 1994), p. 12; 1993: USIS, *Economic Backgrounder,* 11 April 1994; and Press Release of the Office of the US Trade Representative, 4 February 1995.

aspects of its import regime, including a reduction of trade barriers and the gradual opening of its market to US exports.[3]

In spite of these two agreements, the United States is still frustrated by the wide restrictions applied to a wide range of economic activities by foreigners in China with respect to currency exchange, investment, imports and services as well as the lack of IPR protection. Because of these, in early 1995, the United States has threatened China with the imposition of US trade sanctions on Chinese imported goods for China's failure to implement the MOU on IPR and to provide market access for intellectual property-based products. Though this latest trade dispute was resolved just in time to avoid the imposition of sanctions, trade friction between the United States and China is expected to continue, and may even worsen, as long as the trade imbalance persists, in spite of the fact that the two economies are basically compatible trade partners in terms of their development.

The trade friction between the United States and China has profound implications for Australia, which are compounded by the fact that Australia is increasingly looking towards, and dependent on, trade with Asian nations. To begin with, both the United States and Australia are integral parts of the East Asian Industrial Belt or, in more general terms, of the Asia-Pacific region, a position which potentially puts them into competition for the Asian market. In the past, a conflict of interest between them has not occurred because the United States has mainly provided the industrial export market for Asian countries, for example, for Japan since the mid-1950s, for the Asian NICs since the mid-1960s, and for China and for ASEAN countries since the late 1970s, while Australia has largely confined itself to providing raw materials, fuel and food for these countries.

However, as the United States is under increasing pressure to address its trade imbalance with Japan and China through export expansion it tends to compete with Australian goods with regard to a number of commodities, especially in the food and agricultural sectors of these two Asian markets. If China's demand for agricultural imports remains static, any readjustment of the trade flow between the United States and China necessarily has serious repercussions on Australia's agricultural exports to that country. But even if China's demand for agricultural imports grows, the United States and Australia are likely to face much more intensified competition for their relative shares in China's market. Since agricultural exports still make up a large share of Australia's overall export earnings, even relatively slight adjustments in its share of the Chinese market will have serious repercussions for its overall balance of trade and the state of its economy. And since the United States is subsidizing its farmers while Australia is not, the issue of competition for agricultural exports is a fairly emotive one for the Australians and has the potential to undermine relations between the partners in the APEC (Asia-Pacific Economic Cooperation) forum.

The purpose of this chapter is to examine the ramifications of the US-China trade conflict for Australian exports. The discussion turns first to an overview of Australia-China economic relations focusing mainly on trade and investment relations. This is followed by an examination of the ramifications of US-China trade friction for Australia using a simple analytical framework. In order to narrow the discussion manageable proportions, the discussion focuses almost exclusively on Australian food and agricultural exports.

AUSTRALIA-CHINA ECONOMIC RELATIONS

Merchandise Trade

Table 11.2 summarizes Australia-China bilateral trade since the late 1970s when China adopted the open-door and reform policy. It shows that between 1978 and 1979 and between 1993 and 1994 two-way trade increased in nominal terms on average by 13 percent annually — a growth rate which is almost twice that of world trade during the same period. However, the pattern of growth in Australia-China trade was rather uneven in that period for, while

Table 11.2 Australia-China, Hong Kong:
Bilateral Commodity Trade, 1977–1994 (A$ Millions)

	China			Hong Kong			Aggregate
	Exports	Imports	Balance	Exports	Imports	Balance	Balance
1979–80	845	199	645	281	380	−99	546
1980–81	671	269	401	309	395	−86	315
1981–82	602	284	317	436	500	−64	253
1982–83	643	278	364	349	485	−136	228
1983–84	609	311	297	603	550	53	350
1984–85	1061	373	688	839	657	182	870
1985–86	1497	435	1062	721	676	45	1107
1986–87	1592	588	1003	1086	800	286	1289
1987–88	1277	850	426	1927	845	1082	1508
1988–89	1230	1026	204	1889	888	1001	1205
1989–90	1192	1240	−48	1323	847	476	428
1990–91	1347	1502	−155	1573	741	832	677
1991–92	1458	1975	−517	2105	792	1313	796
1992–93	2268	2557	−289	2596	796	1800	1511
1993–94	2589	3120	−531	2785	801	1984	1453

Source: Australian Bureau of Statistics, *International Merchandise Trade Australia*,
Canberra, AGPS, 1995, Cat. No. 5422.

Australia's imports of Chinese goods increased more or less steadily, Australia's
exports to China fluctuated widely in a general upward trend.[4]

During the first phase of the Chinese economic reforms (1979–84) Australian
exports to China are marked by a slump which is largely explained by the fact
there had been an impressive growth of real agricultural output in China.
Since agricultural imports were regarded as a residual in the domestic supply-
demand commodity balance and were justified only as a buffer against domestic
shortages, the greater output of China's agricultural sector, as a result of the
rural reforms, meant that real agricultural imports declined correspondingly
during this period.[5] Exports to China during the 1985–87 period increased
rapidly in response to stagnant agricultural output in China. They declined,
however, since 1987. Internal factors, such as the collapse of wool and wheat
exports due to supply difficulties in Australia, as well as external factors, such
as the competition of subsidized agricultural products from the United States,[6]
as well as factors within China, such as its economic slowdown following the
Tiananmen Square incident and its subsequent austerity programme to counter
inflation, each to a greater or lesser extent, helped to suppress the growth of
Australian agricultural exports to China during this period.

However, Australia's exports to China recovered from 1989 onwards and
rose rapidly in the third phase of China's economic reforms since 1992. For
example, from 1991 to 1992 and from 1993 to 1994 they almost doubled largely
as a result of the 13 percent growth rate of China's economy during this
period.

Australia's exports to China are made up of a small number of bulk commodities dominated initially by agricultural products. However, since the late 1970s there has been a trend towards product diversification with a shift away from mainly agricultural goods to mineral and manufactured goods exports.[7] For example, in 1981 agricultural products accounted for around 80 percent of Australia's exports to China. By 1984, however, their share had declined to only about one-third. Conversely, mineral and manufactured exports increased their shares to 42 percent and 25 percent respectively.

Within the primary sector, Australia's exports to China are heavily concentrated on only a few commodities. In the agricultural sector they consist mainly of wheat, barley, wool and sugar, whereas in the mineral sector they are dominated by iron ore, coal and gold (see Table 11.3). With respect to the manufacturing sector, elaborately transformed manufactured goods (ETM) have made a significant stride ahead in recent years and in 1994 accounted for over 75 percent of all manufactured goods exports to China.

Table 11.3 Major Australian Exports to China (A$ Millions)

	1989	1990	1991	1992	1993	1994[1]
Iron ore & conc.	162.3	136.7	372.9	396.0	468.8	249.7
Coal: Coking	23.8	29.5	20.8	26.1	46.0	14.4
Steaming	–	2.9	–	–	4.4	2.7
Wool, excl. tops	148.1	90.3	333.0	519.4	505.3	376.4
Tops	49.6	47.9	47.0	50.2	74.0	55.2
Wheat	315.0	158.4	263.5	60[2]	100[2]	n.a.
Barley, unmilled	41.0	135.1	73.0	88.1	39.0	n.a.
Manufactures	196.2	170.1	203.7	328.0	559.2	308.2
STM	117.0	88.4	86.7	150.2	135.6	75.0
ETM	75.6	81.7	117.0	187.8	423.6	233.2

Note: 1. Year up to August.
2. These Australian data are confidential, figures are based on Chinese custom statistics.
3. STM stands for simply transformed manufactured goods.

Source: Department of Foreign Affairs and Trade, *China, November 1994*, Canberra, AGPS, 1994a, pp. 35–6.

In contrast to the pattern of exports, Australia's imports from China consist almost exclusively of manufactured goods, especially labour-intensive manufactures, such as textiles, clothing and footwear (TCF). In the early 1980s, TCF accounted for about 60 percent of China's exports to Australia, but with the growing sophistication of Chinese manufacturers the TCF share has fallen to around 43 percent in the period 1993–94. On the other hand there has been a significant increase in the share of electrical equipment and machinery in recent years.[8]

According to Australian statistics, Australia's trade balance with China has turned from surplus into deficit since 1989 (see Table 11.2). However, as opposed to US statistics, there has been no attempt to remove the distortion in Australia-China trade statistics caused by Hong Kong's resurgent entrepôt function for China.[9] Specifically, a significant proportion of Australian goods re-exported via Hong Kong to China is not counted as part of Australian exports to China. Similarly, Chinese goods which are re-exported to Australia through Hong Kong are not counted as Chinese exports and Hong Kong goods processed in China and re-exported to Australia are included in the figures on China's exports to Australia. Thus a real picture of the Australia-China trade balance cannot be gleaned from the Australian trade statistics. However, the real picture can be inferred if Hong Kong and China are treated as a single market for Australia products. As shown in Table 11.2 Australia's trade with the combined China-Hong Kong market is definitely skewed in Australia's favour.

Table 11.4 indicates the growing importance of Greater China and other Asian NICs to Australia's trade. It shows that Australia maintains a fairly persistent trade pattern: on the one hand, it maintains a trade surplus with Japan, Greater China and other Asian NICs (South Korea and Singapore), and on the other hand, it incurs persistent deficits with the United States and the European Union (EU). Australia uses its trade surplus with East Asian countries and the rest of the world to finance its deficit with the United States and Europe.

Table 11.4 Australia's Trade Balance[1] (US$ Billions)

Country	1987	1988	1989	1990	1991	1992	1993
Japan	1.47	2.17	1.44	2.92	4.70	3.36	2.38
China	0.59	0.17	−0.04	−0.08	−0.20	−0.32	−0.44
Hong Kong	0.33	0.91	0.56	0.32	0.84	1.06	1.26
Taiwan	−0.44	−0.40	−0.49	−0.18	0.21	0.19	0.15
South Korea	0.31	0.59	0.72	1.19	1.61	1.41	1.53
Singapore	0.03	0.20	0.25	0.79	1.12	1.62	1.03
Greater China	0.48	0.68	0.03	0.06	0.85	0.93	0.97
China & Asian NICs	0.82	1.47	1.00	2.04	3.58	3.96	3.53
United States	−2.78	−3.72	−5.31	−5.14	−5.29	−5.48	−5.73
European Union	−2.88	−3.83	−4.85	−4.63	−3.99	−3.61	−4.23
Rest of the world	2.90	3.33	3.80	4.64	4.12	3.55	4.05

Note: 1. Imports valued at FOB.
Source: IMF, Director of Trade Statistics Yearbook, 1994, pp. 105–7.

Since the early 1990s, however, there have been slight but perhaps significant shifts in Australia's trade pattern: its surplus with Japan started to show a declining trend, while its surplus with Greater China and other Asian NICs increased. More precisely, since the early 1990s, Australia's trade surplus with

China and other Asian NICs has actually exceeded the size of its trade surplus with Japan. This indicates the growing importance of these countries and especially of Greater China in financing Australia's trade with the United States and the EU.

Australia's trade relations with China and Hong Kong are somewhat asymmetric. For example, in the early 1990s, both China and Hong Kong were among Australia's top ten export markets. For the period 1990–91 and 1993–94, while Japan's share in Australia's export declined, the combined share of Hong Kong and China in Australia's exports increased from 6 to 8 percent and same as the United States it was ranked as the second most important export market for Australia right behind Japan.[10] In the same period, however, Australia's share of China's and Hong Kong's import market slipped from 3.5 percent to 2.9 percent.[11] Australia's trade intensity with China and Hong Kong follows a similar pattern. On the import side China's and Hong Kong's import intensities with Australia declined in the early 1990s. In contrast China/Hong Kong's export intensities with Australia increased. This shows the growing importance of Australia as an export market for China and Hong Kong.

Services Trade

In line with the global trend of relatively faster growth of the services trade than that of merchandise trade, the share of services in Australian total exports increased from 18 percent in the period 1983–84 to 22 percent in 1993–94. Services exports are now more or less of equal importance with agricultural, mineral and manufactured exports. Each roughly accounted for about one quarter of Australian total exports in 1994.[12]

Australia is a net importer of services and hence its services trade balance has suffered persistent deficits over the last ten years. However, more recently its services trade deficit has narrowed significantly due to stronger growth of service exports, especially to North-east Asia. Due to their proximity, North-east Asia and the ASEAN countries are currently Australia's largest services export markets followed by the EU and United States. In the period 1992–93 they accounted for 45 percent of all of Australia's service exports. Within north-east Asia, Japan is the largest destination for Australian services exports, accounting for about 19 percent, followed by China/Hong Kong with 6.1 percent as well as Taiwan and Korea with smaller shares. The combined share of Greater China and Singapore in Australia's total service exports in the years 1992–93 was 22.1 percent which exceeded Japan's share.[13]

In the Asian market, Australia's largest services exports have been travel and education services. North-east Asia accounted for more than one quarter of short-term arrivals in Australia. Japan has the biggest share in Australia travel service exports. However, most recently there was a noteable slowdown in the number of Japanese tourists to Australia whereas the share of travellers from China/Hong Kong, Taiwan and South Korea continued to soar.

The main education service export markets for Australia in North-east Asia have been Hong Kong and China which are the top two sources of full-fee-paying overseas students and accounted for around 40 percent of foreign student spending in Australia in the early 1990s.[14] Chinese student arrivals in Australia have, however, slumped since 1992 due to tighter visa requirements by the Australian government.

With the liberalization of the services trade following the Uruguay Round and the increased liberalization of China's services market, it is expected that Australian exports of other services to China, in particular banking, insurance, accounting, legal and other professional services, are likely to soar in the near future.

Foreign Direct Investment

Australia is a net capital importing country: its FDI inflow in 1992–93 was almost four times its FDI outflow. The United States is the leading foreign direct investor in Australia and accounted for 32 percent of the total stock of FDI in the years 1992–93 followed by the United Kingdom and Japan. The FDI inflow from other north-east Asian countries has started to increase recently, but is still comparatively negligible compared to that of Japan.

According to China's MOFTEC statistics, Australia is one of the most popular destinations for Chinese FDI ranking second after Canada (see Table 11.5). By the end of 1993, according to the Australia Bureau of Statistics, China's investments in 134 projects in Australia were worth US$333 million.[16]

Table 11.5 Top 10 Destinations of China's FDI,[1] 1979–93 (in US$ Millions)

1. Canada	368.5
2. Australia	322.4
3. United States	320.9
4. Hong Kong	135.1
5. Russia	95.2
6. Thailand	48.5
7. New Zealand	43.2
8. Chile	21.5
9. Malaysia	19.6
10. Macao	15.9
World Total	1687.0

Note: 1. Approved amount.
Source: *Almanac of China's Foreign Economic Relations and Trade*, Beijing, China's Outlook Press, 1994, pp. 870–3.

But this accounted for only 0.5 percent of Australia's total FDI inflow in that year.[17] Chinese FDIs in Australia centre in the resource sector since the motive of China's FDI is to secure a stable supply of raw materials to fuel its industrialization drive. The Mount Channer iron ore project and the Portland Aluminium Smelter are China's two largest projects worth A$220 million, accounting for almost half of Chinese FDI stock in Australia.

In contrast, the bulk of Australia's FDI outflow went to the United States and the UK. Cumulative FDIs in north-east Asia amounted to less than 4 percent of Australia's FDIs in the early 1990s.[18] Most of Australia's FDI in North-east Asia went to Hong Kong and Japan. The former was the fifth largest destination for Australian overseas investments with a stock of A$3.1 billion in 1992–93 which accounted for less than 3 percent of Australia's total investment.[19] At the end of 1992, Australia was the seventh largest investor in Hong Kong's manufacturing sector,[20] and over 90 percent of this is concentrated in the non-metallic mineral products industry and in the printing and publishing industry.[21]

Australia is the eighth largest direct foreign investor in China.[22] The sum of its approved FDI there stood at US$1.46 billion in early 1995[23] and that of realized investments at around US$340.4 million by the end of 1993 (Table 11.6). However, Australia's FDI in China was equivalent to only one percent of Australia's FDI abroad. Australia's investment in China covered a wide range of commodities, but were mainly confined to the manufacturing sector. More recently some Australian food processors, such as Cadbury-Schweppes and Fosters Brewing Group, and mining companies, such as BHP and Amcor and banks such as the ANZ, have become increasingly active in the Chinese investment market.

Table 11.6 Australia's FDI in China (in US$ Millions)

Year	Approved	Realized
1979–82	8.4	n.a.
1983	79.6	5.6
1984	4.2	0.4
1985	14.1	14.4
1986	31.6	78.8
1987	47.4	5.0
1988	17.4	4.2
1989	n.a.	46.5
1990	17.8	25.2
1991	n.a.	14.9
1992	n.a.	35.1
1993	640.8	110.3

Source: *Almanac of China's Foreign Economic Relations and Trade,* various issues, and *Zhongguo tongji nianjian* (China Statistical Yearbook), various issues.

IMPLICATIONS FOR AUSTRALIA

Analytical Framework

Theoretically the US-China trade accord on IPR and market access could only benefit Australia's exports if any trade concessions reached in the memorandums are implemented on an MFN basis. For example, in the past the US-Japan trade conflict and its resolution has resulted in improved access to the Japanese market for Australia's exports in general and for Australia's beef, rice and legal services exports to Japan in particular.[24] However, Australia's exports may be discriminated against in China's market if the United States largely assesses the degree of openness of China's market on the basis of the success of its own industry in increasing its market share in China, and if China, in order to reduce the threat of trade sanctions by the United States, gives US products favourable consideration in the sourcing of its imports.

Thus the implications of a US-China trade accord for Australia may cause both trade creation and trade diversion for Australia's exports. A comprehensive assessment of these two effects necessitates the use of a computable general equilibrium model. In view of the scope and constraints of this chapter as well as limits on data availability a less demanding analytical framework is adopted in the following discussion.

Assuming that initially the matrix of China's trade with the United States (US), Australia (AUS) and the rest of the world (ROW) is as follows:

Imports of	China	US	Exports by AUS	ROW	Total
China	*	X_{12}	X_{13}	X_{14}	X_1
US	X_{21}	*	X_{23}	X_{24}	X_2
AUS	X_{31}	X_{32}	*	X_{34}	X_3
ROW	X_{41}	X_{42}	X_{43}	*	X_4

where X_{ij} = imports of ith country from jth country and X_i = total imports of ith country.

The hypothetical change of Australia's exports as a result of the implementation of a US-China trade accord may be depicted as follows:

$$Y_{13} = X_{13} - d_{13} + e_{13} + e'_{13}$$
$$Y_{23} = X_{23}$$
$$Y_{43} = X_{43} + r_{43}$$

where Y_{ij} = hypothetical change of imports of country i from country j
   d_{ij} = diversion of the ith country's imports from country j, and

eij = increase in i's imports from j caused by i country's improved market access;

e'ij = increase in i's imports from j caused by increase of i's GNP;

rij = increase in j's export to i due to strict enforcement of IPR in third country, such as China, which used to supply i'

If the US-China trade accord is administered without discrimination, the trade diversion effect, namely d_{13}, will be zero and in this case Australia's exports to China could only be expected to increase. If there is some discrimination, its net impact on Australia's exports depends on the relative sizes of the trade diversion effects (d_{13}) and trade creation effects (e_{13}, e'_{13} and r_{43}).

The Trade Diversion Effect

The size of the trade diversion effect for Australia depends on a number of factors including the number of products in which Australia is competing with the United States on China's market and the degree of competitiveness of these products in relation to the comparable US product.

Whereas food and agricultural products accounted for one third of Australia's exports to China in 1993, they made up only about 10 percent of US exports to China (see Table 11.7). The probability of the trade diversion or the displacement of Australia's imports by US imports in China's food and agricultural market can be measured by the index of export similarity developed by Finger and Kreinin. The F-K index is defined by the formula:

$$S (ab,c) = {}_{[} -i \text{ minimum } [X_i (ac), X_i (bc)]_{]} \times 100$$

— where S (ab,c) measures the similarity of export patterns of countries a and b to market c, and Xi(ac) is the share of commodity i in a's exports to c. If the commodity structure i in a's exports are identical to b's, the F-K index will equal unity. If a's and b's exports are completely different the index will be equal to zero. The index can be used to measure the degree of similarity in the basket of goods exported by Australia and competing exporting countries such as the United States. The greater the similarity in the commodity structure of their food and agricultrural exports the greater the probability of Australia's goods being displaced by those of the United States in China's market. Table 11.7 presents the commodity composition of the food and agricultural exports of both countries to China. It reveals that Australia's composition of food and agricultural goods is quite different from that of the United States since the F-K index is only 35.5 percent.

Australia's exports are heavily concentrated on SITC 26, namely textile

Table 11.7 Food and Agricultural Exports by Australia
and the US to China (%),[1] 1993

SITC		Australia	US
01	Meat	0.5	3.9
02	Dairy products & bird eggs	0.6	0.4
03	Fish, crustaceans & molluscs	1.4	3.6
04	Cereals	26.2	28.4
05	Vegetables and fruits	0.1	1.3
06	Sugar & honey	5.2	0.2
07	Coffee, tea, cocoa & spices	0.3	0.2
08	Feeding stuff for animals	0.7	2.9
1	Beverages & tobacco	Negl.	4.3
21	Hides, skin & furskin, raw	3.7	2.1
22	Oil seed & oleaginous fruits	Negl.	2.2
23	Crude rubber	Negl.	0.9
24	Cork & wood	Negl.	13.4
25	Pulp & waste paper	Negl.	7.1
26	Textile fibres	55.3	3.2
4	Animal & vegetable oils	2.9	0.5
64	Paper & paper board	2.9	25.6

Note: 1. Food and agriculture cover SITC 00–09, 1, 21–27, 4 and 64. China has
switched from SITC to HS system in trade classification since 1992. Due
to the difficulty in reconciling the product coverage between the two systems,
SITC 00, 09 and 29 have not been included.

Source: General Administration of Customs, *China Customs Statistics Yearbook 1993*,
Vol. I, 1994, Hong Kong: Economic Information Agency, pp. 87–90.

fibres and their wastes, and category 04, namely cereals and cereal preparations,
whereas US food and agricultural exports are more diversified and, with the
exception of cereals, leaned more towards timber products (SITC, 64, 24 and
25). Hence the threat of competition for Australia should not be overrated.

Table 11.8 identifies those of Australia's main exports which are most
similar to those of the United States. It shows that they cover a wide range of
products but are mainly confined to cereals, crude animal materials and
timber products.

The export similarity index only indicates the probability that Australia's
exports may be displaced by similar exports from the United States. To find
out whether, and if so to what extent, US products will displace Australia's
exports requires the knowledge of elasticity of substitution between Australian
and US imports in China's market. This depends on the extent to which
imports from the two countries are differentiated in the Chinese market. The
degree of differentiation should ideally be measured in terms of cross elasticities
of Chinese import demand with respect to the price of imports from Australia
and those from the United States. The higher these cross elasticities the lower

Table 11.8 Major Competing Agricultural Commodities[1] Exported to China by the United States and Australia (in US$ Millions)

CCCCS[2]	Commodity	Export value Australia	US
1. Cereals			
10.01	Wheat	90.3	304.5
11.01	Wheat flour	0.8	0.8
10.03	Barley	77.4	5.2
2. Dairy products			
04.01	Fresh milk	0.5	0.3
04.02	Milk, cream, preserved	2.0	1.4
04.05	Butter	0.1	0.2
3. Vegetable fat			
1516.2000	Margarine	2.6	0.4
4. Meat			
02.01 & 02.02	Beef	2.2	1.1
5. Cocoa			
1806.3100	Chocolate & cocoa	2.2	1.9
6. Animal feeds			
2301.1010	Flour & meals of meat & bones	2.3	0.6
23.09	Animal feed	3.4	10.0
7. Hides & Skin			
41.01	Raw hides & skin of bovine or equine animals	8.9	13.1
8. Timber products			
4411	Fibreboard of wood	4.4	10.4
4801–9	Paper	19.2	281.8

Note: 1. US$1 million and above.
        2. Commodity Classification for China Custom Statistics which was based on Harmonized Commodity Description and Coding System (HS).
Source: General Administration of Customs (1994), op. cit., Vol. II.

is the differentiation between Australia and US products. It can also be indirectly inferred from a comparison of the change in Australia's relative market share and relative price in China. If these are highly correlated the substitution elasticity must be quite high.

In the following sections, we first examine Australia's market share of food and agricultural products in general and then that of selected groups of commodities in which the United States and Australia are competing with each other on China's market.

Between 1990 and 1993 Australia's share in China's food and agricultural imports in terms of value surged from 6.8 percent to 9.2 percent whereas those of the United States slipped from 21.3 percent to 15.6 percent (see Table 11.9). To identify the cause of these changes, a modified constant market share analysis (CMS) can be used.[25] Accordingly, the change in Chinese imports from each competitor is decomposed into three elements, namely the change

Table 11.9 China's Food and Agricultural Imports from Australia and the
United States Current Prices, 1990 and 1993 (in US$ Millions)

	Australia	US	World
1990 imports from	564.3	1769.31	8323.9
1993 imports from	654.8	1111.0	7122.2
Changes in imports 1990–93:	90.5	–658.3	–
of which, due to change in total			
import demand	–81.5	–255.4	–
Due to shift in commodity			
composition	–127.9	–82.6	
Due to change in 'competitiveness'	301.7	–320.3	–

Source: UN, *Commodity Trade Statistics,* 1990 and General Administration of Customs
(1994), op. cit., Vol. I.

in imports due to changes in China's total import demand; the change in
imports due to a shift in China's commodity composition of import demand;
and the residual factor, namely changes in the 'competitiveness' of each
competitor's supply. The results of the decompostion are shown in Table 11.9.

The major finding is that both countries suffered from declining Chinese
import demand for food and agricultural products during this period, as well
as from a shift in China's import demand structure. The United States, however,
was hit relatively harder because of their unfavourable initial export
composition and a reduction in their 'competitiveness'. Australia, on the other
hand, was able to increase its sales to China thanks to its improved
'competitiveness'.

Looking at the group of commodities in which Australia and the United
States are competing with each other in China's market, however, we find that
out of the nine commodities considered, Australia lost its volume share in only
two commodities, namely wheat and barley, whereas it expanded its share in
others (see Table 11.10). However, the two commodities in which Australia lost
ground happen to be Australia's main food and agricultural exports (see
Table 11.7). Thus Australia's overall market share in terms of volume in the
competitive commodities groups must have declined. In contrast, the US
market share in the competitive commodities groups all expanded, with the
single exception of beef. But since the latter does not constitute a major
agricultural export of the United States to China, America's share in China's
market in terms of volume in the competitive commodities group must have
increased significantly. To shed light on the factors behind the different export
performance between Australia and the United States in these commodities,
Table 11.11 compares the change in Australia's relative share with the change
in relative prices. This shows that out of the six commodities for which
comparative data for relative shares and prices are available the change of

Table 11.10 Market Share Comparison: Australia and the US (in %)[1]

	Volume share		Relative prices[2]	
	1990	1993	1990	1993
1. Wheat				
Australia	11.1	9.6	1.02	1.12
US	31.3	40.3	0.94	0.91
2. Wheat flour				
Australia	0.0	13.3	n.a.	0.81
US	2.3	9.7	1.34	1.15
3. Barley				
Australia	68.7	59.9	1.02	1.01
US	0.0	4.1	n.a.	1.00
4. Dairy products				
Australia	7.2	8.6	1.45	0.88
US	3.6	11.5	1.23	0.68
5. Margarine				
Australia	47.6	48.2	0.99	1.08
US	2.4	6.2	2.36	1.23
6. Beef				
Australia	25.1	59.6	1.36	0.70
US	22.3	20.3	1.04	1.02
7. Chocolate & cocoa				
Australia	10.7	68.1	1.64	0.96
US	4.7	16.8	1.51	1.17
8. Bovine, equine hides, raw				
Australia	8.1	10.8	1.46	1.51
US	30.6	31.9	1.52	0.82

Note: 1. Some products are excluded due to difficulties in reconciling the HS system in 1993 with the SITC Rev. 3 system used in 1992 by China.
2. The ratio of Australian and US price to the average world price.

Table 11.11 Australia's Relative Share and Price[1] in China's Imports of Agricultural Products

	Share		Price	
	1990	1993	1990	1993
1. Wheat	0.35	0.24	1.09	1.23
2. Wheat flour	–	1.37	–	0.70
3. Barley	–	14.61	–	1.01
4. Dairy products	2.00	0.75	1.18	1.29
5. Margarine	19.80	7.77	0.42	0.88
6. Beef	1.13	2.93	1.31	0.69
7. Chocolate & cocoa	2.28	4.05	1.09	0.82
8. Bovine & equine hides, raw	0.27	0.34	0.96	1.84

Note: 1. Volume share and prices of Australia divided by those of the US.
2. ' – ' means not applicable.
Source: See Table 11.10.

Australia's relative share in five commodities can be explained by their relative price change. For example, the loss of ground of one of Australia's largest agricultural exports to China, namely wheat, to the United States is largely explained by the relatively lower price competitiveness of Australian exports in relation to US product. The latter, in turn, is attributed by most analysts in Australia to US wheat export subsidies.[26] The significance of the above findings can be summarized as follows: firstly, Australia's food and agricultural exports have performed very well in general inspite of the US-China trade accord during the 1990–93 period. Its performance in commodities which were also exported by the United States, however, was relatively poor compared to the US performance, which, however, can largely be explained by Australia's declined price competitiveness. Hence, there is as yet no evidence that Australia's exports have been discriminated against in Chinese market.

Secondly, the confirmed positive relationship between the relative market shares of Australia and the United States, on the one hand, and their relative prices, on the other, indicates that Australian and US products are highly substitutable in the Chinese market. Thus, when circumstances require, Chinese importers may substitute Australia's imports by those from the United States. Thus, the perceived threat of damage to Australian interests should not be dismissed easily. It is compounded by the fact that China's trade regime is still very much a state trading system where the government maintains various links with trading enterprises which makes it easier to discriminate among suppliers on non-commercial grounds.

Trade Creation Effects

The trade creation effects of a US-China trade accord for Australia consist of the direct trade creation (e_{13} and r_{43}) as well as of the indirect trade creation (e'_{13}). e_{13} is the increase in Chinese imports from Australia as a result of improved market access in China for those Australian products which do not compete with US goods. The size of this effect depends on the share of these commodities in Australia's total exports to, and the height of import barriers for these commodities in, China. As mentioned earlier, almost two-thirds of Australia's food and agricultural exports in 1993 were non-competing products with the US (see Table 11.7), with the major items being wool and sugar.

Wool is Australia's largest export item to China and in 1993 it accounted for 54 percent of Australia's food and agricultural exports there (see Table 11.7). Exports of wool to China have increased rapidly in recent years due to the shift of a considerable number of wool processing plants from the Asian NCs to China. Australia is the world's largest producer and exporter of greasy wool. Australian wool, produced from a 80 percent Merino sheep stock, is famous for its quality and is most suitable for garment manufacture.[27] In 1993

Australia held 59 percent of Chinese wool imports, ahead of such other major competitors as New Zealand, Uruguay, Kazakhstan and Mongolia. The US share was negligible.

Sugar is Australia's third largest food and agricultural export item to China, after wool and cereals, accounting for about 5 percent of Australia's total food and agricultural exports where in 1993 it had a market share of 31 percent, second only to Cuba, the dominant supplier. The US market share was again negligible as it is not self-sufficient in sugar production. Australia has a comparative advantage in sugar production because of its land area and its climatic conditions. It not only exports to China but in 1991 held 16 percent of total world sugar exports.[28] Most Australian raw sugar is produced in Queensland.

China's import demand for sugar has increased significantly lately due to a combination of factors, such as its development of excess capacity to refine sugar for domestic demand and re-exports. This is done in order to capture the price premium between refined and raw sugar.[29] China is a major producer of raw sugar but its output has fallen in the last few years. On the other hand, its demand for refined sugar has increased recently owing to a rise in per capita consumption of food and beverages driven by rapid income growth.

Both wool and sugar are currently subject to a wide range of tariff barriers and non-tariff barriers (NTBs), as well as domestic supports in China which are aimed at increasing domestic production and achieving food and agricultural sufficiency.[30] Upon entry into WTO, China will be bound by the Uruguay Round Agreement which should benefit Australia's agricultural imports into China. For, under this agreement, all NTBs are to be replaced by tariff equivalents and import bans by some minimum access during the implementation period and both tariffs and domestic supports are to be lowered.

However, the Uruguay Round Agreement provides only broad guidelines for improved market access and allows countries considerable flexibility in the method of their implementation. Hence, Australia should not solely rely on improved market access in China due to the Uruguay Round Agreement but it needs to hold regular bilateral market access discussions with China. Undoubtedly, Australia can benefit substantially from the spill-over effects of any market access discussion between China and third countries, such as the United States.

The strict enforcement of IPR in China as a result of a US-China accord should also benefit Australian exports of IPR-based products which are quite substantial and consist mainly of audio-visual materials, computer software, and specialized machinery and equipment. The information technology and telecommunications industry has lately become one of Australia's largest and fastest-growing exports covering computer and telecommunications hardware, and communications and networking equipment and services, such as contract software. These export items are now worth more than wheat exports and amount to about two-thirds of the export value of coal, Australia's single largest export item.[31]

By far the largest benefit to be expected for Australia's exports should come from the fall-out of US-China market access negotiations through the indirect trade creation effect. The internationalization of China's domestic market should help China to reap both the static and dynamic gain of trade as well as an improved FDI environment which should lead to a higher rate of growth of its economy and real income. In most Asian countries the latter is accompanied by dietary changes which include the switch from the traditional staple rice to an alternative staple, typically wheat; the switch from staple starch foods, such as rice and wheat, to more high-protein livestock and dairy products; and a switch away from raw to processed foods. These changes have been well documented in several studies,[32] the significance of which is enormous for food exporters to China, such as Australia. This is because firstly, in view of its huge population, China is likely to become the world's largest food market if its internationalization proceeds. Secondly, China's comparative advantage in agricultural production has worsened rapidly in recent years[33] due to its declining area of arable and pasture land per capita caused by growing industrialization and faster economic growth, as well as higher costs of agricultural production due to environmental degradation.[34] These factors render China's food self-sufficiency programme increasingly uneconomical and, hence, the growth in the demand for food can be expected to be met largely by imports in future. Thus, both Australia and the United States can benefit substantially from this trend.

SUMMARY AND CONCLUSIONS

To summarize, Australia-China trade grew much faster than world trade since China adopted its open-door and reform policy in the late 1970s. There has been a significant diversification in both the commodity composition of Australia exports to, and imports from, China. The importance of agricultural products has declined while that of minerals and manufactured goods in Australia's exports to China has risen. Some diversification of China's export commodity composition to Australia has also occurred: the share of TCF declined while that of electrical machinery and equipment increased. Australia-China bilateral trade relations also experienced a significant transformation. While Japan's share of Australian exports declined, Hong Kong-China has become the second largest export market for Australia. Its trade surplus with Greater China and other Asian NICs now exceeds its surplus with Japan.

Australia has also become an increasingly important market for HongKong-China exports. However, Australia's share in HongKong-China's import market has declined.

The impact of any US-China bilateral trade negotiation and accord on Australian exports of food and agricultural products depends primarily on the degree of competitiveness between Australia and US export items to that country. The bulk of Australia exports of food and agricultural products to China is not directly competing with US products, hence the threat to Australia of trade diversion as a result of a US-China trade accord is expected to be limited.

However, such an accord may have an adverse impact on those Australia exports which are competing with US exports, such as cereals, meat, dairy products, processed food and some animal raw materials. However, so far there is little evidence of any discrimination by China against Australia's exports on non-commercial grounds in these products. However, this possibility cannot be excluded. It is therefore in Australia's interest to monitor any US-China trade agreement closely. However, on the whole, Australia stands to gain substantially from both the direct and indirect trade creation effects generated by any US-China trade negotiations and/or agreement.

NOTES

1. IMF, *Direction of Trade Statistics Yearbook,* 1994, p. 420.
2. A. Butler, 'Trade imbalances and economic theory: The case for a US-Japan trade deficit', *Federal Reserve Bank of St. Louis Review,* March/April, 1991, pp. 16–21.
3. USIS, *Economic Backgrounder,* 11 April 1994.
4. R. Garnaut, *Australia and the Northeast Asian Ascendancy* (Canberra, AGPS, 1990), p. 71.
5. J.C.H. Chai, 'Factors influencing agricultural trade', in Y.Y. Kueh and R.F. Ash (eds.), *Economic Trends in Chinese Agriculture* (Oxford: Clarendon Press, 1993), pp. 733–4.
6. Department of Foreign Affairs and Trade, *Australia and Northeast Asia in the 1990s: Accelerating Change,* Canberra, AGPS, 1992, p. 51.
7. Department of Foreign Affairs and Trade, *China, November 1994,* Canberra, AGPS, 1994, p. 35.
8. Ibid, p. 36.
9. J.C.H. Chai and C.C.L. Kwong (forthcoming), 'Economic relations with China', in Henry Ho and L.C. Chau (eds.), *The Economic System of Hong Kong,* 2nd ed., Hong Kong, Asia Research Services.
10. Australian Bureau of Statistics, *International Merchandise Trade Australia,* Canberra, AGPS, 1995.
11. IMF (1994), pp. 105–6.
12. Department of Foreign Affairs and Trade, *Trade in Services Australia 1993/4,* Canberra, AGPS, 1995, pp. 14–5.
13. Ibid, p. 31.
14. Department of Foreign Affairs and Trade, *Australia and Northeast Asia in the 1990s: Accelerating Change,* Canberra, AGPS, 1992, p. 56.

15. Australia Bureau of Statistics, *International Investment Position, Australia,* Canberra, AGPS, 1994, p. 28.
16. Department of Foreign Affairs and Trade, *China November 1994,* p. 27.
17. Australian Bureau of Statistics (1994), op. cit., p. 28.
18. Department of Foreign Affairs and Trade (1992), op. cit., p. 64.
19. Australian Bureau of Statistics (1994), op. cit., p. 20.
20. Department of Foreign Affairs and Trade (1992), op. cit., p. 25.
21. Ibid, p. 25.
22. Department of Foreign Affairs and Trade, *China November 1994,* p. 38.
23. *The Australian,* 16 May 1995.
24. Department of Foreign Affairs and Trade, *The US-Japan Relationship and Its Implication for Australia,* Canberra, AGPS, 1994, p. 20.
25. J.C.H. Chai, 'Factors influencing agricultural trade', op. cit., p. 385.
26. T. Voon, 'Chinese demand for Australian wheat: Applications of market share models', *Australian Economic Papers,* Vol. 33, No. 63 (1994), p. 229; and I. Roberts and N. Andrews, 'US agriculture: Perspectives on support programmes', *Commodities Forecast and Issues,* Vol. 1 & 2, (Canberra: ABARE, 1994), pp. 217–33.
27. Department of Foreign Affairs and Trade (1994), op. cit., p. 236.
28. Ibid, p. 218.
29. Ibid, p. 215.
30. B. Phillips, J.N.Winton and H.D.B.H Gunasekera, ' Liberalizing primary trade in the APEC region', *Agriculture and Resources Quarterly,* Vol. 5 No. 2 (1993), pp. 198–200.
31. Department of Foreign Affairs and Trade, *Trade in Services Australia 1993/4,* p. 6.
32. J.C.H. Chai, 'Consumption and living standard in China', *The China Quarterly,* September 1992, pp. 721–49 ; R. Garnaut and G.N. Ma, *Grain in China,* Canberra, DFAT, AGPS, 1992; E. Li and S.N. Samuel, 'Income elasticities and socio-demographic factors influencing demand for selected processed and beverage products in urban China', *Australian Journal of Agribusiness,* 1994, pp. 63–74; and J. Laurenceson, *Chinese Urban Food Consumption,* unpublished Honours Thesis, 1994.
33. J.C.H. Chai, 'Factors influencing agricultural trade', op.cit., pp. 361–388.
34. C. Tisdell, 'Asian development and environmental dilemmas', *Contemporary Economic Policy,* Vol. 13, No. 1 (1994), pp. 38–49.

12

Sino-American Relations: An Asian Perspective

*Radha Sinha**

INTRODUCTION

Nations, like human beings, acting in their self-interest aim at maximizing their gains (or minimizing their losses) over a period of time subject, of course, to constraints. Within the national boundary, the government — as the 'guardian' of the national interest — acting within physical, social, economic and moral constraints, tries to 'maximize' its own objective function. In democratic countries, this objective function may consist of the 'maximum welfare of the maximum number'; in authoritarian countries, it is the maintenance of the regime that gets precedence. Nevertheless, in reality, in democratic countries where elections are expensive, those elected must often depend on the 'political donations' of big business. Therefore, the promotion of big business interests receives priority, without which the survival (or at least re-election) of those elected may be put at risk. At the same time, even authoritarian governments cannot totally ignore the interests of the governed, if revolutionary upheavals are to be avoided. Under the circumstances, governments pursuing several, and often conflicting, objectives, have to determine a ranking of priorities, and attach weights to them for implementation.[1] Similarly, states aiming to maximize their objective function in the international setting are faced with multiple and conflicting objectives, keeping in view both the domestic and external constraints.[2] The objectives may simply be regime maintenance at home, independently or with foreign support, or hegemonic control overseas.

In the past, it was often the lack of domestic resources that motivated countries to foreign invasion and colonization. Even the much vaunted idea of 'free trade', in its early stages, was developed and promoted largely 'by the

* The author is thankful to Brian Bridges, Y.Y. Kueh and Dean Meyers, for their critical comments and help in drafting this chapter. He is also thankful to Dick Nanto of the Congressional Research Service of the US Library of Congress for helping with necessary research materials.

essentially mercantilist hope of achieving a virtual industrial monopoly for Great Britain . . .'³ Even Adam Smith saw colonies as a 'means of disposing of surplus produce obtained by extending the division of labour beyond the scope which the domestic market would support.'⁴ He also visualized 'a British commonwealth, with an imperial parliament, of quasi-independent countries, modelled upon the empire of ancient Athens'.⁵

Similar views were expressed by J.R. McCulloch, another ardent classical economist.⁶ Yet others, such as Edward Gibbon Wakefield, also a free-trade philosopher, went further in suggesting that 'an industrial system could not be made viable by free trade alone; England might grow and prosper, without crises or social unrest, only if she also turned to colonization'.⁷ Robert Torrens also advocated the creation of a 'British commercial league — a commercial Zollverein [a duty-free area]'; and differential duties in favour of the British colonies. He argued:

> By extending our colonial system, and opening new and expanding markets in our trans marine dependencies, coupled with the rigid enforcement of the principle of reciprocity, we may arm ourselves with accumulating force to break down hostile tariffs, and to establish free trade throughout the world.⁸

It also needs emphasizing that the early developers Great Britain, France, Germany, the United States or Japan, invariably ignored 'free trade' as a tool of development policy in their early stages of economic development. As Johnson stressed, even in England the heyday of free trade lasted for less than half a century, beginning with the repeal of the Corn laws and the Navigation Acts in the 1840s (that is, after industrialization had proceeded for nearly three quarters of a century and the country had become the 'workshop' of the world), and coming to a decline with the 'powerful policy movement' in the wake of the Great Depression.⁹ However, as Sinha has pointed out:¹⁰

> The colonies rarely had the autonomy to decide their commercial or economic policies. The short interlude of free trade was also the period of considerable 'diplomatic and military aid to commerce' in the name of 'freedom of the seas' leading to the forced opening of China and Japan by the then leading powers including the United States.¹¹ The partition of the African continent among the Western powers also came during this period. These wars of annexation 'were applauded by such Radicals as Joseph Hume'.¹²

Admittedly, the post-Second World War years did see trade liberalization by reductions in tariffs, but the gains were largely offset by non-tariff barriers.¹³ Even during the 1960s, the major economic powers such as the United States, the United Kingdom, Japan and the European Economic Community (EEC) maintained trade barriers with respect to agriculture and textiles. Gradually the list became increasingly bigger, to include steel, steel products, machine tools, footwear, automobiles and consumer electronics. High tariffs and tariff escalation on developing-country semi-processed and processed products has been a common feature of the post-war world. Competitive subsidization, particularly of agriculture, public procurement and 'informal' protection, have also continued.[14] As Johnson argued, contemporary commercial policy has much in common with its 'mercantilist ancestry' in its emphasis on protection against imports to promote national income, wealth and employment, as well as in a concern for a balance of payments surplus achieved more by import restrictions, than export promotion.[15] Thus, as Johnson stressed, mercantilism has remained a potent force in popular and political thinking.

It is against this background that this chapter argues that much of the contemporary talk of free trade and opening of the market, and the creation of a 'Free Trade Area' or eventually a 'Trade Bloc' in Asia, or elsewhere, all fall much in the Wakefield-Torrens line of thinking.

In Asia in particular, Japan, the dominant industrial power in the region in view of its vulnerabilities (that is, the lack of raw materials and a relatively small domestic market), has always seen the region in much the same way as Wakefield-Torrens saw the British colonies. Even after defeat in the Pacific War, Japanese big business continued to assert that the old 'East Asian Co-Prosperity Sphere' was essentially right.[16] In the early post-war years, 'the idea of regional economic integration impressed many [US] officials as the key to Japanese recovery'.[17] Even George Kennan advocated the creation for Japan of a new 'empire in the South'.[18] As Schaller stresses, '. . . *Japan's business and political leaders held fast to an economic strategy first developed in the 1930s. They encouraged and abetted the United States in its eagerness to restore Japan as a great trading nation. Although the fruits of this labor were not harvested until a decade after the Occupation ended, the course was charted by 1947* (italics mine).'[19]

With rapid economic growth and increasing confidence, Japanese government and business have continued to incorporate the south-east Asian economies into Japan's 'economic zone of influence' through foreign aid, trade and foreign investment. Other influences, such as donations to regional universities, research institutes, scholarships and fellowships, and political donations by big business, all are being used to promote a somewhat benign 'Co-Prosperity Sphere'.

The problem, of course, is that the post-war world also witnessed the emergence of a unified China as a major economic and political power, with potential superpower credentials, and no economic integration can be really effective in East Asia unless China is a party to it. A further, perhaps the most complicating, factor is the attitude of the United States to the region. The United States, which for 'cold-war' reasons, had underwritten the prosperity of the region (including that of Japan) is not likely to sit aside and let Japan alone gain from the rapidly increasing prosperity of the region, or allow Japan to create a Japanese 'hegemony' in the region. During the 'cold war', it was tactically important for the United States to placate Japan. With the disintegration of the Soviet Union and the failure of the successor state of Russia to put its house in order, there is no immediate reason for the United States to placate Japan. By the same token, Japan does not need US protection, at least not until China becomes an economic and military superpower which might threaten Japan. In the interim, both Japan and the United States would aim at increasing their influence in China, because China is seen both as an opportunity and a threat.

With the rapid growth and modernization of its major industries and its military, China may not directly threaten the US mainland, but it can certainly undermine US interests in Asia. Therefore, the United States will need Japan as a counter-balance to China. Japan will also need the US security umbrella, lest China become ambitious. Japan has increasingly worried about the Chinese military threat; this is reflected in the 1995 *Defense White Paper*. Japan is also openly encouraging the security integration of the south-east Asian countries (now including Vietnam) as a counter to a potential Chinese threat.[20] However, Japan cannot underestimate its economic opportunities in China; consequently, its protests regarding the Chinese military build-up or recent nuclear tests have been rather feeble.[21] In addition, Japan cannot offend China, except marginally, for fear of a Chinese veto against Japan's permanent membership in the United Nations Security Council.

Japan, already a major military power, has to tread softly also because China and the other East Asian countries have not forgotten the humiliation suffered during their colonization and the wartime atrocities committed by the Japanese army. Occasional assertions by noted politicians that Japan was not an aggresssor or that the scale of atrocities has been exaggerated, continue to undermine official apologies by the Japanese government. Most Asians also believe that Japan will re-emerge as a major military superpower (and a nuclear one) in the foreseeable future.[22] Hence, the east and southeast Asian nations would not agree to an uncontested superpower role for Japan in East Asia. The countries in the region fear both Japan and China, and would like to keep a US presence in the region.[23] China, itself, might like the United States to stay in the region to block Japanese 'hegemonic' ambitions. Under the circumstances, no paper on Sino-American relations can be adequate unless Japan is also brought into consideration. It is the triad, China-Japan-the United States, that will determine the fate of the region for the foreseeable future.

Nature and Evolution of Sino-American Relations

As is well known, the history of European trade with the East — China, India and the Spice Islands — dates back to Roman times, if not earlier. An almost insatiable European demand for luxuries, silk, cotton textiles and spices had to be paid for in gold and silver, for the Asians did not need much that was produced in Europe. Writing about the sixteenth and seventeenth centuries, a French historian wrote:

> The Mediterranean as a whole operated as a machine for accumulating precious metals, of which, be it said, it could never have enough. It hoarded them only to lose them to India, China, and the East Indies. The great discoveries may have revolutionized routes and prices, but they did not alter the fundamental situation [the European adverse balance of trade with the East]'[24]

Even after the arrival of gold and silver from the Americas in the 1550s, the trade balance with the East did not much improve. The import of treasure had, in fact, created a greater demand for Eastern luxuries. There began an increasing outcry against the import and use of Chinese silk and Indian cotton goods, and prohibitive legislation was passed, as early as 1700, in several European countries to keep such imports out. But the demand for such products continued unabated. By the second half of the century, however, the import of gold from America became comparatively insignificant.[25] Imports of American treasure dwindled much further after the second decade of the seventeenth century.[26] This created further problems in paying the traders in the East with gold and silver. In this context of a trade deficit, the emergence of the opium trade during the first three decades of the nineteenth century came as a great blessing to European traders. The political control of India by the British East India Company enabled the company licensees and the American clippers alike to bring increasing imports of opium into China.[27] In the first decade of the nineteenth century, as much as 600 000 lb. of opium was imported into China by British traders alone. By 1839 it had reached 4 million lb.[28]

As Fairbank suggests, 'it became the marijuana/heroin of the time'.[29] Arguably, 'the issue was not simply opium but the fact that the Chinese wanted to restrict, and the West to expand, their intercourse. The West prevailed [by sheer superior force].'[30] As Tuchman points out : 'Throughout the process of the opening of China, the United States followed through portals cut out by the British, avoiding aggression and inheriting the advantages.'[31] This was a typical 'free-ride' by the United States, an accusation that it raises frequently these days against Japan and other allies. As Fairbank highlights:

> The Opium war of 1839–42 [and of 1856–60] [was] a classical inequity. Opium sales to China were necessary to balance the triangular trade that moved Canton teas to London, and London goods and investments to India. The leading British opium merchants on the China coast, headed by Dr. William Jardine of Jardine Matheson & Company, helped Palmerston work out the aims and strategy of the war. They leased vessels to the British fleet, along with pilots and translators, and from their continued sales of opium accumulated the silver that the British expedition bought and used for its expenditures in China. It was an opium-colored war, even though the basic issue was whether Peking would accept relations with Britain as between equal states.[32]

It needs reminding that the forced opening of China (or later Japan) was being done in the name of *high principles* (that is, 'freedom of trade' and 'freedom of the seas').

Possibly, it could be seen as a re-run of the crusades, which were essentially conceived as religious wars, yet, the take-over of the lucrative trade routes with Asia from the infidels worked as an important incentive for Venice and Genoa to provide assistance with men and money.[33] Commenting on the first four crusades, Roberts writes:

> Its religious impulse could still move men, but the first four crusades had clearly shown the unpleasant face of greed and cupidity. They were the first examples of European overseas imperialism, both in their characteristic mixture of noble and ignoble aims and in the abortive colonialism . . . In Syria and Palestine, Europeans were not simply pushing forward their frontier in a movement of settlements as in Spain or on the pagan marches of Germany. *They were attempting to transplant western institutions to a remote and exotic setting, to seize lands and goods no longer easily available in the West, and they could do all this with clear consciences because their opponents were infidels* . . . (italics mine)[34]

The Chinese case was not so different. As Fairbank points out, on the authority of Joseph Fletcher, a reputed scholar on central Asia, the Anglo-Chinese settlement at Nanking was 'remarkably similar' to what the Chinese authorities had already conceded to Kokand, a central Asian principality.[35] Clearly, the West was not after a reasonable settlement. As Fairbank stresses:

> . . . Britain and the United states, and France, were expansive maritime powers from another world, addicted to sea power, violence, law and treaty rights, and for them the first treaty settlement of 1842–44 was only the beginning of encroachment. Imperialism supervened.[36]

American 'Isolationism'

In order to have a proper perspective of the US role in Asia, certain popular misconceptions ought to be set aside before we go any further. Contrary to what an average American believes, *'the United States has never been truly isolationist. Even in the period between the two world wars, America was only isolationist toward Europe; in the Western Hemisphere, the United States was openly interventionist; and in the Far East, Washington played an active role'* (italics mine).[37]

Largely the work of John Quincy Adams, the Monroe Doctrine unveiled before the US Congress in 1823 unilaterally declared that any act of intervention by the European powers in the affairs of the newly independent Latin American countries would be treated as an unfriendly act by the US government. Sounding a highly principled act — a newly independent country (the United States) guaranteeing foreign non-intervention in the affairs of other newly independent neighbours must be seen as noble — the doctrine opened the way for the United States' annexation of foreign territories in North America. Not able to call upon European support, Mexico gradually lost Texas, Utah, Nevada, California and most of Arizona. Hawaii was annexed in 1898.[38] By this time, American policymakers had begun to view US expansion in the Far East as equally important as that in Latin America.[39] The Philippines was occupied in 1898, and shortly thereafter was annexed as a colony. On the ruthless suppression of the Filipinos, Mark Twain, in disgust, suggested that the American flag ought to be redesigned with 'the white stripes painted with black and the stars replaced by the skull and crossbones'.[40]

However, the American government, like that of any imperialistic power, did not feel a sense of guilt. President McKinley 'stressed the altruistic rather than economic causes'.[41] In a speech given in Boston on 17 February 1899, he claimed:

> The Philippines, like Cuba and Puerto Rico, were entrusted to our hands by the war, and to that great trust, under the providence of God and in the name of human progress and civilization, we are committed . . . We could not discharge the responsibilities upon us until these colonies became ours, either by conquest or by treaty. *Our concern was not for conquests or trade or empire, but for the people whose interests and destiny, without our willing it, had been put in our hands* (italics mine).[42]

This was the reiteration of the same *mission civilisatrice* which the Europeans had used time and again in the imperial conquest of non-European lands. It was the same European mission of civilizing the barbarians that Christian missionaries proliferated in China and elsewhere, 'asserting by their presence China's [and many others'] need for salvation'.[43] Gradually, the US government also began to open the doors for American businesses in those countries. The policy came to be known as 'dollar diplomacy' from the time of President Theodore Roosevelt's securing access for American bankers in Santo Domingo in 1905. President Taft called this policy 'substituting dollars for bullets. It is one that appeals alike to idealistic sentiments, to the dictates of sound policy and strategy, and to legitimate commercial ends.'[44]

Another popular misconception is that it is only now (that is, in the post-Second World War period) that US policymakers began to give East Asia a prominence in American diplomacy. It was as early as 1905 that President Theodore Roosevelt had declared that '. . . Our future history will be more determined by our position on the Pacific facing China than by our position on the Atlantic facing Europe.'[45]

In short, defeat in the Opium War brought great humiliation to the Chinese government. Peasant uprisings were rather common in China from very early times.[46] A defeat at the hands of the 'foreign barbarians' was a different matter, however. It destroyed whatever legitimacy the imperial system was left with.

As Tuchman stresses:

> In the years following the First Opium War disasters multiplied, taxes were increased upon the peasantry, corruption in the governing mandarinate became systematic, respect for authority declined, power decentralized, banditry flourished, sovereignty rotted at the center. In 1850 all these decays and discontents coalesced in a great popular uprising known as the Taiping Rebellion which was to last 15 years and cost 29 million lives before it was over. Drawing strength from the oppressed, the Taipings succeeded in establishing a rival capital at Nanking. The recurring moment seemed at hand when the Mandate of Heaven had been withdrawn from a dynasty proven unworthy. But the foreigners, in order to ensure the privileges they had exacted by the treaty, shored up the Government. With their aid Nanking was retaken to the accompanying massacre of 100,000 Taipings.[47]

The pattern that was established, of the foreign powers keeping alive a corrupt and inefficient government in order to retain the privileges gained for foreigners, has been repeated time and again, and continues to our present days in most developing countries.

Those progressive Chinese who, drawing inspiration from the Meiji 'modernizers', attempted to remodel China on Western lines were circumvented by the reactionary mandarinate around Empress Dowager Tsu Hsi. China lost territories to the British and the French in 1885 and to Japan in 1895 during the 'rampant' age of imperialism. America, however, 'caught between hunger [for wealth and power] and principle' as Tuchman suggests:

> . . . had joined in the exploitation of China without compromising her scruples against taking territory. In 1898 this combination of profit and principles was elevated to a doctrine of foreign policy by John Hay. Called the Open Door (though not by him), it managed to sound generous, high-minded and somewhat protective of China while meaning, if anything at all, that the door of penetration should be opened equally to everybody.
>   . . . American infiltration of China by this time was a two-pronged affair of business and gospel. Agents of Standard Oil purveying kerosene for every household lamp in China may have found more receptive customers, but the missionaries were to leave a greater mark on relations between the two countries.[48]

The Boxer Rebellion of 1899–1900, virtually the last gasp of the anti-imperialist struggle, was much less organized than the Taiping and was led by the fanatics of secret societies in China. Riding on the wave of xenophobia, they murdered missionaries, their families and Chinese 'collaborators'. However, the reprisal, when it came, was no less despicable. An American minister wrote that foreign soldiers and civilians from general to private, from minister to attaché, from bishop to missionary, had 'stolen, sacked, pillaged, and generally disgraced themselves'.[49] But it was only China which was declared to have committed crimes 'against civilization' and was required to pay a huge indemnity; and her customs revenue was held as security.[50]

In the face of increasing public discontent with Qing rule and the realization that without 'modernization' China could not get back her dignity, a reform movement ultimately culminated in the establishment of a Republic in 1911. Even in the best of times, the central government's power remained curtailed both by the war-lords, who controlled the countryside, and by the fact that the 'treaty ports' remained under foreign powers. Life in republican China was no better than that in a 'semi-colonial' country; 'foreigners did not control the polity, though their privileges impaired its sovereignty'.[51]

Inter-War Diplomacy and China

With the coming of the First World War, Japan was quick to expand its influence in China at the expense of the Germans, going far beyond the British — then a political ally of Japan — request for 'protection of the sea route'.[52] The Okuma cabinet was determined to take over German privileges in China. Anticipating Japanese incursions into Chinese territory, Yuan Shih-K'ai, then the Republic's president, approached the United States to take over the German interests in China temporarily, prior to their being ultimately handed over to China. The United States replied that *'it would be quixotic in the extreme to allow the question of China's territorial integrity to entangle the United States in international difficulties* (Italics mine)'.[53]

Although blatant interventionism in China was opposed by some groups within the Japanese government, yet it did not prevent Foreign Minister Kato putting forward a long list of demands, known as the Twenty-One Demands, before China. If accepted, they would have constituted a virtual Chinese capitulation to becoming a Japanese protectorate. Contrary to the Japanese caution to keep these demands secret, Yuan leaked them, hoping that some foreign intervention might save the integrity of China. Unfortunately, no assistance came.[54]

Britain even advised compliance. 'President Wilson considered the Twenty-One Demands offensive', but his Secretary of State, Robert Lansing, defined the 'American interest in the Far East as commercial rather than political', and was even sympathetic 'with the Japanese aspirations for colonization'.[55] Lansing felt that not allowing a sphere of influence to Japan would undercut the American stand on the Monroe Doctrine. Lansing thought of buying off Japan by turning over the Philippines to it. This idea was turned down by the President.[56] Subsequently, Lansing, in his efforts to appease Japan, reached the Lansing-Ishii Agreement of November 1917. The United States, while not giving up the Open Door Policy, conceded that Japan had 'special interests in China'.[57] However, when Japan moved into Manchuria and set up a puppet government called Manchukuo in 1931, the United States refused to recognize it. The League of Nations declared the Japanese action illegal, and the Japanese angrily stormed out of the League. The League had earlier sounded out the

American Secretary of State, Henry Stimson, regarding the possibility of an embargo against Japan for its aggression in China, but the League was simply rebuffed.[58] President Hoover rejected the recommendation of his Secretary of War, Patrick Hurley, to be tough with Japan, and categorically stated that 'he would fight for [the] Continental United States as far as any body, but he would not fight for Asia.'[59] Eventually, America had to fight a war with Japan because European interests were at risk, but not to prevent the dismemberment of China. Other countries were not prepared to fight Japan, either. The British were always sympathetic to Japan although they had not renewed the Anglo-Japanese Treaty because of American and Canadian pressure. Britain also viewed a powerful Japan as a safeguard against Russian expansionism in the East. Publicly, France supported the view of the League of Nations, but privately let Japan know that the French appreciated Japan's problems in China.[60] The League did not have any enforcement machinery other than the military power of the major states, and in this instance no major power was willing to take up the Chinese case. The Soviet Union would have joined in a collective action but was not willing to act alone.

US Economic Interests in China in the Inter-War Period

Trade

Lack of substantial business interests in China was, perhaps, another reason for America's not taking determined action against Japan over Manchuria in 1931, over the Amau Doctrine,[61] or over the Japanese continued march into southern China. In 1937, China was taking only 10 percent of US exports to the Far East, Japan's share was as high as 53 percent (Table 12.1). Therefore, US businessmen were opposed to sanctions against Japan on account of its invasion of China.[62] One commentator went so far as to suggest that Japan's take-over of China might mean greater prosperity for US businesses. He argued:

> . . . she [Japan] will be in the market for many years to come for capital goods, for raw materials and for loans . . . If Japan can secure capital, create order and develop Chinese resources, the market will blossom like a rose. Japan might become rich by the new trade, and so might some Americans.[63]

As late as mid-1937, the *Wall Street Journal* was saying that '. . . our relations with China are less important than our relations with Japan'.[64] By this time, however, the United States government had begun to consider trade restrictions, particularly on the export of arms, on Germany and Japan under the Neutrality Act. The US Chamber of Commerce said the ' proposal to break off an important trade connection' was not based on 'mature reflection'.[65] As late as 1940, a *Fortune* magazine poll indicated that only 19 percent of businessmen were willing to intervene in China to counter Japanese

Table 12.1 United States Trade With the Far East, 1937

(Value in US$ Millions; share in percent)

Region or country	Exports		Imports	
	Value	Share	Value	Share
South and South-east Asia	174	31.7	679	67.9
British India	44	8.0	96	9.6
British Malaya	9	1.6	242	24.2
British Ceylon	2	0.3	21	2.1
Netherlands Indies	23	4.2	115	11.5
French Indochina	3	0.5	77	7.7
Philippine Islands (US)	85	15.5	126	12.6
Thailand	4	0.7	1	0.1
Other	4	0.7	1	0.1
East Asia	375	68.3	321	32.1
China	50	9.1	104	10.4
Hong Kong (Br.)	20	3.6	9	0.9
Kwangtung (Japanese)	16	2.9	4	0.4
Japan	289	52.6	204	20.4
Grand Total	549	100.0	1000	100.0

Source: US Department of Commerce, *Foreign Commerce and Navigation of the United States*, 1940, p. xv.

aggression.[66] It was only in 1941 with the Japanese march into South-east Asia and the loss of sources of raw materials that American business began to see Japan as a threat to US interests in the Pacific.

US foreign investment in China

If trade with China was not important for the United States, its capital investment in China was even less so. According to Remer, in 1931 the total foreign investment in China amounted only to $3.2 billion (at 1932 dollar parity), of which nearly 37 percent was the share of Great Britain, and 35 percent of Japan, against only 6 percent for the United States.[67] Nearly a third of total US investments were in exports and imports. Among public utilities, the Shanghai Power Company and the Shanghai Telephone Company were those in which Americans had controlling interests, but shares were subscribed by British, Chinese and Japanese nationals. US investment in manufacturing was largely limited to the manufacturing of Chinese carpets in Tientsin and Peking. Some of their manufacturing plants were involved in importing, assembling and operating motor cars, and manufacturing electrical equipment, shipping containers and cigarettes.[68] Total US investment in China represented around 6 percent of total foreign investment in manufacturing in China. The

Japanese share was 44 percent.[69] Clearly, the US stake in China was important neither in terms of trade nor investment.

Victim of American Ignorance

The stage for Japan's march into Asia was set in the 1860s and 1870s as is reflected in the *Seikan Ron* ('Conquer Korea Argument') between 1869 and 1873 or in 1890 when Prime Minister Yamagata Aritomo made a distinction between Japan's 'line of sovereignty' and 'line of interest or advantage'.[70] Taken in its proper perspective, it simply meant that Japan was not going to be satisfied purely by defending its sovereignty; it needed a foothold in Asian countries to promote its own imperialistic interests, not unlike other contemporary imperialists. Gradual annexation of Formosa, Korea and subsequently the creation of Manchuoko, all pointed in the same direction. As seen earlier, no major power, not even the United States, was prepared to fight for the integrity of China, even as late as the early 1930s. The American inaction was rooted in various causes: firstly, the Americans really felt that Japan, being a world power — proven by Japan's victory over China and Russia — needed a sphere of influence, in much the same way as the British, French or the Americans themselves had their own spheres. Secondly, subjugating weaker countries, outside the European cultural zone, was not seen as immoral. The Japanese, by modernizing themselves, were already considered equal![71] Thirdly, many Americans and Europeans had felt that China was too 'backward' and divided to govern itself. Fourthly, America did not have much economic interest in China. Finally, American policymakers were only barely informed about the Chinese situation.[72] This was clearly reflected in their failure to formulate a realistic policy to support China in its anti-Japanese struggle. Much of the information coming through missionaries and a few scholars was largely sentimental about 'Free China'.[73] According to Fairbank:

> The epitaph for America's China policy in the 1940s should begin by noting the American profound ignorance of the Chinese situation. They were preoccupied with their official contacts with the Nationalists and their own logistic war efforts in China. They sensed the Nationalist deterioration but had little detailed knowledge of it. The CCP [Chinese Communist Party] side of the picture was meanwhile almost entirely blank to the Americans. The few observers who got to Yenan responded to the upbeat optimism and determination of the CCP, but there were no American observers in North China except for a very few journalists, who however had very limited observations. The result was that the CCP power was completely underestimated. In 1948 the American estimate was that the Nationalists could not defeat the CCP, but neither could the CCP defeat the Nationalist. This view showed a total incomprehension of reality of China.[74]

On the basis of such ignorance, the Americans came to back the Nationalists and not only lost the war in China but also lost any opportunity to moderate the CCP in its early days. The American mind fails to comprehend to this day that much of the use of terms such as 'communism' and 'socialism' in developing countries was synonymous with 'nationalism' and 'anti-colonialism'. This was as true of China and Vietnam — as of India. As Fairbank stresses, '[T]he extent of Mao's Sinification of Marxism or the creation of national communism could not be adequately appreciated by outsiders [read Americans] who did not know the gruesome details of Mao's relationship with Stalin'.[75]

Grave errors of judgement in understanding the Chinese communists not only delayed the emancipation of China from Japanese aggression but also embittered the communists towards the United States, with serious implications for the world. As Tuchman, suggests:

> Their future alignment in international affairs was, not, in 1944, necessarily fixed. What course Chinese Communism might have taken if an American connection had been brought to bear is a question that lost opportunities have made forever unanswerable. The only certainty is that it could not have been worse.[76]

The question that one has to look for is, why did the United States government opt for the Nationalists in spite of continued warning by Stilwell of the military weaknesses of the Nationalists. As Tuchman suggests:

> It was essentially a decision for counter-revolution. The same choice was made in former colonial territories where, contrary to the late President's [Roosevelt] intent, American forces were actively helping to restore the French rule in Indochina against a strong movement against independence. In charters and declarations American aims were democratic but, in practice, executants opted for the old regime. In China the decision was not merely futile; it aligned America in the popular eye with the oppressor and the landlord and tax collector, it disheartened the liberal forces and violently antagonized the future rulers. While many suspected that the effort was misguided, American policy could not readjust. . . There was no feasible alternative. To abandon the legal government for the Communists was not within American capacity and would have meant political suicide at home.[77]

The American decision to oppose Communist China's admission to the United Nations soured US-China relations all the more. Perhaps, this also led, at least indirectly, to the Chinese involvement in the Korean War. At the end of the Second World War, Korea, though independent of the Japanese occupation, found itself divided at the 38th parallel. The North, under Soviet influence, became communist; the South under US influence, became capitalist. Originally, it was hoped that the two parts would be reunited and given independence eventually.[78] However, in 1947 the US-sponsored initiative in the UN General Assembly for Korean unification failed because of Soviet opposition. However, in a UN-supervised Assembly election in South Korea, President Syngman Rhee's party was routed, with only 48 against 120 from other parties, mostly from the left. The new Assembly was, in the overwhelming majority, in favour of unification, even on North Korean terms. Perhaps these results encouraged the North to invade the South. The United States 'pushed through a resolution in the UN Security Council branding the North Koreans as aggressors, demanding a cessation of hostilities, and requesting a withdrawal behind the thirty-eighth parallel'.[79] The Soviet Union did not have the chance to veto the resolution as it had refused to take part in the UN proceedings against the United States insistence on the continuation of Chiang Kai-shek's representation in the United Nations rather than Communist China. Contrary to his assurances to Stalin, President Truman authorized General MacArthur to invade North Korea. This attempt at 'rolling back communism in Asia' alarmed the Chinese leadership. They transmitted a series of warnings to America that China would not 'sit back with folded hands and let the Americans come to the border'.[80] On being ignored by the United States, the Chinese publicly declared that if the US forces continued their advance in the North, China would enter the conflict. General MacArthur and his supporters in Congress began to advocate strategic bombing of the Chinese mainland. The British were so alarmed by the prospect of another major conflagration in the Far East that Prime Minister Attlee came to Washington in December 1950 to plead with President Truman to opt for a negotiated settlement. President Truman, too worried about domestic opposition, disagreed.[81] As Ambrose highlights:

> A negotiated settlement with the Chinese would bring the wrath of the Republicans on their heads, and the congressional elections were a few days away. If peace came, there would be no N.S.C.68 and the American foreign policy would be back where it was before the Korean War — much bluster and little muscle.[82]

The Chinese leadership, which had not yet fully consolidated, having taken over in China only a few months before, wanted to give peaceful solution a chance. So, on being invited, they came to the United Nations. They arrived on 24 November 1950 to be greeted with the news that MacArthur, in his characteristic hyperbole, had promised to bring 'the boys "home by Christmas" after they had all been to the Yalu'. The Chinese delegation immediately returned home. The European allies were furious. The French government openly charged that MacArthur had 'launched his offensive at this time to wreck the negotiations'.[83] Within two weeks of entering the war the Chinese 'volunteers' reversed the fortunes of war, clearing the American forces out of North Korea.[84] Yet again, the chance of a negotiated, mutually acceptable peace between the United States and China was thrown to the wind. Even Truman, in his later life, 'came to think that the Korean War, which he had much supported, began the militarization of American foreign policy'.

Moynihan does not fully agree with Truman, yet he concedes to Truman that in 'Korea, as in Vietnam, we . . . confused the national interest with an ideological preference'.[85]

The indefensible US policy of not allowing Communist China its legitimate seat in the United Nations continued.[86] This increasingly created a sense of disenchantment among developing countries with America's democratic credentials. Whatever doubt remained in the minds of developing countries' leaders vanished as a result of the US involvement in Indochina in defence of European colonialism, and nearly two decades later, the overthrow of the democratically-elected Allende government in Chile, to protect the interests of an American multinational. The latter incident, though important, does not belong here in this chapter. However, Indochina certainly does. President F.D. Roosevelt was 'a sincere opponent of the old-style colonialism and wanted the British out of India, the Dutch out of the Netherlands East Indies, the Americans out of the Philippines, and the French out of Indochina'.[87] However, during the high tide of anti-communism during the Truman era, anti-communism took precedence over all other American ideals.

In 1952 President Eisenhower, with his Second World War reputation and anti-communist rhetoric, was elected by a landslide. With him came John Foster Dulles, the cold-war warrior, who was 'absolutely certain of his own and his country's goodness. Dulles' unshakable beliefs were based on general American ideas. They differed hardly at all from those of Truman, Acheson, Main Street in Iowa City or Madison Avenue in New York City.'[88] With them also came Vice President Nixon, at one time 'a McCarthyite congressman' who had denounced the Truman Administration for 'loving China'. Even while campaigning for vice president in 1952 he had charged that '. . . China would not have become Communist — if the Truman Administration had backbone.'[89] It was no surprise that the Eisenhower administration was totally opposed to a negotiated settlement in Vietnam.

President Kennedy, who in theory believed in a negotiated settlement, in practice opted for a graduated expansion of the US involvement in Vietnam — both overt and covert — a policy which continued until the early years of the Nixon administration. President Nixon added a new dimension by 'a secret escalation of ongoing cross-border operations from Vietnam to Cambodia [officially a neutral country]'.[90] The covert 'pacification or neutralization program' was intensified.[91] However, none of the American actions succeeded in breaking the morale of North Vietnam's leadership, who launched a major conventional offensive in 1972. In response, the Nixon administration further intensified bombing the North, including Hanoi, and mined Haiphong harbour.

Presumably, this brought the North Vietnamese leaders to Paris to negotiate a 'peace with honor', to use Nixon's phrase, and a peace accord was signed on 27 January 1973. This, as Sulzberger, a veteran journalist wrote, 'theoretically put a formal end to the Vietnam War, but what it failed to accomplish was a means of swiftly withdrawing U.S. troops . . . '[92] It was a queer irony of fate that the Americans ultimately lost South Vietnam to communism in Paris in 1973, which they could possibly have saved if they had not undermined the Geneva Accord of 1954.

The Chinese, as stated earlier, were at the Geneva Conference of 1954. John Foster Dulles had refused even to shake hands with Chou En-lai (Zhou Enlai). Yet, when the time came to extricate America from the Vietnam War, President Nixon, at one time a young McCarthyite congressman, 'self-invited' himself to China in July 1971. Admittedly, it was not just Vietnam that made President Nixon go to China; he had already conceded in 1967 in a *Foreign Affairs* article that 'any American policy toward Asia must eventually comes to grips with the reality of China'.[93] The Chinese leadership had also begun to put out feelers from 1968 onwards. Even before assuming office, President Nixon had sent a message to China though the French President, General de Gaulle, that he was in favour of 'normalization of relations'. He also 'foresaw the admission of Peking to the United Nations'. President Nixon's visit certainly opened the way for normalization of the relationship. However, it is known that Sino-American contacts continued after 1955 either 'by proxy through third world countries' or bilateral talks even at ambassadorial levels in third countries or at international conferences.[94] As Barnett stresses, '. . . from 1959 it was Washington rather than Peking that pressed for agreement on secondary issues, such as the exchange of newsmen and an increase in other nonofficial contacts. On these issues, its position became increasingly flexible.'[95] President Kennedy had talked not only of broadening non-official contacts but also of the possibility of providing food to China [in the famine years in the wake of the Great Leap Forward] and the need for including China in the disarmament talks. '*But Kennedy, fearful of the domestic political costs of dealing with the controversial China issue, deferred consideration of substantial changes in China policy* (italics mine).'[96] A Senate Foreign Relations Committee hearing on China policy in 1966 found considerable public support for a new China policy, and in response President Johnson came out in favour of a reconciliation; however, too engrossed with Vietnam, he did very little.[97] In this context, President Nixon's idea of normalization of relations with China had nothing original to it. Nevertheless, he succeeded in changing the policies because of his credentials as a one-time McCarthyite communist-hater. Besides, by this time there was enormous opposition to the Vietnam War in America because increasing numbers of American young men were returning home in coffins.[98]

Although the Nixon administration had already begun to change its position from 1970, the US policy on the Chinese non-entry into the United Nations suffered a major setback on 25 October 1971, when, by a snap vote in the General Assembly, Communist China was admitted to the United Nations and the Nationalist Chinese (Formosa) were forced out by a two-thirds majority (76 for and 35 against).[99]

Soon after came the visit to China by President Nixon, and the Mao-Nixon meeting opened the way to normalization of US relations with China.[100] With Deng Xiaoping's coming to power and his launching of market-oriented reforms, a sense of euphoria was created among US businessmen. This hardly materialized. However, with a short interruption — in the wake of the Tiananmen incident—Sino-American relations are still on track, although threats of trade sanctions on grounds of infringements of human rights, or the violation of intellectual property rights, have become common. China's most-favoured-nation (MFN) treatment in the United States is subject to annual review, and its entry into the newly created World Trade Organization (WTO) is still being opposed by the Clinton administration.

The growing economic power of China is seen as both an opportunity and a threat by the United States, Japan and other east Asian countries. With her growing economic might — in terms of purchasing power parity, the Chinese gross domestic product is rated as the third highest, following only the United States and Japan — China is not only a vast potential market, it is also able to modernize its military. The disintegration of the Soviet Union and its need for foreign exchange has given a golden opportunity to China to update its military equipment. This frightens her neighbours, particularly Japan, because China has continued with her nuclear tests. America is concerned also about its huge trade deficit with China, but much more so about the huge budget deficit at home. The latter imposes economic austerity, and as a part of it a reduction in the military budget and the reduction in foreign military bases; while strategic prudence requires maintaining a presence in Asia. This dilemma is not easy to solve; unless of course, the United States is prepared to live with a militarily more powerful Japan, an idea which most Asians, including the Chinese, detest.

RECENT TRENDS OF CHINA's TRADE

With the economic reforms of 1978, both foreign trade and foreign capital came to be liberalized in China. As a result, in eight out of the thirteen years between 1980 and 1992, the rate of growth in exports was higher than 15 percent per annum, occasionally even higher than 30 percent. Increases in imports were also substantial.

By 1993, China accounted for nearly 2.9 percent of world exports.[101] However, unlike many developing countries, its pattern was substantially diversified. For instance, in 1992 only 35 percent of exports were destined to developed market economies, and 60 percent to developing market economies

Table 12.2 Direction of Chinese Exports and Imports
by Main Regions, 1992 (in percent)

Region or country	Exports	Imports
Developed Market Economies	35.3	46.5
Total Europe	9.8	14.1
EEC	8.9	12.0
USA and Canada	10.9	13.2
Japan	13.8	16.7
Others	0.9	2.4
Countries in Eastern Europe	3.6	5.4
Socialist countries in Asia	0.9	0.3
Developing Market Economics	60.1	38.5
OPEC	2.5	2.5
American developing countries	1.3	2.3
African developing countries	1.5	0.6
West Asia	2.1	1.3
South and southeast Asian countries	55.1	34.1
WORLD TOTAL	100.0	100.0

Source: UNCTAD, *Handbook of International Trade and Development Statistics 1993* (1994), Tables 3.4 and 3.5.

(see Table 12.2). Its exports to socialist countries had come down to less than 4 percent. This was a remarkable turn-around. Of the 35 percent of exports going to developed market economies, the share of Japan was nearly 14 percent, the United States and Canada 11 percent, and the EC (now the European Union) nearly 9 percent. Thus, for exports, China did not depend on any one particular country or group.

Among developing market economies, pride of place went to Asian developing market economies, to which were directed as much as 55 percent of the total exports of China. The rest were divided among other developing countries. China's exports to Asian socialist economies were less than one percent. In the case of imports, inevitably the share of developed market economies was high (46 percent). Yet, not unlike exports, China has not been dependent on any one country or group for its imports. Japan's share at 17 percent has been certainly the largest, the United States and Canada together totalled 13 percent. The share of the European Union (EU) is a little less than that of North America. It does seem that China, with its experience of being a semi-colonized country, is intentionally avoiding being dependent on any one developed country. In so far as the imports from developing market economies are concerned, once again, many of the imports (34 out of 39 percent) come from Asian market economies. Thus, looking at both the direction of exports and the sources of imports, it is obvious that China is very much integrated with Asian developing countries, a certainly prudent policy. This also indicates that China is gearing itself to play an important part in regional groups such as APEC. Arguably, it might be in the interest of the small countries in the region to have China in such a group, because this might impose some group-obligations on China, while at the same time it might act as a counter-balancing force against the two other large countries, the United States and Japan. In the foreseeable future, the Chinese leadership may continue to harbour suspicions against both the United States and Japan and will hesitate to allow them to play a dominant role in the Chinese economy, but it may let smaller technologically rich countries such as South Korea play a significant role in China's economic development. This does provide a valuable opportunity for such smaller countries.

The Nature of China's Trade With Japan and the United States

It has already been stated that in terms of both China's exports and imports, Japan is a little more important than the United States. However, to compare the economic contributions of one country with those of another, one has not only to look into the nature of foreign trade, but also of foreign investment and foreign aid. Let us first have a look at the nature of trade between China and Japan, on the other hand, and China and the United States on the other.

It is clear from Table 12.3, that China, as one would expect of a developing country, is neither a large market for exports or a source of imports for either Japan or the United States. Only 5 percent of Japan's total exports go to China, and nearly 9 percent of total imports come from China. As for both US exports and imports, China is even less important.

However, as Table 12.4 indicates, China's total exports (in terms of value) to the United States exceeds those to Japan by more than 50 percent. On the other hand, Chinese imports from the United States approximate half of those from Japan. The end result is that China's trade balance with the United States is more than four times that of Japan. On the whole, the estimated import/cover ratio suggests that for every $100 worth of exports from Japan to China, Japan imports only $119 worth of imports from China, while the United States imports as much as $143 worth of merchandise from China for every $100 exported to China. Thus, in the context of trade, the US market is more open to Chinese goods than that of Japan. Arguably, therefore, the United States is making a much larger net transfer of resources to China through foreign trade than Japan does.

China's composition of exports to the two trading partners (Japan and the United States) also shows similar tendencies. For instance, manufactures account for only two-thirds of Japanese imports from China, while ninety-five

Table 12.3 China's Share in Japan's and the United States Trade, 1993

Commodities	China's share in Japan's trade (%)		China's share in US trade (%)	
	Exports	Imports	Exports	Imports
Agricultural	8.1	6.8	1.1	2.2
Raw materials	15.9	4.0	1.7	1.1
Food	–	8.0	0.8	2.2
Mining products	12.4	4.0	2.5	0.6
Fuels	–	4.4	–	0.4
Manufactures	4.7	12.3	2.1	6.9
Iron and steel	20.3	–	–	–
Chemicals	5.2	3.8	.1.8	–
Machinery and transport equipment	3.7	3.8	2.6	2.4
Other non-elect. machinery	8.9	–	3.3	–
Electrical machinery	–	9.7	–	7.1
Office and telecom equipment	2.6	4.4	1.3	3.6
Automotive prod.	2.3	–	1.7	–
Other transport equipment	2.6	–	5.7	–
Textiles	16.3	29.8	–	12.1
Clothings	–	49.8	–	18.4
Other consumer goods	–	14.7	–	21.4
Footwear	–	36.1	–	40.9
Toys and games	–	22.8	–	39.3
Total	4.8	8.5	1.9	5.8

Source: GATT, *International Trade: Trends and Statistics 1994*, (1995), Tables II.12, II.13, II.54, and II.55.

percent of US imports from China consist of manufactures (Table 12.4). Among the 'manufactures' group, machinery and transport equipment account for only 11 percent of Japanese imports from China, while they account for 20 percent of US imports of machinery. In the case of electrical machinery, office and telecommunications equipment, Japanese imports amount to only 9 percent of total imports of manufactures from China. For the United States, these two groups account for 16 percent of the total import of manufactures. This again shows that the United States is prepared to import more capital goods from China than Japan. Under the circumstances, the US assistance towards the diversification of Chinese industries is somewhat more impressive than that of Japan.

Foreign Investment in China

The inflow of foreign investment into China is given in Table 12.5. It shows

Table 12.4 China's Exports and Imports to Japan and the
United States, 1993

(US$ Billions)

Commodities	China's trade with Japan's		China's Trade with the US	
	Exports	Imports	Exports	Imports
Agriculture	4.0	0.3	0.8	0.6
Raw materials	0.7	0.3	0.1	0.2
Food	3.3	–	0.7	0.4
Mining Products	2.6	0.6	0.4	0.5
Fuels	2.2	–	0.3	–
Manufactures	13.7	16.2	32.1	7.5
Iron and steel	–	2.9	–	–
Chemicals	0.7	1.0	–	0.8
Machinery and transport equipment	1.6	9.5	6.3	5.8
Other non-electrical machinery	–	4.0	–	1.4
Electrical Machinery	0.5	–	1.8	–
Office and telecom equipment	0.7	2.2	3.4	0.9
Automotive Prod.	–	1.8	–	0.8
Other transport equipment	–	0.6	–	2.3
Textiles	1.2	1.1	1.0	–
Clothings	6.3	–	6.6	–
Other Consumer goods	3.2	–	15.6	–
Footwear	0.7	–	4.8	–
Toys and games	0.5	–	4.8	–
Total	20.4	17.2	33.7	8. 8
TRADE SURPLUS	3.2	–	13.2	–
IMPORT COVER RATIO*	119.1	–	–	142.9

Note: * Import/Cover Ratio = Export/Import multiplied by 100 to convert into an index. It simply implies that for every $100 worth of exports to a particular country, how much is imported by the exporting country. In the case of this table, it seems that for every $100 worth of exports to China, Japan imports only $119 worth of goods as against $143 for the United States exports and imports, China is even less important for the United States. Only 2 percent of total US exports go to China and nearly 6 percent of US total imports come from China. Even in the case of manufactures, Japan imports more (12 percent of total imports) from China than the US (7 percent). The United States also exports much less of manufactures (2 percent of its exports, as against 5 percent in the case of Japan).

Source: GATT, International Trade: *Trend and Statistics 1994*, (1995), Tables II.12, II.13, II.54, and II.55

that 63 percent of all equity capital inflow into China during the period 1984–93 came from Hong Kong.[102] In the case of equity, the shares of both Japan and the United States are roughly the same, at around 8 percent of the total. This is closely followed by Taiwan, with nearly 7 percent. The share of Singapore is 1.5 percent and that of Germany one percent. Thus, nearly three-quarters of all foreign investment into China comes from only three countries: Hong Kong, Taiwan and Singapore.

In the case of loans, the most significant contribution is that of Japan, at 38 percent. The share of the United States is only 8 percent, against Hong Kong's 10 percent. Clearly, the availability of loans from Japan allows China to import Japanese capital goods, which she badly needs. But because of the yen appreciation, the cost of such loans is rising fast for China (and for the other developing countries in the region). The cost of debt-servicing is high also because a major proportion of the loans from Japan are not on concessional terms. According to the data on Japanese foreign aid provided by Evans, between 1984 and 1993 loans and export credits on concessional terms given by Japan to China totalled US$9 billion ($5.7 billion in loans and $3.4 billion in export credits).[103] Perkin's data in Table 12.5, however, mentions a total for Japanese loans to China at US$23.8 billion. Thus, only 38 percent of Japanese loans to China have been on concessional terms. As Evans' table points out, in

Table 12.5 Cumulative Foreign Investment (Actuals) in China, 1984–1993

Source	Equity		Loans		Total	
	\multicolumn — (Value in US$ Billions; Share in Percentage)					
	Value (%)	Share (%)	Value (%)	Share (%)	Value (%)	Share (%)
Hong Kong*	39.3	63.3	6.4	10.3	45.7	36.0
United States	5.1	8.3	1.6	2.6	6.7	5.3
Japan	5.0	8.1	23.8	38.2	28.8	22.7
Taiwan**	4.2	6.7	–	–	4.2	3.3
Germany	0.7	1.1	2.1	3.4	2.8	2.2
Singapore	0.9	1.5	0.6	0.9	1.5	1.2
Britain	0.6	0.9	2.6	4.1	3.1	2.5
France	0.4	0.6	4.4	7.1	4.8	3.8
Italy	0.3	0.5	1.3	2.1	1.5	1.2
Canada	0.3	0.4	1.2	2.0	1.5	1.2
Total	62.2	100.0	64.7	100.0	126.9	100.0

*   Hong Kong includes Macao
** 1992 and 1993 only
Source: Ian Perkin, 'Reality of China's "Foreign" Investor' *Sunday Morning Post*, 8 January 1995. Figures may not add up to 100 because of rounding up.

the period under consideration, the United States did not provide any bilateral foreign aid to China; its export credit has also been relatively insignificant at US$315 million over the entire period. In addition to concessional loans and export credits, Japan also gave China another US$1.6 billion in terms of grants. Thus, the Japanese contribution through bilateral assitance to China has been quite substantial.

Essentially, comparing the relative performance of resource transfers from Japan and the United States to China (or for that matter any other developing country), is not easy. The nature of the data and its sources are not always uniform, nor are they well-defined. For instance, Perkin's data mentioned in Table 12.5 do not make it clear whether the equity includes foreign direct investment (FDI); perhaps it does. On the other hand, Japanese official sources, while mentioning the cumulative total of DFI-transfers from Japan into China at $6.2 billion for the period 1951–93, refer not to actual direct foreign investment but to the amount based on 'approval and notification'. This would, certainly, overestimate the actual foreign capital transferred from Japan. Similarly, the figure for loans given by Perkin does not say whether it includes concessional loans or not. Perhaps it does. During the same period (1984–93), Evans suggests a sum of US$1.6 billion as grants and US$3.4 billion as export credits. The latter ought to be part of Perkin's figure for loans. Japan also transferred nearly US$11 billion as trade deficits with China between 1984 and 1993. Therefore, the gross transfer of resources from Japan to China between 1984 and 1993 would come to approximately US$41 billion.[104]

However, during this period (1984–93), the United States did not provide any foreign aid to China; export credits, too, as suggested earlier, were meagre. According to Perkin's data, the United States' contribution through equity and loans was only US$7 billion, not an impressive figure. On the other hand, during this period, the US total trade deficit with China amounted to $70 billion. If this figure is added to the equity and loan figures, total US gross resource transfers to China would come to an impressive figure of $77 billion, or $36 billion more than Japan. A lot has been written on the 'correctness' of the Japanese ODA. Evans' paper is one of the examples; there are many others. But most studies tend to take a partial view by taking account of foreign aid or foreign investment alone.

'Trade versus Aid' has been a long-debated issue in development economics, and the consensus is in favour of trade rather than aid. Trade provides foreign exchange resources unencumbered by foreign conditions or foreign priorities, leaving the country to decide its own priorities. This luxury is not available with aid, or even with foreign investment. Under the circumstances, those who concentrate their attention purely on aid or foreign investment grossly underestimate the contribution Sino-American economic relations are making towards the economic development of China. Besides, China also gains from the US trade deficits with East and South-east Asia, with which China has a significant part of its trade.

It would, therefore, be necessary for China to take serious note of US sensitivities on trade, defence and human rights issues. On the other hand, the United States must see its trade deficit with China as an investment for the future; a richer China will certainly be a bigger trading partner and potentially a more secure, and therefore a sober, ally.

CONCLUSION

The Sino-American relationship has moved, over a century and a half, through several phases. In the beginning, America shared with its forebears the early Anglo-Saxon *mission civilisatrice*, and as a 'free-rider' shared the loot of the blatant European imperialism of the nineteenth century. However, occassional bouts of *moralism* prevented it from acquiring territorial possessions in China. It also donated part of its share of the Boxer indemnity to the missionaries for the education of Chinese young scholars in America.

The second stage came during the first half of the twentieth century, which can be called a period of benign neglect of China. The United States neither made a lot of money in China, nor did it wish to fight to defend the integrity of China against the gradual dismemberment of that country by Japan, the new imperialists in the race for power, territory and glory.

The third period, from the end of the Second World War to the beginning of rapprochement with China during the Nixon presidency, can be called, in the words of Senator Frank Church, the period of 'the illusion of American omnipotence'. This period will be remembered as a period of lost opportunities. Had America taken the early overtures of the Chinese communists seriously, or had it not supported the dying colonial regime in Indochina, it might have gone down in history as the emancipator of the colonized peoples of the world. Instead, it became 'entrapped and enthralled', as Senator Frank Church stesses, in the 'fantasy that it lay within its power to control other countries through the covert [and sometimes overt] manipulation of their affairs.'[105]

The final phase, which concerns the contemporary situation, can be called a period of constructive dialogue. The contemporary Sino-American relationship is still in its infancy and needs to be nurtured from both sides. For a satisfactory relationship between China and the United States, both countries will have to make hard choices. The Clinton administration rightly realizes that a reduction in the fiscal deficit has to be one of its main priorities. With a very conservative Congress, President Clinton's task has become inordinately difficult. The reduction in military expenditure, once anathema, now with the disintegration of the Soviet empire, is being seriously undertaken. In this repect, while the need for modernization of the Chinese military is perfectly justifiable, China can assist the US government by not accelerating its military programmes unduly. It is also imperative for China that it must settle maritime disputes about various islands in the South China Sea in a peaceful way, as it has repeatedly suggested it would.

Much the same is true of the Taiwan issue. The conservatives within the United States will keep on needling China by raising the spectre of an independent Taiwan. Taiwan, or at least some sections of the Taiwanese population, might have the illusion that the United States will come to Taiwan's rescue if military confrontation with China became a real possibility. Hungary and Poland had similar misconceptions; nobody came to their rescue when the Soviet tanks rolled in. On the other hand, it is self-defeating for China to think in terms of military adventures, even with respect to a 'recalcitrant province'. A show of force not only makes its neighbours worried about China's military might, but also provides an opportunity for the conservatives in America to raise doubts about the genuine desire of China to live in peace with its neighbours. America does have a security interest in East Asia and the Pacific; so has China. It is imperative, therefore, that these two countries have regular consultations on strategic issues, either bilaterally or multilaterally. A recent US Defense Department study claims that, '[I]t is worth noting in this context that the United States regards the high seas as an international commons. Our strategic interest in maintaining the lines of communications linking Southeast Asia, Northeast Asia, and the Indian Ocean makes it essential that we resist any maritime claims beyond those permitted by the Law of the Sea Convention.'[106] This is certainly a sentiment which China or any party to an international convention must reciprocate. Unfortunately, in the past, for instance in the mining of the Nicaraguan harbour, it was the United States which infringed international law, and even before the judgement of the International Court went against it, it refused to accept the jurisdiction of the International Court.[107]

Similarly, notwithstanding the lack of infrastructure and the lack of adequate understanding of international business practices, a reduction in trade barriers in China ought to be another Chinese priority. China can also assist by buying much more capital goods from the United States, to assist in the reduction of the US trade deficit. This, in view of the significant depreciation of the US dollar, makes good sense. Besides depending on capital goods and technology, a developing country ought to diversify its sources as far as possible; depending on one country might lead to excessive charges for replacements of parts and accessories. As suggested earlier, it is clear that China is trying to diversify its trade, and that there is an opportunity for American businessmen to take advantage of this. In this regard, however, some of the US restrictions on the export of advanced technology have to be relaxed. China needs such technology for civilian uses, although it is difficult these days to easily differentiate between military and civilian uses. On the other hand, past experience suggests that such sanctions have slowed down rather than prevented the development of military technology in China, or for that matter in other developing countries. Under the circumstances, it may be wise for the United States to allow the flow of advanced technology for civilian use under some kind of international supervision. Some halting steps in this direction have been taken by President Clinton, and it would be wise to relax such restrictions further.

It might also be necessary to tone down rhetoric on other trade matters, such as the question of intellectual property rights. Enormous losses to American or non-American businesses are well-known. However, United States Trade Representative (USTR) officials concede that: 'China has fulfilled most of its obligations under the 1992 IPR agreement by enacting new IPR laws . . .'[108] In their view, it is the enforcement machinery which is either inadequate or inefficient. In a developing country which, until recently, had a centrally planned economy, learning to run a country on Western business lines must take time. Inadequacy and inefficiency of administration is often endemic in developing countries. While pressures for improving the situation must continue, it is unnecessary to make it a cause for introducing unilateral actions such as Super 301, which, being illegal under GATT (now WTO) rules, undermines multilateral agreements. This creates doubts, in the minds of China or other US trading partners, that the US administration is not serious about its international obligations. Besides, many US domestic regulation agencies, for example the Environmental Protection Agency (EPA), cannot enforce domestic regulations effectively.

Another major dispute between China and America relates to human rights. These are universal rights and claiming 'exemption' on grounds either of an earlier stage of development or 'Asian values' is tantamount to a licence for exploitation of the 'underclass'. However, there are certain issues which must be clarified. Firstly, human rights can be used as a trade protection measure. Child labour is an evil and it must be eradicated as soon as possible. But stopping child labour may also increase costs of production, because adult labour is more expensive and can be unionized more easily. In this respect, opposition to child labour can come from sources which might like to use it purely as a trade protection measure. Secondly, trade sanctions against human rights violations can be discriminatory. Any country must use trade, or any other kind of sanction connected with human rights violations, universally and not make it punitive for some, while others go free. Thirdly, certain human rights are clearly universally accepted as something inherently desirable, but there may be others which are debatable. For instance, many developed countries have given up the death penalty as a punishment for murder or other serious crimes; but it prevails in several states in America.[109] Finally, the definition of human rights itself may be controversial. For instance, the Atlantic Charter guaranteed 'four freedoms' for mankind, one of them was the 'Freedom from Want'. Not only do nearly a billion people not have enough to eat in developing countries, but many in the richer countries have nutritional levels comparable to the poor in developing countries. Besides, there are many cases in which the United States government has aided and abetted human rights violations, or has at least been a bystander while genocide has been in full swing. Can such countries have the moral fervour to introduce sanctions on other countries which violate human rights?

Given the way the political game is played in the United States, it becomes difficult to distinguish between reality and rhetoric. The latter is often for domestic consumption. Other countries use rhetoric for similar purposes, but the United States has some special features which make rhetoric a more common phenomenon than in other democratic countries. For instance, an American president is elected for a four-year term which can be renewed only once. Senate elections take place every two years for a third of its seats. A president, therefore, has to campaign for elections every two years. The frequency of elections gives the American president little time to make hard choices and stick by them. Another major problem with the US system of government is the lack of continuity in policymaking. In any democratic country the political masters keep on changing but the civil service is permanent, maintaining the continuity in policies. In the case of the United States, the most senior-level civil servants come and go with the presidents. This leads to a rapid turnover of senior officials, leading to a lack of continuity in policymaking. Besides, many of these senior officials are recruited from industries or sectional interests. On top of these, there is a complex set of people such as the lobbyists, political action committees and other interest groups. With such pressures pulling in different directions, it is difficult for a president to deliver much, unless of course the person has extraordinary abilities. Even persons like Presidents Kennedy and Johnson failed, against their own best judgement, to let communist China take its legitimate seat in the United Nations for fear of their conservative constituents. The problem is that the American system of government is the outcome of its history, its culture and traditions. Change may come, but only slowly. The same arguments apply to other countries. For instance, China was not a democratic country for most of its history; it will take time for democracy to take root. Foreign pressures may even be counterproductive. Changes through the exchange of scholars, students, businessmen, government employees, journalists and so on, all can influence the direction which China will take. Anybody wishing well for China must be patient, as well as cautious. Countries of the West, including Japan, which exploited China and deprived it of its legitimate place in the world, have the least right to moralize.

NOTES

1. For instance, the objectives of economic growth, equality of income and political power, environmental protection, full employment, economic stability, people's participation and many others cannot be easily attained simultaneously and may even be conflicting.
2. Experts on international relations suggest that all governments pursue some of the common objectives such as autonomy, welfare, security and regime maintenance. But for developing countries another objective, nation building, is added. See K.J. Holsti, 'The comparative analysis of foreign policy for Southeast Asian States', in David Wurfel and Bruce Burton (eds.), *The Political Economy of the Foreign Policy in Southeast Asia* (Houndmills: Macmillan, 1990), p. 15.
3. Bernard Semmel, *The Rise of Free Trade Imperialism* (London: Cambridge University Press, 1970), p. 9.
4. D.P. O'Brien, *The Classical Economists* (Oxford: Clarendon Press, 1975), p. 171.
5. Semmel (1970), op. cit., p. 28.
6. This idea came to be known as the 'vent for surplus' — a term coined by John Stuart Mill, but he did not support the idea behind the concept.
7. Semmel (1970), op. cit., p. 10.
8. R. Torrens, *The Budget* (London: Elder Smith, 1844), p. 66.
9. Harry G. Johnson, *On Economics and Society* (Chicago: Chicago University Press, 1975), p. 271.
10. Radha Sinha, 'Economic reforms in developing countries: Some conceptual issues', *World Development,* Vol. 23, No. 4 (April 1995), pp. 557–576.
11. Harold U. Faulkner, *The Decline of the Laissez Faire, 1897–1917* (New York: M.E. Sharpe Inc., 1951), p. 54.
12. Semmel (1970), p. 206.
13. Jagdish Bhagwati, *Protectionism* (Cambridge, MA: The MIT Press, 1989), p. 3.
14. W. Max Corden, *Protection and Liberalization: A Review of Analytical Issues,* Occasional Paper No. 54 (Washington DC: International Monetary Fund, 1987), p. 3.
15. Johnson, *On Economics and Society,* op. cit., p. 271.
16. Quoted in J. Halliday and G. McCormack, *Japanese Imperialism Today: Co-prosperity in Greater East Asia* (Harmondsworth: Pelican, 1973), pp. 117–8.
17. Michael Schaller, *The American Occupation of Japan: The Origins of the Cold War in Asia* (New York: Oxford University Press, 1985), p. 142.
18. Ibid., p.vii.
19. Ibid., p. 298.
20. Brian Bridges, 'Here comes a new phase of China-Japan rivalry', *International Herald Tribune,* Tuesday 1 August 1995.
21. For instance, between 1989 and 1993, the annual average of Japan's grant aid to China was only 6.3 percent of the total aid. Between 1984 and 1993, the average annual loans amounted to $2.6 billion compared with the grant-aid of less than one hundred million a year.
22. A recent public opinion poll conducted by the *Yomuiri Shimbun* in cooperation with Gallup, showed that as many as 56 percent of South Koreans, 39 percent of Malaysians, 35 percent of Chinese, 33 percent of Thais and Vietnamese and 23 percent of Indonesians think that Japan is already a major military power or will emerge as one. As many as 85 percent of Koreans, 61 percent of Thais, 49 percent of Indonesians and 45 percent of Chinese felt that Japan will also become a major nuclear power. See *The Daily Yomiuri,* 23 and 24 May 1995.
23. Of late, both the Association of South East Asian Nations (ASEAN) and the European Union (EU) have created a new framework for dialogue in the form of the Asia-Europe Meeting (AEM) to attain a 'sense of political balance'. See

Yukifumi Takeuchi, 'Europe revives its sense of Asia's importance', *Asahi Evening News,* Sunday, 5 November 1995, p. 3.

24. Fernand Braudel, *The Mediterranean World in the Age of Philip II* (Glasgow: Fontana Collins, 1976), (Translated from the French by Sian Reynolds) Second Impression, p. 464.
25. Ibid., p. 476
26. Ibid., p. 536.
27. Barbara W. Tuchman, *Sand Against the Wind: Stilwell and the American Experience in China 1911–45* (London: Macdonald Futura Publishers, 1981), p. 33.
28. George M. Beckmann, *The Modernization of China and Japan* (New York: Harper and Row, 1965), p. 123.
29. John King Fairbank, *The Great Chinese Revolution, 1800–1985* (London: Chatto and Windus, 1987), p. 85. See also Wolfram Eberhard, *A History of China* (Berkeley: University of California Press, 1948), pp. 298–9.
30. Tuchman (1981), op. cit., p. 34.
31. Ibid., p.35.
32. Fairbank (1987), op. cit., p. 92.
33. As Tuchman suggests: 'The wealth of Venice and Genoa was made in trade with the infidels of Syria and Egypt despite papal prohibition' in *A Distant Mirror: The Calamitous 14th. Century* (New York: Alfred A. Knof, 1979), p. 38. See also J.M. Roberts, *The Pelican History of the World* (Harmondsworth: Penguin Books, 1981), pp. 349–50. Roberts suggests that the immediate beneficiaries of the Fourth Crusade 'were the Venetians and Genoese to whose history the wealth and commerce of Byzantinum was now annexed' (p. 350).
34. Roberts (1981), op. cit., pp. 500–1.
35. In 1935, Peking had agreed that Kokand could station a political representative at Kashgar and commercial agents in five cities; Kokand officials were to have consular, judicial and police powers over foreigners (mostly from Kokand) in their respective areas as well as the power to levy customs duties from them. The Qing government also gave indemnity to those Kokand traders that had been dispossessed by the Chinese officials. For details see J.K. Fairbank (1987) pp. 89–90.
36. Ibid., p. 93.
37. James Chase and Caleb Carr, America Invulnerable: *The Quest for Absolute Security From 1812 to Star Wars* (New York: Summit Books, 1988).
38. The history of US intervention in Latin America is too long to be narrated in this chapter. A few examples may suffice. By violating unilaterally the Clayton-Bulmer Treaty of 1850 with Britain, the United States got exclusive right of transit in Nicaragua. In 1898 the Americans went to war with Spain to 'liberate' Cuba from Spanish domination. Cuba was not annexed but American troops were stationed between 1898 and 1902; subsequently, by introducing the Platt Amendment to the Cuban constitution, she obtained the right to intervene in Cuban affairs, establish military bases and a naval base at Guantanamo Bay. As a result of the war with Spain, Puerto Rico and Guam were ceded to America. In order to build the Panama Canal, the Americans stage-managed an independence movement and subsequent independence in Panama, a Colombian territory. The United States obtained the right to maintain public order in Panama and sent in US troops in 1908, 1912, 1918 and more recently in order to kidnap Noriega. The American government took over the right of collection of customs duties of the Dominican Republic when it defaulted in paying back its loan to an American finance company. When Jose Santos Zelaya, the leader of a Liberal government in Nicaragua attempted to side-step and negotiate loans with a British company for the construction of a canal through its own territory, an insurrection was organized by the US government, which led to the overthrow of the government. The information

contained in this footnote came from Jenny Pearce, *Under the Eagle: US Intervention in Central America and the Caribbean,* (London: Latin American Bureau, 1981).

39. Chase and Carr (1988), op. cit., p. 128.
40. Quoted in Chase and Carr, ibid., p. 133.
41. Faulkner (1951), op. cit., p. 69.
42. *The Boston Herald,* 17 February 1899, quoted in Faulkner (1951), op. cit., p. 69.
43. Tuchman (1981), op. cit., p. 36.
44. Message to the Congress, 3 December 1912.
45. Tuchman (1981), op. cit., p. 42.
46. Eberhard (1948), op. cit., pp. 246–250.
47. Tuchman (1981), op. cit., p 35.
48. Ibid., p. 38.
49. Quoted in Tuchman (1981), op.cit., p. 40.
50. Subsequently, having been inspired by the Christian missionaries, the US Congress decided to devote half of the Boxer indemnity for the education of Chinese scholars in the United States. To a limited extent this turned out to be beneficial in creating the new leadership. By 1925, nearly a thousand young Chinese were sent to America for higher education. See Fairbank (1987), op. cit., p. 187. Many more Chinese students, ranging between five and fifteen thousand, visited Japan annually (p. 152).
51. Ibid., p. 177. However, much of the progressive liberal education came from American and European universities; so did science and technology education (pp.197–98).
52. Beckmann (1965), op. cit., p. 353.
53. Ibid., p. 354.
54. Ibid., pp. 355–7.
55. Chace and Carr (1988), op. cit., p. 165.
56. Ibid., p. 165.
57. Quoted in Beckmann (1965), op. cit., p. 360.
58. Chase and Carr (1988), op. cit., pp. 202–3; see also Beckmann (1965), pp. 447–449.
59. Chase and Carr (1988), op. cit., pp. 203. Dean Meyers claims that in his researches he has come across information that President Roosevelt had begun, as early as 1937, to provide material support to Chiang Kai-shek through French Indo-China, in spite of public opposition to US involvement in China. The fact that President Roosevelt was upset with Japan and held a sympathetic attitude to China is well known. It is also known that President Roosevelt, with respect to the Neutrality Act, began to make a distinction between the shipment of arms under the American flag and the sale of such arms to China. [Tuchman (1981), op. cit., p. 223]. Yet, even after the sinking of the USS. Panay, President Roosevelt was anxious to 'keep Americans out of trouble'. The American embassy in Nanking was supplying exact information about the location of the embassy staff so that they might not be bombed during the Japanese air raids. The sinking of the USS Panay was a deliberate attack, but no serious action was taken because the Japanese had apologized and accepted the American demand for indemnities in full. Tuchman (1981), pp. 227–28. The first partial embargo on scrap iron and steel and certain grades of aviation fuel, introduced on 26 July 1940, was not extended on oil 'for fear of touching off a Japanese advance to the Indies'. — Ibid., pp. 270–1. Any kind of substantial help began to come into China only after the Lend-Lease was signed in 1941.
60. Paul Kennedy, *The Rise and Fall of the Great Powers* (London: Unwin Hyman, 1988), p. 334.
61. This Doctrine, announced by Japanese Foreign Minister Eiji Amau in April 1934, stipulated that Japan had a special interest in Asia, and it precluded other foreign powers providing any assistance to China.

62. For instance see William Johnstone, *The United States and Japan's New Order* (Oxford: Oxford University Press, 1941), pp. 218–7. The author suggests that as late as 1940 even US businessmen living in China were opposed to a total embargo against Japan, and even fewer supported going to war against Japan. For some other references see Jonathan Marshall, 'Southeast Asia and US-Japan relations: 1940–1941', Pacific Research and World Empire Telegram, March-April, 1973, p. 4n.

63. Tyler Dennet, 'Alternative American policies in the Far East', *Foreign Affairs,* 1938, p. 392.

64. Quoted in Marshall (1973), op. cit., p. 4.

65. Ibid., p. 4.

66. *Fortune,* September 1940, p. 114.

67. C.F. Remer, *Foreign Investement in China,*1933, Table 7, p. 77. During this period the total US foreign investment abroad was estimated by the Department of Commerce at US$15 000 million. In China, it amounted to only $196.8 million or eqivalent to only 1.3 of total US foreign investment. Ibid., p. 77.

68. Ibid., pp. 282–290.

69. Ibid., calculated on the basis of Table 10, p. 86.

70. Richard Storry, *Japan and the Decline of the West in Asia 1894–1943* (London: Macmillan, 1979), pp. 15–6.

71. It might, however, need reminding that the Japanese suggestion to include 'the racial equality' clause in the League of Nations Charter was not accepted because of the opposition of Britain, then the closest ally of Japan, and Australia, her present-day closest ally.

72. The situation was also complicated by what Daniel Bell calls the American 'tendency to convert concrete issues into ideological problems, to invest them with moral color and high emotional charge'. See Daniel Bell, *The End of Ideology,* (Cambridge, MA: Harvard University Press, 1988, (first published in 1960)). See also Allan Bloom who, commenting on President Reagan's 'evil empire' rhetoric said: 'What was offensive to contemporary ears in President Reagan's use of the word "evil" was its cultural arrogance, the presumption that he, and America, knew what is good; its closedness to the dignity of other ways of life, its implicit contempt for those who do not share our ways. The political corollary is that he is not open to negotiation. *The opposition to good and evil is not negotiable and is a cause of war. Those who are interested in 'conflict resolution' find it much easier to reduce the tension between values than the tension between good and evil* (italics mine). See Allan Bloom, *The Closing of the American Mind* (New York: Simon and Schuster, 1987), p.142.

73. Dean Meyers has brought to my notice that in March 1938, a major two-phase conference on the Chinese Crisis was held by the Institute of Pacific Relations, which brought together a body of considerable informed opinion.

74. Fairbank (1987), op. cit., p. 268. There were a few exceptions. The most well-known was Professor Owen Lattimore, who certainly knew a lot about China. He lived there in various capacities, as businessman, newspaperman, traveller and scholar since 1920 and had written books on Mongolia, Manchuria and China's outer provinces. Lattimore's report to the Atlantic Conference 'gave a revealing view of China's resentments' against the United States and Britain. [Tuchman (1981), op. cit., pp. 289–90.]

75. Fairbank (1987), op. cit., p. 260. In fact, President Roosevelt had, as a part of the Yalta Agreement, arranged a Soviet-Chinese Treaty between the USSR and the Nationalist government. The latter had also agreed to return to the Russians their *imperialistic rights* in north-east China along the railways (p. 261).

76. Tuchman (1981), op. cit., p. 622. It is also known that Chou had suggested that he 'would serve under General Stilwell and would obey' (p. 410).

77. Tuchman (1981), op. cit., p. 672–3.
78. Stephen E. Ambrose, *Rise to Globalism: American Policy since 1938* (Fourth edition) (Harmondsworth: Penguin Books, 1985), p. 48. Some of the details in this section are largely based on this book.
79. Ibid., p. 119.
80. Ambrose (1985), op. cit., p. 123. I gather from Dean Meyers that the recently released Russian and Chinese archives suggest that both the Russians and the Chinese were in complicity with the North Korean leadership in their attack on the South on 25 June 1950. These materials indicate that Mao had assured Stalin that if the attack broke down, the Chinese forces would enter the war.
81. Richard M. Freeland, *The Truman Doctrine and the Origins of the McCarthyism* (New York: New York University Press, 1985), p. 356.
82. Ambrose (1985), op. cit., p. 124.
83. Ibid., p. 125.
84. Truman threatened, at least indirectly, to use the atom bomb against China. This alarmed the allies so much that the British Prime Minister flew to Washington and obtained the assurance 'that as long MacArthur held on there [in South Korea] there would be no atom bombs dropped.' See Ambrose, op. cit., p. 126. However, in his memoirs Dean Rusk firmly counters such suggestions that President Truman ever in any way countenanced the use of the atom bomb against China.
85. Daniel Patrick Moynihan, *Came the Revolution: Argument in the Reagan Era* (San Diego: Harcourt Brace Jovanovich, 1988), pp. 207–8.
86. Indefensibility of such a policy has been commented on by many in the United States. For instance, George Ball, who was Under Secretary of State to both presidents Kennedy and Johnson has stressed that, '[F]or many years, under the Truman, Eisenhower, Kennedy, and Johnson Administrations, our policy of trying to exclude Peking from taking over representation of China in New York had made no sense.' See George W. Ball, *Diplomacy For A Crowded World: An American Foreign Policy* (London: Bodley Head, 1976), p. 26.
87. Ambrose (1985), op. cit., p. 42.
88. Ambrose (1985), op. cit., p. 134.
89. Ball (1976), op. cit., p. 20.
90. Ibid., p. 298.
91. For example, Bill Colby, the director of the programme, himself told a Senate hearing that 20 587 had been killed, 28 978 imprisoned, and 17 717 were converted to act as agents for the South Vietnamese government. To this, one must add over 40 000 killed by South Vietnam's own covert operation called *Phung Hoang*, a mythical bird, a harbinger of peace. Many American veterans claim that the Phoenix Program was literally an assassination program. Ibid., p. 311.
92. C.L. Sulzberger, *The World and Richard Nixon* (New York: Prentice Hall Press, 1987), p. 112.
93. Richard Nixon, 'Asia after Vietnam', *Foreign Affairs,* Vol. 46, No. 1, (October 1967), p. 111.
94. A. Doak Barnett, *China and the Major Powers in East Asia* (Washington DC: Brookings Institution, 1977), pp. 178–179.
95. Ibid., p. 190.
96. Ibid.
97. Ibid., pp. 190–1.
98. The total number of American boys dead in combat during the entire period of the Vietnam War was 58 000 and wounded 300 000.
99. Derek Mercer, *Chronicle of the 20th Century* (London: Chronical, 1988), p. 1971.
100. The visit was arranged through the good offices of Romania and Pakistan; Japan was not even consulted. Until then, Japan had conformed to the US policies

towards China; the Nixon visit set the scene for a Japanese independent diplomacy towards China.

101. *The Economist,* 18–24 November 1995, p. 139.
102. It is possible that some of these are coming from the Japanese or US subsidiaries operating in Hong Kong, but the present author does not have access to a detailed breakdown of Hong Kong's investment into China according to the parent companies.
103. Peter C. Evans, 'Japan and the United States diverge on assistance to China', Japan Economic Institute (JEI), 19 May 1995, Table 1, p. 3.
104. In this figure, both the equity and loans are taken from Perkin, and the grants from Evans. Trade deficits have been calculated on the basis of various issues of JEI reports. This figure would be much lower if the transfers were reported in net terms.
105. Senator Frank Church quoted in John Prados, *Presidents' Secret Wars: CIA and Pentagon Covert Operations From World War II Through Iranscam* (New York: William Morrow, 1986), p. 337.
106. US Department of Defense, Office of International Security Affairs, *United States Security Strategy for the East Asia-Pacific Region,* 1995, p. 20.
107. Moynihan (1988), pp. 143–4.
108. Wayne M. Morrison, 'The China-U.S. trade dispute on intellectual property rights' CRS Report for Congress, Congress Research Service (CRS), 21 February 1995, CRS–4.
109. Anthony Lewis, 'Executing more innocents', *Asahi Evening News,* Friday 15 December 1995, p. 8.

13

China in the World Economy*

Marcus Noland

INTRODUCTION AND OVERVIEW

Since the inception of economic reforms in the late 1970s, China's economic performance has been nothing short of spectacular. Between 1979 and 1994, China's real growth rate has averaged more than 9 percent annually (Figure 13.1). Agriculture has been decollectivized, the management of state-controlled firms has been decentralized, and property rights reforms have facilitated an explosion of business outside central government control. Goods and factor markets have been liberalized to a significant extent: most prices are now determined by markets, state control of labour markets has been reduced, and previously repressed capital markets have experienced rapid, if uneven, development. China nevertheless retains a significant state-owned sector, and problems associated with lack of reform in this sector, combined with the relatively primitive nature of macroeconomic policy instruments, have led to a stop-start pattern of growth and problems with inflation. The time path of Chinese economic growth is subject to considerable uncertainty.[1]

The level of output in China is likewise subject to considerable uncertainty, and various attempts to measure the purchasing power adjusted level of GDP have generated a wide range of estimates.[2] Indeed, the estimate of Chinese GDP per capita reported in the most widely cited source, the Penn World Tables, changed by 40 percent in successive versions of the Tables. Thus any attempt to put the size of the Chinese economy into international perspective is subject to enormous uncertainty. With this caveat, an estimate of the Chinese share of world output derived from purchasing power adjusted data reported by the United States Central Intelligence Agency is reported in Table 13.1.

As can be seen in the first column of Table 13.1, China accounted for just under 9 percent of world output in 1993, making it the world's third largest economy following the United States and Japan. The remaining columns show China's share ten years hence under various scenarios.[3] The Chinese growth

* Copyright© 1997 by the Institute for International Economics. All rights reserved.

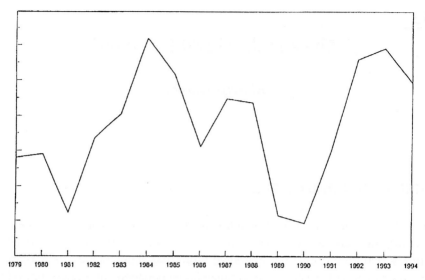

1979 1980 1981 1982 1983 1984 1985 1986 1987 1988 1989 1990 1991 1992 1993 1994

Figure 13.1   GDP Growth Rate in China, 1979–1994

Table 13.1 World Income Shares, 1993 and 2003

	1993	2003		
		Low	Medium	High
North America	26.3	22.8	24.0	25.5
United States	21.9	18.2	19.2	20.6
Canada	2.1	1.9	2.0	2.0
Mexico	2.3	2.7	2.8	2.9
Asia-Pacific	26.1	28.1	31.0	33.6
Japan	8.8	7.6	8.1	8.8
China	8.8	10.8	13.0	15.5
Rest of Asia-Pacific	8.5	8.4	9.9	10.8
Korea	1.5	1.4	1.9	2.1
Taiwan	1.0	1.0	1.2	1.3
Hong Kong	0.6	0.5	0.7	0.8
Singapore	0.3	0.4	0.4	0.5
Malaysia	0.4	0.5	0.6	0.7
Thailand	0.8	0.9	1.2	1.4
Philippines	0.4	0.4	0.5	0.5
Indonesia	0.9	1.0	1.3	1.4
Australia	2.2	1.9	2.0	2.1
New Zealand	0.3	0.3	0.3	0.3
Western Europe	22.5	18.3	19.1	19.9
Latin America	6.0	5.6	5.9	6.1
Rest of the world	19.1	19.2	20.0	21.9

Note: Shares are calculated from purchasing power adjusted national income figures.
Source: Marcus Noland, 'Implications of Asian economic growth', *Asia Pacific Economic Cooperation Working Paper Series,* No. 94–5 (Washington: Institute for International Economics, 1994).

rate is subject to the greatest uncertainty due to questions about the character of Chinese economic policy in the post-Deng era. The bottom line is that even under the slow growth scenario, China clearly emerges as the world's second largest economy in the next decade. This conclusion is further reinforced if the figures for Hong Kong's share of output are added to China's.

These are the two central points that must be kept in mind in analysing China in the world economy: the reform process is incomplete and China is huge. The inevitable bumps along the way in the reform process that the rest of the world could largely ignore in the case of a smaller economy cannot be overlooked in the case of China. A few examples should suffice. China is the world's largest importer of sugar and cooking oil, and the number of commodities for which it is the world's largest importer may soon include wheat, corn, barley and cotton as China grows and incomes rise. In April 1995 China reimposed import quotas on sugar, vegetable oil, grain, and cotton; China is sufficiently large that actions of this sort can wreak havoc on global markets. Internally, China has opened commodity futures markets, but the pricing of futures can be rendered impossible if the government remains willing to undertake significant price controls.

Other examples from the financial markets include the (eventually resolved) dispute over CITIC Shanghai's refusal to pay $40 million in debts owed to fourteen brokers on the London Metals Exchange, and the same firm's refusal to comply with an unfavourable arbitral ruling in the Revpower case. On 23 February 1995, on the same day Nick Leeson was blowing up Barings, Shanghai International lost something on the order of US$100–120 million (the approximate value of the firm) by trading twenty times the regulatory limit in government bond futures. The government's response was in effect to erase the final eight minutes of trading.

North Korea has defaulted on debts and has tried to pay off creditors with fish instead of cash, but North Korea's total merchandise trade is only around $2 billion and the world can easily absorb erratic economic policy by a marginal participant in the world economy. China is not North Korea. China's sheer size means that the rest of the world has to take developments in China very seriously, if for no other reason than developments in China are the single biggest potential threat to the stability of the international economy. Just imagine a Mexican-style crisis in China.

CHINA'S EXTERNAL ECONOMIC RELATIONS

China's participation in international trade has grown rapidly during the period of reform, and its share of world trade has risen from 0.6 percent in 1977 to 2.5 percent in 1993, making it the world's eleventh-largest trading nation (Figure 13.2). Chinese economic reforms not only spurred an enormous growth in trade, but the reforms have transformed the commodity composition as well, aligning China's pattern of trade more closely with its true pattern of comparative advantage (Table 13.2). Between 1980 and 1992, the share of exports accounted for by the light manufactures of SITC 8 rose from 16 percent to 40 percent. Similarly, imports of capital equipment (SITC 7) rose from 25 percent to 39 percent during this period.

China has also become a major player in international capital markets. China is now the leading developing country destination for foreign direct investment. The stock of inward foreign direct investment now exceeds $100 billion, though some of this is due to 'round-tripping' as Chinese investment is routed through Hong Kong to take advantage of the more favourable treatment of foreign investors. Firms with foreign equity participation accounted for two-thirds of the increase in Chinese exports in 1992 and 1993.

With regard to portfolio investment, external debt does not appear to be a problem: World Bank figures estimate annual repayments of the order of $12–14 billion, well within China's service capacity, though some private analysts argue the burden is higher.

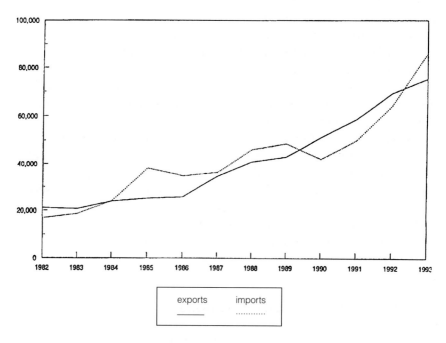

Figure 13.2   Merchandise Trade (US$ billions)

Table 13.2 Changes in Chinese Export and Import Shares

	Exports		Imports	
	1980	1992	1980	1992
Food and live animals	0.15	0.10	0.15	0.04
Beverages and tobacco	0.00	0.01	0.00	0.01
Crude materials, inedible, except fuels	0.09	0.04	0.18	0.06
Mineral fuels, lubricants and related materials	0.21	0.06	0.01	0.04
Animal and vegetable oils, fats and waxes	0.00	0.00	0.01	0.01
Chemicals and related products	0.06	0.05	0.10	0.13
Manufactured goods	0.20	0.19	0.25	0.25
Machinery and transport equipment	0.03	0.15	0.25	0.39
Miscellaneous manufactured articles (includes textile and apparel)	0.16	0.40	0.03	0.08
Others	0.09	0.01	0.01	0.01
Total	1.00	1.00	1.00	1.00

Source: Statistics Canada, *World Trade Database*, 1980–1992.

China is a major recipient of multilateral and bilateral official lending. The United States has recently questioned whether China should continue to receive concessional finance through the International Development Agency (IDA), the World Bank soft loan window. IDA funds have accounted for about a quarter of China's US$22 billion in World Bank loans since 1980, and China has been receiving approximately US$1 billion annually from IDA for the last several years. The United States appears to be isolated on this issue, though Japanese attitudes may be changing in light of its dispute with China over nuclear testing.

The rapid growth of China's international trade has posed particular problems for high income countries, including the United States. Imports have been concentrated in labour-intensive manufactures, and economic theory suggests that this exerts downward pressure on the wages of low-skilled labour.[4] Moreover, China has a rapidly growing bilateral trade surplus with the United States, even according to Chinese data, and even when the miscounting of re-exports through Hong Kong are taken into account (Table 13.3). Nor can this growing Chinese surplus be explained away as a function of the relocation of production from Hong Kong and Taiwan to China as was conceivable a few years ago (Table 13.4). Differences in political values, the growing bilateral imbalance, and the concentration of imports in light manufactures all act as political lightning rods in the United States. What is

Table 13.3 US-China Bilateral Trade Balances (US$ Billions)

	US data	Chinese data	Adjusted US data	Adjusted Chinese data
1989	6.18	−3.5	2.75	1.78
1990	10.43	−1.4	6.49	5.38
1991	12.68	−1.8	8.87	6.75
1992	18.26	−0.3	11.39	11.28
1993	22.76	6.3	14.59	19.85

Source: K.C. Fung, 'Accounting for Chinese trade: Some national and regional considerations', paper presented at Conference on Research in Income and Wealth, Geography and Ownership as Bases for Economic Accounting, Washington, 19–20 May 1995, Table 15.

Table 13.4 Bilateral US-Chinese Economic Area Trade Balances (US$ Billions)

	Chinese Economic Area	PRC	Hong Kong	Taiwan
1987	−25.9	−2.8	−5.9	−17.2
1988	−20.6	−3.5	−4.6	−12.6
1989	−22.6	−6.2	−3.4	−13.0
1990	−24.4	−10.4	−2.8	−11.2
1991	−23.7	−12.7	−1.1	−9.8
1992	−28.4	−18.3	−0.7	−9.3
1993	−31.4	−22.8	0.3	−8.9
1994	−37.4	−29.5	1.7	−9.6

Note: Customs valuation.
Source: US Department of Commerce.

truly striking about US trade politics is how China policy has been driven by exporters, not import-competing interests.

The potential for Sino-American economic conflict is likely to worsen. Table 13.5 reports the shares of US trade accounted for by different trade partners, and projections of how these shares might change obtained by plugging the Table 13.1 figures, estimates of per capita income, measures of distance and other factors into a gravity model of bilateral trade.[5] As indicated in Table 13.4, China's share of US trade is likely to grow significantly, and China may become the United States' fifth largest trade partner after Canada, Mexico, Japan, and the European Union.

Beginning in May 1992 and four times since, the US Treasury has cited China for manipulating its currency 'to prevent balance of payments adjustment and gain unfair advantage' under section 3004 of the 1988 Trade Act. Trade frictions are likely to be exacerbated by import surges and illegal behaviour.

Table 13.5 US Trade Shares

	1993	2003		
		Low	Medium	High
North America	28.3	27.5	30.3	31.5
Canada	20.5	16.5	18.2	19.2
Mexico	7.8	10.8	12.1	12.5
ASIA-PACIFIC	35.2	34.7	37.6	41.1
Japan	14.7	12.2	13.2	15.0
China	3.8	4.2	5.3	6.7
Rest of Asia-Pacific	16.6	16.4	19.1	21.6
Korea	3.0	2.5	3.4	4.1
Taiwan	3.9	3.7	4.5	5.3
Hong Kong	1.9	1.6	2.1	2.6
Singapore	2.3	2.3	2.6	3.0
Malaysia	1.6	1.8	2.1	2.4
Thailand	1.2	1.2	1.5	1.9
Philippines	0.8	0.8	0.9	1.0
Indonesia	0.8	0.8	1.0	1.1
Australia	1.1	0.9	1.0	1.1
New Zealand	0.2	0.2	0.2	0.2
Western Europe	22.2	17.4	18.5	20.2
Latin America	6.8	5.9	6.3	7.0
Rest of the world	7.5	6.9	7.3	8.1

Source: Marcus Noland, 'Implications of Asian economic growth', *Asia Pacific Economic Cooperation Working Paper Series*, No. 94–5 (Washington: Institute for International Economics, 1994).

To cite one example, China's share of the US bicycle market increased from 14.6 percent in 1993 to 23.7 percent in 1994, and in April 1995 three American manufacturers filed an anti-dumping suit against China. This suit follows the imposition of anti-dumping duties on Chinese bicycles in Canada, Mexico and the EU.[6]

Evasion of textile and apparel restrictions has also been a point of contention. China circumvents its bilateral textile and apparel quotas, mainly by transhipping products through third countries which are also covered by bilateral quotas. In other words, the Chinese substitute their products for the unfulfilled quotas of third countries. A US Customs Service study put the value of these transhipments at $2 billion. The main transhipment points are the high wage locations of Hong Kong, Taiwan, Macao and Singapore. Textile and apparel imports from these four countries were $8.5 billion in 1993. In other words, the Treasury figure implies that nearly 25 percent were transhipped.

A bilateral agreement on this issue was signed in January 1994. Government sources indicate that the problem appears to be getting worse, however. According to the Customs Service, there appears to be roughly US$10 billion in Chinese textiles and apparel floating around the world not properly accounted for. For example, Chinese customs officials reported US$13 billion in exports to 120 countries in 1992. Eighty-one countries alone reported US$23.7 billions in imports from China in the same year. (MOFTEC reports US$7.7 billion in textile and apparel exports in 1992, making the discrepancy even bigger.)

China reports $6.4 billion of textile and apparel exports to Hong Kong in 1992. Hong Kong reports $8.6 billion in consumption imports (a enormous figure), and $9.7 billion in re-exports. Even allowing for high re-export mark-ups, these discrepancies are huge.

The US Customs Service found that half of the 36 fastest growing apparel suppliers to the US market had no significant domestic production for export, but reported a significant increase in imports from China. Kenya, for example has recently experienced a 790 percent growth rate in apparel imports from China, and a 212 percent growth in exports to the United States. Other countries, including Belize, the Czech Republic, Ecuador and Qatar, exhibit similar triple-digit growth rates. All in all, the Customs Service estimates that at least $200 million of illegally transhipped apparel is coming into the United States through these countries.

Transhipping is currently subject to criminal prosecution, and Customs and the Justice Department have launched a major campaign to prosecute transhippers. There was recently a major conviction involving a Chinese state-owned firm. In May 1995 the United States cut China's cotton underwear quota by 35 percent and also reduced some other quotas because of illegal transhipping though Hong Kong, and mislabelling them as video rewinders and metal furniture.

This sort of problem is not limited to the United States. In April 1995 the EU announced that it was deducting 9.3 million garments (less than 1 percent of the Chinese quota) for three years because of illegal transhipping through Hong Kong, Dubai, Morocco, Bangladesh and Kenya.[7]

The point is simple: although as an economist and as a consumer I might benefit from illegal behaviour of this sort, differences over political values combined with illegal acts which arguably disadvantage some of the poorer members of American society may do significant harm to China's image in the United States. The result may be a significant worsening of US-China relations. A recent public opinion survey found that both the élite and the general public believe by substantial majorities that the United States has vital national interests at stake in China.[8] This view of China's growing importance is not translated into warm feelings, however: China's ranking is in the lowest quartile of regions and countries, below the EU, Japan and Russia, and just above the Cedras dictatorship in power in Haiti at the time of the poll. Moreover, this is not partisan. Both liberal Democrats and conservative Republican politicians in the United States have expressed antipathy towards China, and China's image in the United States will further suffer by comparison next year [1996] when Taiwan directly elects its president for the first time. Such a political atmosphere poses a potential threat to China's diplomatic interests. The US Congress recently voted overwhelmingly to support the admittance into the US of Taiwan's President Lee Teng-hui to receive an honorary degree at his alma mater, Cornell University.[9] Ironically, the *brouhaha* over the Lee visit may actually improve China's prospects for getting into the World Trade Organization — having caused a diplomatic flare-up, the US may now take a softer line.

PROSPECTS FOR CHINA IN THE WORLD ECONOMY

> Great powers do not want to be snubbed or shunned. The most critical junctures in human history have always been the moments when a new power struggles to its feet and begins to take a fresh look at the existing world order. We cannot repeat mistakes made at the turn of the last century, when a newly-industrialized and united Germany and Japan came on the world scene but were excluded from established international systems. And we certainly cannot afford to make that mistake with a country that has one fifth of the world's citizens, that suffered a 200 year history of colonial oppression and territorial losses, that is about to become the world's largest producer of acid rain, and that possesses a nuclear arsenal.
>
> — Lawrence H. Summers, Undersecretary of the Treasury[10]

The outside world has limited abilities to affect the development of the Chinese economy — the outcomes of the major economic policy issues that China faces will largely be determined internally. To give but one example: if the political leadership in China began to fear that centrifugal forces were pulling the country apart, there might well be a retrenchment of economic reform, and the Chinese government would become less responsive to the interests of foreigners and to fulfilling international obligations. In such circumstances there would probably not be a general deal that foreigners could do to reverse such a tendency.

Thus the overarching goals of US economic policy towards China are to promote political and economic liberalization within China (which the Clinton administration explicitly views as linked), integrate China into global institutions, and pursue US commercial interests (which the administration largely identifies as exporters' interests).

The administration regards technical assistance as the primary channel through which it can influence economic reform in China (and by extension encourage political liberalization). Among the avenues of technical assistance which have recently been created (or revitalized) has been the US-China Joint Economic Committee led by the Treasury Department, with working groups on financial reform and the foreign exchange system. The Securities and Exchange Commission has a group that works on securities regulation, and the Treasury and the Federal Reserve Board have a group to provide assistance on banking regulation and the implementation of monetary policy.

The US government's direct influence is undoubtedly greater on the question of China's integration into world economic institutions, where the most prominent issue is China's accession to the WTO. The US (and other countries) are understandably cautious on this issue because of China's enormous size and the likely precedential effect that the terms of China's accession will have on the protocols of approximately twenty other economies in transition which wish to join the WTO.

To join the WTO a signatory must agree to uphold the basic requirements of membership: transparency of the trade regime; uniform, non-discriminatory application of trade rules; and national treatment for goods and, to a more limited extent, services providers. In the case of China, foreigners have encountered significant difficulties in a lack of transparency in the application of trade restrictions, as well as non-uniform application of trade policy in different parts of China.

In these negotiations the United States has tended to put more emphasis on obtaining access to the Chinese market (this would be consistent with the US domestic political emphasis on exports), while the EU has put more emphasis on securing liberal safeguard provisions to protect against imports from China.[11] (Japan has tended to align itself more closely with the US position.) Ironically, the US insistence on market access (which is, after all, trade-expanding and welfare-enhancing) has been criticized in China, while the EU's demands for safeguards (which restrict trade and reduce welfare) has received less opprobrium.

Beyond these fundamental issues, the main points of contention regarding China's application to join the WTO have been whether China will enter as a developed or developing country (and thereby the length of the transitional period granted for bringing domestic practices into compliance with treaty obligations) as well as the issue of trading rights and the role of state-owned firms and state trading monopolies.

China has argued that it should be allowed to enter the WTO as a developing country, and China is a developing country on any measure of per capita income. The United States has argued, however, that significant parts of China are sufficiently developed such that it would be folly to permit China the additional leeway granted developing countries. (China's case is complicated by the fact that Taiwan has indicated that it is prepared to join the WTO as a developed country.) The likely outcome will be to classify China as a developing country for some WTO obligations and a developed country for others.

China maintains state trading monopolies, and unless foreigners are freely allowed to import and export, concessions on tariffs and other impediments to trade would be meaningless. The current negotiations centre on the dismantling of these monopolies, and foreign monitoring of the operations of state-owned firms to ensure that they do not run foul of the WTO's anti-subsidy provisions.

With regard to market access, the United States has asked China to join the 'zero for zero' group which eliminated tariffs on construction equipment, medical equipment, steel, beer, distilled spirits, pharmaceuticals, paper, toys, and furniture, and which greatly reduced tariffs on chemicals and electronics. The European Union has requested that China bind industrial product tariffs at 20 to 25 percent. Although neither demand is likely to be satisfied, China will undoubtedly increase market access as part of its WTO accession.

The situation in services is more complicated. China has resisted opening up its telecommunications services market to foreign providers on national security grounds. However, without a modern telecommunications system, concessions in other areas, such as banking, are less valuable. Again, the most likely outcome is a highly detailed set of provisions specifying which forms of telecommunications are open to foreign participation. In the insurance negotiation, the Chinese proposal is excessively vague. This has led some foreign observers to wonder if the timidity exhibited by the Chinese negotiators is not evidence of the great deal of uncertainty surrounding policy in the post-Deng era, and the unwillingness of the Chinese negotiators to 'stick their necks out' until some of this uncertainty is clarified. For these reasons most observers in the United States do not foresee a rapid resolution of the China WTO issue.

Lastly, China is also a participant in the Asia Pacific Economic Cooperation (APEC). The major achievements of APEC thus far have been the holding of the first pan-Asian meeting of heads of government (ironically held in the United States in November 1993) and the declaration a year later of a commitment by the leaders to free trade and investment in the Asia-Pacific region. Concrete progress towards this goal has been less evident, however, and observers are looking to the upcoming Osaka meeting to see if APEC will be more than a talking shop.

Were the APEC countries to actually implement free trade and investment in the region, the results could be quite impressive. One recent study concluded that the static income gains to China of such an agreement would be 2.2 percent of real GDP, while the dynamic gains would be even larger.[12] (Interestingly China is shown to experience an income gain even if it were excluded from any such arrangement — the impact on the other Asian economies would be sufficiently large that China itself would gain through the spillover from the others' income boost.) Another study, undertaken by the Australian government, put the gains to China of an APEC free trade agreement at 4.2 to 5.5 percent of GDP depending on model and specification.[13]

CONCLUSIONS

Integrating large, rapidly emerging countries into the international order is always problematic. In the case of China, this is made more difficult by differences in political values, and the fact that the rapid growth of the Chinese economy is likely to force significant adjustment costs onto the incumbent powers due to the complementarity of their economies. As a consequence, one must expect that China will be involved in intermittent trade conflict with the United States and others for the foreseeable future. Moreover, due to China's size, the inevitable mishaps that may accompany the process of reform could well have international ramifications.

From this perspective it becomes highly important that China be brought into international bodies such as the WTO to try to contain and intermediate these prospective frictions. At the same time, China must assume the obligations that come with membership — otherwise China's entry may eviscerate these groups.

These issues require hard bargaining, and, given the uncertainty surrounding the future political leadership in Beijing, both Chinese and foreign negotiators may have a tendency to be cautious. This suggests that a prolonged period of transition may be in the offing before China is firmly integrated into international economic institutions on a more permanent and stable basis.

NOTES

1. One consequence of these difficulties is that growth may be overstated. Inflation was officially 24.2 percent in 1994, but many observers believe the true figure is higher. The basket of goods and their weights in the price index are not reported and apparently subject to change, and the sampling techniques used to assemble the underlying data is poor. The industrial and producer price deflators diverge significantly after 1992, and an unofficial recalculation puts real GDP growth at 9.0 in 1993 and 7.8 in 1994, significantly below the official values reported in Figure 13.1.
2. Nicholas R. Lardy, *China in the World Economy* (Washington: Institute for International Economics, 1994), Table 1.3.
3. See Marcus Noland, 'Implications of Asian economic growth', *Working Papers on Asia Pacific Economic Cooperation 94–5* (Washington: Institute for International Economics, 1994) for further details on the underlying scenarios and the derivation of the projections.

4. There is considerable academic debate in the United States as to whether this indeed has been occurring. For opposing views, see Robert Z. Lawrence and Matthew J. Slaughter, 'International trade and American wages in the 1980s: Giant sucking sound or small hiccup?' *Brookings Papers on Economic Activity,* No. 2 (1993), pp. 161–226 and Edward E. Leamer, 'A trial economist's view of US wages and "globalization" ', paper presented at the Brookings Institution Conference on *Imports, Exports, and the American Worker* (Washington, 2–3 February 1995).

5. Again, see Noland (1994), op. cit., for details of this estimation.

6. *Financial Times,* 7 April 1995.

7. *Financial Times,* 19 April 1995.

8. John E. Rielly, *American Public Opinion and US Foreign Policy 1995* (Chicago: Chicago Council on Foreign Relations, 1995).

9. The vote in the House of Representatives was 396 to 0, and the tally in the Senate was 97 to 1. The sole Senator voting against the resolution had previously announced that he would not stand for re-election, and reportedly has two sons doing business in Shanghai. Chinese confusion over the administration's policy of 'comprehensive engagement' is readily understandable. At the same time, China must surely grant the average American a similar degree of perplexity over Chinese outrage about Lee's visit, at precisely the moment when China and Taiwan are deepening high-level contacts.

10. Lawrence H. Summers, 'An assessment of American economic thinking and policy toward China', *United States-China Relations,* Vol. 23, No. 2 (1995), pp. 1–8.

11. The US also faces a legal issue on the apparent conflict between US application of the WTO to China and the Jackson-Vanik amendment which inhibits the extension of unconditional MFN treatment to communist countries. Most legal observers in the United States believe that this conflict can be finessed when the time comes.

12. Jeffrey D. Lewis, Sherman Robinson and Zhi Wang, 'Beyond the Uruguay Round: The implications of an Asian Free Trade Area' (Washington: World Bank, 1995), mimeo.

13. Office of National Assessments, 'APEC liberalization gains' (Canberra, 1994), mimeo.

Index